SKILLS For SUCCESS

with Microsoft® PowerPoint 2010

COMPREHENSIVE

TOWNSEND | MURRE WOLF | VARGAS

Prentice Hall

Boston   Columbus   Indianapolis   New York   San Francisco   Upper Saddle River
Amsterdam   Cape Town   Dubai   London   Madrid   Milan   Munich   Paris   Montréal   Toronto
Delhi   Mexico City   São Paulo   Sydney   Hong Kong   Seoul   Singapore   Taipei   Tokyo

Library of Congress Cataloging-in-Publication Data

Townsend, Kris.
  Skills for success with PowerPoint 2010 comprehensive / by Kris Townsend.
      p. cm.
  Includes bibliographical references.
  ISBN 978-0-13-508832-6 (alk. paper)
  1. Presentation graphics software.   2. Microsoft PowerPoint (Computer file)
I. Title.
T385.T685 2010
005.5'8—dc22   2010019634

Editor in Chief: *Michael Payne*
AVP/Executive Acquisitions Editor: *Stephanie Wall*
Product Development Manager: *Eileen Bien Calabro*
Editorial Project Manager: *Virginia Guariglia*
Development Editor: *Ginny Munroe*
Editorial Assistant: *Nicole Sam*
AVP/Director of Online Programs, Media: *Richard Keaveny*
AVP/Director of Product Development, Media: *Lisa Strite*
Editor—Digital Learning & Assessment: *Paul Gentile*
Product Development Manager, Media: *Cathi Profitko*
Media Project Manager, Editorial: *Alana Coles*
Media Project Manager, Production: *John Cassar*
Director of Marketing: *Kate Valentine*
Senior Marketing Manager: *Tori Olsen Alves*
Marketing Coordinator: *Susan Osterlitz*

Marketing Assistant: *Darshika Vyas*
Senior Managing Editor: *Cynthia Zonneveld*
Associate Managing Editor: *Camille Trentacoste*
Production Project Manager: *Camille Trentacoste*
Senior Operations Supervisor: *Natacha Moore*
Senior Art Director: *Jonathan Boylan*
Art Director: *Anthony Gemmellaro*
Text and Cover Designer: *Anthony Gemmellaro*
Manager, Rights and Permissions: *Hessa Albader*
Supplements Development Editor: *Tina Minchella*
Full-Service Project Management: *MPS Content Services, a Macmillan Company*
Composition: *MPS Content Services, a Macmillan Company*
Printer/Binder: *Quad/Graphics-Taunton*
Cover Printer: *Lehigh/Phoenix*
Typeface: *Minion 10.5/12.5*

Credits and acknowledgments borrowed from other sources and reproduced, with permission, in this textbook appear on appropriate page within text.

Microsoft® and Windows® are registered trademarks of the Microsoft Corporation in the U.S.A. and other countries. Screen shots and icons reprinted with permission from the Microsoft Corporation. This book is not sponsored or endorsed by or affiliated with the Microsoft Corporation.

Many of the designations by manufacturers and seller to distinguish their products are claimed as trademarks. Where those designations appear in this book, and the publisher was aware of a trademark claim, the designations have been printed in initial caps or all caps.

Prentice Hall
is an imprint of

www.pearsonhighered.com

10 9 8 7 6 5 4 3 2
ISBN-10: 0-13-508832-1
ISBN-13: 978-0-13-508832-6

Contents in Brief

Common Features

| Chapter 1 | Common Features of Office 2010 | 2 |
| | More Skills | 26 |

PowerPoint

Chapter 1	Getting Started with PowerPoint 2010	30
	More Skills	54
Chapter 2	Format a Presentation	64
	More Skills	88
Chapter 3	Enhance Presentations with Graphics	98
	More Skills	122
Chapter 4	Present Data using Tables, Charts, and Animation	132
	More Skills	156
Chapter 5	Enhance PowerPoint Presentations	166
	More Skills	190
Chapter 6	Add Multimedia Objects to a Presentation	200
	More Skills	224
Chapter 7	Customize Graphics and Draw on Slides	234
	More Skills	258
Chapter 8	Create Custom Templates	268
	More Skills	292
Chapter 9	Create Accessible Presentations and Write Macros	302
	More Skills	326
Chapter 10	Finalize Presentations	336
	More Skills	360

Glossary 370

Index 375

Table of Contents

Common Features

Chapter 1	**Common Features of Office 2010**	**2**
Skill 1	Start Word and Navigate the Word Window	6
Skill 2	Start Excel and PowerPoint and Work with Multiple Windows	8
Skill 3	Save Files in New Folders	10
Skill 4	Print and Save Documents	12
Skill 5	Open Student Data Files and Save Copies Using Save As	14
Skill 6	Type and Edit Text	16
Skill 7	Cut, Copy, and Paste Text	18
Skill 8	Format Text and Paragraphs	20
Skill 9	Use the Ribbon	22
Skill 10	Use Shortcut Menus and Dialog Boxes	24

More Skills

More Skills 11	Capture Screens with the Snipping Tool	26
More Skills 12	Use Microsoft Office Help	26
More Skills 13	Organize Files	26
More Skills 14	Save Documents to Windows Live	26

PowerPoint

Chapter 1	**Getting Started with PowerPoint 2010**	**30**
Skill 1	Open, View, and Save Presentations	34
Skill 2	Edit and Replace Text in Normal View	36
Skill 3	Format Slide Text	38
Skill 4	Check Spelling and Use the Thesaurus	40
Skill 5	Insert Slides and Modify Slide Layouts	42
Skill 6	Insert and Format Pictures	44
Skill 7	Organize Slides Using Slide Sorter View	46
Skill 8	Apply Slide Transitions and View Slide Shows	48
Skill 9	Insert Headers and Footers and Print Presentation Handouts	50
Skill 10	Add Notes Pages and Print Notes	52

More Skills

More Skills 11	Type Text in the Outline Tab	54
More Skills 12	Use Keyboard Shortcuts	54
More Skills 13	Move and Delete Slides in Normal View	54
More Skills 14	Design Presentations for Audience and Location	54

Chapter 2	**Format a Presentation**	**64**
Skill 1	Create New Presentations	68
Skill 2	Change Presentation Themes	70
Skill 3	Apply Font and Color Themes	72
Skill 4	Format Slide Background with Styles	74
Skill 5	Format Slide Backgrounds with Pictures and Textures	76
Skill 6	Format Text with WordArt	78
Skill 7	Change Character Spacing and Font Color	80
Skill 8	Modify Bulleted and Numbered Lists	82
Skill 9	Move and Copy Text and Objects	84
Skill 10	Use Format Painter and Clear All Formatting Commands	86

More Skills

More Skills 11	Edit Slide Masters	88
More Skills 12	Save and Apply Presentation Templates	88
More Skills 13	Create Slides from Microsoft Word Outline	88
More Skills 14	Design Presentations with Contrast	88

Chapter 3	**Enhance Presentations with Graphics**	**98**
Skill 1	Insert Slides from Other Presentations	102
Skill 2	Insert, Size, and Move Clip Art	104
Skill 3	Modify Picture Shapes, Borders, and Effects	106
Skill 4	Insert, Size, and Move Shapes	108
Skill 5	Add Text to Shapes and Insert Text Boxes	110
Skill 6	Apply Gradient Fills and Group and Align Graphics	112

Skill 7	Convert Text to SmartArt Graphics and Add Shapes	114
Skill 8	Modify SmartArt Layouts, Colors, and Styles	116
Skill 9	Insert Video Files	118
Skill 10	Apply Video Styles and Adjust Videos	120

More Skills

More Skills 11	Compress Pictures	122
More Skills 12	Save Groups as Picture Files	122
More Skills 13	Change Object Order	122
More Skills 14	Design Presentations Using Appropriate Graphics	122

Chapter 4   Present Data Using Tables, Charts, and Animation — 132

Skill 1	Insert Tables	136
Skill 2	Modify Table Layouts	138
Skill 3	Apply Table Styles	140
Skill 4	Insert Column Charts	142
Skill 5	Edit and Format Charts	144
Skill 6	Insert Pie Charts	146
Skill 7	Apply Animation Enhance and Emphasis Effects	148
Skill 8	Modify Animation Timing and Use Animation Painter	150
Skill 9	Remove Animation and Modify Duration	152
Skill 10	Navigate Slide Shows	154

More Skills

More Skills 11	Prepare Presentations to Be Viewed Using Office PowerPoint Viewer	156
More Skills 12	Insert Hyperlinks in a Presentation	156
More Skills 13	Create Photo Albums	156
More Skills 14	Design Presentations with Appropriate Animation	156

Chapter 5   Enhance PowerPoint Presentations — 166

Skill 1	Use the Research Task Pane	170
Skill 2	Copy and Paste between Programs	172
Skill 3	Customize Character Spacing	174
Skill 4	Clear Formatting	176
Skill 5	Adjust Line Spacing	178
Skill 6	Change Text Direction and Case	180
Skill 7	Divide Text into Columns	182
Skill 8	Align Text and Shapes	184
Skill 9	Duplicate Slides	186
Skill 10	Replace Fonts	188

More Skills

More Skills 11	Create Custom Slide Shows and Add Sections	190
More Skills 12	Change and Reset Pictures	190
More Skills 13	Equalize Character Height	190
More Skills 14	Format Slide Title Backgrounds	190

Chapter 6   Add Multimedia Objects to a Presentation — 200

Skill 1	Edit Videos	204
Skill 2	Change Video Options	206
Skill 3	Insert Hyperlinks	208
Skill 4	Insert and Edit Excel Charts	210
Skill 5	Link Files with Paste Special	212
Skill 6	Add Action Settings to Shapes	214
Skill 7	Create Slides with Timed Breaks	216
Skill 8	Insert Sound Effects	218
Skill 9	Insert Watermarks	220
Skill 10	Create SmartArt Organization Charts	222

More Skills

More Skills 11	Record and Play Narrations	224
More Skills 12	Add Rehearsal Timings	224
More Skills 13	Insert Songs	224
More Skills 14	Download and Apply Microsoft Office Templates	224

Chapter 7   Customize Graphics and Draw on Slides — 234

Skill 1	Create Custom Shapes	238
Skill 2	Group Objects and Export Custom Shapes	240
Skill 3	Use the Ruler to Apply Indents and Align Objects	242
Skill 4	Animate Graphics Using Motion Paths	244
Skill 5	Recolor and Customize Pictures	246
Skill 6	Modify and Link to Photo Albums	248
Skill 7	Add Captions and Convert Text to SmartArt	250
Skill 8	Modify Graphics to Reduce Presentation File Sizes	252

Skill 9	Insert Symbols	254
Skill 10	Edit Notes and Handouts Masters	256

More Skills

More Skills 11	Save Slides as Image Files	258
More Skills 12	Export Customized SmartArt as a Picture	258
More Skills 13	Create SmartArt with the Nested Target Layout	258
More Skills 14	Create Text Effects by Combining WordArt and Shapes	258

Chapter 8	**Create Custom Templates**	**268**
Skill 1	Create Custom Templates	272
Skill 2	Customize Slide Layouts	274
Skill 3	Set Transparent Colors and Organize Slide Masters and Layouts	276
Skill 4	Customize Slide Master Elements	278
Skill 5	Create Custom Layouts	280
Skill 6	Add Custom SmartArt Placeholders	282
Skill 7	Work with Multiple Slide Masters	284
Skill 8	Use Templates to Create New Presentations	286
Skill 9	Insert Slides from Multiple Slide Masters	288
Skill 10	Organize Slide Elements Using the Selection Pane	290

More Skills

More Skills 11	Create Photo Albums from Templates	292
More Skills 12	Create Quiz Shows from Templates	292
More Skills 13	Add Online Templates to Existing Presentations	292
More Skills 14	Customize the Quick Access Toolbar	292

Chapter 9	**Create Accessible Presentations and Write Macros**	**302**
Skill 1	Work with Language and Translation Tools	306
Skill 2	Make Presentations More Accessible	308
Skill 3	Prepare Presentations for Kiosks and Save as Slide Shows	310
Skill 4	Remove Personal Information and Prepare Presentations for Sharing on the Internet	312
Skill 5	Display the Developer Tab and Add ActiveX Controls	314

Skill 6	Create and Debug Macros	316
Skill 7	Write and Test VBA Statements	318
Skill 8	Add and Edit Comments	320
Skill 9	Import Slides from Other File Formats and Check Compatiblity	322
Skill 10	Set Passwords and Add Digital Signatures	324

More Skills

More Skills 11	Create Multilevel Lists	326
More Skills 12	Edit Macros in Visual Basic for Applications	326
More Skills 13	Add XML and Save Forms as XML Documents	326
More Skills 14	Insert Signature Lines	326

Chapter 10	**Finalize Presentations**	**336**
Skill 1	Use Reviewer Feedback to Improve Presentations	340
Skill 2	Reorder and Hide Slides	342
Skill 3	Collect Information Using the Clipboard Pane	344
Skill 4	Paste from Webpages	346
Skill 5	Create Citations in Word	348
Skill 6	Cite Sources on a Bibliography Slide	350
Skill 7	Animate Chart Elements	352
Skill 8	Mark up Slides During Presentations and Use the Laser Pointer	354
Skill 9	Change Presentation Resolution	356
Skill 10	Package Presentations to CD	358

More Skills

More Skills 11	Download and Run PowerPoint Viewer	360
More Skills 12	Add an Agenda and Change the Orientation of Slides	360
More Skills 13	Use Presenter View	360
More Skills 14	Prepare Equipment and Software for Presentations	360

Glossary		370
Index		375

About the Authors

Kris Townsend is an Information Systems instructor at Spokane Falls Community College in Spokane, Washington. Kris earned a bachelor's degree in both Education and Business, and a master's degree in Education. He has also worked as a public school teacher and as a systems analyst. Kris enjoys working with wood, snowboarding, and camping. He commutes to work by bike and enjoys long road rides in the Palouse country south of Spokane.

This book is dedicated to the students at Spokane Falls Community College. Their adventures, joys, and frustrations guide my way.
—KRIS TOWNSEND

Stephanie Murre Wolf is a Technology and Computer Applications instructor at Moraine Park Technical College in Wisconsin. She is a graduate of Alverno College and enjoys teaching, writing curriculum, and authoring textbooks. In addition to classroom instruction, Stephanie actively performs corporate training in technology. She is married and has two sons; together, the family enjoys the outdoors.

This book is dedicated to my sons, Sam and Silas, and my husband, Mike. Your support is appreciated and your positive attitudes are an inspiration.
—STEPHANIE MURRE WOLF

Alicia Vargas is an Associate Professor of Business Information Technology at Pasadena City College in California. She holds a bachelor's and a master's degree in Business Education from California State University, Los Angeles and has authored numerous textbooks and training materials on Microsoft Word, Microsoft Excel, and Microsoft PowerPoint.

This book is dedicated to my parents, Mary and Luis Perez, who inspired me to pursue my education and achieve my goals, and to my son Phil, for whom I hope I have done the same.
—ALICIA VARGAS

Contributors

We'd like to give a special thank you to Rebecca Lawson from Lansing Community College for her help in co-authoring several of the chapters in this book.

We'd like to thank the following people for their work on Skills for Success:

Instructor Resource Authors

Cheri Adams	Wichita Technical College	Ram Raghuraman	Joliet Junior College
Ernest Gines	Tarrant County College—Southeast Campus	Mark Renslow	Globe University
Andrea Leinbach	Harrisburg Area Community College	Candice Spangler	Columbus State Community College
LeAnn Moreno	Southeast Technical College		

Technical Editors

Lisa Bucki		Linda Pogue	Northwest Arkansas Community College
Kelly Carling		Steve Rubin	California State University—Monterey Bay
Hilda Wirth Federico	Jacksonville University		
Janet Pickard	Chattanooga State Tech Community College		

Reviewers

Darrell Abbey	Cascadia Community College	Tara Cipriano	Gateway Technical College
Laura Aagard	Sierra College	Paulette Comet	Community College of Baltimore County—Catonsville
John Alcorcha	MTI College		
Barry Andrews	Miami Dade College	Susana Contreras de Finch	College of Southern Nevada
Natalie Andrews	Miami Dade College	Gail W. Cope	Sinclair Community College
Wilma Andrews	Virginia Commonwealth University School of Business	Lennie Coper	Miami Dade College
		Chris Corbin	Miami Dade College
Bridget I. Archer	Oakton Community College	Janis Cox	Tri-County Technical College
Tahir Aziz	J. Sargeant Reynolds	Tomi Crawford	Miami Dade College
Greg Balinger	Miami Dade College	Martin Cronlund	Anne Arundel Community College
Terry Bass	University of Massachusetts, Lowell	Jennifer Day	Sinclair Community College
Lisa Beach	Santa Rosa Junior College	Ralph DeArazoza	Miami Dade College
Rocky Belcher	Sinclair Community College	Carol Decker	Montgomery College
Nannette Biby	Miami Dade College	Loorna DeDuluc	Miami Dade College
David Billings	Guilford Technical Community College	Caroline Delcourt	Black Hawk College
Brenda K. Britt	Fayetteville Technical Community College	Michael Discello	Pittsburgh Technical Institute
Alisa Brown	Pulaski Technical College	Kevin Duggan	Midlands Technical Community College
Eric Cameron	Passaic Community College	Barbara Edington	St. Francis College
Gene Carbonaro	Long Beach City College	Donna Ehrhart	Genesee Community College
Trey Cherry	Edgecombe Community College	Hilda Wirth Federico	Jacksonville University
Kim Childs	Bethany University	Tushnelda Fernandez	Miami Dade College
Pualine Chohonis	Miami Dade College	Arlene Flerchinger	Chattanooga State Tech Community College

Hedy Fossenkemper	*Paradise Valley Community College*
Kent Foster	*Withrop University*
Penny Foster-Shiver	*Anne Arundel Community College*
Arlene Franklin	*Bucks County Community College*
George Gabb	*Miami Dade College*
Barbara Garrell	*Delaware County Community College*
Deb Geoghan	*Bucks County Community College*
Jessica Gilmore	*Highline Community College*
Victor Giol	*Miami Dade College*
Melinda Glander	*Northmetro Technical College*
Linda Glassburn	*Cuyahoga Community College, West*
Deb Gross	*Ohio State University*
Rachelle Hall	*Glendale Community College*
Marie Hartlein	*Montgomery County Community College*
Diane Hartman	*Utah Valley State College*
Betsy Headrick	*Chattanooga State*
Patrick Healy	*Northern Virginia Community College—Woodbridge*
Lindsay Henning	*Yavapai College*
Kermelle Hensley	*Columbus Technical College*
Diana Hill	*Chesapeake College*
Rachel Hinton	*Broome Community College*
Mary Carole Hollingsworth	*GA Perimeter*
Stacey Gee Hollins	*St. Louis Community College—Meramec*
Bill Holmes	*Chandler-Gilbert Community College*
Steve Holtz	*University of Minnesota Duluth*
Margaret M. Hvatum	*St. Louis Community College*
Joan Ivey	*Lanier Technical College*
Dr. Dianna D. Johnson	*North Metro Technical College*
Kay Johnston	*Columbia Basin College*
Warren T. Jones, Sr.	*University of Alabama at Birmingham*
Sally Kaskocsak	*Sinclair Community College*
Hazel Kates	*Miami Dade College*
Gerald Kearns	*Forsyth Technical Community College*
Charles Kellermann	*Northern Virginia Community College—Woodbridge*
John Kidd	*Tarrant County Community College*
Chris Kinnard	*Miami Dade College*
Kelli Kleindorfer	*American Institute of Business*
Kurt Kominek	*NE State Tech Community College*
Dianne Kotokoff	*Lanier Technical College*
Cynthia Krebs	*Utah Valley University*
Renuka Kumar	*Community College of Baltimore County*
Jean Lacoste	*Virginia Tech*
Gene Laughrey	*Northern Oklahoma College*
David LeBron	*Miami Dade College*
Kaiyang Liang	*Miami Dade College*
Linda Lindaman	*Black Hawk College*
Felix Lopez	*Miami Dade College*
Nicki Maines	*Mesa Community College*
Cindy Manning	*Big Sandy Community and Technical College*
Patri Mays	*Paradise Valley Community College*
Kathy McKee	*North Metro Technical College*
Norma McKenzie	*El Paso Community College*
Lee McKinley	*GA Perimeter*
Sandy McCormack	*Monroe Community College*
Eric Meyer	*Miami Dade College*
Kathryn Miller	*Big Sandy Community and Technical College, Pike Ville Campus*
Gloria A. Morgan	*Monroe Community College*
Kathy Morris	*University of Alabama, Tuscaloosa*
Linda Moulton	*Montgomery County Community College*
Ryan Murphy	*Sinclair Community College*
Stephanie Murre Wolf	*Moraine Park Technical College*
Jackie Myers	*Sinclair Community College*
Dell Najera	*El Paso Community College, Valle Verde Campus*
Scott Nason	*Rowan Cabarrus Community College*
Paula Neal	*Sinclair Community College*
Bethanne Newman	*Paradise Valley Community College*
Eloise Newsome	*Northern Virginia Community College—Woodbridge*
Karen Nunan	*Northeast State Technical Community College*
Ellen Orr	*Seminole Community College*
Carol Ottaway	*Chemeketa Community College*
Denise Passero	*Fulton-Montgomery Community College*
Americus Pavese	*Community College of Baltimore County*
James Gordon Patterson	*Paradise Valley Community College*
Cindra Phillips	*Clark State CC*
Janet Pickard	*Chattanooga State Tech Community College*
Floyd Pittman	*Miami Dade College*
Melissa Prinzing	*Sierra College*
Pat Rahmlow	*Montgomery County Community College*
Mary Rasley	*Lehigh Carbon Community College*
Scott Rosen	*Santa Rosa Junior College*
Ann Rowlette	*Liberty University*

Contributors continued

Kamaljeet Sanghera	*George Mason University*
June Scott	*County College of Morris*
Janet Sebesy	*Cuyahoga Community College*
Jennifer Sedelmeyer	*Broome Community College*
Kelly SellAnne	*Arundel Community College*
Teresa Sept	*College of Southern Idaho*
Pat Serrano	*Scottsdale Community College*
Amanda Shelton	*J. Sargeant Reynolds*
Gary Sibbits	*St. Louis Community College—Meramec*
Janet Siert	*Ellsworth Community College*
Gary R. Smith	*Paradise Valley Community College*
Karen Smith	*Technical College of the Lowcountry*
Robert Smolenski	*Delaware County Community College*
Robert Sindt	*Johnson County Community College*
Patricia Snyder	*Midlands Technical College*
Pamela Sorensen	*Santa Rosa Junior College*
Eric Stadnik	*Santa Rosa Junior College*
Mark Stanchfield	*Rochester Community and Technical College*
Diane Stark	*Phoenix College*
Neil Stenlund	*Northern Virginia Community College*
Linda Stoudemayer	*Lamar Institute of Technology*
Pamela Stovall	*Forsyth Technical Community College*
Linda Switzer	*Highline Community College*
Margaret Taylor	*College of Southern Nevada*
Martha Taylor	*Sinclair Community College*
Michael M. Taylor	*Seattle Central Community College*
Roseann Thomas	*Fayetteville Tech Community College*
Ingrid Thompson-Sellers	*GA Perimeter*
Daniel Thomson	*Keiser University*
Astrid Hoy Todd	*Guilford Technical Community College*
Barb Tollinger	*Sinclair Community College*
Cathy Urbanski	*Chandler Gilbert Community College*
Sue Van Boven	*Paradise Valley Community College*
Philip Vavalides	*Guildford Technical Community College*
Pete Vetere	*Montgomery County Community College—West Campus*
Asteria Villegas	*Monroe College*
Michael Walton	*Miami Dade College*
Teri Weston	*Harford Community College*
Julie Wheeler	*Sinclair Community College*
Debbie Wood	*Western Piedmont Community College*
Thomas Yip	*Passaic Community College*
Lindy Young	*Sierra Community College*
Matt Zullo	*Wake Technical Community College*

Instructors – You asked for it so here it is!

A Microsoft® Office textbook that recognizes how students learn today-

Skills for Success

with Microsoft® PowerPoint 2010 *Comprehensive*

- **10 x 8.5 Format –** Easy for students to read and type at the same time by simply propping the book up on the desk in front of their monitor

- **Clearly Outlined Skills –** Each skill is presented in a single two-page spread so that students can easily follow along

- **Numbered Steps and Bulleted Text –** Students don't read long paragraphs or text, but they will read information presented concisely

- **Easy-to-Find Student Data Files –** Visual key shows students how to locate and interact with their data files

Start Here – Students know exactly where to start and what their starting file will look like

Outcome – Shows students up front what their completed project will look like

Skills List – A visual snapshot of what skills they will complete in the chapter

Sequential Pagination – Saves you and your students time in locating topics and assignments

Skills for Success

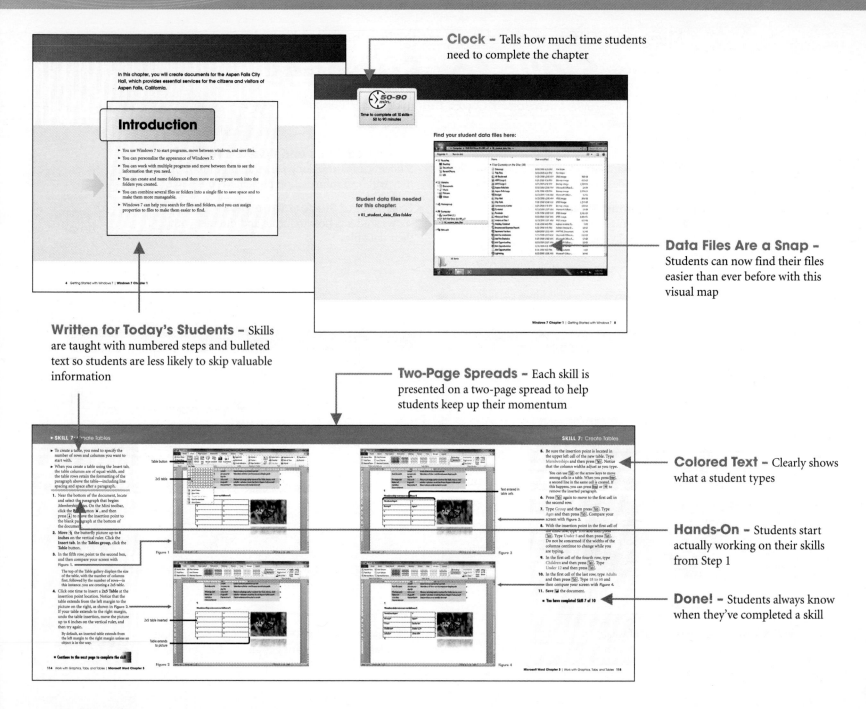

Clock – Tells how much time students need to complete the chapter

Data Files Are a Snap – Students can now find their files easier than ever before with this visual map

Written for Today's Students – Skills are taught with numbered steps and bulleted text so students are less likely to skip valuable information

Two-Page Spreads – Each skill is presented on a two-page spread to help students keep up their momentum

Colored Text – Clearly shows what a student types

Hands-On – Students start actually working on their skills from Step 1

Done! – Students always know when they've completed a skill

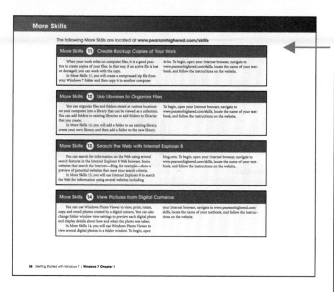

More Skills – Additional skills included online

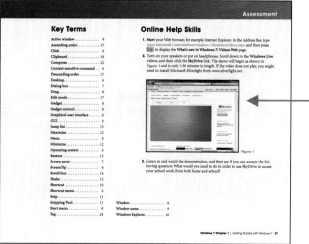

Online Project – Students practice using Microsoft Help online to help prepare them for using the applications on their own

End-of-Chapter Material – Several levels of assessment so you can assign the material that best fits your students' needs

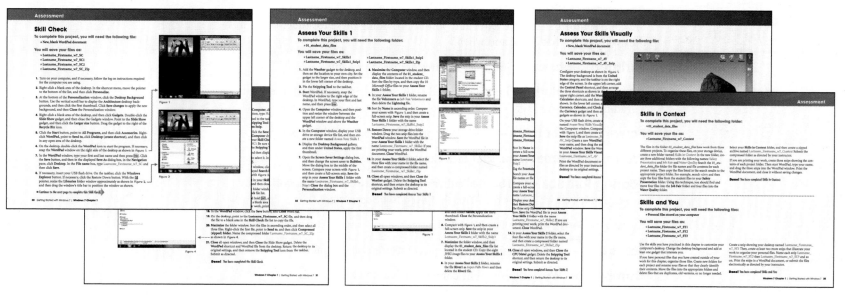

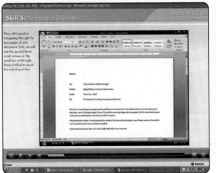
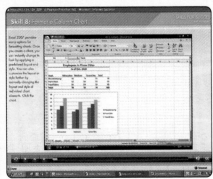

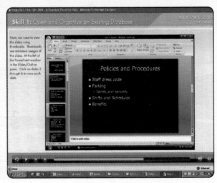

Videos! – Each skill within a chapter comes with a video that includes audio, which demonstrates the skill

NOTE: These videos are only available with *Skills for Success with Office 2010 Volume 1*

Instructor Materials

All Instructor materials available on the IRCD

Instructor's Manual – Teaching tips and additional resources for each chapter

Assignment Sheets – Lists all the assignments for the chapter, you just add in the course information, due dates and points. Providing these to students ensures they will know what is due and when

Scripted Lectures – Classroom lectures prepared for you

Annotated Solution Files – Coupled with the scoring rubrics, these create a grading and scoring system that makes grading so much easier for you

Power Point Lectures – PowerPoint presentations for each chapter

Prepared Exams – Exams for each chapter

Scoring Rubrics – Can be used either by students to check their work or by you as a quick check-off for the items that need to be corrected

Syllabus Templates – For 8-week, 12-week, and 16-week courses

Test Bank – Includes a variety of test questions for each chapter

Companion Website – Online content such as the More Skills Projects, Online Study Guide, Glossary, and Student Data Files are all at www.pearsonhighered.com/skills

SKILLS

For SUCCESS

with Microsoft®

PowerPoint 2010

COMPREHENSIVE

Common Features of Office 2010

▶ The programs in Microsoft Office 2010—Word, Excel, PowerPoint, and Access—share common tools that you use in a consistent, easy-to-learn manner.

▶ Common tasks include opening and saving files, entering and formatting text, and printing your work.

Your starting screen will look like this:

SKILLS
myitlab
Skills 1-10 Training

At the end of this chapter, you will be able to:

Skill 1 Start Word and Navigate the Word Window
Skill 2 Start Excel and PowerPoint and Work with Multiple Windows
Skill 3 Save Files in New Folders
Skill 4 Print and Save Documents
Skill 5 Open Student Data Files and Save Copies Using Save As
Skill 6 Type and Edit Text
Skill 7 Cut, Copy, and Paste Text
Skill 8 Format Text and Paragraphs
Skill 9 Use the Ribbon
Skill 10 Use Shortcut Menus and Dialog Boxes

MORE SKILLS

More Skills 11 Capture Screens with the Snipping Tool
More Skills 12 Use Microsoft Office Help
More Skills 13 Organize Files
More Skills 14 Save Documents to Windows Live

Outcome

Using the skills listed to the left will enable you to create documents similar to this:

Visit Aspen Falls!

Aspen Falls overlooks the Pacific Ocean and is surrounded by many vineyards and wineries. Ocean recreation is accessed primarily at Durango County Park. The Aspen Lake Recreation Area provides year round fresh water recreation and is the city's largest park.

Local Attractions
- Wine Country
  - Wine Tasting Tours
  - Wineries
- Wordsworth Fellowship Museum of Art
- Durango County Museum of History
- Convention Center
- Art Galleries
- Glider Tours

Aspen Falls Annual Events
- Annual Starving Artists Sidewalk Sale
- Annual Wine Festival
- Cinco de Mayo
- Vintage Car Show
- Heritage Day Parade
- Harvest Days
- Amateur Bike Races
- Farmer's Market
- Aspen Lake Nature Cruises
- Aspen Falls Triathlon
- Taste of Aspen Falls
- Winter Blues Festival

Contact Your Name for more information.

You will save your files as:

Lastname_Firstname_cf01_Visit1
Lastname_Firstname_cf01_Visit2
Lastname_Firstname_cf01_Visit3

In this chapter, you will create documents for the Aspen Falls City Hall, which provides essential services for the citizens and visitors of Aspen Falls, California.

Common Features of Office 2010

- ▶ Microsoft Office is the most common software used to create and share personal and business documents.

- ▶ Microsoft Office is a suite of several programs—Word, PowerPoint, Excel, Access, and others—that each have a special purpose.

- ▶ Because of the consistent design and layout of Microsoft Office, when you learn to use one Microsoft Office program, you can use most of those skills when working with the other Microsoft Office programs.

- ▶ The files you create with Microsoft Office need to be named and saved in locations where they can be easily found when you need them.

**Time to complete all
10 skills – 50 to 90 minutes**

Find your student data files here:

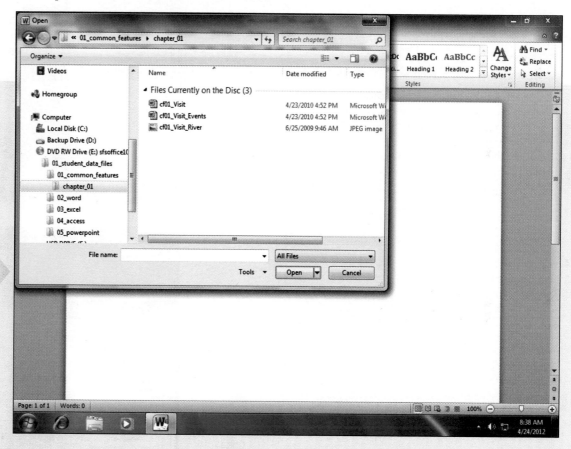

Student data files needed for this chapter:

- cf01_Visit
- cf01_Visit_Events
- cf01_Visit_River

► The Word 2010 program can be launched by clicking the Start button, and then locating and clicking the *Microsoft Word 2010* command.

► When you start Word, a new blank document displays in which you can type text.

1. In the lower left corner of the desktop, click the **Start** button 🚀.

2. In the lower left corner of the **Start** menu, click the **All Programs** command, and then compare your screen with **Figure 1**.

   The Microsoft Office folder is located in the All Programs folder. If you have several programs installed on your computer, you may need to scroll to see the Microsoft Office folder.

3. Click the **Microsoft Office** folder, and then compare your screen with **Figure 2**.

   Below the Microsoft Office folder, commands that open various Office 2010 programs display.

4. From the **Start** menu, under the **Microsoft Office** folder, click **Microsoft Word 2010**, and then wait a few moments for the Microsoft Word window to display.

5. If necessary, in the upper right corner of the Microsoft Word window, click the Maximize button 🗖.

■ **Continue to the next page to complete the skill**

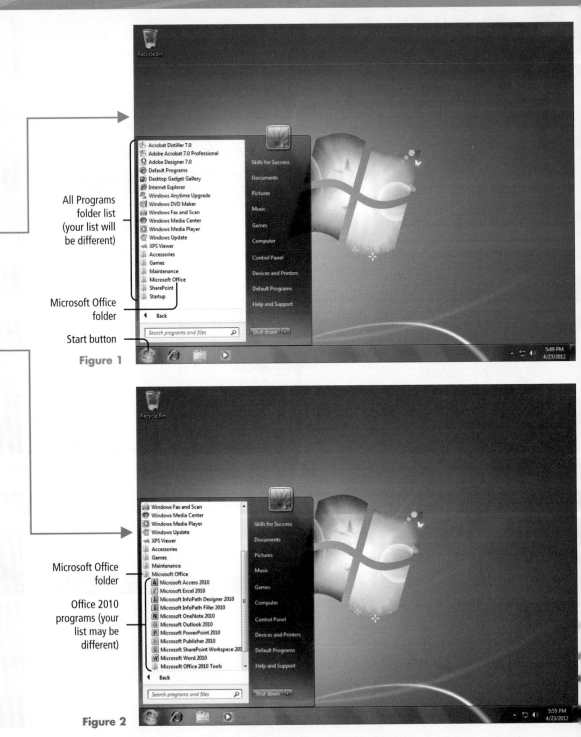

All Programs folder list (your list will be different)

Microsoft Office folder

Start button

Figure 1

Microsoft Office folder

Office 2010 programs (your list may be different)

Figure 2

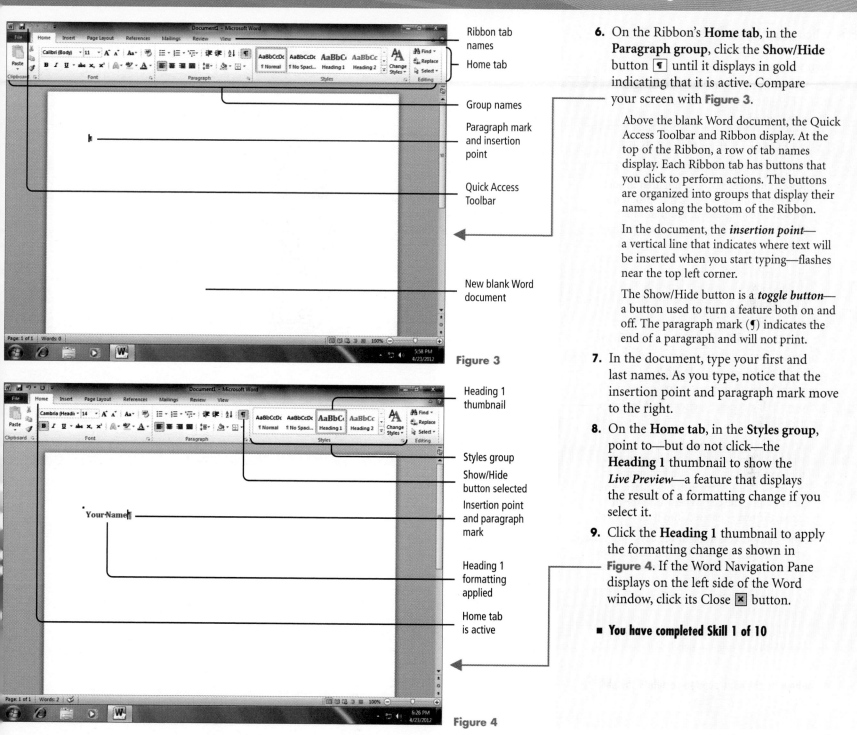

Figure 3

Figure 4

6. On the Ribbon's **Home tab**, in the **Paragraph group**, click the **Show/Hide** button ¶ until it displays in gold indicating that it is active. Compare your screen with **Figure 3**.

> Above the blank Word document, the Quick Access Toolbar and Ribbon display. At the top of the Ribbon, a row of tab names display. Each Ribbon tab has buttons that you click to perform actions. The buttons are organized into groups that display their names along the bottom of the Ribbon.
>
> In the document, the *insertion point*— a vertical line that indicates where text will be inserted when you start typing—flashes near the top left corner.
>
> The Show/Hide button is a *toggle button*— a button used to turn a feature both on and off. The paragraph mark (¶) indicates the end of a paragraph and will not print.

7. In the document, type your first and last names. As you type, notice that the insertion point and paragraph mark move to the right.

8. On the **Home tab**, in the **Styles group**, point to—but do not click—the **Heading 1** thumbnail to show the *Live Preview*—a feature that displays the result of a formatting change if you select it.

9. Click the **Heading 1** thumbnail to apply the formatting change as shown in **Figure 4**. If the Word Navigation Pane displays on the left side of the Word window, click its Close ☒ button.

■ **You have completed Skill 1 of 10**

► When you open more than one Office program, each program displays in its own window.

► When you want to work with a program in a different window, you need to make it the active window.

1. Click the **Start** button ⬢, and then compare your screen with **Figure 1**.

   Your computer may be configured in such a way that you can open Office programs without opening the All Programs folder. The Office 2010 program commands may display as shortcuts in the Start menu's pinned programs area or the recently used programs area. Your computer's taskbar or desktop may also display icons that start each program.

2. From the **Start** menu, locate and then click **Microsoft Excel 2010**. Depending on your computer, you may need to double-click—not single click—to launch Excel. Compare your screen with **Figure 2**. If necessary, click the Maximize button ▣.

   A new blank worksheet displays in a new window. The first *cell*—the box formed by the intersection of a row and column—is active as indicated by the thick, black border surrounding the cell. When you type in Excel, the text is entered into the active cell.

   The Quick Access Toolbar displays above the spreadsheet. The Excel Ribbon has its own tabs and groups that you use to work with an Excel spreadsheet. Many of these tabs, groups, and buttons are similar to those found in Word.

   On the taskbar, two buttons display—one for Word and one for Excel.

■ **Continue to the next page to complete the skill**

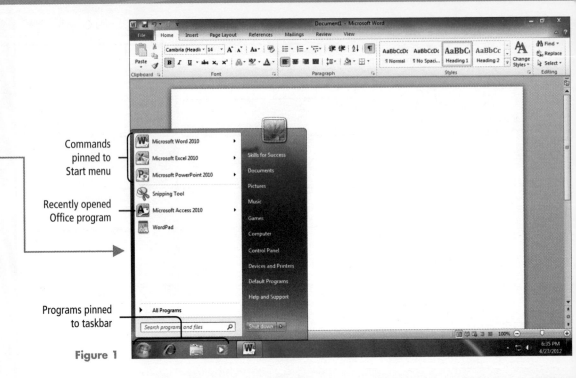

Commands pinned to Start menu

Recently opened Office program

Programs pinned to taskbar

Figure 1

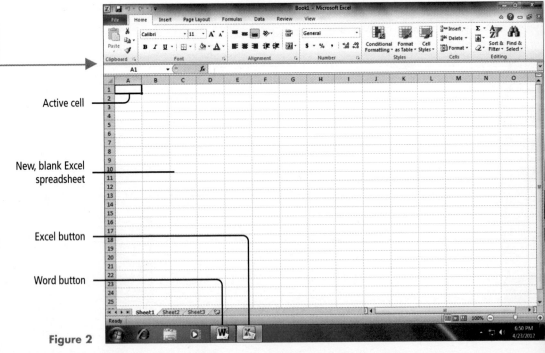

Active cell

New, blank Excel spreadsheet

Excel button

Word button

Figure 2

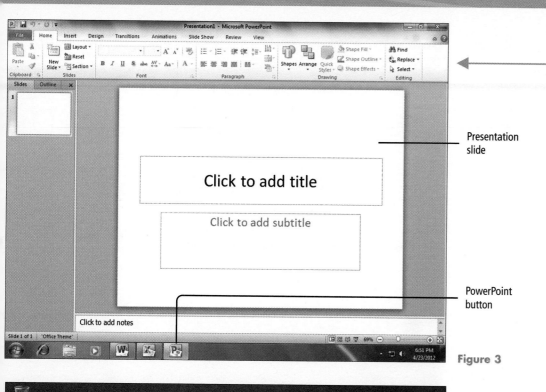

Presentation slide

PowerPoint button

Figure 3

3. From the **Start** menu 💿, locate and then click **Microsoft PowerPoint 2010**. Compare your screen with **Figure 3**. If necessary, Maximize ⬜ the Presentation1 - Microsoft PowerPoint window.

> A new, blank presentation opens in a new window. The PowerPoint window contains a slide in which you can type text. PowerPoint slides are designed to be displayed as you talk in front of a group of people.

4. In the upper right corner of the **PowerPoint** window, click the **Close** button ❌.

5. On the taskbar, click the **Word** button to make it the active window. With the insertion point flashing to the right of your name, press Enter, and then type Skills for Success Common Features Chapter

6. In the upper right corner of the **Document1 - Microsoft Word** window, click the **Minimize** button ➖.

> The Word window no longer displays, but its button is still available on the taskbar.

7. With the Excel window active, in the first cell—cell **A1**—type your first name. Press Tab, and then type your last name.

8. Press Enter, type =TODAY() and then press Enter to calculate the current date and to display it in the cell.

9. In the **Excel** window, click the **Restore Down** button ⬜ and then compare your screen with **Figure 4**.

> The window remains open, but it no longer fills the entire screen. The Maximize button replaced the Restore Down button.

▪ **You have completed Skill 2 of 10**

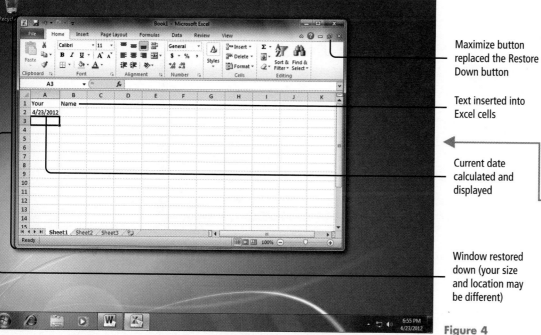

Maximize button replaced the Restore Down button

Text inserted into Excel cells

Current date calculated and displayed

Window restored down (your size and location may be different)

Figure 4

► A new document or spreadsheet is stored in the computer's temporary memory (**RAM**) until you save it to your hard drive or USB flash drive.

1. If you are saving your work on a USB flash drive, insert the USB flash drive into the computer now. If the Windows Explorer button 📁 flashes on the taskbar, right-click the button, and then on the Jump List, click Close window.

2. On the taskbar, click the **Word** button to make it the active window. On the **Quick Access Toolbar**, click the **Save** button 💾.

   For new documents, the first time you click the Save button, the Save As dialog box opens so that you can name the file.

3. If you are to save your work on a USB drive, in the Navigation pane scroll down to display the list of drives, and then click your USB flash drive as shown in **Figure 1**. If you are saving your work to another location, in the Navigation pane, locate and then click that folder or drive.

4. On the **Save As** dialog box toolbar, click the **New folder** button, and then immediately type Common Features Chapter 1

5. Press Enter to accept the folder name, and then press Enter again to open the new folder as shown in **Figure 2**.

   The new folder is created and then opened in the Save As dialog box file list.

■ **Continue to the next page to complete the skill**

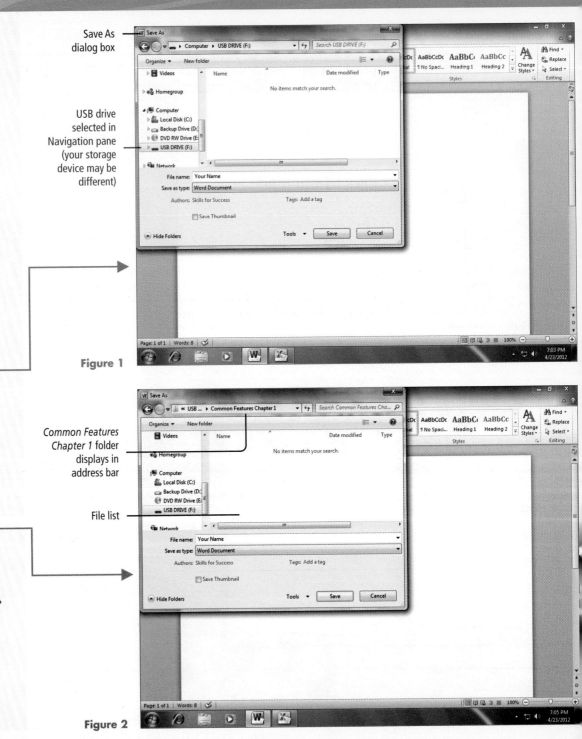

Save As dialog box

USB drive selected in Navigation pane (your storage device may be different)

Figure 1

Common Features Chapter 1 folder displays in address bar

File list

Figure 2

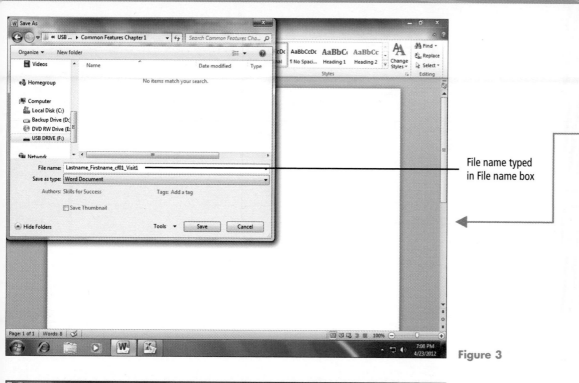

File name typed in File name box

Figure 3

6. In the **Save As** dialog box, click in the **File name** box one time to highlight all of the existing text.

7. With the text in the **File name** box still highlighted, type Lastname_Firstname_ cf01_Visit1

8. Compare your screen with **Figure 3**, and then click **Save**.

   After the document is saved, the name of the file displays on the title bar at the top of the window.

9. On the taskbar, click the **Windows Explorer** button . In the folder window **Navigation** pane, open the drive on which you are saving your work, and then click the **Common Features Chapter 1** folder. Verify that *Lastname_Firstname_ cf01_Visit1* displays in file list.

10. On the taskbar, click the **Excel** button to make it the active window. On the Excel **Quick Access Toolbar**, click the **Save** button .

11. In the **Save As** dialog box **Navigation** pane, open the drive where you are saving your work, and then click the **Common Features Chapter 1** folder to display its file list.

    The Word file may not display because the Save As box typically displays only files created by the program you are using. Here, only Excel files will typically display.

12. Click in the **File name** box, replace the existing value with Lastname_Firstname_ cf01_Visit2 and then click the **Save** button.

13. On the taskbar, click the **Windows Explorer** button, and then compare your screen with **Figure 4**.

■ **You have completed Skill 3 of 10**

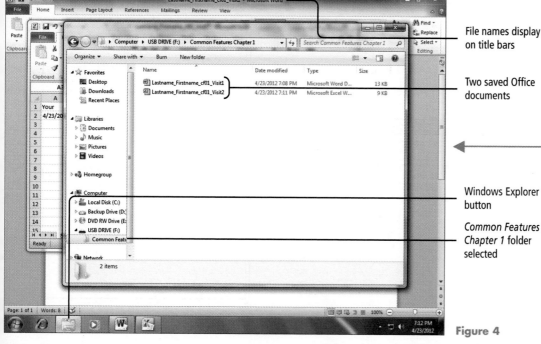

File names display on title bars

Two saved Office documents

Windows Explorer button

Common Features Chapter 1 folder selected

Figure 4

► Before printing, it is a good idea to work in *Page Layout view*—a view where you prepare your document or spreadsheet for printing.

1. On the taskbar, click the **Excel** button, and then click the **Maximize** button.

2. On the Ribbon, click the **View tab**, and then in the **Workbook Views group**, click the **Page Layout** button. Compare your screen with **Figure 1**.

   The worksheet displays the cells, the margins, and the edges of the paper as they will be positioned when you print. The *cell references*—the numbers on the left side and the letters across the top of a spreadsheet that address each cell—will not print.

3. On the Ribbon, click the **Page Layout tab**. In the **Page Setup group**, click the **Margins** button, and then in the **Margins** gallery, click **Wide**.

4. Click the **File tab**, and then on the left side of the Backstage, click **Print**. Compare your screen with **Figure 2**.

   The Print tab has commands that affect your print job and a preview of the printed page. Here, the cell references and *grid lines*—lines between the cells in a table or spreadsheet—do not display because they will not be printed.

5. In the **Print Settings**, under **Printer**, notice the name of the printer. You will need to retrieve your printout from this printer. If your instructor has directed you to print to a different printer, click the Printer arrow, and choose the assigned printer.

■ **Continue to the next page to complete the skill** ►

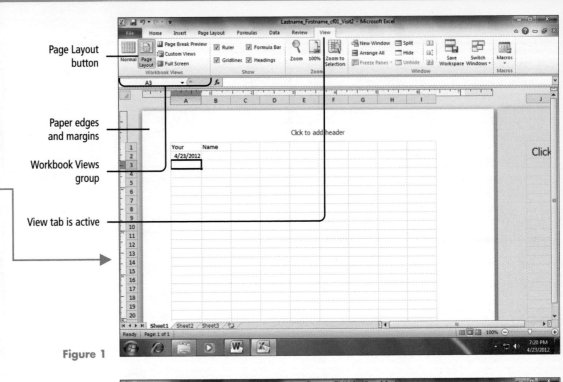

Page Layout button
Paper edges and margins
Workbook Views group
View tab is active

Figure 1

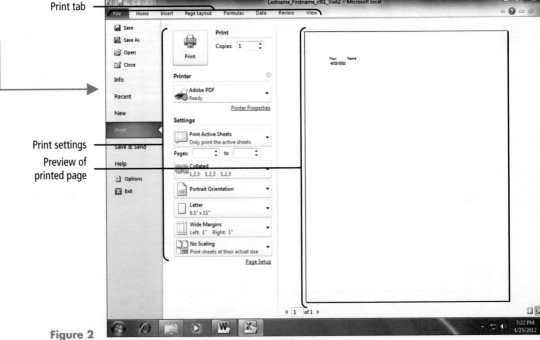

Print tab
Print settings
Preview of printed page

Figure 2

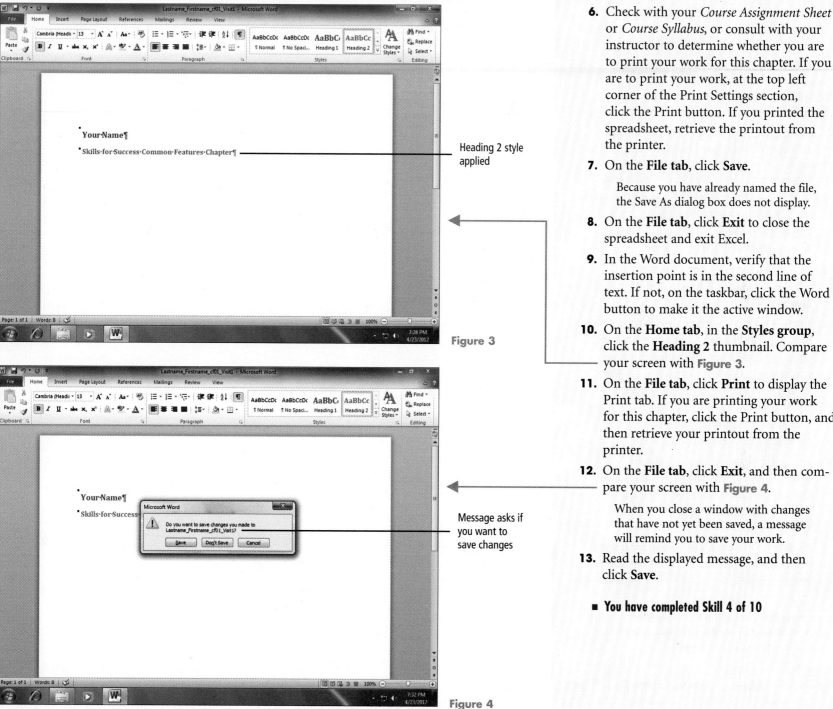

Heading 2 style applied

Figure 3

Message asks if you want to save changes

Figure 4

6. Check with your *Course Assignment Sheet* or *Course Syllabus,* or consult with your instructor to determine whether you are to print your work for this chapter. If you are to print your work, at the top left corner of the Print Settings section, click the Print button. If you printed the spreadsheet, retrieve the printout from the printer.

7. On the **File tab**, click **Save**.

   Because you have already named the file, the Save As dialog box does not display.

8. On the **File tab**, click **Exit** to close the spreadsheet and exit Excel.

9. In the Word document, verify that the insertion point is in the second line of text. If not, on the taskbar, click the Word button to make it the active window.

10. On the **Home tab**, in the **Styles group**, click the **Heading 2** thumbnail. Compare your screen with **Figure 3**.

11. On the **File tab**, click **Print** to display the Print tab. If you are printing your work for this chapter, click the Print button, and then retrieve your printout from the printer.

12. On the **File tab**, click **Exit**, and then compare your screen with **Figure 4**.

    When you close a window with changes that have not yet been saved, a message will remind you to save your work.

13. Read the displayed message, and then click **Save**.

■ **You have completed Skill 4 of 10**

▸ This book often instructs you to open a student data file so that you do not need to start the project with a blank document.

▸ The student data files are located on the student CD that came with this book. Your instructor may have provided an alternate location.

▸ You use Save As to create a copy of the student data file onto your own storage device.

1. If necessary, insert the student CD that came with this text. If the AutoPlay dialog box displays, click Close ⊠.

2. Using the skills practiced earlier, start **Microsoft Word 2010**.

3. In the **Document1 - Microsoft Word** window, click the **File tab**, and then click **Open**.

4. In the **Open** dialog box **Navigation** pane, scroll down and then, if necessary, open ▷ Computer. In the list of drives, click the CD/DVD drive to display the contents of the student CD. If your instructor has provided a different location, navigate to that location instead of using the student CD.

5. In the file list, double-click the **01_student_data_files** folder, double-click the **01_common_features** folder, and then double-click the **chapter_01** folder. Compare your screen with **Figure 1**.

6. In the file list, click **cf01_Visit**, and then click the **Open** button. Compare your screen with **Figure 2**.

   If you opened the file from the student CD, the title bar indicates that the document is in *read-only mode*—a mode where you cannot save your changes.

■ **Continue to the next page to complete the skill**

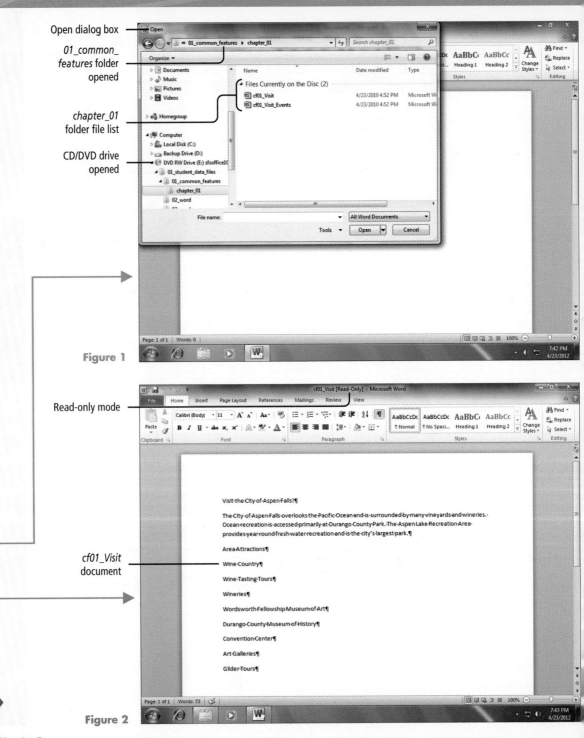

Open dialog box

01_common_features folder opened

chapter_01 folder file list

CD/DVD drive opened

Figure 1

Read-only mode

cf01_Visit document

Figure 2

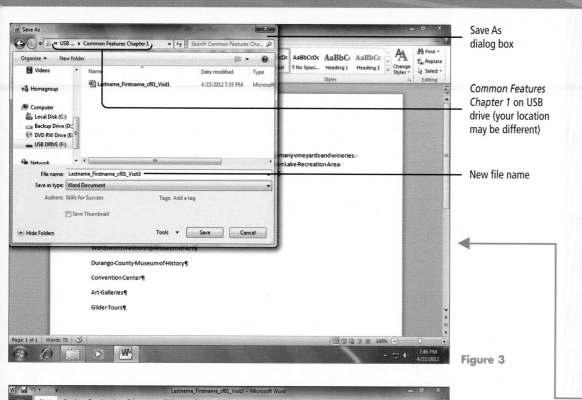

Save As dialog box

Common Features Chapter 1 on USB drive (your location may be different)

New file name

Figure 3

7. If the document opens in Protected View, click the Enable Editing button.

   Protected View is a view applied to documents downloaded from the Internet that allows you to decide if the content is safe before working with the document.

8. Click the **File tab**, and then click **Save As**.

   Because this file has already been saved with a name in a specific location, you need to use Save As to create a copy with a new name and location.

9. In the **Save As** dialog box **Navigation** pane, navigate to the **Common Features Chapter 1** folder that you created previously—open ▷ the drive on which you are saving your work, and then click the **Common Features Chapter 1** folder.

10. In the **File name** box, replace the existing value with Lastname_Firstname_cf01_ Visit3 Be sure to use your own first and last names.

11. Compare your screen with **Figure 3**, and then click the **Save** button.

12. On the title bar, notice the new file name displays and *[Read-Only]* no longer displays.

13. On the taskbar, click the **Windows Explorer** button. Verify that the three files you have saved in this chapter display as shown in **Figure 4**.

14. In the Windows Explorer window, navigate to the **student CD**, and then display the **chapter_01** file list.

15. Notice that the original student data file—*cf01_Visit*—is still located in the **chapter_01** folder, and then **Close** ✕ the Windows Explorer window.

■ **You have completed Skill 5 of 10**

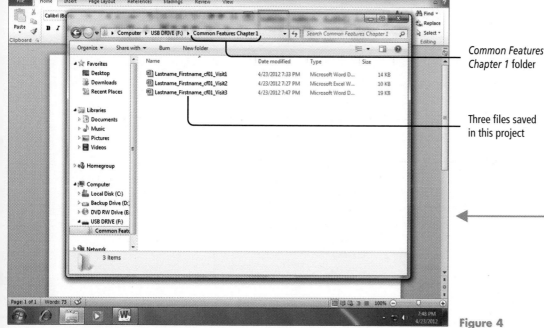

Common Features Chapter 1 folder

Three files saved in this project

Figure 4

► To *edit* is to insert text, delete text, or replace text in an Office document, spreadsheet, or presentation.

► To edit text, you need to position the insertion point at the desired location or select the text you want to replace.

1. With the **Word** document as the active window, in the first line, click to the left of the word *Aspen*. Press [Bksp] 12 times to delete the words *the City of*. Be sure there is one space between each word as shown in **Figure 1**. ─────────

    The Backspace key deletes one letter at a time moving from right to left.

2. In the second line of the document, click to the left of the words *The City of Aspen Falls*. Press [Delete] 12 times to delete the phrase *The City of*.

    The Delete key deletes one letter at a time moving from left to right.

3. In the line *Area Attractions*, double-click the word *Area* to select it. Type Local and then compare your screen with **Figure 2**. ──

    When a word is selected, it is replaced by whatever you type next.

■ **Continue to the next page to complete the skill**

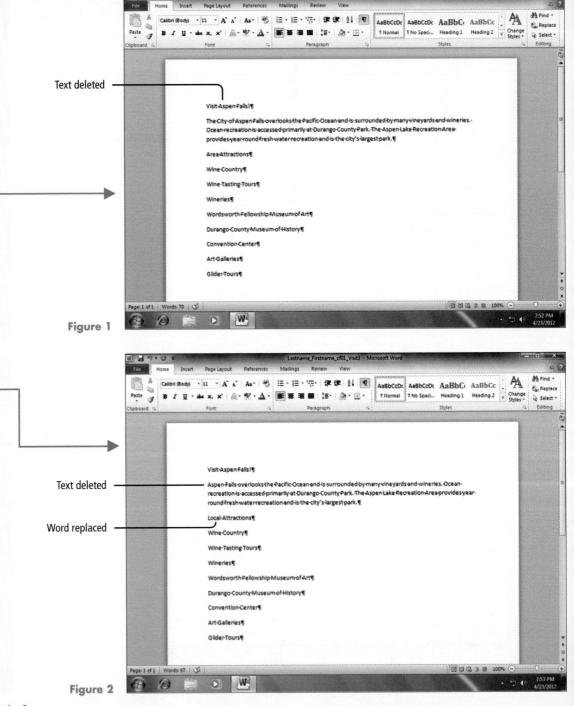

Text deleted

Figure 1

Text deleted

Word replaced

Figure 2

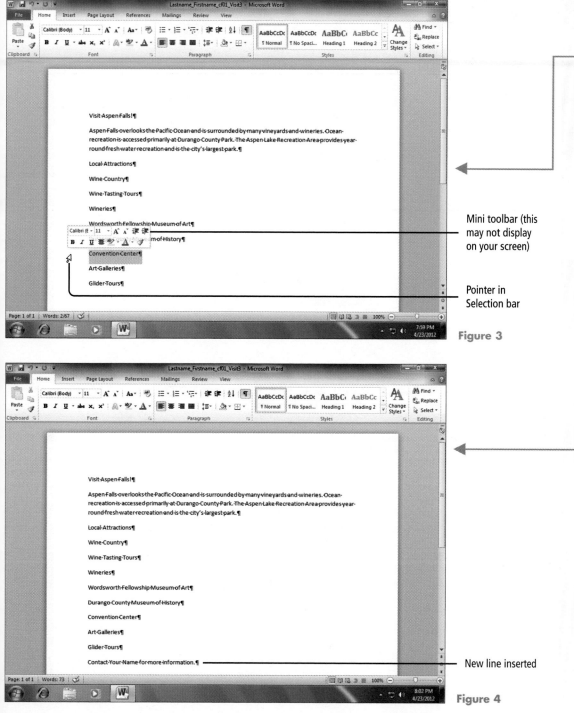

Figure 3

Mini toolbar (this may not display on your screen)

Pointer in Selection bar

New line inserted

Figure 4

4. Place the pointer approximately 1 inch to the left of the line *Convention Center*. When the 🔄 pointer displays as shown in **Figure 3**, click one time.

Placing the pointer in the Selection bar and then clicking is a way to select an entire line with a single click. After selecting text, the **Mini toolbar**—a toolbar with common formatting buttons—may display briefly as you move the mouse.

5. With the entire line still selected, press Delete to delete the line.

6. On the **Quick Access Toolbar**, click the **Undo** button 🔄 one time. Notice the *Convention Center* line displays again.

When you perform an incorrect action, clicking the Undo button often returns your document to its previous state.

7. At the end of the last line—*Glider Tours*—click between the last word and the paragraph formatting mark (¶). Press Enter to insert a new line.

8. With the insertion point in the new line, type Contact Your Name for more information. Be sure to use your first and last names in place of *Your* and *Name*. Compare your screen with **Figure 4**.

9. On the **Quick Access Toolbar**, click **Save** 🖫.

When a document has already been saved with the desired name, click the Save button—the Save As dialog box is not needed.

■ **You have completed Skill 6 of 10**

▶ The *copy* command places a copy of the selected text or object in the *Clipboard*—a temporary storage area that holds text or an object that has been cut or copied.

▶ You can move text by moving it to and from the Clipboard or by dragging the text.

1. Click the **File tab**, and then click **Open**. In the **Open** dialog box, if necessary, navigate to the student files and display the contents of the chapter_01 folder. Click **cf01_Visit_Events**, and then click **Open**.

2. On the right side of the Ribbon's **Home tab**, in the **Editing group**, click the **Select** button, and then click **Select All**. Compare your screen with **Figure 1**.

3. With all of the document text selected, on the left side of the **Home tab**, in the **Clipboard group**, click the **Copy** button 🗐.

4. In the upper right corner of the Word window, click **Close** ✖. You do not need to save changes—you will not turn in this student data file.

5. In **Lastname_Firstname_cf01_Visit3**, click to place the insertion point to the left of the line that starts *Contact Your Name*.

6. On the **Home tab**, in the **Clipboard group**, point to—but do not click—the **Paste** button. Compare your screen with **Figure 2**.

   The Paste button has two parts—the upper half is the Paste button, and the lower half is the Paste button arrow. When you click the Paste button arrow, a list of paste options display.

▪ **Continue to the next page to complete the skill**

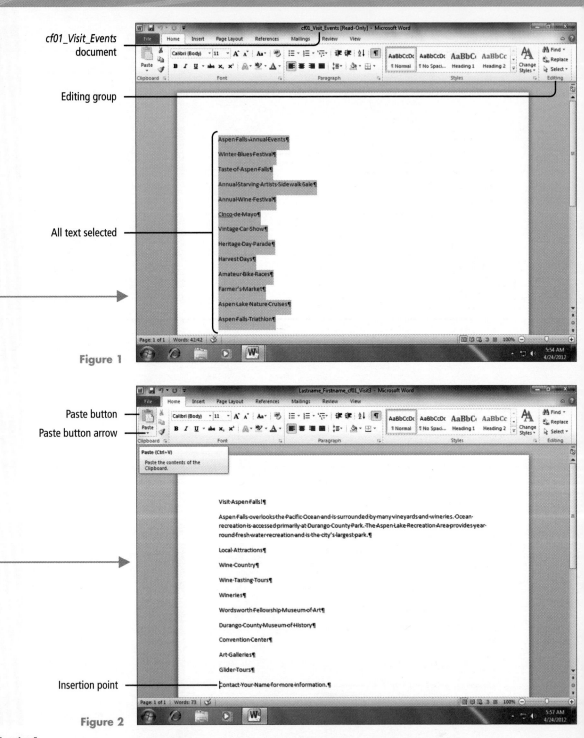

cf01_Visit_Events document

Editing group

All text selected

Figure 1

Paste button

Paste button arrow

Insertion point

Figure 2

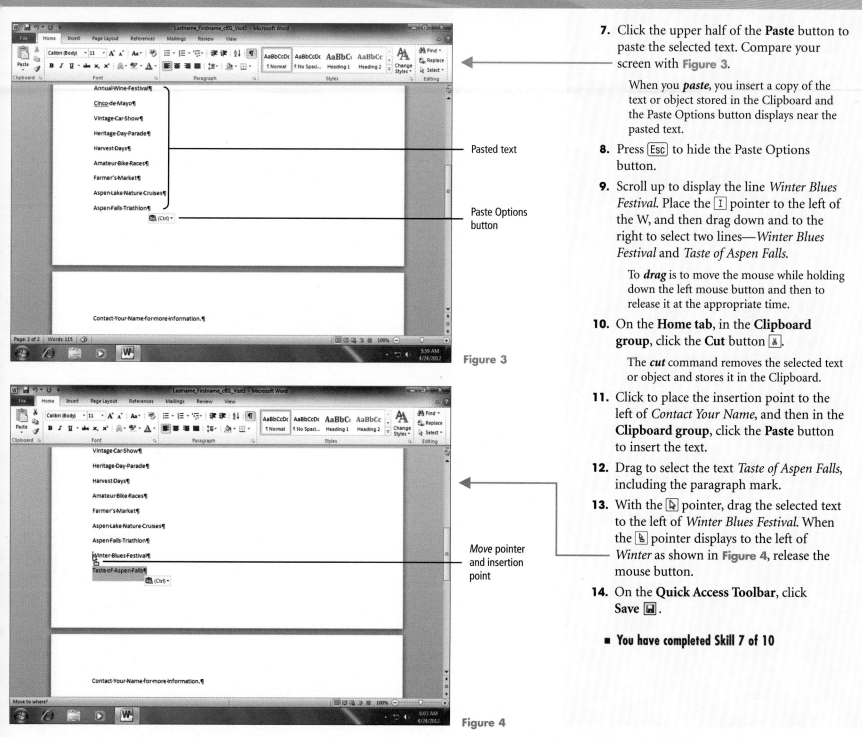

Pasted text

Paste Options
button

Figure 3

Move pointer
and insertion
point

Figure 4

7. Click the upper half of the **Paste** button to paste the selected text. Compare your screen with **Figure 3**.

   When you *paste*, you insert a copy of the text or object stored in the Clipboard and the Paste Options button displays near the pasted text.

8. Press [Esc] to hide the Paste Options button.

9. Scroll up to display the line *Winter Blues Festival*. Place the [I] pointer to the left of the W, and then drag down and to the right to select two lines—*Winter Blues Festival* and *Taste of Aspen Falls*.

   To *drag* is to move the mouse while holding down the left mouse button and then to release it at the appropriate time.

10. On the **Home tab**, in the **Clipboard group**, click the **Cut** button [✄].

    The *cut* command removes the selected text or object and stores it in the Clipboard.

11. Click to place the insertion point to the left of *Contact Your Name*, and then in the **Clipboard group**, click the **Paste** button to insert the text.

12. Drag to select the text *Taste of Aspen Falls*, including the paragraph mark.

13. With the [▷] pointer, drag the selected text to the left of *Winter Blues Festival*. When the [▷] pointer displays to the left of *Winter* as shown in **Figure 4**, release the mouse button.

14. On the **Quick Access Toolbar**, click **Save** [💾].

■ **You have completed Skill 7 of 10**

▶ To *format* is to change the appearance of the text—for example, changing the text color to red.

▶ Before formatting text, you first need to select the text that will be formatted.

▶ Once text is selected, you can apply formatting using the Ribbon or the Mini toolbar.

1. Scroll to the top of the document, and then click anywhere in the first line, *Visit Aspen Falls.*

2. On the **Home tab**, in the **Styles group**, click the **Heading 1** thumbnail.

    When no text is selected, the Heading 1 style is applied to the entire paragraph.

3. Click in the paragraph, *Local Attractions,* and then in the **Styles group**, click the **Heading 2** thumbnail. Click in the paragraph, *Aspen Falls Annual Events,* and then apply the **Heading 2** style. Compare your screen with **Figure 1**.

4. Drag to select the text *Visit Aspen Falls!* Immediately point to—but do not click—the Mini toolbar to display it as shown in **Figure 2**. If necessary, right-click the selected text to display the Mini toolbar.

■ **Continue to the next page to complete the skill**

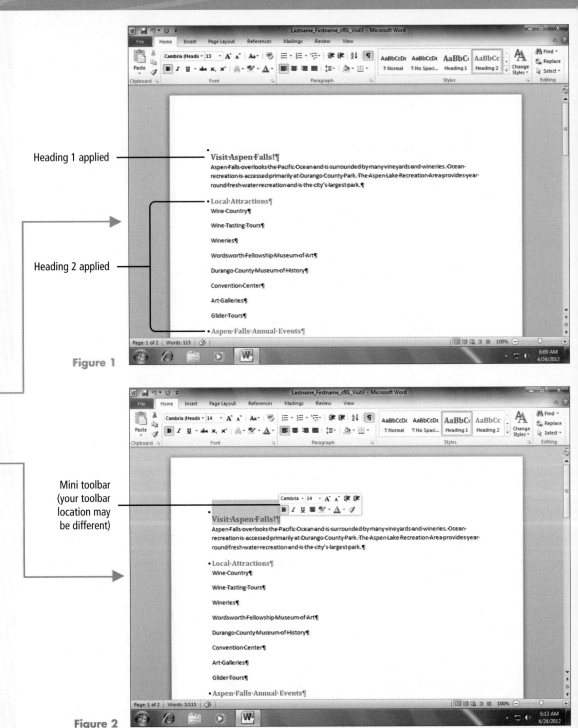

Heading 1 applied

Heading 2 applied

Figure 1

Mini toolbar (your toolbar location may be different)

Figure 2

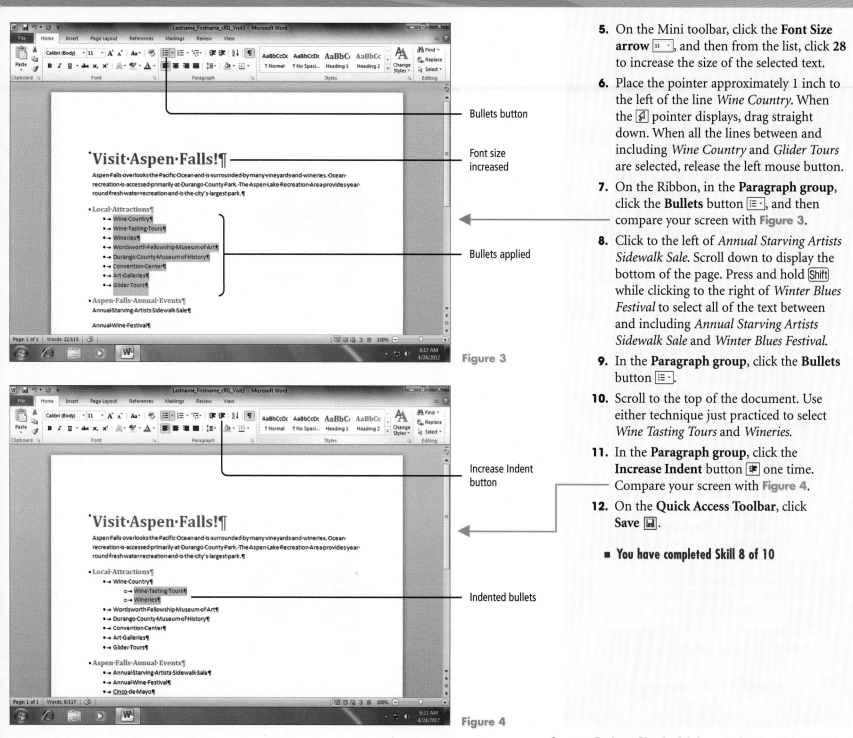

Figure 3

Figure 4

5. On the Mini toolbar, click the **Font Size arrow** ⊞⁻, and then from the list, click **28** to increase the size of the selected text.

6. Place the pointer approximately 1 inch to the left of the line *Wine Country*. When the ⬧ pointer displays, drag straight down. When all the lines between and including *Wine Country* and *Glider Tours* are selected, release the left mouse button.

7. On the Ribbon, in the **Paragraph group**, click the **Bullets** button ⊞⁻, and then compare your screen with **Figure 3**.

8. Click to the left of *Annual Starving Artists Sidewalk Sale*. Scroll down to display the bottom of the page. Press and hold ⇧Shift while clicking to the right of *Winter Blues Festival* to select all of the text between and including *Annual Starving Artists Sidewalk Sale* and *Winter Blues Festival*.

9. In the **Paragraph group**, click the **Bullets** button ⊞⁻.

10. Scroll to the top of the document. Use either technique just practiced to select *Wine Tasting Tours* and *Wineries*.

11. In the **Paragraph group**, click the **Increase Indent** button ⊞ one time. Compare your screen with **Figure 4**.

12. On the **Quick Access Toolbar**, click **Save** 🖫.

■ **You have completed Skill 8 of 10**

▶ Each Ribbon tab contains commands organized into groups. Some tabs display only when a certain type of object is selected—a graphic, for example.

1. Press and hold Ctrl, and then press Home to place the insertion point at the beginning of the document.

2. On the **Ribbon,** to the right of the **Home tab**, click the **Insert tab**. In the **Illustrations group**, click the **Picture** button.

3. In the **Insert Picture** dialog box, navigate as needed to display the contents of the student files in the **chapter_01** folder. Click **cf01_Visit_River**, and then click the **Insert** button. Compare your screen with **Figure 1**.

   When a picture is selected, the Format tab displays below Picture Tools. On the Format tab, in the Picture Styles group, a *gallery*— a visual display of choices from which you can choose—displays thumbnails. The entire gallery can be seen by clicking the More button to the right and below the first row of thumbnails.

4. On the **Format tab**, in the **Picture Styles group**, click the **More** button ▼ to display the **Picture Styles** gallery. In the gallery, point to the fourth thumbnail in the first row—**Drop Shadow Rectangle**—to display the ScreenTip as shown in **Figure 2**.

   A *ScreenTip* is informational text that displays when you point to commands or thumbnails on the Ribbon.

5. Click the **Drop Shadow Rectangle** thumbnail to apply the picture style.

■ **Continue to the next page to complete the skill** ▶

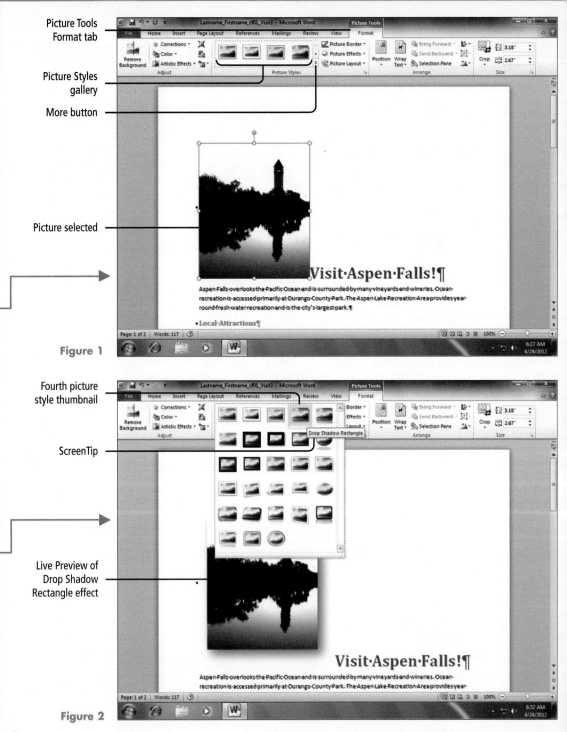

Picture Tools Format tab

Picture Styles gallery

More button

Picture selected

Figure 1

Fourth picture style thumbnail

ScreenTip

Live Preview of Drop Shadow Rectangle effect

Figure 2

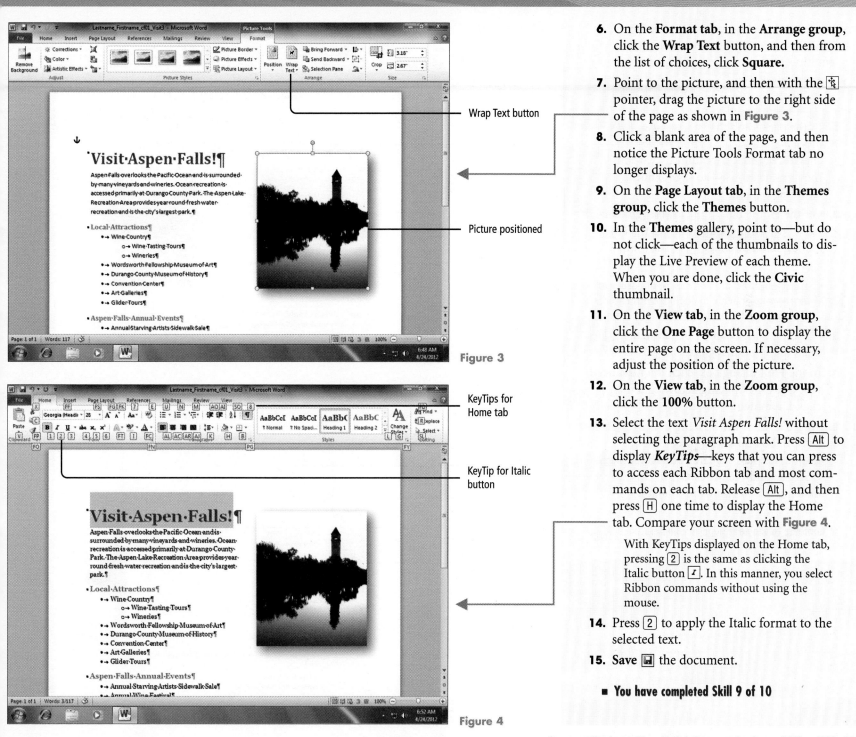

Wrap Text button

Picture positioned

Figure 3

KeyTips for
Home tab

KeyTip for Italic
button

Figure 4

6. On the **Format tab**, in the **Arrange group**, click the **Wrap Text** button, and then from the list of choices, click **Square.**

7. Point to the picture, and then with the pointer, drag the picture to the right side of the page as shown in **Figure 3**.

8. Click a blank area of the page, and then notice the Picture Tools Format tab no longer displays.

9. On the **Page Layout tab**, in the **Themes group**, click the **Themes** button.

10. In the **Themes** gallery, point to—but do not click—each of the thumbnails to display the Live Preview of each theme. When you are done, click the **Civic** thumbnail.

11. On the **View tab**, in the **Zoom group**, click the **One Page** button to display the entire page on the screen. If necessary, adjust the position of the picture.

12. On the **View tab**, in the **Zoom group**, click the **100%** button.

13. Select the text *Visit Aspen Falls!* without selecting the paragraph mark. Press [Alt] to display *KeyTips*—keys that you can press to access each Ribbon tab and most commands on each tab. Release [Alt], and then press [H] one time to display the Home tab. Compare your screen with **Figure 4**.

    With KeyTips displayed on the Home tab, pressing [2] is the same as clicking the Italic button [I]. In this manner, you select Ribbon commands without using the mouse.

14. Press [2] to apply the Italic format to the selected text.

15. **Save** the document.

■ **You have completed Skill 9 of 10**

▶ Commands can be accessed in *dialog boxes*—boxes where you can select multiple settings.

▶ You can also access commands by right-clicking objects in a document.

1. In the paragraph that starts *Aspen Falls overlooks the Pacific Ocean*, **triple-click**—click three times fairly quickly without moving the mouse—to highlight the entire paragraph.

2. On the **Home tab**, in the lower right corner of the **Font group**, point to the **Font Dialog Box Launcher** 🖿 as shown in **Figure 1**. ⎯⎯⎯⎯⎯⎯⎯

   The 🖿 buttons at the lower right corner of most groups open a dialog box with choices that may not be available on the Ribbon.

3. Click the **Font Dialog Box Launcher** 🖿 to open the Font dialog box.

4. In the **Font** dialog box, click the **Advanced tab**. Click the **Spacing arrow**, and then click **Expanded**.

5. To the right of the **Spacing** box, click the **By spin box up arrow** three times to display *1.3 pt*. Compare your screen with **Figure 2**, and then click **OK** to close the dialog box and apply the changes.

■ **Continue to the next page to complete the skill**

Font Dialog Box Launcher

Font dialog box preview

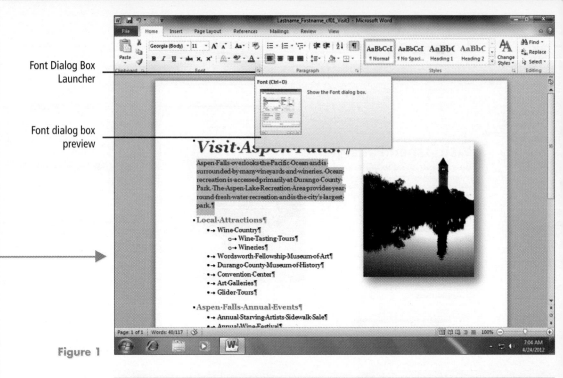

Figure 1

Font dialog box

Advanced tab

Spacing arrow

Spin box arrows

Paragraph selected

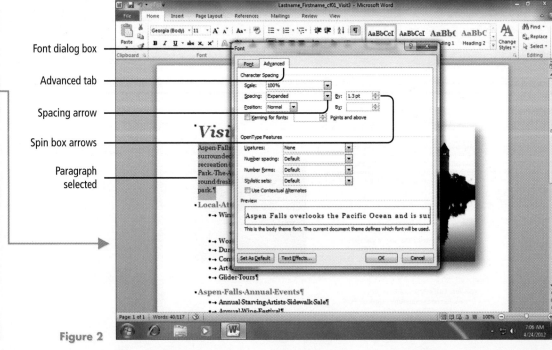

Figure 2

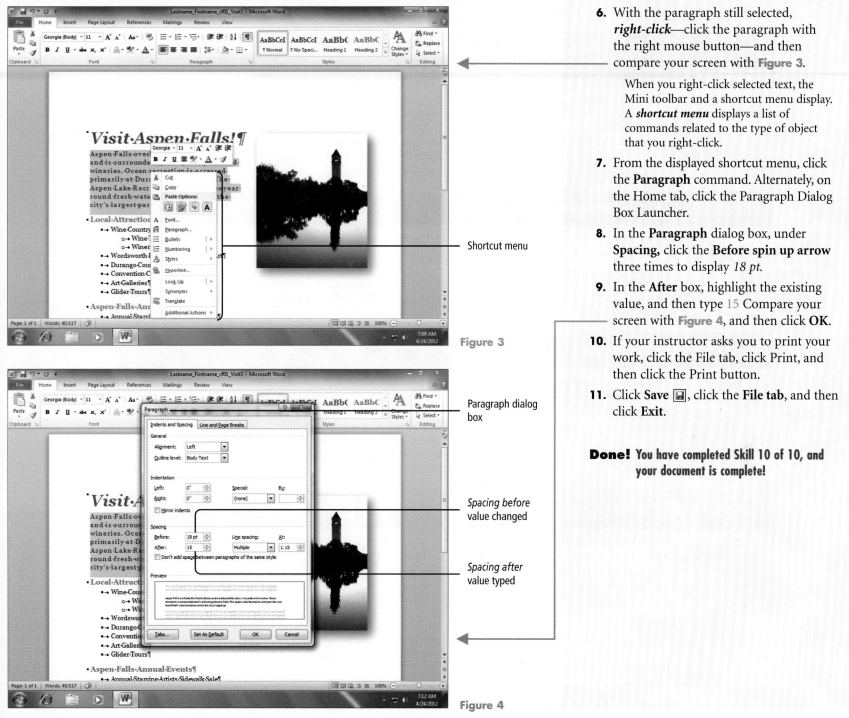

Figure 3

Figure 4

6. With the paragraph still selected, *right-click*—click the paragraph with the right mouse button—and then compare your screen with **Figure 3**.

> When you right-click selected text, the Mini toolbar and a shortcut menu display. A *shortcut menu* displays a list of commands related to the type of object that you right-click.

7. From the displayed shortcut menu, click the **Paragraph** command. Alternately, on the Home tab, click the Paragraph Dialog Box Launcher.

8. In the **Paragraph** dialog box, under **Spacing,** click the **Before spin up arrow** three times to display *18 pt.*

9. In the **After** box, highlight the existing value, and then type 15 Compare your screen with **Figure 4**, and then click **OK**.

10. If your instructor asks you to print your work, click the File tab, click Print, and then click the Print button.

11. Click **Save** 🖫, click the **File tab,** and then click **Exit**.

Done! You have completed Skill 10 of 10, and your document is complete!

More Skills

The following More Skills are located at **www.pearsonhighered.com/skills**

More Skills Capture Screens with the Snipping Tool

Some of the work that you do in this book cannot be graded without showing your computer screens to the grader. You can use the Snipping Tool to create pictures of your screens. Snip files can be printed or submitted electronically.

In More Skills 11, you will use the Snipping Tool to create a picture of your screen and then copy the picture into a Word document.

To begin, open your web browser, navigate to www.pearsonhighered.com/skills, locate the name of your textbook, and then follow the instructions on the website.

More Skills Use Microsoft Office Help

Microsoft Office 2010 has a Help system in which you can search for articles that show you how to accomplish tasks.

In More Skills 12, you will use the Office 2010 Help system to view an article on how to customize the Help window.

To begin, open your web browser, navigate to www.pearson highered.com/skills, locate the name of your textbook, and then follow the instructions on the website.

More Skills Organize Files

Over time, you may create hundreds of files using Microsoft Office. To find your files when you need them, they need to be well-organized. You can organize your computer files by carefully naming them and by placing them into folders.

In More Skills 13, you will create, delete, and rename folders. You will then copy, delete, and move files into the folders that you created.

To begin, open your web browser, navigate to www.pearsonhighered.com/skills, locate the name of your textbook, and then follow the instructions on the website.

More Skills Save Documents to Windows Live

If your computer is connected to the Internet, you can save your Office documents to a drive available to you free of charge through Windows Live. You can then open the files from other locations such as home, school, or work.

In More Skills 14, you will save a memo to Windows Live.

To begin, open your web browser, navigate to www.pearsonhighered.com/skills, locate the name of your textbook, and then follow the instructions on the website.

Key Terms

Cell. 8

Cell reference 12

Clipboard 18

Copy 18

Cut. 19

Dialog box 24

Drag. 19

Edit 16

Format 20

Gallery. 22

Grid line 12

Insertion point. 7

KeyTip. 23

Live Preview 7

Mini toolbar 17

Page Layout view 12

Paste 19

Protected View. 15

RAM 10

Read-only mode. 14

Right-click 25

ScreenTip 22

Shortcut menu. 25

Toggle button. 7

Triple-click 24

Online Help Skills

1. **Start** ⊙ Word. In the upper right corner of the Word window, click the **Help** button ⊙. In the **Help** window, click the **Maximize** ▭ button.

2. Click in the search box, type Create a document and then click the **Search** button. In the search results, click **Create a document**.

3. Read the article's introduction, and then below **What do you want to do**, click **Start a document from a template**. Compare your screen with **Figure 1**.

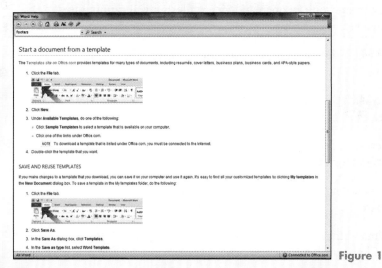

Figure 1

4. Read the Start a document from a template section to see if you can answer the following: What types of documents are available as templates? On the New tab, under Available Templates, what are the two general locations that you can find templates?

Matching

Match each term in the second column with its correct definition in the first column by writing the letter of the term on the blank line in front of the correct definition.

____ **1.** A feature that displays the result of a formatting change if you select it.

____ **2.** A line between the cells in a table or spreadsheet.

____ **3.** A mode where you can open and view a file, but you cannot save your changes.

____ **4.** A view where you prepare your document or spreadsheet for printing.

____ **5.** Quickly click the left mouse button two times without moving the mouse.

____ **6.** To insert text, delete text, or replace text in an Office document, spreadsheet, or presentation.

____ **7.** A command that moves a copy of the selected text or object to the Clipboard.

____ **8.** A command that removes the selected text or object and stores it in the Clipboard.

____ **9.** To change the appearance of the text.

____ **10.** A menu that displays a list of commands related to the type of object that you right-clicked on.

A Copy

B Cut

C Double-click

D Edit

E Format

F Grid line

G Live Preview

H Page Layout

I Read-only

J Shortcut

Multiple Choice

Choose the correct answer.

1. The flashing vertical line that indicates where text will be inserted when you start typing.
   - **A.** Cell reference
   - **B.** Insertion point
   - **C.** KeyTip

2. A button used to turn a feature both on and off.
   - **A.** Contextual button
   - **B.** On/Off button
   - **C.** Toggle button

3. The box formed by the intersection of a row and column.
   - **A.** Cell
   - **B.** Cell reference
   - **C.** Insertion point

4. Until you save a document, it is stored only here.
   - **A.** Clipboard
   - **B.** Live Preview
   - **C.** RAM

5. The combination of a number on the left side and a letter on the top of a spreadsheet that addresses a cell.
   - **A.** Coordinates
   - **B.** Cell reference
   - **C.** Insertion point

6. A temporary storage area that holds text or an object that has been cut or copied.
   - **A.** Clipboard
   - **B.** Dialog box
   - **C.** Live Preview

7. A toolbar with common formatting buttons that displays after you select text.
   - **A.** Gallery toolbar
   - **B.** Mini toolbar
   - **C.** Taskbar toolbar

8. Informational text that displays when you point to commands or thumbnails on the Ribbon.
   - **A.** Live Preview
   - **B.** ScreenTip
   - **C.** Shortcut menu

9. A visual display of choices from which you can choose.
   - **A.** Gallery
   - **B.** Options menu
   - **C.** Shortcut menu

10. An icon that displays on the Ribbon to indicate the key that you can press to access Ribbon commands.
    - **A.** KeyTip
    - **B.** ScreenTip
    - **C.** ToolTip

Topics for Discussion

1. You have briefly worked with three Microsoft Office programs: Word, Excel, and PowerPoint. Based on your experience, describe the overall purpose of each of these programs.

2. Many believe that computers enable offices to go paperless—that is, to share files electronically instead of printing and then distributing them. What are the advantages of sharing files electronically, and in what situations would it be best to print documents?

Getting Started with PowerPoint 2010

▶ Microsoft Office PowerPoint is a presentation graphics software program that you can use to present information effectively to your audience.

▶ You can use PowerPoint to create electronic slide presentations and handouts.

Your starting screen will look similar to this:

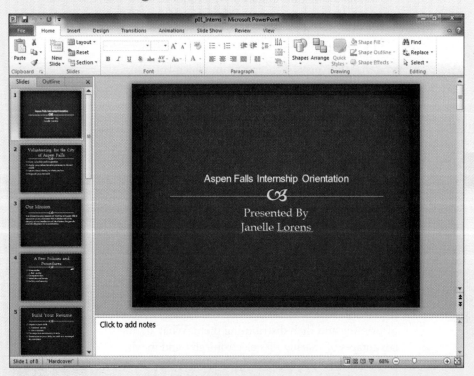

SKILLS
Skills 1-10 Training

At the end of this chapter, you will be able to:

Skill 1 Open, View, and Save Presentations
Skill 2 Edit and Replace Text in Normal View
Skill 3 Format Slide Text
Skill 4 Check Spelling and Use the Thesaurus
Skill 5 Insert Slides and Modify Slide Layouts
Skill 6 Insert and Format Pictures
Skill 7 Organize Slides Using Slide Sorter View
Skill 8 Apply Slide Transitions and View Slide Shows
Skill 9 Insert Headers and Footers and Print Presentation Handouts
Skill 10 Add Notes Pages and Print Notes

MORE SKILLS

More Skills 11 Type Text in the Outline Tab
More Skills 12 Use Keyboard Shortcuts
More Skills 13 Move and Delete Slides in Normal View
More Skills 14 Design Presentations for Audience and Location

Outcome

Using the skills listed to the left will enable you
to create a presentation like this:

You will save this presentation as:

Lastname_Firstname_p01_Interns

In this chapter, you will create documents for the Aspen Falls City Hall, which provides essential services for the citizens and visitors of Aspen Falls, California.

Introduction

- ▶ There are four views in PowerPoint—Normal, Slide Sorter, Slide Show, and Reading.

- ▶ Normal view is used to edit and format your presentation.

- ▶ In Slide Sorter view, you can organize your presentation by moving and deleting slides.

- ▶ In Slide Show view, your presentation displays as an electronic slide show.

- ▶ Reading view is optimized for viewing presentations on a computer screen— for example, during an online conference.

Time to complete all
10 skills – 60 minutes

Find your student data files here:

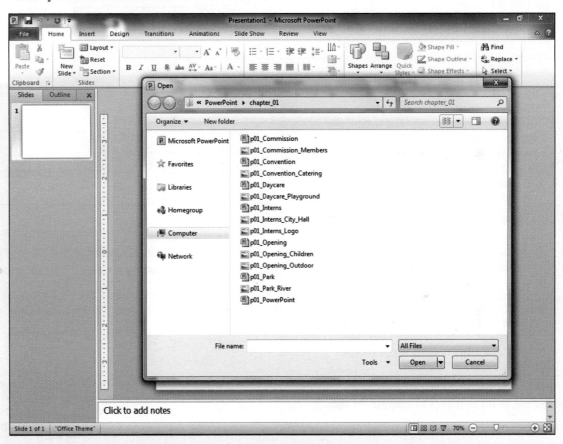

**Student data files needed
for this chapter:**

- p01_Interns
- p01_Interns_Logo
- p01_Interns_City_Hall

► When you start PowerPoint 2010, a new blank presentation displays.

► Save your changes frequently so that you do not lose any of your editing or formatting changes.

1. Click the **Start** button ⊕. From the **Start** menu, locate, and then start **Microsoft PowerPoint 2010**.

2. Take a moment to identify the main parts of the PowerPoint window as shown in **Figure 1** and described in the table in **Figure 2**.

    The PowerPoint window is divided into three parts—the Slide pane, the left pane containing the Slides and Outline tabs, and the Notes pane. The status bar displays the View and Zoom buttons and indicates the presentation design, the displayed slide number, and the number of slides in the presentation.

3. In the upper left corner of the PowerPoint window, click the **File tab**, and then click **Open**. In the **Open** dialog box, navigate to your student data files. Select **p01_Interns** and then click the **Open** button—or press Enter—to display **Slide 1** in the Slide pane.

    A *slide* is an individual page in a presentation and can contain text, pictures, tables, charts, and other multimedia or graphic objects.

■ **Continue to the next page to complete the skill**

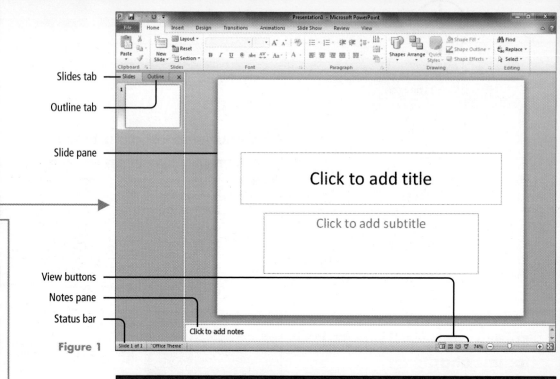

Figure 1

Microsoft PowerPoint Screen Elements	
Screen Element	**Description**
Notes pane	An area of the Normal View window used to type notes that can be printed below a picture of each slide.
Outline tab	An area of the Normal View window that displays the presentation outline.
Slide pane	An area of the Normal View window that displays a large image of the active slide.
Slides tab	An area of the Normal View window that displays all of the slides in the presentation in the form of miniature images.
Status bar	A horizontal bar at the bottom of the presentation window that displays the current slide number, number of slides in a presentation, View buttons, Theme, and Zoom slider. The status bar can be customized to include other information.
View buttons	Buttons that change the presentation window view.

Figure 2

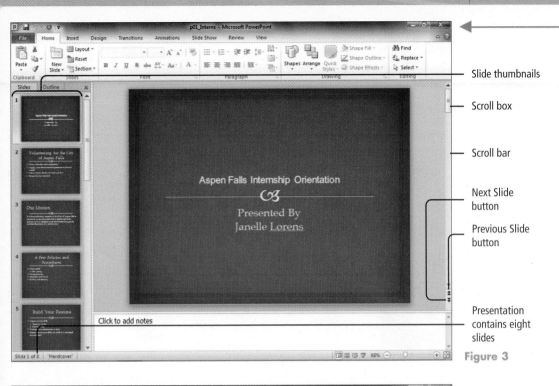

Slide thumbnails

Scroll box

Scroll bar

Next Slide button

Previous Slide button

Presentation contains eight slides

Figure 3

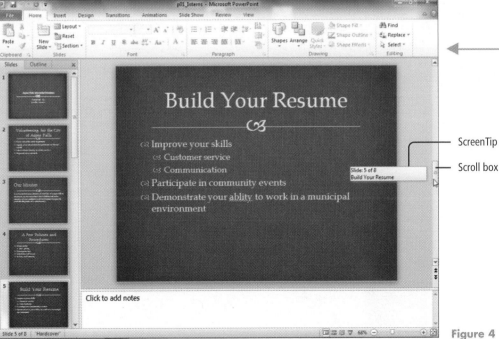

ScreenTip

Scroll box

Figure 4

4. Compare your screen with **Figure 3**.

At the left side of the PowerPoint window, on the Slides tab, the slide *thumbnails*—miniature images of presentation slides—and slide numbers display. A scroll bar to the right of the slide thumbnails is used to view additional slides. You can click a slide thumbnail to display it in the Slide pane. At the right side of the window, another scroll bar displays a scroll box and the Next Slide and Previous Slide buttons used to navigate in your presentation.

5. At the left of the PowerPoint window, on the **Slides tab**, click **Slide 2** to display it in the Slide pane. Click the slide thumbnails for **Slides 3** through **5** to view each slide. As you view each slide, notice that the vertical scroll bar at the right side of the PowerPoint window moves, indicating the relative location in the presentation of the slide that you are viewing.

6. At the right side of the PowerPoint window, point to the vertical scroll box, and then hold down the mouse button. A ScreenTip displays the slide number and slide title, as shown in **Figure 4**. Drag down to display **Slide 8**.

7. Drag the scroll box up to display **Slide 1**.

8. On the **File tab**, click **Save As**. Navigate to the location where you are saving your files, create a folder named PowerPoint Chapter 1 and then using your own name, save the presentation as Lastname_ Firstname_p01_Interns

■ **You have completed Skill 1 of 10**

▶ In ***Normal view***, the PowerPoint window is divided into three areas—the Slide pane, the left pane containing the Slides and Outline tabs, and the Notes pane.

▶ Individual lines of bulleted text on a slide are referred to as ***bullet points***.

▶ Bullet points are organized in list levels similar to an outline. A ***list level*** is identified by the indentation, size of text, and bullet assigned to that level.

▶ You can use the Replace command to change multiple occurrences of the same text in a presentation.

1. Display **Slide 3**, which contains two ***placeholders***—boxes with dotted borders that are part of most slide layouts and that hold text or objects such as charts, tables, and pictures.

2. Near the end of the paragraph, click to the left of the letter *c* in the word *community* so that the insertion point displays before the word *community*, as shown in **Figure 1**. ──────────

3. Type family-oriented and then press [Spacebar] to insert the text to the left of the word *community*.

4. Display **Slide 2**, click at the end of the last bullet point—*Expand your network*—and then press [Enter].

5. Press [Tab] to create a second-level, indented bullet point. Type Professional contacts and then press [Enter]. Type Mentors and friends and then compare your slide with **Figure 2**. ──────────

   Pressing [Enter] at the end of a bullet point results in a new bullet point at the same list level.

■ **Continue to the next page to complete the skill** ▶

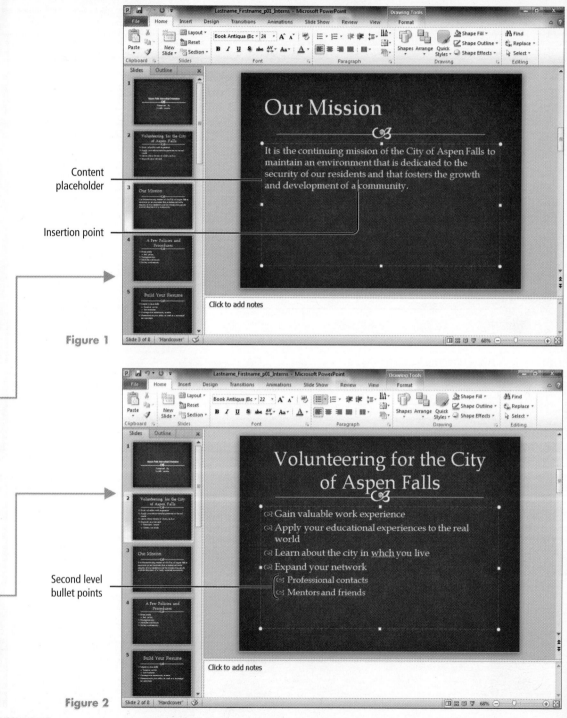

Content placeholder

Insertion point

Figure 1

Second level bullet points

Figure 2

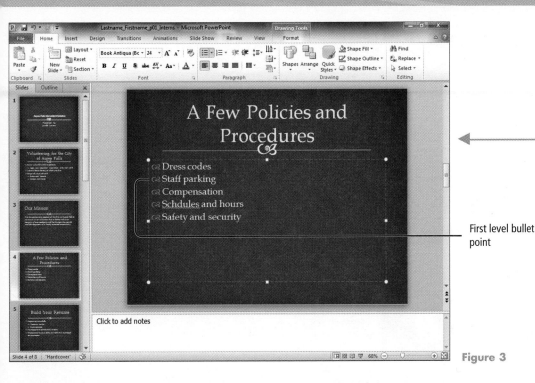

First level bullet point

Figure 3

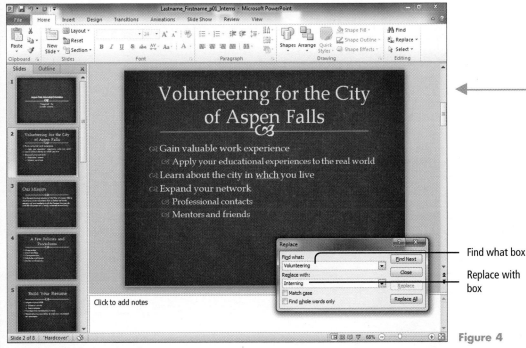

Find what box

Replace with box

Figure 4

6. Click anywhere in the second bullet point—*Apply your educational experiences to the real world*. On the **Home tab**, in the **Paragraph group**, click the **Increase List Level** button.

The selection is formatted as a second-level bullet point, indicated by the indent, smaller font size, and new bullet symbol.

7. Display **Slide 4**. Click anywhere in the second bullet point—*Staff parking*. On the **Home tab**, in the **Paragraph group**, click the **Decrease List Level** button. Compare your screen with **Figure 3**.

A first-level bullet point is applied to *Staff parking* at the same level as the other bullet points on this slide, as indicated by the bullet symbol and the increased font size.

8. Display **Slide 2** and notice the word *Volunteering* in the title placeholder.

There is more than one instance in the presentation in which the word *Volunteering* is used instead of the word *Interning*.

9. On the **Home tab**, in the **Editing group**, click the **Replace** button. In the **Find what** box, type Volunteering and then click in the **Replace with** box. Type Interning and then compare your screen with **Figure 4**.

10. In the **Replace** dialog box, click the **Replace All** button to display a message box indicating that two replacements were made. Click **OK** to close the message box, and then in the **Replace** dialog box click the **Close** button. **Save** the presentation.

■ **You have completed Skill 2 of 10**

► A *font*, which is measured in *points*, is a set of characters with the same design and shape.

► Font styles and effects emphasize text and include bold, italic, underline, shadow, small caps, and outline.

► The horizontal placement of text within a placeholder is referred to as *text alignment*. Text can be aligned left, centered, aligned right, or justified.

1. Display **Slide 1** and drag to select the title text—*Aspen Falls Internship Orientation*

2. On the Mini toolbar, click the **Font Size** arrow ⟨⁴⁴ ·⟩, and then click **32**.

3. With the title text still selected, on the **Home tab**, in the **Font group**, click the **Font** arrow ⟨Calibri (Headings) ·⟩. Scroll the **Font** gallery, and then point to **Consolas** to display the Live Preview of the selected text in the font to which you are pointing, as shown in **Figure 1**. ────────

4. In the **Font** gallery, click **Consolas**.

5. With the title text still selected, in the **Font group**, click the **Dialog Box Launcher** ⟨▣⟩ to display the Font dialog box, as shown in **Figure 2**. ────────

   The Font dialog box provides additional font style and effect formatting options.

6. Under **Effects**, select **Small Caps**, and then click **OK**.

   With small caps, lowercase characters are capitalized but are smaller than characters that were typed as capital letters.

■ **Continue to the next page to complete the skill** ➤

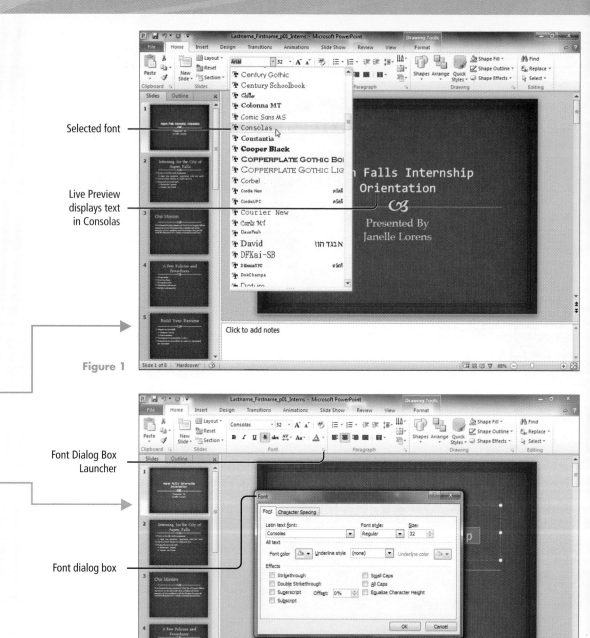

Selected font

Live Preview displays text in Consolas

Figure 1

Font Dialog Box Launcher

Font dialog box

Figure 2

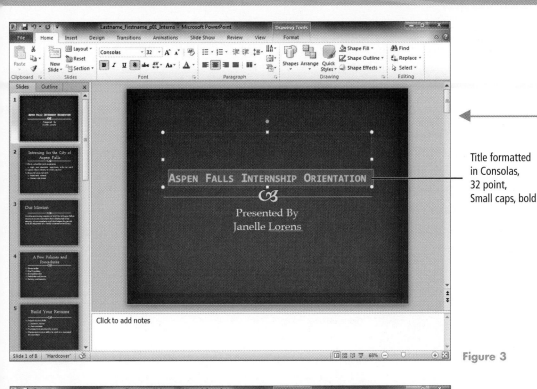

Title formatted in Consolas, 32 point, Small caps, bold

Figure 3

Title center aligned

Paragraph centered with line spacing of 1.5

Figure 4

7. With the title still selected, in the **Font group**, click the **Bold** button ⊞, and then click the **Italic** button ⊡.

8. If necessary, select the title. On the **Home tab**, in the **Font group**, click the **Italic** button ⊡ to turn off the italic formatting. Compare your slide with **Figure 3**.

> You can use the Mini toolbar, the Ribbon, or the Font dialog box to apply font styles and effects.

9. Display **Slide 3** and click the title text to select the title placeholder.

10. On the **Home tab**, in the **Paragraph group**, click the **Center** button ▤ to center align the title text.

11. Click anywhere in the content placeholder that contains the paragraph. In the **Paragraph group**, click the **Center** button ▤ to center align the paragraph within the content placeholder.

12. In the **Paragraph group**, click the **Line Spacing** button ⌑▾. In the displayed list, click **1.5** to increase the space between lines in the paragraph. Compare your slide with **Figure 4**.

13. **Save** ⊟ the presentation.

■ **You have completed Skill 3 of 10**

- PowerPoint compares slide text with the words in the Office 2010 main dictionary. Words that are not in the main dictionary are marked with a red wavy underline.
- You can correct spelling errors using the shortcut menu or the spell check feature.
- The *thesaurus* is a research tool that provides a list of *synonyms*—words with the same meaning—for text that you select.

1. Display **Slide 5**. Notice that the word *ablity* is flagged with a red wavy underline, indicating that it is misspelled.

2. Point to *ablity* and click the right mouse button to display the shortcut menu with suggested solutions for correcting the misspelled word, as shown in **Figure 1**.

3. From the shortcut menu, click **ability** to correct the spelling of the word.

4. Display **Slide 1**. In the subtitle, notice that the name *Lorens* is flagged as misspelled, although it is a proper name and is spelled correctly.

    Proper names are sometimes flagged as misspelled even though they are correctly spelled.

5. Right-click **Lorens**, and from the shortcut menu, click **Ignore All**. Compare your slide with **Figure 2**.

    The Ignore All option instructs PowerPoint to ignore all occurrences of a word that is not in the main dictionary but that is spelled correctly. Thus, the red wavy underline is removed.

■ **Continue to the next page to complete the skill**

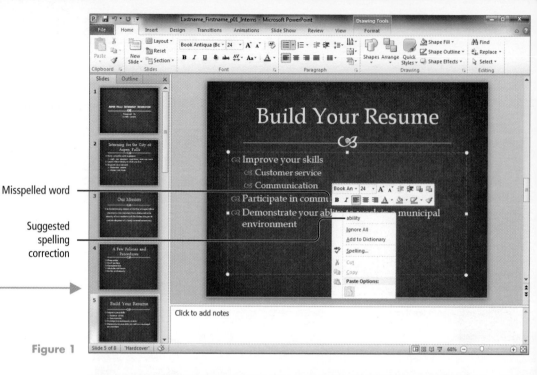

Misspelled word

Suggested spelling correction

Figure 1

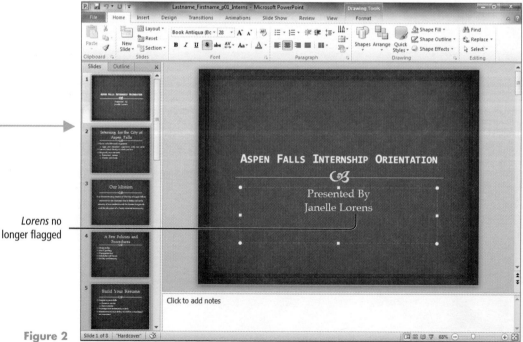

Lorens no longer flagged

Figure 2

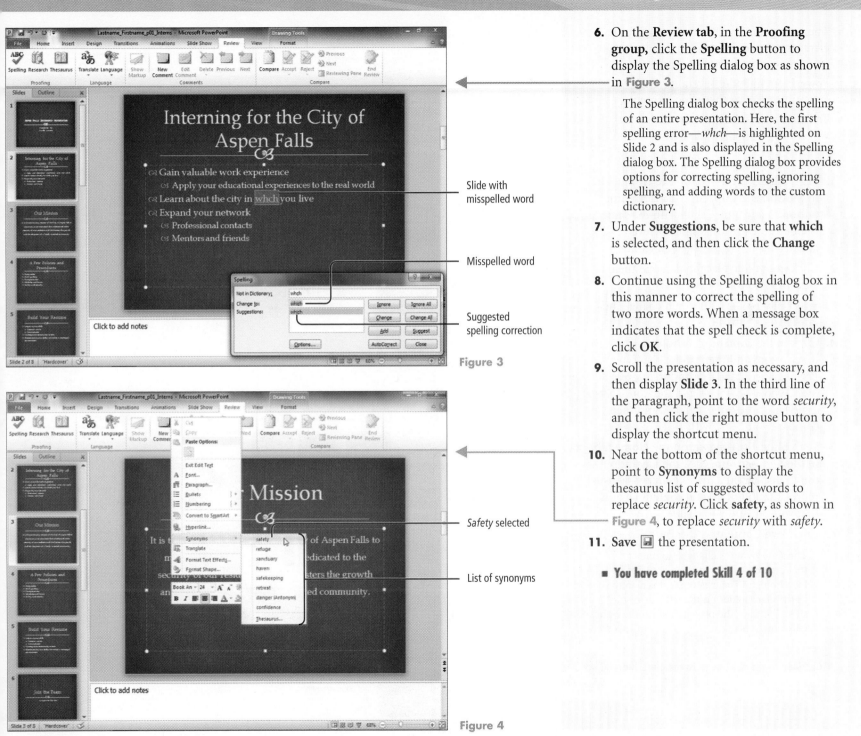

Figure 3

Figure 4

Slide with misspelled word

Misspelled word

Suggested spelling correction

Safety selected

List of synonyms

6. On the **Review tab**, in the **Proofing group,** click the **Spelling** button to display the Spelling dialog box as shown in **Figure 3**.

> The Spelling dialog box checks the spelling of an entire presentation. Here, the first spelling error—*whch*—is highlighted on Slide 2 and is also displayed in the Spelling dialog box. The Spelling dialog box provides options for correcting spelling, ignoring spelling, and adding words to the custom dictionary.

7. Under **Suggestions**, be sure that **which** is selected, and then click the **Change** button.

8. Continue using the Spelling dialog box in this manner to correct the spelling of two more words. When a message box indicates that the spell check is complete, click **OK**.

9. Scroll the presentation as necessary, and then display **Slide 3**. In the third line of the paragraph, point to the word *security*, and then click the right mouse button to display the shortcut menu.

10. Near the bottom of the shortcut menu, point to **Synonyms** to display the thesaurus list of suggested words to replace *security*. Click **safety**, as shown in **Figure 4**, to replace *security* with *safety*.

11. **Save** ⊟ the presentation.

■ **You have completed Skill 4 of 10**

► The arrangement of the text and graphic elements or placeholders on a slide is referred to as its *layout*.

► PowerPoint includes several predefined layouts used to arrange slide elements.

► To insert a new slide, display the slide that will come before the slide that you want to insert.

1. With **Slide 3** displayed, on the **Home tab**, in the **Slides group**, click the **New Slide** button to add a new slide with the same layout as the previous slide. If several slide layouts display, click Title and Content.

2. Click in the title placeholder, and then type Your Role as a City Intern

3. Select the title text, and then change the **Font Size** to **48**.

4. Click in the content placeholder. Type Job descriptions and then press Enter. Type Performance standards and then press Enter. Type Evaluations and then press Enter. Type Full-time opportunities and then compare your slide with **Figure 1**.

5. With **Slide 4** still active, on the **Home tab**, in the **Slides group**, click the **Layout** button to display the *Layout gallery*—a visual representation of several content layouts that you can apply to a slide.

6. Click **Two Content** as shown in **Figure 2**.

   The slide layout is changed to one that includes a title and two content placeholders. The existing text is arranged in the placeholder on the left side of the slide. For now, the placeholder on the right will remain blank.

   ■ **Continue to the next page to complete the skill** ▶

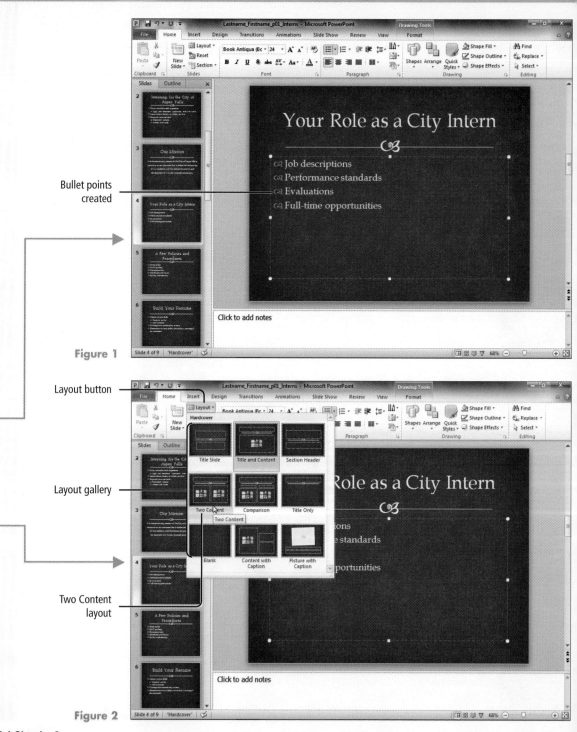

Bullet points created

Figure 1

Layout button

Layout gallery

Two Content layout

Figure 2

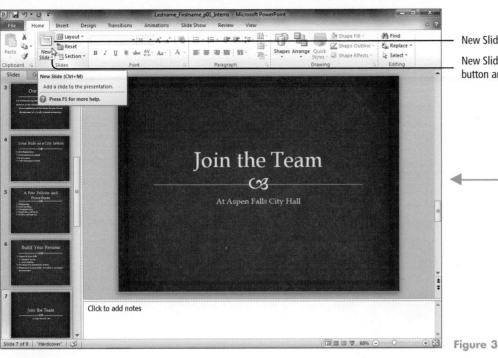

New Slide button

New Slide button arrow

Figure 3

Content with Caption layout

Figure 4

7. If necessary, use the scroll box to display **Slide 7**. On the **Home tab**, in the **Slides group**, point to the **New Slide** button and notice that it is divided into two parts as shown in **Figure 3**.

When you click the upper part of the New Slide button, a new slide is inserted with the same layout as the previous slide. When you click the lower part of the New Slide button—the *New Slide button arrow*—a gallery displays in which you can select a layout for the slide that you want to insert.

8. Click the **New Slide button arrow** to display the **Layout** gallery, and then click **Content with Caption** as shown in **Figure 4**. If you inserted a new slide without displaying the gallery, on the Home tab, in the Slides group, click Layout, and then click Content with Caption.

9. Click in the title placeholder, and then type Interning at City Hall

10. Select the title, and then change the **Font Size** 44 · to **24** and **Center** ≡ the text.

11. Click in the placeholder below the title. Type As an Aspen Falls intern, you will learn about municipal government and expand your horizons by applying your business management skills

12. Select the sentence that you typed, and then **Center** ≡ the text, change the **Font Size** 44 · to **18**, and apply **Italic** *I*. In the **Paragraph group**, click the **Line Spacing** button ‡≡·, and then click **1.5**.

13. **Save** 🖫 the presentation.

■ **You have completed Skill 5 of 10**

▶ In PowerPoint, *clip art* refers to images included with Microsoft Office or from Microsoft Office Online.

▶ *Pictures* are images created with a scanner, digital camera, or graphics software saved with a graphic file extension such as .jpg, .tif, or .bmp.

1. Display **Slide 4**. In the content placeholder on the right, click the **Insert Picture from File** button 🖾 as shown in **Figure 1**.

2. In the **Insert Picture** dialog box, navigate to your student files for this chapter, click **p01_Interns_Logo**, and then click **Insert**.

   The inserted picture is selected, as indicated by the *sizing handles*—circles or squares surrounding a selected object that are used to adjust its size. When you point to a circular sizing handle, a diagonal resize pointer— ⬉ or ⬈ —displays, indicating that you can resize the image proportionally, both vertically and horizontally. When you point to a square sizing handle, a vertical resize pointer ↕ or horizontal resize pointer ↔ displays, indicating the direction in which you can size the image.

3. Notice the **Picture Tools** contextual tool displays as shown in **Figure 2**.

   Contextual tools enable you to perform commands related to the selected object, and they display one or more contextual tabs that contain related groups of commands used for working with the selected object. The Format contextual tab contains four groups.

■ **Continue to the next page to complete the skill**

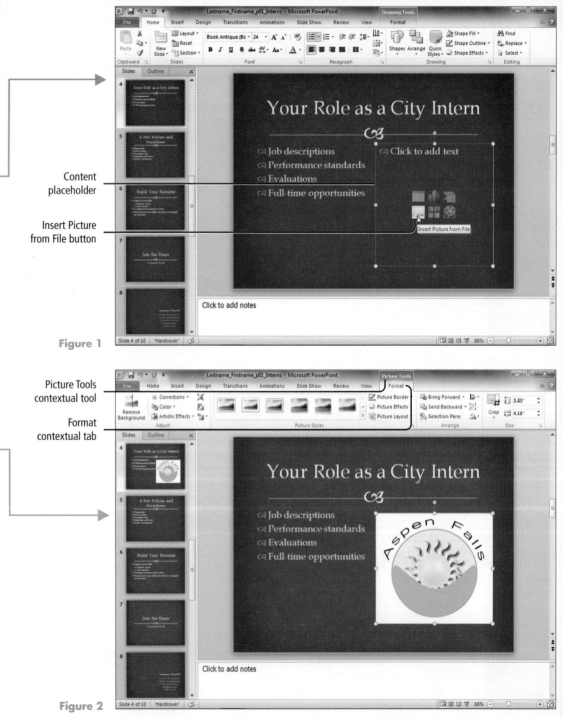

Content placeholder

Insert Picture from File button

Figure 1

Picture Tools contextual tool

Format contextual tab

Figure 2

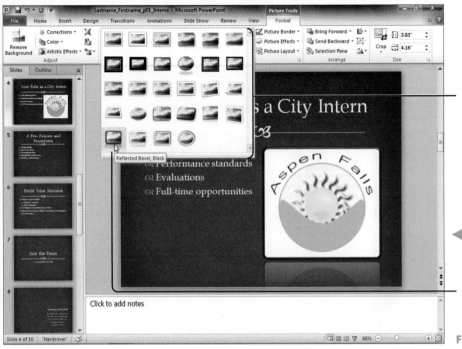

Picture Styles gallery

Reflected Bevel, Black picture style selected

Figure 3

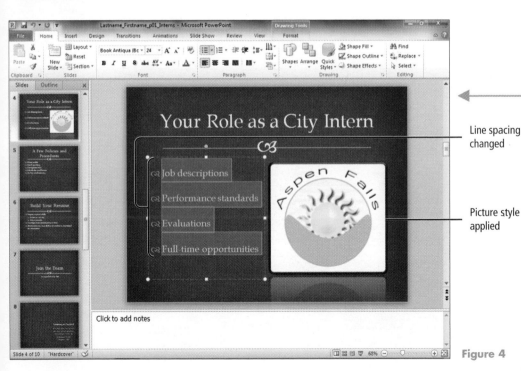

Line spacing changed

Picture style applied

Figure 4

4. On the **Format tab**, in the **Picture Styles group**, click the **More** button ⊡ to display the **Picture Styles** gallery.

A *picture style* is a prebuilt set of formatting borders, effects, and layouts applied to a picture.

5. In the **Picture Styles** gallery, move your pointer over several of the picture styles and use Live Preview to see the effect of the style on your picture and to display the ScreenTip identifying the style.

6. Using the ScreenTips to verify your selection, point to the picture style—**Reflected Bevel, Black**—as shown in **Figure 3**.

7. Click **Reflected Bevel, Black** to apply the style to the picture.

8. In the left placeholder, select the four bullet points. On the **Home tab**, in the **Paragraph group**, click the **Line Spacing** button ⧉, and then click **2.0**. Compare your slide with **Figure 4**.

The additional line spacing balances the text with the picture.

9. Display **Slide 8**. In the content placeholder on the left, click the **Insert Picture from File** button 🖾. In the **Insert Picture** dialog box, navigate to your student files for this chapter, click **p01_Interns_City_Hall**, and then click **Insert**.

10. On the **Format tab**, in the **Picture Styles group**, click the third style—**Metal Frame**.

11. **Save** 🖫 the presentation.

■ **You have completed Skill 6 of 10**

▶ *Slide Sorter view* displays all of the slides in your presentation as thumbnails.

▶ Slide Sorter view is used to rearrange and delete slides, to apply formatting to multiple slides, and to get an overall impression of your presentation.

▶ In Slide Sorter view, you can select multiple slides by holding down Shift or Ctrl.

1. In the lower right corner of the PowerPoint window, locate the **View** buttons as shown in **Figure 1**, and then click the **Slide Sorter** button ▦ to display all of the slide thumbnails.

2. If necessary, scroll the presentation so that Slides 7 through 10 are visible. Click **Slide 7** and notice that a thick outline surrounds the slide, indicating that it is selected. Hold down Shift and click **Slide 10** so that Slides 7 through 10 are selected.

   Using Shift enables you to select a group of sequential slides.

3. With the four slides selected, hold down Ctrl and then click **Slides 7** and **8**. Notice that only Slides 9 and 10 are selected, as shown in **Figure 2**.

   Using Ctrl enables you to select or deselect individual slides.

■ **Continue to the next page to complete the skill**

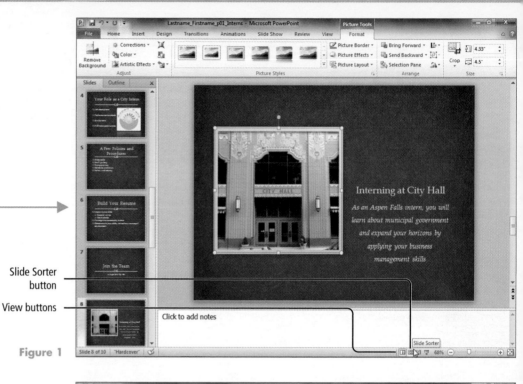

Slide Sorter button

View buttons

Figure 1

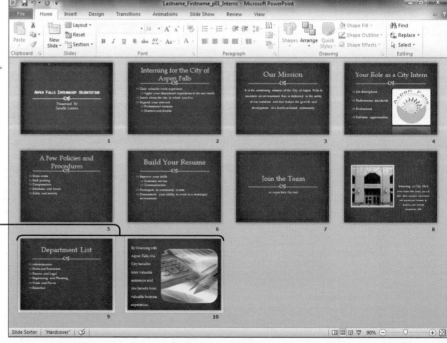

Selected slides

Figure 2

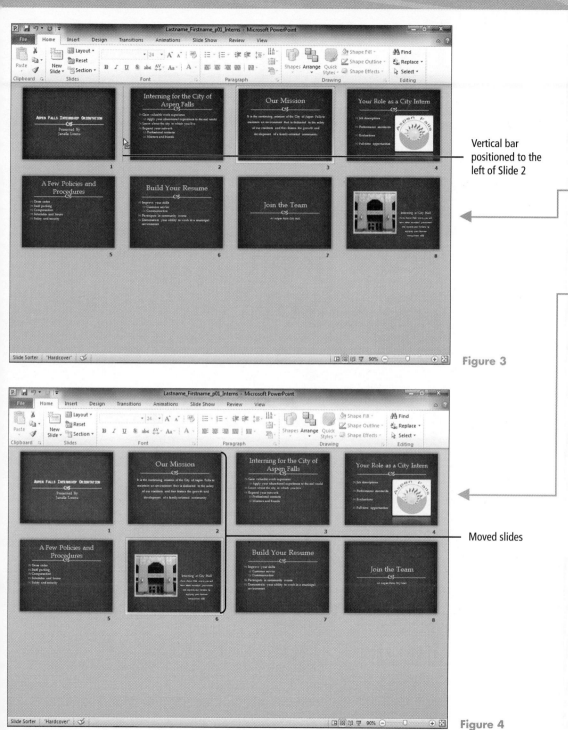

Figure 3

Figure 4

4. Press Delete to delete Slides 9 and 10 and notice that your presentation contains eight slides.

5. If necessary, use the scroll bar so that **Slide 3** is visible. Click **Slide 3** to select it.

6. Point to **Slide 3**, hold down the left mouse button, and then drag the slide to the left until the displayed vertical bar is positioned to the left of **Slide 2**, as shown in Figure 3. Release the mouse button to move the slide.

7. Point to **Slide 8**, and then drag so that the vertical bar is displayed to the left of **Slide 6**. Release the mouse button to move the slide, and then compare your screen with Figure 4.

8. Double-click **Slide 1** to return the presentation to Normal view with Slide 1 displayed.

9. **Save** 🖫 the presentation.

■ **You have completed Skill 7 of 10**

Vertical bar positioned to the left of Slide 2

Moved slides

► When a presentation is viewed as an electronic slide show, the entire slide fills the computer screen, and when your computer is connected to a projection system, an audience can view your presentation on a large screen.

► *Slide transitions* are motion effects that occur in Slide Show view when you move from one slide to the next during a presentation.

► You can choose from a variety of transitions, and you can control the speed and method with which the slides advance during a presentation.

1. With **Slide 1** displayed, click the **Transitions tab**. In the **Transition to This Slide group**, click the **More** button ⏷ to display the **Transitions** gallery as shown in **Figure 1**.

   The slide transitions are organized in three groups—Subtle, Exciting, and Dynamic Content.

2. Click several of the transitions to view the transition effects, using the **More** button ⏷ as necessary to display the gallery.

3. In the **Transition to This Slide group**, click the **More** button ⏷, and then under **Exciting**, click **Zoom**.

4. In the **Transition to This Slide group**, click the **Effect Options** button, and then compare your screen with **Figure 2**.

   The Effect Options menu lists the directions from which a slide transition displays.

5. Click **Out** to change the direction from which the slide transitions.

■ **Continue to the next page to complete the skill**

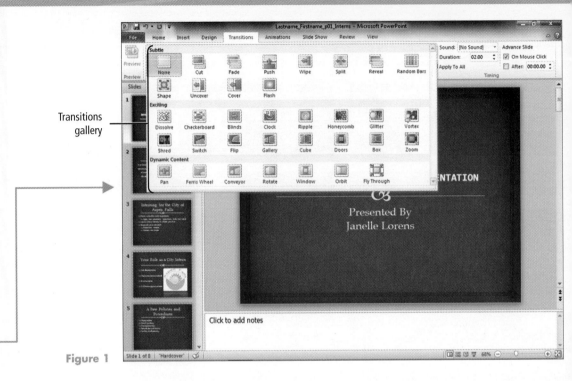

Transitions gallery

Figure 1

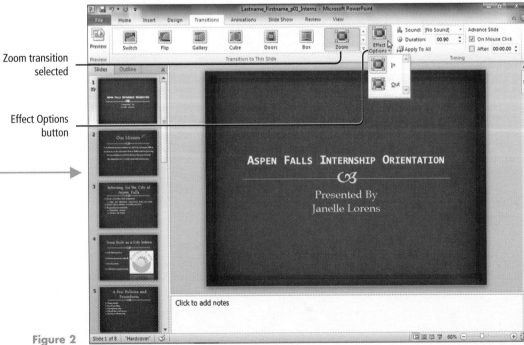

Zoom transition selected

Effect Options button

Figure 2

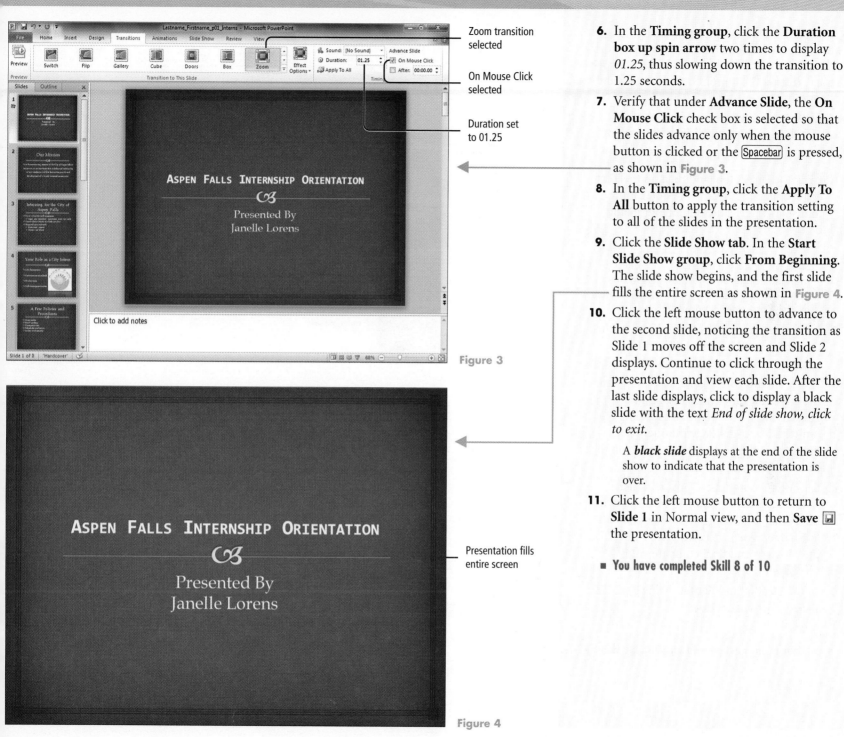

Zoom transition
selected

On Mouse Click
selected

Duration set
to 01.25

Figure 3

Presentation fills
entire screen

Figure 4

6. In the **Timing group**, click the **Duration box up spin arrow** two times to display *01.25*, thus slowing down the transition to 1.25 seconds.

7. Verify that under **Advance Slide**, the **On Mouse Click** check box is selected so that the slides advance only when the mouse button is clicked or the Spacebar is pressed, as shown in Figure 3.

8. In the **Timing group**, click the **Apply To All** button to apply the transition setting to all of the slides in the presentation.

9. Click the **Slide Show tab**. In the **Start Slide Show group**, click **From Beginning**. The slide show begins, and the first slide fills the entire screen as shown in Figure 4.

10. Click the left mouse button to advance to the second slide, noticing the transition as Slide 1 moves off the screen and Slide 2 displays. Continue to click through the presentation and view each slide. After the last slide displays, click to display a black slide with the text *End of slide show, click to exit.*

A **black slide** displays at the end of the slide show to indicate that the presentation is over.

11. Click the left mouse button to return to **Slide 1** in Normal view, and then **Save** 🖫 the presentation.

■ **You have completed Skill 8 of 10**

► A *header* is text that prints at the top of each sheet of slide handouts. A *footer* is text that displays at the bottom of every slide or that prints at the bottom of a sheet of slide handouts.

► *Slide handouts* are printed images of a single slide or multiple slides on a sheet of paper.

1. Click the **Insert tab**, and then, in the **Text group**, click the **Header & Footer** button to display the Header and Footer dialog box.

> In the Header and Footer dialog box, the Slide tab is used to insert a footer on each individual slide. For most projects in this textbook, you will insert headers and footers on the Notes and Handouts tab.

2. In the **Header and Footer** dialog box, click the **Notes and Handouts tab**, and then compare your screen with **Figure 1**.

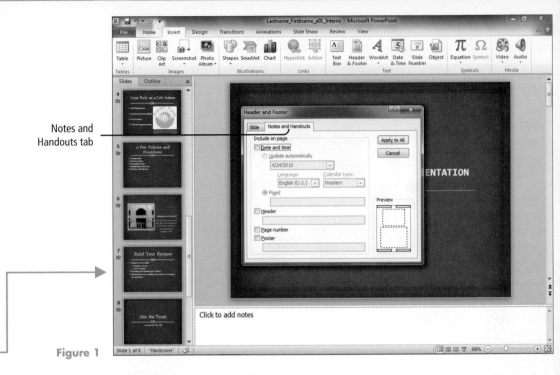

Figure 1

3. Under **Include on page**, if necessary, *clear* the Date and time check box and the Header check box so that these items are omitted. Select the **Page number** check box so that the page number prints on the slide handouts.

4. Select the **Footer** check box, and then notice that the insertion point displays in the Footer box. Using your own first and last name, type Lastname_Firstname_ p01_Interns and then compare your screen with **Figure 2**.

5. In the **Header and Footer** dialog box, click the **Apply to All** button.

■ **Continue to the next page to complete the skill**

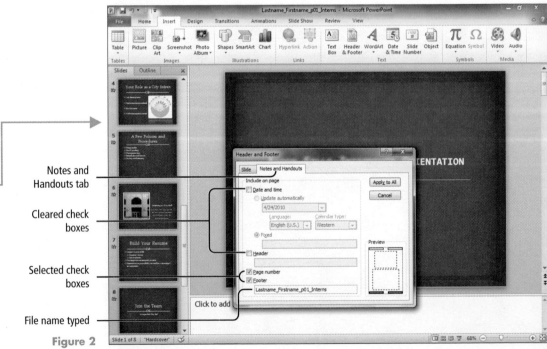

Figure 2

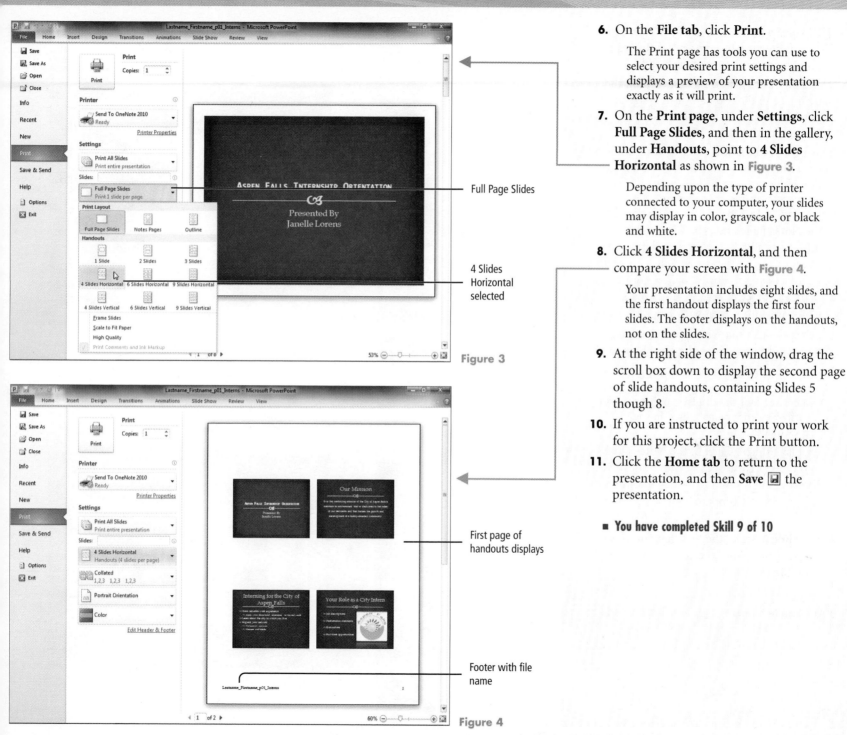

Full Page Slides

4 Slides Horizontal selected

Figure 3

First page of handouts displays

Footer with file name

Figure 4

6. On the **File tab**, click **Print**.

The Print page has tools you can use to select your desired print settings and displays a preview of your presentation exactly as it will print.

7. On the **Print page**, under **Settings**, click **Full Page Slides**, and then in the gallery, under **Handouts**, point to **4 Slides Horizontal** as shown in Figure 3.

Depending upon the type of printer connected to your computer, your slides may display in color, grayscale, or black and white.

8. Click **4 Slides Horizontal**, and then compare your screen with Figure 4.

Your presentation includes eight slides, and the first handout displays the first four slides. The footer displays on the handouts, not on the slides.

9. At the right side of the window, drag the scroll box down to display the second page of slide handouts, containing Slides 5 though 8.

10. If you are instructed to print your work for this project, click the Print button.

11. Click the **Home tab** to return to the presentation, and then **Save** 🖫 the presentation.

■ **You have completed Skill 9 of 10**

► The ***Notes pane*** is an area of the Normal View window used to type notes that can be printed below a picture of each slide.

► ***Notes pages*** are printouts that contain the slide image in the top half of the page and speaker notes typed in the Notes pane in the lower half of the page.

► During a presentation, refer to your notes to review important points that you want to make while running a slide show.

1. Display **Slide 3**. Below the slide, click in the **Notes** pane and type There are numerous advantages to completing an internship with the Aspen Falls City Hall. Browse the city website to view comments made by interns from previous years. Compare your screen with **Figure 1**.

2. Select the text that you typed in the **Notes** pane, and then change the **Font Size** to **18**.

> In the Notes pane, the size of the text does not change. When you print the notes, the increased font size displays so that you can easily view the printed notes during the presentation.

3. Display **Slide 6**. Click in the **Notes** pane and type Ask your advisor for additional information on opportunities in other city departments. Compare your screen with **Figure 2**.

4. On **Slide 6**, select the text that you typed in the **Notes** pane, and then change the **Font Size** to **18**.

■ **Continue to the next page to complete the skill**

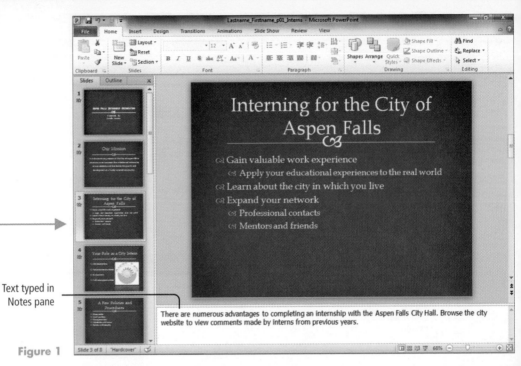

Text typed in Notes pane

Figure 1

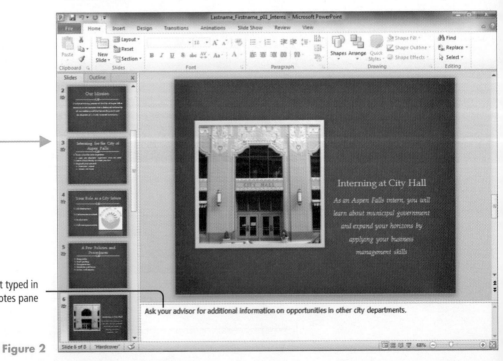

Text typed in Notes pane

Figure 2

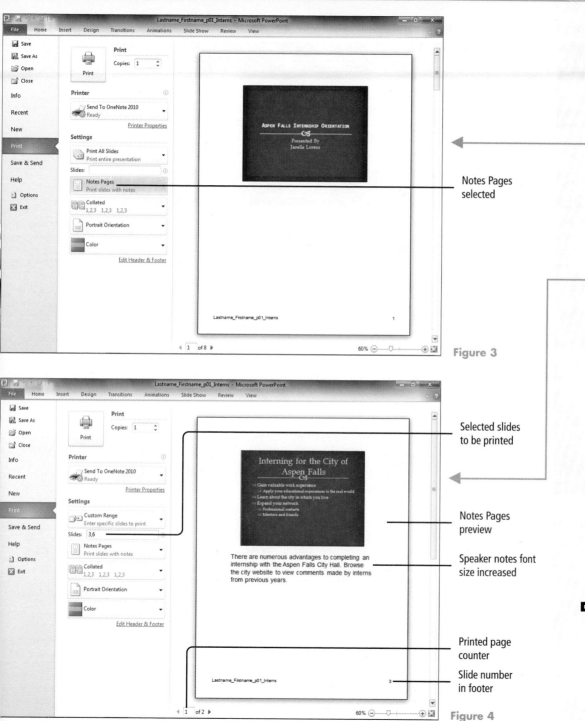

Figure 3

Figure 4

5. Display **Slide 1**, and then click the **File tab**. Click **Print** and notice that under **Settings**, the previous print selection—*4 Slides Horizontal*—displays.

6. Under **Settings**, click **4 Slides Horizontal**, and then under **Print Layout**, click **Notes Pages**. Compare your screen with **Figure 3**.

Because notes were not typed for Slide 1, the slide displays at the top of the Notes Page, and the lower portion of the Notes Page is blank.

7. Under **Settings**, click **Print All Slides**, and then click **Custom Range**. In the **Slides** box, type 3,6 and then compare your screen with **Figure 4**.

To print individual slides, in the Slides box, type the slide numbers, separated by commas. To print sequential slides, type the first and last slide numbers, separated by a hyphen.

When selected slides are printed, page numbers in the headers or footers display the slide number. Here, the upper part of the Notes Page displays Slide 3, and the lower part displays the notes in 18 point font size. Below the Notes Page, a page counter indicates that two pages will print.

8. If your instructor asks you to print this project, click the Print button.

9. Click the **Home tab**, **Save** 🖫 the presentation, and then **Exit** PowerPoint. Submit the printout or file as directed by your instructor.

Done! You have completed Skill 10 of 10 and your presentation is complete!

The following More Skills are located at **www.pearsonhighered.com/skills**

More Skills Type Text in the Outline Tab

The Outline tab is used when you want to create several slides that are composed primarily of text.

In More Skills 11, you will open a presentation and then type text in the Outline tab for two slides.

To begin, open your web browser, navigate to www.pearsonhighered.com/skills, locate the name of your textbook, and follow the instructions on the website.

More Skills Use Keyboard Shortcuts

You can use keyboard shortcuts to apply commands instead of clicking buttons on the Ribbon or shortcut menu.

In More Skills 12, you will open a presentation and use keyboard shortcuts to apply font styles, change text alignment, and save a presentation.

To begin, open your web browser, navigate to www.pearsonhighered.com/skills, locate the name of your textbook, and follow the instructions on the website.

More Skills Move and Delete Slides in Normal View

Slides can be moved in Normal view using the Slides tab. You can select multiple slides using Ctrl and Shift, and then delete or drag the selected slides to a new location in the presentation.

In More Skills 13, you will open a presentation, select and delete one slide, and then select and move a slide.

To begin, open your web browser, navigate to www.pearsonhighered.com/skills, locate the name of your textbook, and follow the instructions on the website.

More Skills Design Presentations for Audience and Location

When you design a presentation, you should consider the size of the room in which the presentation will be viewed and the number of people who will be present.

In More Skills 14, you will review design tips for presenting in a large room, and then you will open a presentation and review formatting changes that will improve the readability of the presentation when viewed by a large audience.

To begin, open your web browser, navigate to www.pearsonhighered.com/skills, locate the name of your textbook, and follow the instructions on the website.

Key Terms

Black slide. 49

Bullet point 36

Clip art 44

Contextual tools 44

Font 38

Footer 50

Header. 50

Layout 42

Layout gallery 42

List level 36

Normal view. 36

Notes Page 52

Notes pane 52

Picture. 44

Picture style 45

Placeholder. 36

Point 38

Sizing handle 44

Slide. 34

Slide handout. 50

Slide Sorter view 46

Slide transition 48

Synonym. 40

Text alignment. 38

Thesaurus. 40

Thumbnail 35

Online Help Skills

1. **Start** 🅿 PowerPoint. In the upper right corner of the PowerPoint window, click the **Help** button 🔘. In the **Help** window, click the **Maximize** 🔲 button.

2. Click in the search box, type sections and then click the **Search** button 🔍. In the search results, click **Organize your slides into sections**.

3. Read the article's introduction, *Overview of sections*, and then below **In this article**, click **Add and name a section**. Compare your screen with **Figure 1**.

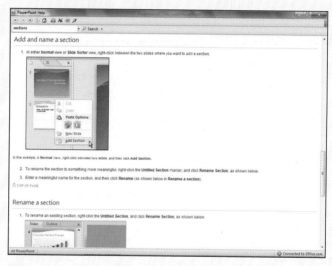

Figure 1

4. Scroll down to read the entire article and then see if you can answer the following: What is the purpose of dividing a presentation into sections?

Matching

Match each term in the second column with its correct definition in the first column. Write the letter of the term on the blank line in front of the correct definition.

____ **1.** The PowerPoint view in which the window is divided into three panes—the Slide pane, the left pane containing the Slides and Outline tabs, and the Notes pane.

____ **2.** Levels of text on a slide identified by the indentation, size of text, and bullet assigned to that level.

____ **3.** An individual line of bulleted text on a slide.

____ **4.** A box with dotted borders that is part of most slide layouts and that holds text or objects such as charts, tables, and pictures.

____ **5.** A feature that changes the horizontal placement of text within a placeholder.

____ **6.** A set of characters with the same design and shape.

____ **7.** A circle or square surrounding a selected object that is used to adjust its size.

____ **8.** A slide that displays at the end of the slide show to indicate that the presentation is over.

____ **9.** An area of the Normal View window used to type notes that can be printed below a picture of each slide.

____ **10.** A printout that contains the slide image in the top half of the page and speaker notes typed in the Notes pane in the lower half of the page.

A Black slide

B Bullet point

C Font

D List level

E Normal

F Notes page

G Notes pane

H Placeholder

I Sizing handle

J Text alignment

Multiple Choice

Choose the correct answer.

1. A research tool that provides a list of synonyms.
   - **A.** Reviewer
   - **B.** Spell check
   - **C.** Thesaurus

2. Words with the same meaning.
   - **A.** Synonyms
   - **B.** Antonyms
   - **C.** Prepositions

3. The arrangement of the text and graphic elements or placeholders on a slide.
   - **A.** Layout
   - **B.** Gallery
   - **C.** Design

4. Images included with Microsoft Office or from Microsoft Office Online.
   - **A.** Pictures
   - **B.** Vector graphics
   - **C.** Clip art

5. Tools used to perform specific commands related to a selected object.
   - **A.** Contextual tools
   - **B.** ScreenTips
   - **C.** Tool galleries

6. A prebuilt set of formatting borders, effects, and layouts applied to a picture.
   - **A.** Artistic effects
   - **B.** Picture styles
   - **C.** Picture designs

7. A motion effect that occurs in Slide Show view when you move from one slide to the next during a presentation.
   - **A.** Animation
   - **B.** Slide transition
   - **C.** Custom effect

8. Text that prints at the top of a sheet of slide handouts or notes pages.
   - **A.** Page numbers
   - **B.** Header
   - **C.** Footer

9. Text that displays at the bottom of every slide or that prints at the bottom of a sheet of slide handouts.
   - **A.** Page numbers
   - **B.** Header
   - **C.** Footer

10. Printed images of a single slide or multiple slides on a sheet of paper.
    - **A.** Notes
    - **B.** Slide handout
    - **C.** Footer

Topics for Discussion

1. PowerPoint 2010 provides a number of slide transitions that you can apply to your presentation. Do you think that it is important to apply one consistent transition to the entire presentation instead of applying a different transition to each slide? Why or why not?

2. When you applied the transition to the slides in the project in this chapter, you verified that the slides should advance when the mouse is clicked instead of advancing automatically after a few seconds. Why do you think that presentation slides should be advanced when the speaker clicks the mouse button instead of automatically?

Skill Check

To complete this presentation, you will need the following files:

- p01_Park
- p01_Park_River

You will save your presentation as:

- **Lastname_Firstname_p01_Park**

1. **Start** PowerPoint. From your student files, open **p01_Park**. Save the file in your **PowerPoint Chapter 1** folder as Lastname_Firstname_p01_Park

2. On **Slide 1**, select the title text—*Community Park Proposal*. In the **Font group**, click the **Font** arrow, and then click **Garamond**. Click the **Font Size** arrow, and then click **48**. Click the **Font Dialog Box Launcher**. In the **Font** dialog box, select **Small Cap**s, and then click **OK**.

3. In the subtitle, click to the right of the word *Aspen*, and then, adding spaces as necessary, type Falls

4. In the **Editing group**, click **Replace**. In the **Find what** box, type north and then in the **Replace with** box type south Click **Replace All**. Click **OK**, and then **Close** the **Replace** dialog box.

5. Display **Slide 2**. Click in the title, and then in the **Paragraph group**, click **Center**. Select all of the bullet points. In the **Paragraph group**, click the **Line Spacing** button, and then click **1.5**.

6. Click anywhere in the third-bullet point. In the **Paragraph group**, click the **Decrease List Level** button. Click in the last bullet point. In the **Paragraph group**, click the **Increase List Level** button, and then compare your slide with **Figure 1**. ──

7. Display **Slide 3**. On the **Home tab**, in the **Slides group**, click the *lower* part of the **New Slide** button. In the gallery, click **Title Slide**. In the title placeholder, type What will we do with the land at the current park location?

8. In the subtitle placeholder, type Develop or Remodel and then change the subtitle text **Font Size** to **36**. Compare your slide with **Figure 2**. ──

9. On the **Review tab**, in the **Proofing group**, click the **Spelling** button. Click **Change** to accept the spelling for *Municipal*, and then ignore the spelling for *Ramsburg*. **Close** the message box.

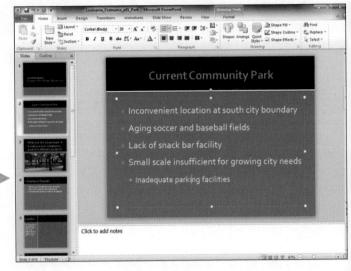

Figure 1

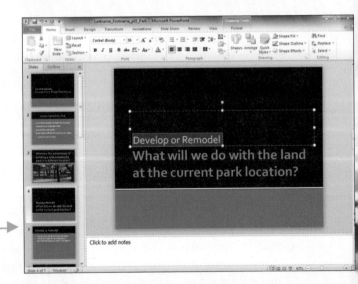

Figure 2

■ Continue to the next page to complete this Skill Check

10. Display **Slide 6**. Right-click the word *entrance*. From the shortcut menu, point to **Synonyms**, and then click **entry**.

11. On the right side of **Slide 6**, click the **Insert Picture from File** button. From your student files, insert **p01_Park_River**. On the left side of the slide, select the text in the content placeholder. On the **Home tab**, in the **Paragraph group**, click the **Line Spacing** button, and then click **1.5**. Compare your slide with **Figure 3**.

12. Display **Slide 3**, and then select the picture. On the **Format tab**, in the **Picture Styles group**, click the **More** button, and then click the eleventh thumbnail—**Compound Frame, Black**.

13. Display **Slide 5**. On the **Home tab**, in the **Slides group**, click the **Layout** button, and then click **Two Content**. In the placeholder on the right, type Remodeling the park will increase the number of recreational facilities and then press Enter. Type Less expensive to remodel than develop

14. In the lower right corner of the PowerPoint window, click the **Slide Sorter** button. Select **Slide 7**, and then press Delete. Point to **Slide 6**, and then drag to position the vertical bar before **Slide 4** to move the slide. On the status bar, locate the View buttons, and then click the **Normal** button.

15. On the **Transitions tab**, in the **Transition to This Slide group**, click the **More** button, and then under **Subtle**, click **Wipe**. In the **Timing group**, click the **Durations box up spin arrow** one time to increase the **Duration** to *01.25*. Click **Apply to All**.

16. On the **Slide Show tab**, in the **Start Slide Show group**, click **From Beginning**, and then press the mouse button to advance through the slide show. When the black slide displays, click the mouse button or press Esc.

17. Display **Slide 2**. In the **Notes pane**, type The growing population in Aspen Falls warrants additional recreation facilities. Select the text and then change the **Font Size** to **18**.

18. On the **Insert tab**, in the **Text group**, click the **Header & Footer** button. Click the **Notes and Handouts tab**. Select the **Page number** check box, and then select the **Footer** check box. In the **Footer** box, type Lastname_Firstname_p01_Park and then click **Apply to All**.

19. **Save** the presentation, and then compare your completed presentation with **Figure 4**.

20. Print the presentation or submit the file as directed by your instructor, and then **Exit** PowerPoint.

Done! You have completed the Skill Check

Figure 3

Figure 4

Assess Your Skills 1

To complete this project, you will need the following files:

- p01_Commission
- p01_Commission_Members

You will save your presentation as:

- Lastname_Firstname_p01_Commission

1. **Start** PowerPoint. From the student files that accompany this textbook, open **p01_Commission**. **Save** the presentation in your **PowerPoint Chapter 1** folder as Lastname_Firstname_p01_Commission

2. On **Slide 1**, center the subtitle, change the font to **Arial** and the font size to **32**, and then apply **Small Caps**.

3. Display **Slide 2**, and then change the layout to **Two Content**. In the placeholder on the right, from your student files, insert the picture **p01_Commission_Members**, and then apply the **Compound Frame, Black** picture style.

4. With **Slide 2** still active, insert a new slide with the **Title and Content** layout. In the slide title, type Commission Responsibilities and then in the content placeholder, type the following four bullet points:

   Review new expansion plans
   Residential and commercial
   Recommend amendments to
      Planning Codes
   Design and development standards

5. Increase the list level of the second and fourth bullet points, and then select all of the bullet points and change the line spacing to **1.5**.

6. Use the thesaurus to change the word *expansion* to *development*.

7. Display **Slide 5**, and then change the layout to **Section Header**.

8. Display the presentation in **Slide Sorter** view, and then move **Slide 5** between **Slides 3 and 4**. Return the presentation to **Normal** view.

9. Apply the **Push** transition with the **From Top** effect option. Change the **Duration** to *01.50*. Apply the transition to all slides, and then view the slide show from the beginning.

10. Display **Slide 5**, and then in the **Notes** pane, type The Planning Commission is actively developing a plan for new construction in the city based on demographic projections through the year 2015. Change the speaker notes font size to **18**.

11. Correct all spelling errors in the presentation.

12. In the **Notes and Handouts** footer, insert the page number and the file name Lastname_Firstname_p01_Commission

13. Display the **Print** page, and then display **6 Slides Horizontal**. Compare your completed presentation with **Figure 1**. **Save** the presentation, and then print or submit the file as directed by your instructor.

Done! You have completed Assess Your Skills 1

Figure 1

Assessment

Assess Your Skills 3 and 4 can be found at **www.pearsonhighered.com/skills**.

Assess Your Skills 2

To complete this presentation, you will need the following files:

- p01_Convention
- p01_Convention_Catering

You will save your presentation as:

- Lastname_Firstname_p01_Convention

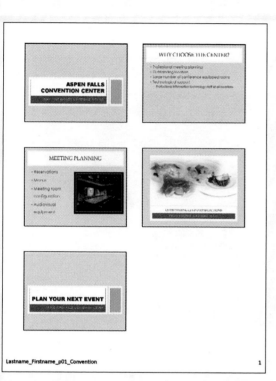

Figure 1

1. **Start** PowerPoint. From your student files, open **p01_Convention**. **Save** the presentation in your **PowerPoint Chapter 1** folder as Lastname_Firstname_p01_Convention

2. Display **Slide 3**. In the first bullet point, after the word *Professional*, type meeting and adjust spacing as necessary. Decrease the list level for the fourth bullet point, and then increase the list level for the fifth bullet point. Replace all instances of Hall with Center and then correct the spelling throughout the presentation.

3. Display **Slide 1**. Change the title font to **Arial Black** and the font size to **36**. Change the title alignment to **Align Text Right**. Select the subtitle, apply **Italic** and **Small Caps**, and then **Align Text Right**.

4. Display **Slide 4**, and then apply the same formatting to the title and subtitle as you did to the title and subtitle on Slide 1.

5. Display **Slide 2**. Select all four bullet points, and then change the line spacing to **1.5**. Apply the **Double Frame, Black** picture style to the picture.

6. With **Slide 2** still selected, insert a new slide with the **Picture with Caption** layout. In the title placeholder, type Outstanding Culinary Selections

7. In the caption placeholder, located below the title, type Professional catering staff Change the caption font size to **18**. In the picture placeholder, from your student files, insert the picture **p01_Convention_Catering**.

8. Display the presentation in **Slide Sorter** view. Delete **Slide 6**, and then move **Slide 4** between Slides 1 and 2. For all slides, apply the **Split** transition with the **Vertical In** effect option. View the slide show from the beginning.

9. Display **Slide 2** in **Normal** view, and then in the **Notes** pane, type The convention center is conveniently located in central Aspen Falls. Change the speaker notes font size to **18**.

10. In the **Notes and Handouts** footer, insert the page number and the file name Lastname_Firstname_p01_Convention

11. Compare your completed presentation with **Figure 1**. **Save** your presentation, and then print or submit the file as directed by your instructor.

Done! You have completed Assess Your Skills 2

Assess Your Skills Visually

To complete this presentation, you will need the following files:

- p01_Daycare
- p01_Daycare_Playground

You will save your presentation as:

- Lastname_Firstname_p01_Daycare

Open the file **p01_Daycare**. Save the file in your **PowerPoint Chapter 1** folder as Lastname_Firstname_p01_Daycare and then format the single slide presentation as a flyer as shown in **Figure 1**. To complete this presentation flyer, change the title font to **Corbel** size **36**. Change the font size for all other text to **18**. In the placeholder on the right, insert the picture **p01_Daycare_Playground** and apply the **Soft Edge Rectangle** picture style. In the Notes and Handouts footer, insert the page number and the file name Lastname_Firstname_p01_Daycare and then print or submit the file as directed by your instructor.

Done! You have completed Assess Your Skills Visually

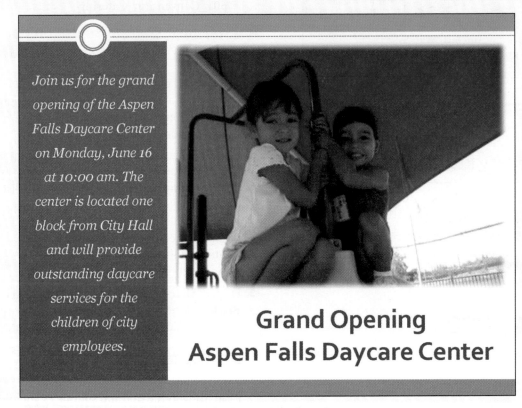

Join us for the grand opening of the Aspen Falls Daycare Center on Monday, June 16 at 10:00 am. The center is located one block from City Hall and will provide outstanding daycare services for the children of city employees.

**Grand Opening
Aspen Falls Daycare Center**

Figure 1

Skills in Context

To complete this presentation, you will need the following files:

- p01_Opening
- p01_Opening_Outdoor
- p01_Opening_Children

You will save your presentation as:

- Lastname_Firstname_p01_ Opening

From your student files, open the **p01_Opening** presentation. Change the layout of Slide 2 to **Picture with Caption** and insert the **p01_Opening_Outdoor** picture in the picture placeholder. Apply an appropriate picture style. In the caption placeholder, change the font, font size, font effects, and line spacing so that the slide is formatted attractively. Insert a new Slide 3 using a layout of your choice. In the title placeholder, type Grand Opening Events and then for the slide content, provide a list of events that will take place at the grand opening ceremony, such as continental breakfast, arts and crafts, children's events, and teacher introductions.

At the end of the presentation, insert a slide using either the Content with Caption or the Picture with Caption layout. Use this slide to remind people of the date and time of the grand opening. Insert the picture **p01_Opening_Children** on this slide and apply an appropriate picture style. Apply slide transitions to all of the slides in the presentation and correct the spelling. Insert the file name and page number in the Notes and Handouts footer. Save your presentation as Lastname_Firstname_p01_Opening and then print or submit electronically.

Done! You have completed Skills in Context

Skills and You

To complete this presentation, you will need the following file:

- p01_PowerPoint

You will save your presentation as:

- Lastname_Firstname_p01_PowerPoint

From your student files, open **p01_PowerPoint**, and then on the first slide, add your name to the subtitle placeholder. Add a slide that describes your reasons for wanting to learn PowerPoint. Add a slide with the Content with Caption layout, and on it, describe how you plan to use PowerPoint personally or professionally. If you have a picture of yourself, add it to this slide, and then change font size and line spacing as necessary. If you do not have a picture of yourself, use a picture that depicts how you plan to use PowerPoint.

Insert a final slide with the Section Header layout and enter text that briefly summarizes in two lines—the title line and the subtitle line—your presentation. Add a footer to the presentation with the file name and page number, and then check spelling in the presentation. Save the presentation as Lastname_Firstname_p01_PowerPoint and then print or submit the file as directed by your instructor.

Done! You have completed Skills and You

CHAPTER 2

Format a Presentation

▶ Formatting is the process of changing the appearance of the text, layout, or design of a slide.

▶ Apply formatting to text and images to enhance your slides in a manner that conveys your message to your audience.

Your starting screen will look similar to this:

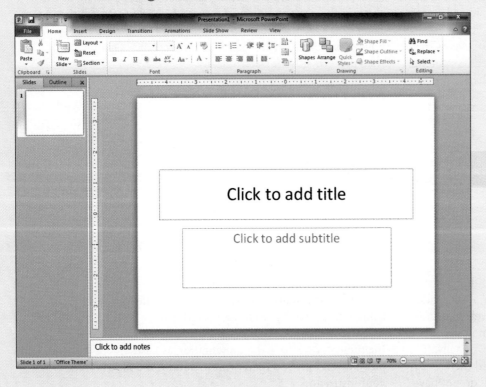

SKILLS

Skills 1-10 Training

At the end of this chapter, you will be able to:

Skill 1 Create New Presentations

Skill 2 Change Presentation Themes

Skill 3 Apply Font and Color Themes

Skill 4 Format Slide Backgrounds with Styles

Skill 5 Format Slide Backgrounds with Pictures and Textures

Skill 6 Format Text with WordArt

Skill 7 Change Character Spacing and Font Color

Skill 8 Modify Bulleted and Numbered Lists

Skill 9 Move and Copy Text and Objects

Skill 10 Use Format Painter and Clear All Formatting

MORE SKILLS

More Skills 11 Edit Slide Masters

More Skills 12 Save and Apply Presentation Templates

More Skills 13 Create Slides from Microsoft Word Outline

More Skills 14 Design Presentations with Contrast

Outcome

Using the skills listed to the left will enable you
to create a presentation like this:

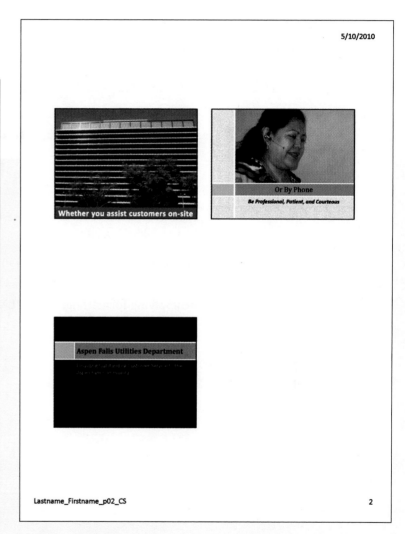

You will save this presentation as:

Lastname_Firstname_p02_CS

In this chapter, you will create presentations for the Aspen Falls City Hall, which provides essential services for the citizens and visitors of Aspen Falls, California.

Introduction

▶ Apply PowerPoint themes to your presentations to create dynamic and professional-looking slides.

▶ Customize your presentation design by changing font colors, bullet symbols, and slide backgrounds.

▶ Before applying formatting, use the Live Preview feature to view the effect of different formatting on your slides.

**Time to complete all
10 skills – 60 minutes**

Student data files needed
for this chapter:

- p02_CS_Building
- p02_CS_Headset
- p02_CS_Representative
- p02_CS_Telephone

Find your student data files here:

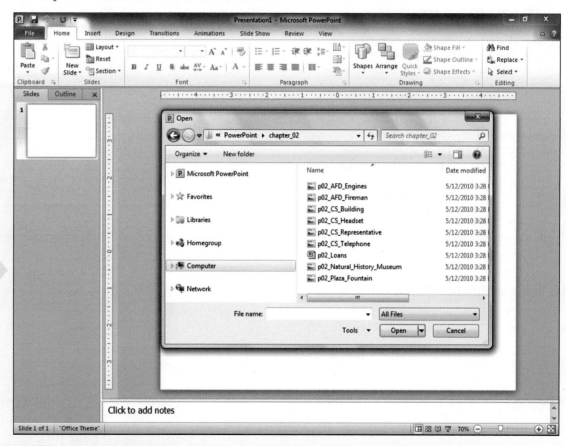

▶ When you start PowerPoint, a new, blank presentation displays.

▶ In a new, blank presentation, black or grey text displays on a white background.

1. **Start** PowerPoint. On the **File tab**, click the **New tab** to display the **New** page as shown in **Figure 1**.

   The New page displays available templates, themes, and templates that you can download from Office.com. A **template** is a file upon which a presentation can be based. On the right side of the New page, a preview of the selected template displays. Here, a preview of the Blank presentation template displays.

2. Under **Available Templates and Themes**, click **Sample templates**, and then click several templates to display the preview of each on the right side of the **New** page.

3. Under **Available Templates and Themes**, click the **Home** button, and then click **Blank presentation**. On the right side of the **New** page, click the **Create** button to display a new blank presentation.

4. Click in the title placeholder, and then type Aspen Falls Utilities Department

5. Click in the subtitle placeholder. Type Customer Service Training and then compare your screen with **Figure 2**.

■ **Continue to the next page to complete the skill**

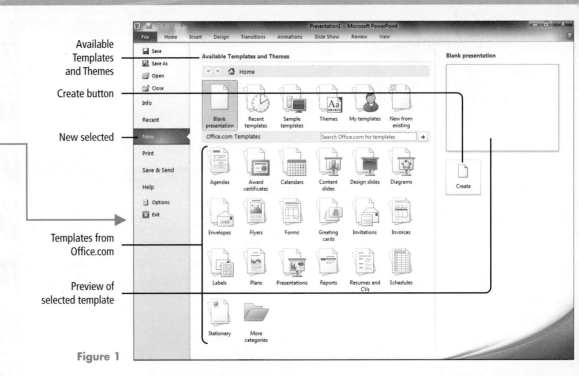

Available Templates and Themes
Create button
New selected
Templates from Office.com
Preview of selected template

Figure 1

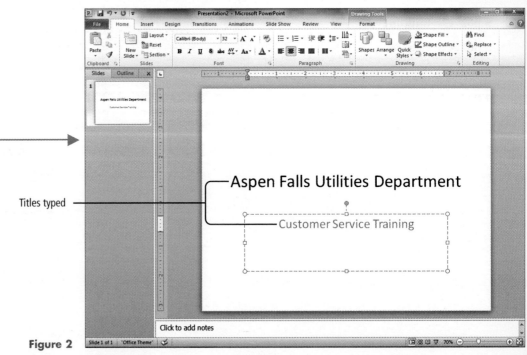

Titles typed

Figure 2

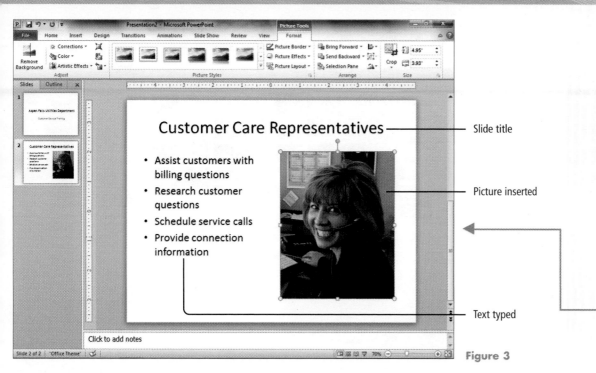

Slide title

Picture inserted

Text typed

Figure 3

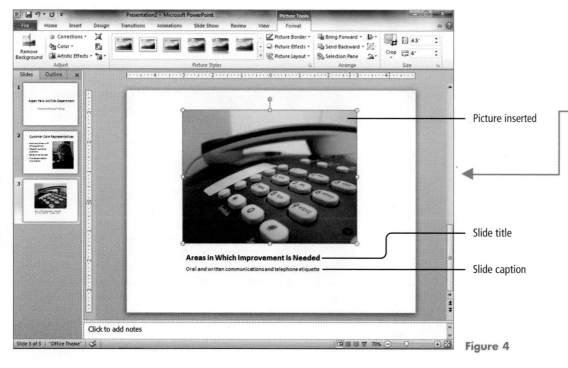

Picture inserted

Slide title

Slide caption

Figure 4

6. On the **Home tab**, in the **Slides group**, click the **New Slide button arrow**. In the gallery, click the **Two Content** thumbnail to insert a slide with the **Two Content** layout. In the title placeholder, type Customer Care Representatives

7. Click in the placeholder on the left, and then type the following four bullet points:
   Assist customers with billing questions
   Research customer questions
   Schedule service calls
   Provide connection information

8. In the placeholder on the right, click the **Insert Picture from File** button, and then from your student files, insert the picture **p02_CS_Representative**. Compare your slide with **Figure 3**.

9. On the **Home tab**, in the **Slides group**, click the **New Slide button arrow**. In the gallery, click **Picture with Caption**. In the title placeholder, type Areas in Which Improvement Is Needed In the text placeholder, type Oral and written communications and telephone etiquette

10. In the picture placeholder, from your student files, insert **p02_CS_Telephone**, and then compare your slide with **Figure 4**.

11. On the Quick Access Toolbar, click **Save**. Navigate to the location where you are saving your files, create a folder named PowerPoint Chapter 2 and then using your own name, save the document as Lastname_Firstname_p02_CS

■ **You have completed Skill 1 of 10**

► The presentation *theme* is a set of unified design elements—colors, fonts, and graphics—that provides a unique look for your presentation.

► The status bar displays the name of the theme applied to the presentation. The Office theme is the default theme applied to new presentations.

► To give the presentation a consistent design, choose one theme for all of the slides in the presentation.

1. Display **Slide 1**. On the **Design tab**, in the **Themes group**, click the **More** button ⊡ to display the **Themes** gallery.

2. Under **Built-In**, point to the second theme—*Adjacency*—and notice that Live Preview displays the current slide with the selected theme as shown in **Figure 1**.

   Under Built-In, the default theme—Office—displays first. After the Office theme, the themes are arranged alphabetically and are identified by their ScreenTips.

3. Under **Built-In**, point to several themes and view the changes to the first slide.

   Each theme includes background colors, font styles, colors, sizes, and slide layouts specific to the theme.

4. Under **Built-In**, locate and click **Median** to apply the theme to all of the slides in the presentation. Compare your screen with **Figure 2**.

■ **Continue to the next page to complete the skill**

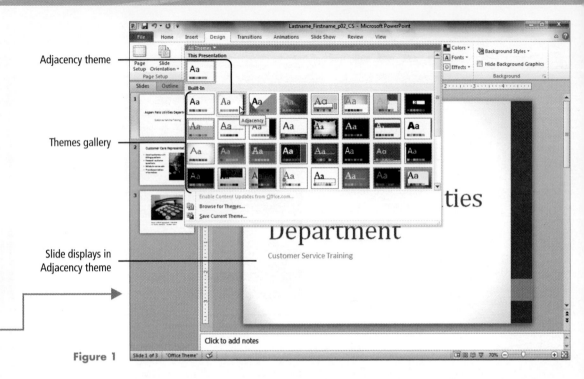

Adjacency theme

Themes gallery

Slide displays in Adjacency theme

Figure 1

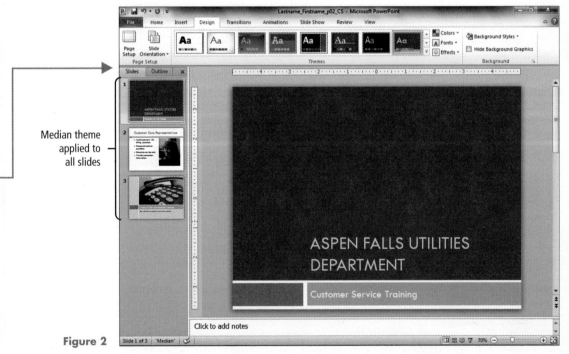

Median theme applied to all slides

Figure 2

Title and caption text formatted

Figure 3

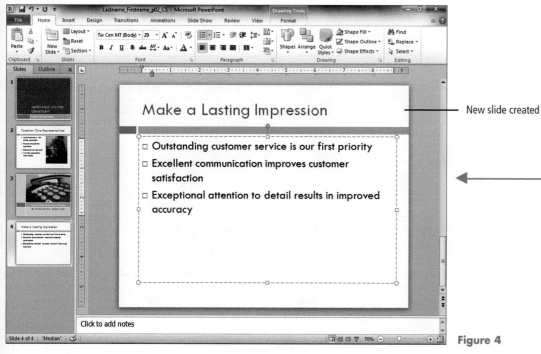

New slide created

Figure 4

5. Display **Slide 3**, and then select the title *Areas in Which Improvement Is Needed.* On the Mini toolbar, click the **Center** button.

6. Select the caption text *Oral and written communications and telephone etiquette.*

7. On the Mini toolbar, click the **Increase Font Size** button two times to change the font size to **20**. On the Mini toolbar, click the **Center** button, and then click the **Italic** button. Compare your slide with **Figure 3**.

After applying a new theme to a presentation, you should review each slide and make formatting changes as necessary. The fonts, layouts, and spacing associated with one theme may require that existing text and objects be resized or moved to display in a manner that is consistent and attractive in the newly applied theme.

8. Insert a **New Slide** with the **Title and Content** layout. In the title placeholder, type Make a Lasting Impression and then in the content placeholder, type the following three bullet points:

Outstanding customer service is our first priority

Excellent communication improves customer satisfaction

Exceptional attention to detail results in improved accuracy

9. Compare your slide with **Figure 4**, and then **Save** the presentation.

■ **You have completed Skill 2 of 10**

► Customize the presentation theme by changing the colors, fonts, effects, and background styles applied to a presentation.

► When you are using several pictures in a presentation, choose theme colors that complement the pictures you selected.

1. Display **Slide 1**. On the **Design tab**, in the **Themes group**, click the **Colors** button to display a list of color themes as shown in **Figure 1**.

> *Theme colors* are composed of a set of coordinated colors that are applied to the backgrounds, objects, and text in a presentation. The Median theme color is selected because the Median theme is applied to the presentation.

2. Point to each of the theme colors, and as you do so, notice the colors applied to **Slide 1**.

3. Click **Foundry** to change the theme colors of the presentation, and then compare your screen with **Figure 2**.

> You can apply a design theme to the presentation—in this case Median—and then change the colors by applying a different theme color. Although the presentation colors change, the overall design of the presentation and the slide layouts continue to be formatted using the Median theme.

■ **Continue to the next page to complete the skill**

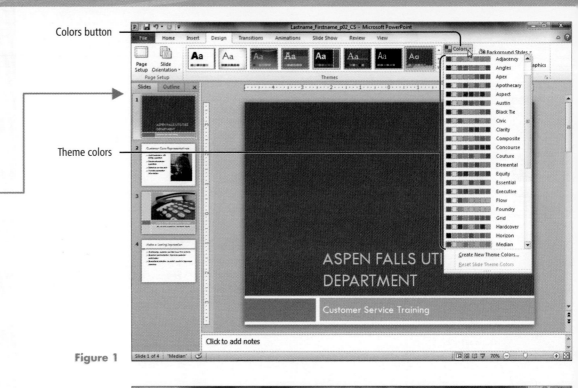

Colors button

Theme colors

Figure 1

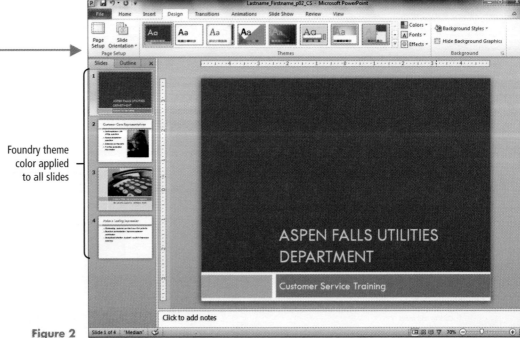

Foundry theme color applied to all slides

Figure 2

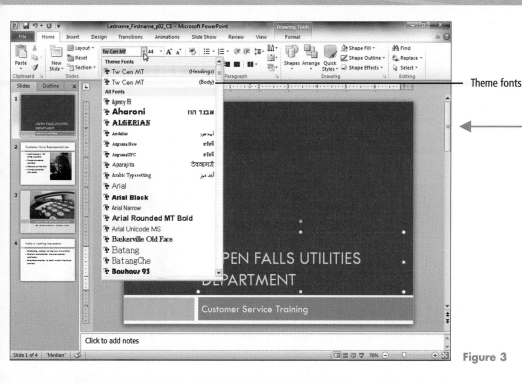

Theme fonts

Figure 3

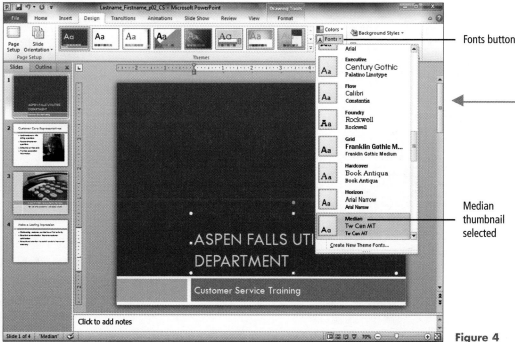

Fonts button

Median thumbnail selected

Figure 4

4. On **Slide 1**, click anywhere in the title placeholder. Click the **Home tab**, and then in the **Font group**, click the **Font button arrow** Calibri (Headings). Notice that at the top of the Font list, under Theme Fonts, *Tw Cen MT (Headings)* and *Tw Cen MT (Body)* display, as shown in **Figure 3**.

> Every presentation theme includes *theme fonts* that determine the font applied to two types of slide text—headings and body. The *headings font* is applied to slide titles, and the *body font* is applied to all other text. Sometimes the heading and body fonts are the same, but they are different sizes. In other font themes, the heading and body fonts are different.

5. Click the **Design tab** to close the Font list, and then in the **Themes group**, click the **Fonts** button.

> The gallery displays fonts in pairs. The first font in each pair is the Headings font, and the second font is the Body font.

6. Scroll the **Theme Fonts** gallery, and notice that the *Median* theme font is selected as shown in **Figure 4**.

7. Point to several of the themes to view the changes to the slide text. Click the **Adjacency** theme, and then scroll through the presentation. Notice that the font changes have been applied to every slide.

> When you apply a new theme font to the presentation, the text on every slide is updated with the new heading and body fonts.

8. **Save** 🔲 the presentation.

■ **You have completed Skill 3 of 10**

► Customize the presentation design by applying a background style to your slides. A ***background style*** is a slide background fill variation that combines theme colors in different intensities or patterns.

► Background styles can be applied to a single slide or to all of the slides in the presentation.

► After you apply a background style, you can reset the background so that the original background associated with the presentation is applied to the slide.

1. Display **Slide 2**. On the **Design tab**, in the **Background group**, click the **Background Styles** button to display the **Background Styles** gallery as shown in **Figure 1**.

> The styles that display are designed to coordinate with the theme color applied to the presentation.

2. Point to each background and view the style applied to the slide, and then click **Style 10**.

> The Style 10 background style is applied to every slide in the presentation.

3. Display **Slide 1**. On the **Design tab**, in the **Background group**, click the **Background Styles** button. Point to the last style— **Style 12**—and then right-click to display the shortcut menu as shown in **Figure 2**.

■ **Continue to the next page to complete the skill**

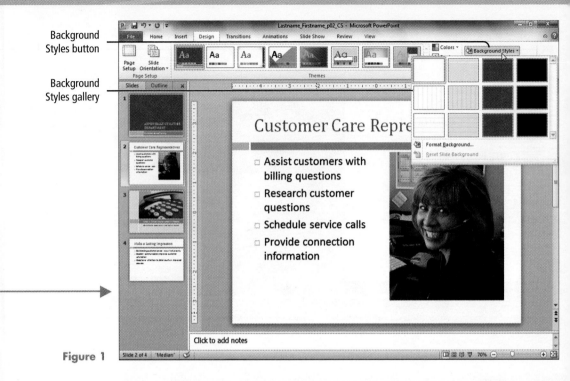

Background Styles button
Background Styles gallery

Figure 1

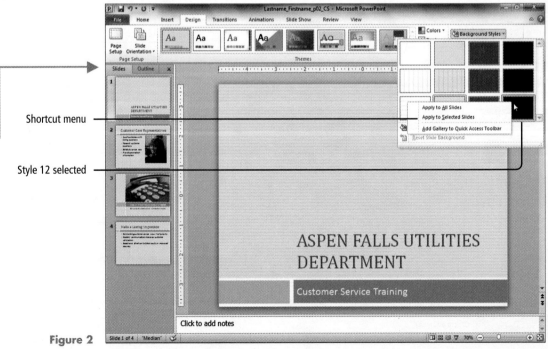

Shortcut menu
Style 12 selected

Figure 2

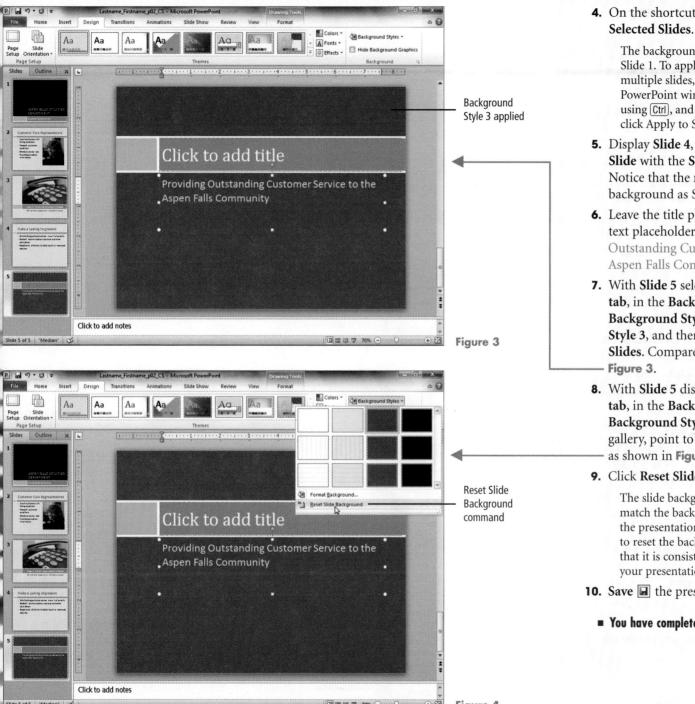

Background
Style 3 applied

Figure 3

Reset Slide
Background
command

Figure 4

4. On the shortcut menu, click **Apply to Selected Slides**.

The background style is applied only to Slide 1. To apply a background style to multiple slides, at the left side of the PowerPoint window, select the slides by using Ctrl, and then on the shortcut menu, click Apply to Selected Slides.

5. Display **Slide 4**, and then insert a **New Slide** with the **Section Header** layout. Notice that the new slide has the same background as Slides 2 through 4.

6. Leave the title placeholder blank. In the text placeholder, type Providing Outstanding Customer Service to the Aspen Falls Community

7. With **Slide 5** selected, on the **Design tab**, in the **Background group**, click the **Background Styles** button. Right-click **Style 3**, and then click **Apply to Selected Slides**. Compare your screen with **Figure 3**.

8. With **Slide 5** displayed, on the **Design tab**, in the **Background group**, click the **Background Styles** button. Below the gallery, point to **Reset Slide Background**, as shown in **Figure 4**.

9. Click **Reset Slide Background**.

The slide background is modified to match the background style applied to the presentation. You can use this feature to reset the background of a slide easily so that it is consistent with the other slides in your presentation.

10. Save 🔲 the presentation.

■ **You have completed Skill 4 of 10**

► A slide can be formatted by inserting a picture or a texture on the slide background.

1. Display **Slide 4**, and then insert a **New Slide** with the **Title Only** layout.

2. On the **Design tab**, in the **Background group**, click the **Background Styles** button, and then click **Format Background**. Compare your screen with **Figure 1**.

3. In the **Format Background** dialog box, if necessary, select the **Picture or texture fill** option button, and then under **Insert from**, click the **File** button.

4. In the **Insert Picture** dialog box, navigate to your student files for this chapter, and then click **p02_CS_Building**. Click **Insert** to insert the picture on the slide background.

5. At the left side of the **Format Background** dialog box, click **Picture Color** to display options for changing picture color.

6. Under **Recolor**, click the **Presets button arrow**, and then click any of the color options. Notice the change to the picture.

7. Under **Recolor**, click the **Presets button arrow** again, and then point to the second color option—**Grayscale**—as shown in **Figure 2**. Click the **Grayscale** thumbnail.

   The background picture displays in *grayscale*—a black-and-white effect achieved through a series of shades of gray from white to black.

8. In the **Format Background** dialog box, click **Close**.

■ **Continue to the next page to complete the skill** ➤

Format Background dialog box

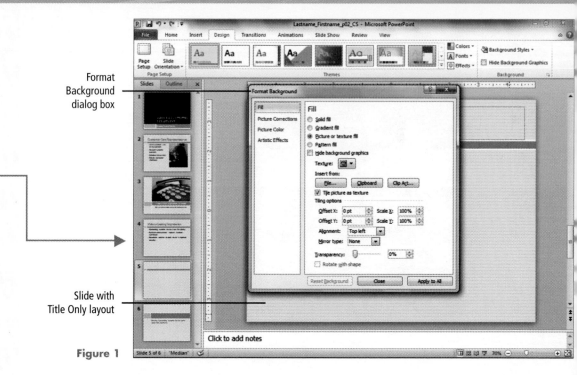

Slide with Title Only layout

Figure 1

Picture Color selected

Presets button arrow

Grayscale color mode

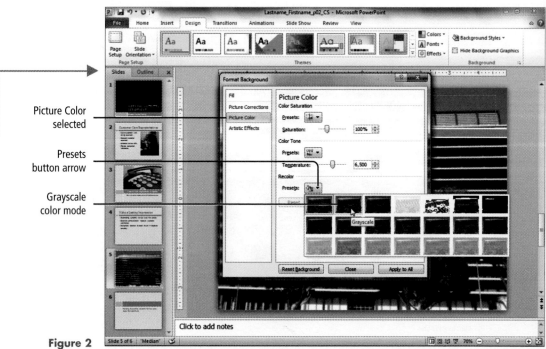

Figure 2

Hide Background
Graphics check
box selected

Figure 3

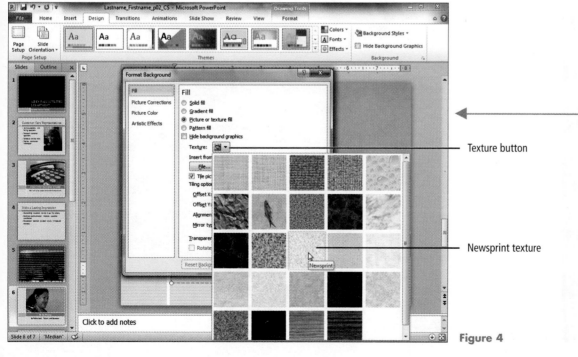

Texture button

Newsprint texture

Figure 4

9. On the **Design tab**, in the **Background group**, select the **Hide Background Graphics** check box, and then compare your screen with **Figure 3**.

> When graphics that are a part of the theme interfere with a background picture, hide the background graphics.

10. With **Slide 5** displayed, insert a **New Slide** with the **Picture with Caption** layout. In the picture placeholder, click the **Insert Picture from File** button. From your student files, insert the picture **p02_CS_Headset**. In the title placeholder, type Or By Phone and then change the **Font Size** to **36** and **Center** the text.

11. In the text placeholder, type Be Professional, Patient, and Courteous and then change the **Font Size** to **28**. **Center** the text.

12. On the **Design tab**, in the **Background group**, click the **Background Styles** button, and then click **Format Background**.

13. In the **Format Background** dialog box, if necessary, select the **Picture or texture fill** option button, and then click the **Texture** button to display the **Texture** gallery. Use the ScreenTips to locate the **Newsprint** texture as shown in **Figure 4**.

> When applying a texture to the slide background, be sure to choose a texture that coordinates with the background colors on the rest of your slides.

14. Click **Newsprint**, and then in the **Format Background** dialog box, click **Close**.

15. Save the presentation.

- **You have completed Skill 5 of 10**

▶ *WordArt* is a text style used to create decorative effects in your presentation.

▶ You can insert new WordArt, or you can convert existing text to WordArt.

1. Display **Slide 1**, and then select the title text. On the **Format tab**, in the **WordArt Styles group**, click the **More** button ⊟ to display the WordArt gallery.

2. Point to several WordArt styles and notice that Live Preview displays the title with the WordArt effect applied.

3. Under **Applies to Selected Text**, in the first row, point to the fourth WordArt style—**Fill - White, Outline - Accent 1**—as shown in **Figure 1**. Click the thumbnail and **Center** ▣ the title text.

4. Select the subtitle text. On the **Format tab**, in the **WordArt Styles group**, click the **More** button ⊟. In the **WordArt** gallery, under **Applies to All Text in the Shape**, click the second WordArt style—**Fill - Black, Background 1, Metal Bevel**—and then **Center** ▣ the text.

5. Display **Slide 5**. On the **Home tab**, in the **Slides group**, click the **Layout** button, and then click the **Blank** thumbnail to change the slide layout.

6. On the **Insert tab**, in the **Text group**, click the **WordArt** button. In the **WordArt** gallery, click the third WordArt style—**Fill - White, Drop Shadow**. Compare your screen with **Figure 2**.

    On the slide, a WordArt placeholder displays *Your text here*.

7. With the WordArt text selected, type Whether you assist customers on-site

    The placeholder expands to accommodate the text.

▪ **Continue to the next page to complete the skill**

Selected WordArt style

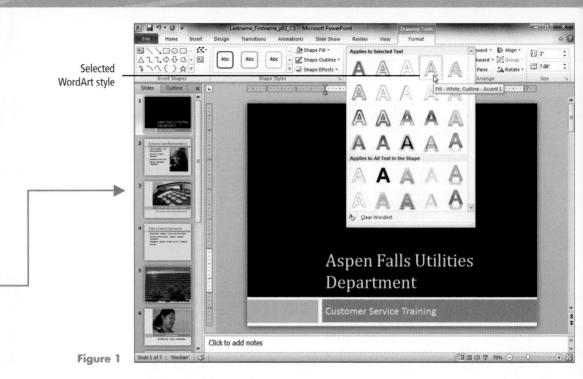

Figure 1

WordArt placeholder

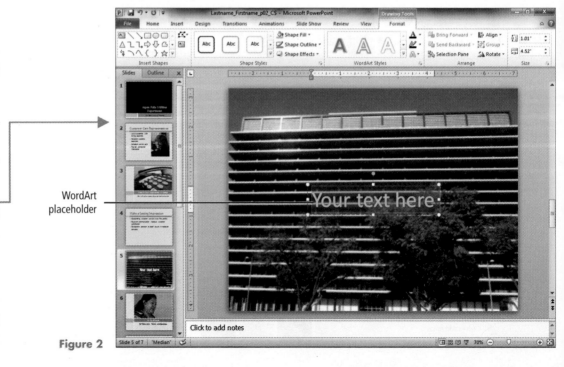

Figure 2

Move pointer

WordArt font size changed to 40

Figure 3

8. Select the **WordArt** text. On the Mini toolbar, click the **Font Size arrow** ⟨ ⟩, and then click **40** to resize the WordArt.

9. Point to the outer edge of the WordArt placeholder to display the ⟨ ⟩ move pointer as shown in **Figure 3**.

10. While holding down the left mouse button, drag down and to the left so that the lower left corner of the WordArt placeholder aligns with the lower left corner of the slide, and then release the mouse button to move the WordArt.

11. With the WordArt still selected, point to its square, center-right sizing handle to display the ⟨ ⟩ pointer. Drag to the right so that the right edge of the WordArt placeholder aligns with the right edge of the slide.

12. On the **Format tab**, in the **Shape Styles group**, click the **Shape Fill** button to display the **Fill** gallery.

The colors in the top row of the Fill gallery are the Foundry theme colors. The colors in the rows below the first row are light and dark variations of the theme colors and coordinate with the color theme. These colors can be used to change the *fill color*— the inside color of text or an object—so that the WordArt text displays prominently against the picture on the background.

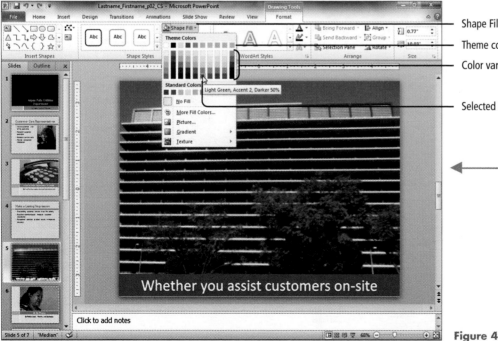

Shape Fill button

Theme colors

Color variations

Selected color

Figure 4

13. Under **Theme Colors**, in the last row, click the sixth color—**Light Green, Accent 2, Darker 50%**—as shown in **Figure 4**.

The WordArt text contrasts with the green fill color and the title is clearly visible on the slide.

14. **Save** ⟨ ⟩ the presentation.

■ **You have completed Skill 6 of 10**

▶ When a selected font displays text that appears crowded in a placeholder, expand the horizontal spacing between characters.

▶ When a selected font displays text with excessive horizontal spacing, condense the spacing between characters.

▶ Change font colors to create contrast and emphasis on a slide.

1. If necessary, display **Slide 5**, and then select the WordArt text at the bottom of the slide. On the **Home tab**, in the **Font group**, click the **Bold** button [B].

   The bold text contrasts well with the dark background of the placeholder, but the characters are spaced tightly together.

2. With the text still selected, on the **Home tab**, in the **Font group**, click the **Character Spacing** button [AV·], and then in the list, click **More Spacing**. In the **Font** dialog box, click the **Spacing** arrow, and then click **Expanded**. In the **By** box, type 1.6 to expand the spacing between characters by 1.6 points. Compare your dialog box with **Figure 1**, and then click **OK** to apply the character spacing.

3. Display **Slide 3**, and then select the title. In the **Font group**, click the **Character Spacing** button [AV·], and then click **Tight** to reduce the amount of space between each character. Compare your slide with **Figure 2.**

■ **Continue to the next page to complete the skill**

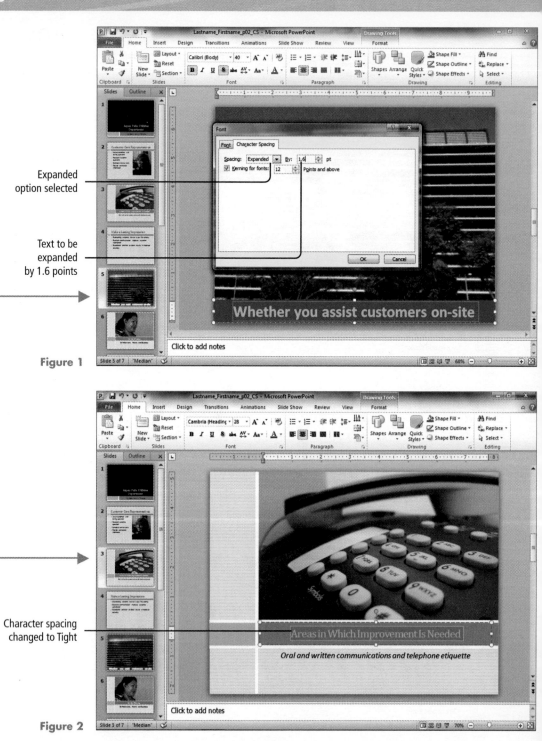

Expanded option selected

Text to be expanded by 1.6 points

Figure 1

Character spacing changed to Tight

Figure 2

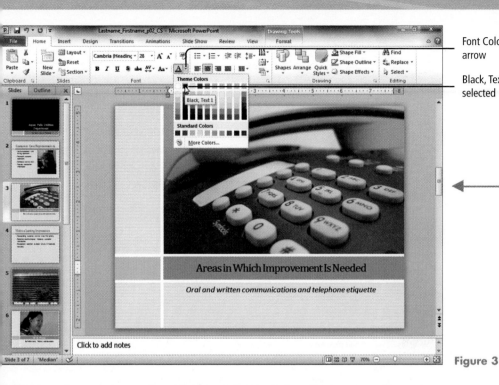

Font Color button arrow

Black, Text 1 selected

Figure 3

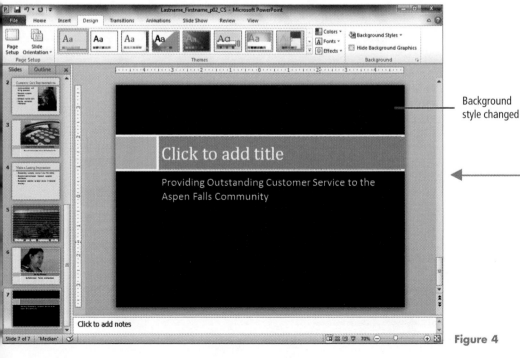

Background style changed

Figure 4

4. With the title still selected, on the **Home tab**, in the **Font group**, click the **Font Color button arrow** [A▾] to display the **Font Color** gallery.

> The colors in the first row of the Font Color gallery are the colors associated with the presentation color theme.

5. In the first row, click the second color— **Black, Text 1**—to change the color of the selected text, as shown in **Figure 3**.

> In the Font group, the Font Color button displays the color that you just applied to the selection. If you want to apply the same color to another selection, you can click the Font Color button without displaying the color gallery.

6. Display **Slide 6**, and then select the title text. On the Mini toolbar, click the **Font Color** button [A▾] to change the font color to black.

7. Display **Slide 7** and notice that the background does not provide sufficient contrast for the subtitle text. On the **Design tab**, in the **Background group**, click the **Background Styles** button. In the gallery, right-click **Style 4**, and then click **Apply to Selected Slides**. Compare your slide with **Figure 4**.

> To create contrast for the text on a slide, change either the font color or the slide background style.

8. **Save** [💾] the presentation.

■ **You have completed Skill 7 of 10**

▶ The presentation theme includes default bullet styles for the bullet points in content placeholders. You can customize a bullet symbol by changing its style, color, and size.

▶ A numbered list can be applied to bullet points in place of bullet symbols.

1. Display **Slide 4**, and then in the content placeholder, select the three bullet points. On the **Home tab**, in the **Paragraph group**, click the **Numbering** button ⊞▾, and then compare your screen with **Figure 1**. If you clicked the Numbering button arrow and a gallery displays, in the first row, click the second Numbering option—1, 2, 3.

    The bullet symbols are replaced by numbers. The default color for the numbers—light green—is based on the Foundry color theme.

2. With the three numbered list items selected, click the **Numbering button arrow** ⊞▾, and then below the gallery, click **Bullets and Numbering**.

3. In the **Bullets and Numbering** dialog box, on the **Numbered tab**, click the **Color** button. Under **Theme Colors**, in the last row, point to the seventh color—**Sky Blue, Accent 3, Darker 50%**—as shown in **Figure 2**. Click to apply the new color.

4. In the **Size** box, replace the number with 100 so that the numbers will be the same size as the text. Click **OK** to apply the changes to the numbers in the list.

■ **Continue to the next page to complete the skill**

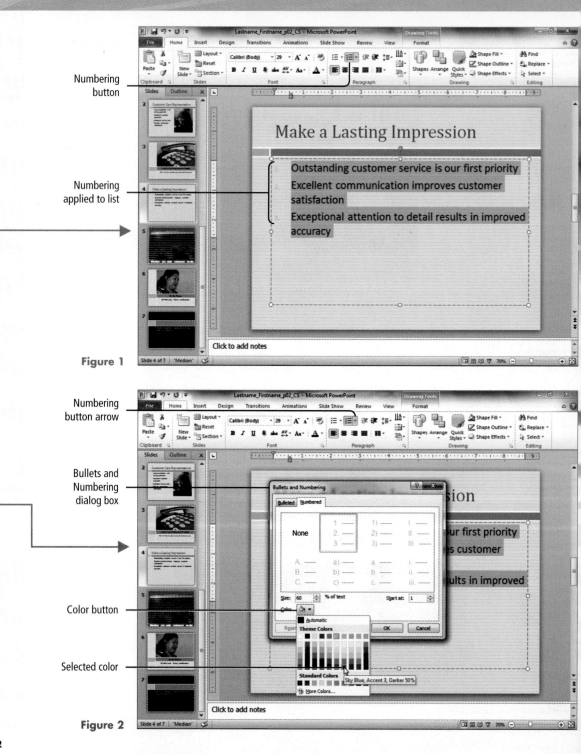

Numbering button

Numbering applied to list

Figure 1

Numbering button arrow

Bullets and Numbering dialog box

Color button

Selected color

Figure 2

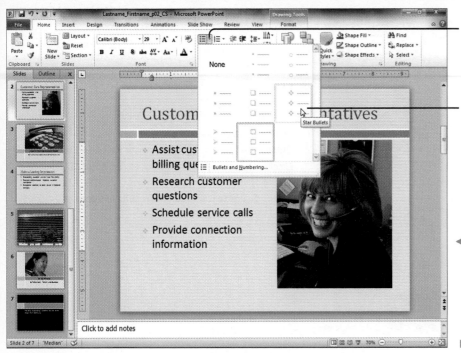

Bullets button arrow

Star Bullets thumbnail

Figure 3

5. Display **Slide 2**. In the content placeholder, select the four bullet points.

6. With the four bullet points selected, on the **Home tab**, in the **Paragraph group**, click the **Bullets button arrow** [≡▾] to display the **Bullets** gallery. If your bullets disappeared, click the Bullets button again, and then repeat Step 6, making sure to click the Bullets *button arrow* instead of the Bullets *button*.

   The gallery displays several bullet characters that you can apply to the selection.

7. Point to the **Star Bullets** thumbnail as shown in **Figure 3**, and then click the thumbnail to change the bullet style for the selection.

8. With the four bullet points selected, click the **Bullets button arrow** [≡▾], and then below the gallery, click **Bullets and Numbering**.

9. In the **Bullets and Numbering** dialog box, on the **Bulleted tab**, in the first row of the bullet gallery, click **Filled Square Bullets**. Click the **Color** button. Under **Theme Colors**, in the last row, click the seventh color—**Sky Blue, Accent 3, Darker 50%**.

10. In the **Size** box, replace the number with 90 and then compare your dialog box with **Figure 4**.

11. Click **OK** to apply the bullet style, color, and size, and then **Save** [💾] the presentation.

   ▪ **You have completed Skill 8 of 10**

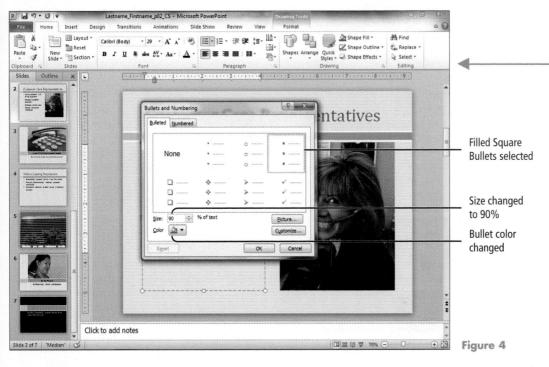

Filled Square Bullets selected

Size changed to 90%

Bullet color changed

Figure 4

► The Cut command removes selected text or graphics from your presentation and places the selection in the Clipboard.

► The Clipboard is a temporary storage area maintained by your operating system.

► The Copy command duplicates a selection and places it in the Clipboard.

1. Display **Slide 4**. In the content placeholder, position the pointer over the number **3**, and notice the pointer that displays as shown in **Figure 1**.

2. With the pointer positioned over the number **3**, click the mouse button, and notice that the number and the related text are selected.

   Clicking a list number or bullet symbol is an efficient way to select the entire point.

3. On the **Home tab**, in the **Clipboard group**, click the **Cut** button ✂ to remove the item from the slide and send it to the Clipboard.

4. In the second numbered list item, click in front of the *E* in the word *Excellent*. In the **Clipboard group**, click the **Paste** button to paste the selection to the new location. Notice that below the pasted text, the Paste Options button displays as shown in **Figure 2**, providing options for formatting pasted text. Also notice that the points are automatically renumbered when the order is changed.

■ **Continue to the next page to complete the skill**

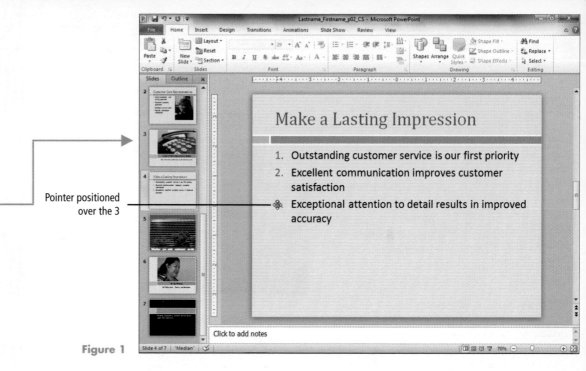

Pointer positioned over the 3

Figure 1

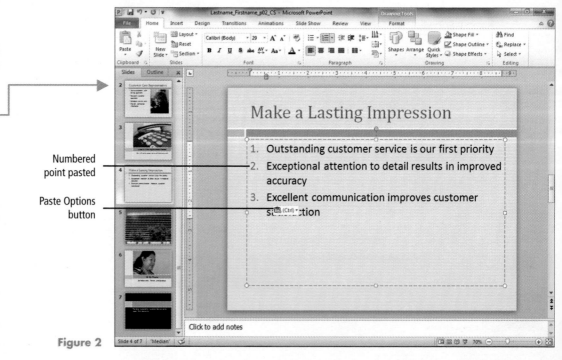

Numbered point pasted

Paste Options button

Figure 2

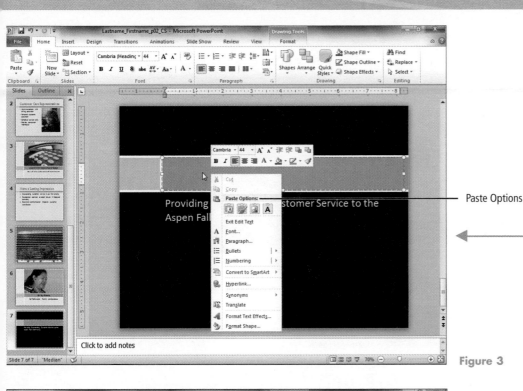

Paste Options

Figure 3

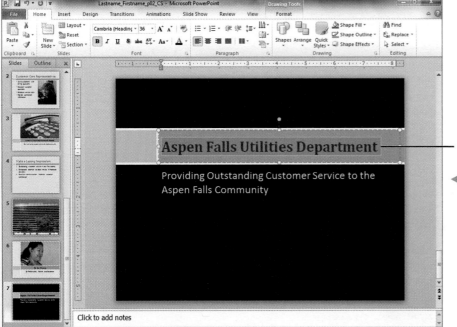

Title pasted and formatted

Figure 4

5. Click the **Paste Options** button 🗐 to view the options.

   Keep Source Formatting applies the original formatting of the pasted text. *Use Destination Theme* applies the formatting of the slide to which the text is pasted. *Picture* pastes the text as a picture. *Keep Text Only* removes all formatting from the selection. The Paste Options button remains on the screen until you perform another action.

6. Display **Slide 1**, and then select the title text. Point to the selection, and then right-click to display the shortcut menu. On the shortcut menu, click **Copy**.

   There are multiple methods you can use to cut, copy, and paste text, including the shortcut menu and the buttons in the Clipboard group. You can also use the keyboard shortcuts—Ctrl+X to cut, Ctrl+C to copy, and Ctrl+V to paste.

7. Display **Slide 7**. Right-click in the title placeholder to display the shortcut menu as shown in **Figure 3**, and then notice the four paste options.

8. On the shortcut menu, under **Paste Options**, point to each button to view how each paste option displays the text, and then click the last button—**Keep Text Only**.

9. Select the title text. Apply **Bold** 🅱, change the **Font Color** 🔺▾ to **Black, Background 1**, and then change the **Font Size** to **36**. Compare your slide with **Figure 4**.

10. **Save** 🖫 the presentation.

■ **You have completed Skill 9 of 10**

▶ *Format Painter* copies *formatting* from one selection of text to another, thus ensuring formatting consistency in your presentation.

▶ Use the Clear All Formatting button to revert to the font formatting associated with the original slide layout.

1. Display **Slide 3**, and then select the word *Oral.* On the **Home tab**, in the **Clipboard group**, click the **Format Painter** button, and then position the pointer anywhere in the Slide pane. Compare your screen with **Figure 1**.

   The pointer displays with a small paintbrush attached to it, indicating that Format Painter is active.

2. Display **Slide 6**. Drag the pointer over the caption text—*Be Professional, Patient, and Courteous.*

   The selected text is now formatted in italic, 20 point, as was the text on Slide 3. Notice that only the formatting was applied; the text was not copied. The pointer is no longer active.

3. If necessary, select the caption text—*Be Professional, Patient, and Courteous.* On the **Home tab**, in the **Font group**, click the **Clear All Formatting** button to revert to the default font formatting for this slide layout.

   Use the Clear All Formatting button to revert to the original formatting on a slide.

4. With the caption text still selected, change the **Font Size** to **28**, and then apply **Bold** and **Italic**. Compare your slide with **Figure 2**.

■ **Continue to the next page to complete the skill**

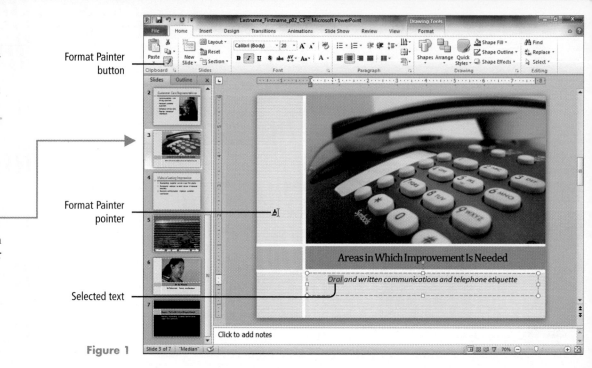

Format Painter button

Format Painter pointer

Selected text

Figure 1

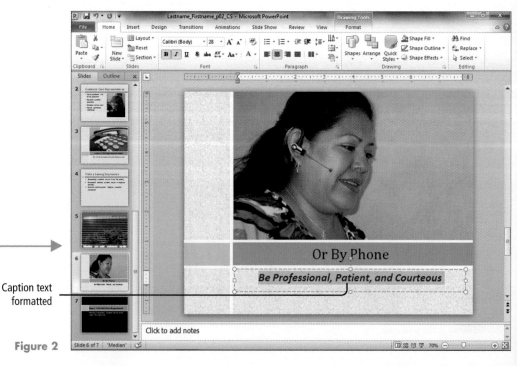

Caption text formatted

Figure 2

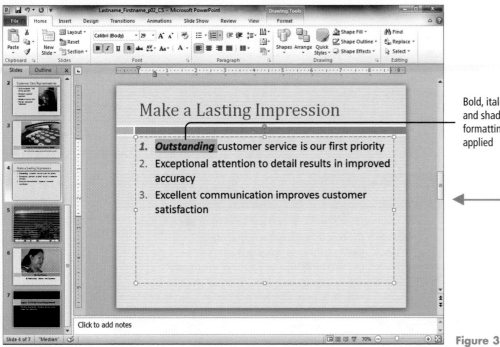

Bold, italic, and shadow formatting applied

Figure 3

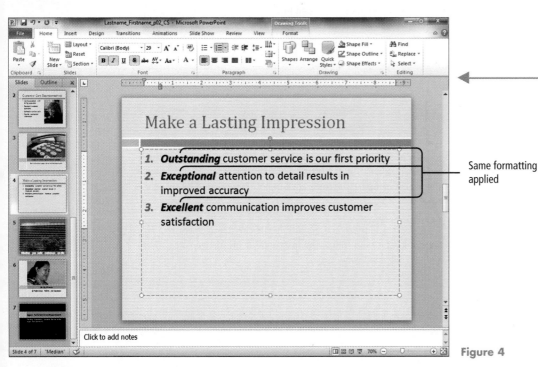

Same formatting applied

Figure 4

5. Display **Slide 4**. In the first item, select the text *Outstanding*. On the **Home tab**, in the **Font group**, click the **Bold** button [B], the **Italic** button [I], and the **Shadow** button [S]. Compare your slide with **Figure 3**.

6. With the text *Outstanding* still selected, on the **Home tab**, in the **Clipboard group**, *double-click* the **Format Painter** button [✓].

    To apply formatting to multiple selections, double-click the Format Painter button.

7. In the second numbered item, click the word *Exceptional* to apply the selected formatting to the text. Notice that the [▲I] pointer is still active.

8. In the third numbered item, click the word *Excellent*. If you were unable to apply the formatting to the word *Excellent*, repeat Step 6, and then try again.

9. To turn off Format Painter, on the **Home tab**, in the **Clipboard group**, click the **Format Painter** button [✓]. Alternately, press [Esc]. Compare your slide with **Figure 4**.

10. Apply the **Wipe** transition with the **Effect Options** changed to **From Top** to all of the slides, and then view the slide show from the beginning.

11. Insert a **Header & Footer** on the **Notes and Handouts** that includes the **Date and time** updated automatically, a **Page number**, and the **Footer** Lastname_Firstname_p02_CS

12. **Save** [💾] the presentation. Print your presentation or submit electronically, as directed by your instructor. **Exit** PowerPoint.

Done! You have completed Skill 10 of 10 and your presentation is complete!

More Skills

The following More Skills are located at **www.pearsonhighered.com/skills**

More Skills Edit Slide Masters

When you are formatting a presentation and want to change the format for every slide in the presentation, modify the slide master. The slide master holds information about the colors, fonts, and other objects that display on your slides.

In More Skills 11, you will edit a slide master by changing its font and bullet styles.

To begin, open your web browser, navigate to www.pearsonhighered.com/skills, locate the name of your textbook, and then follow the instructions on the website.

More Skills Save and Apply Presentation Templates

You can design your own custom presentation and save it as a template so that you can easily apply the template to another presentation.

In More Skills 12, you will save a presentation as a template and then apply the template to another presentation.

To begin, open your web browser, navigate to www.pearsonhighered.com/skills, locate the name of your textbook, and then follow the instructions on the website.

More Skills Create Slides from Microsoft Word Outline

The bullet points in a PowerPoint presentation are based on an outline in which the list levels are assigned to varying outline levels. An outline based on paragraph styles in Microsoft Word can be imported into PowerPoint to create slides.

In More Skills 13, you will import a Microsoft Word outline to create slides in a PowerPoint presentation.

To begin, open your web browser, navigate to www.pearsonhighered.com/skills, locate the name of your textbook, and then follow the instructions on the website.

More Skills Design Presentations with Contrast

Contrast is an important element of slide design because it enables the audience to clearly view presentation text, images, and objects.

In More Skills 14, you will review design principles that will assist you in creating contrast on your slides. You will view two slides and compare the difference in contrast created by using color and images.

To begin, open your web browser, navigate to www.pearsonhighered.com/skills, locate the name of your textbook, and then follow the instructions on the website.

Key Terms

Background style............ 74

Body font 73

Fill color 79

Format Painter............. 86

Grayscale.................. 76

Headings font.............. 73

Template 68

Theme 70

Theme color 72

Theme font................ 73

WordArt 78

Online Help Skills

1. **Start**  PowerPoint. In the upper right corner of the PowerPoint window, click the **Help** button ⊙. In the **Help** window, click the **Maximize** button.

2. Click in the search box, type Overview of themes and then click the **Search** button ⊙. In the search results, click **What is a theme?**

3. Below **In this article**, click **Overview of Office themes**. Compare your screen with **Figure 1**.

Figure 1

4. Scroll down to read the entire article and then see if you can answer the following: How does modifying a presentation theme color result in a dramatic change in a presentation?

Matching

Match each term in the second column with its correct definition in the first column by writing the letter of the term on the blank line in front of the correct definition.

____ **1.** A file upon which a presentation can be based.

____ **2.** A set of unified design elements that provides a look for your presentation, using colors, fonts, and graphics.

____ **3.** A theme that determines the font applied to two types of slide text—headings and body.

____ **4.** A font applied to slide titles.

____ **5.** A font applied to all slide text except titles.

____ **6.** A slide background fill variation that combines theme colors in different intensities or patterns.

____ **7.** A text style used to create decorative effects in a presentation.

____ **8.** The inside color of text or an object.

____ **9.** A command that removes selected text or graphics from a presentation and then moves the selection to the Clipboard.

____ **10.** A temporary storage area maintained by the operating system.

A Background style

B Body font

C Clipboard

D Cut

E Fill color

F Headings font

G Template

H Theme

I Theme font

J WordArt

Multiple Choice

Choose the correct answer.

1. The process of changing the appearance of the text, layout, or design of a slide.
   A. Editing
   B. Designing
   C. Formatting

2. The area of the PowerPoint window in which the name of the applied theme displays.
   A. Status bar
   B. Task pane
   C. Slide pane

3. The default theme in PowerPoint.
   A. Apex
   B. Office
   C. Urban

4. The coordinating set of colors applied to presentation backgrounds, objects, and text.
   A. Theme color
   B. Color palette
   C. Color gallery

5. A black-and-white effect achieved through a series of shades of gray from white to black.
   A. Sepia
   B. Gradient fill
   C. Grayscale

6. A format that you can change to create contrast and emphasis on a slide.
   A. Alignment
   B. Font color
   C. Layout

7. The command used to duplicate a selection.
   A. Format Painter
   B. Cut
   C. Copy

8. The command used to copy formatting from one selection to another.
   A. Format Painter
   B. Cut
   C. Copy

9. A command used to revert to font formatting associated with the original slide layout.
   A. Clear All Formatting
   B. Reset Format
   C. Reset Slide Layout

10. The mouse action necessary when Format Painter is used on multiple selections.
    A. Single-click
    B. Double-click
    C. Triple-click

Topics for Discussion

1. PowerPoint 2010 includes several themes that you can apply to your presentations. What should you consider when choosing a design theme for the presentations that you create?

2. Format Painter is an important tool used to maintain consistent formatting in a presentation. Why is consistency important when you format the slides in your presentations?

Skill Check

To complete this presentation, you will need the following files:

- **New blank presentation**
- **p02_Plaza_Fountain**

You will save your presentation as:

- **Lastname_Firstname_p02_Plaza**

1. **Start** PowerPoint. In the new presentation, type the slide title The Plaza at Aspen Falls and the subtitle Opening Ceremony **Save** the file in your **PowerPoint Chapter 2** folder as Lastname_Firstname_p02_Plaza

2. Insert a **New Slide** with the **Title and Content** layout. In the title placeholder, type Event Activities In the text placeholder, type four bullet points: Ribbon cutting and Welcome address and Continental breakfast and Grand prize raffle

3. On the **Design tab**, in the **Themes group**, click the **More** button. Under **Built-In**, click **Urban**. In the **Themes group**, click the **Fonts** button, and then click **Metro**. Click the **Colors** button, and then click **Equity**. In the **Background group**, click the **Background Styles** button, and then click **Style 10**. Compare your screen with **Figure 1**.

4. Insert a **New Slide** with the **Blank** layout. On the **Design tab**, in the **Background group**, click the **Background Styles** button, and then click **Format Background**. In the **Format Background** dialog box, select **Picture or texture fill**, then under **Insert from**, click the **File** button. From your student files, insert **p02_Plaza_Fountain**. Click **Close**.

5. Insert a **New Slide** with the **Content with Caption** layout. Type the slide title Join the Celebration! In the left placeholder, type four bullet points: July 25 at 10 a.m. and Free events and Retail locations and park will be open and Raffle at 6 p.m.

6. Select the bullet points and change the **Line Spacing** to **1.5**. In the **Paragraph group**, click the **Bullets button arrow**, and then click **Bullets and Numbering**. Click **Arrow Bullets**, and then click the **Color button**. In the last row, click the fifth color—**Orange, Accent 1, Darker 50%**. In the **Size** box, type 80 and then click **OK**. Compare your screen with **Figure 2**.

- Continue to the next page to complete this Skill Check ▶

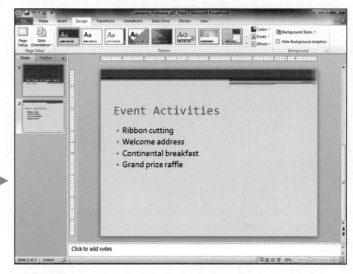

Figure 1

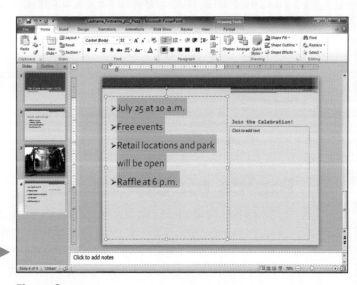

Figure 2

7. On the **Design tab**, in the **Background group**, click the **Background Styles** button, and then click **Format Background**. Select **Picture or texture fill**, and then click the **Texture** button. Click **Newsprint**, and then click **Close**.

8. Display **Slide 2**, and then select the four bullet points. On the **Home tab**, in the **Paragraph group**, click the **Numbering** button.

9. Display **Slide 3**. On the **Design tab**, in the **Background group**, select the **Hide Background Graphics** check box. On the **Insert tab**, in the **Text group**, click **WordArt**. Click the third WordArt style—**Fill - White, Drop Shadow**—and then replace the WordArt text with Ribbon cutting to take place at the fountain

10. Change the **Font Size** to **36**, and then point to the outer edge of the WordArt placeholder. Drag to align the placeholder with the lower left corner of the slide. Size the WordArt so that it extends from the left to the right edge of the slide.

11. On the **Format tab**, in the **Shape Styles group**, click the **Shape Fill** button. Under **Theme Colors**, in the last row, click the sixth color—**Dark Red, Accent 2, Darker 50%**.

12. Select the WordArt text. On the **Home tab**, in the **Font group**, click the **Character Spacing** button, and then click **More Spacing**. Click the **Spacing** arrow, click **Expanded**, and then click **OK**. Compare your screen with **Figure 3**.

13. Display **Slide 1**. On the **Design tab**, in the **Background group**, click the **Background Styles** button, right-click **Style 4**, and then click **Apply to Selected Slides**. Select the title. On the **Format tab**, in the **WordArt Styles group**, click the **More** button, and then under **Applies to Selected Text**, click the last style—**Gradient Fill - Brown, Accent 4, Reflection**.

14. On the **Home tab**, in the **Clipboard group**, click the **Copy** button. Display **Slide 4**, and then click in the text placeholder below the title. In the **Clipboard group**, click the **Paste** button. Change the **Font Size** to **40**, and then **Center** the text.

15. Display **Slide 1**. Select the subtitle. Apply **Bold** and **Italic**, and then on the **Home tab**, in the **Clipboard group**, click the **Format Painter** button.

16. Display **Slide 4**, and then drag the **Format Painter** pointer over the title—*Join the Celebration!*—**Center** the title and change the **Font Color** to **Black, Text 1**.

17. Insert a **Header & Footer** on the **Notes and Handouts** with the **Date and time**, the **Page number**, and the **Footer** Lastname_Firstname_p02_Plaza

18. **Save** the presentation, and then compare your presentation with **Figure 4**. Print or submit electronically.

Done! You have completed the Skill Check

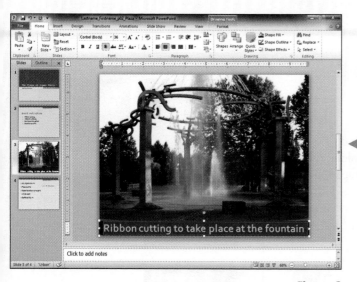

Figure 3

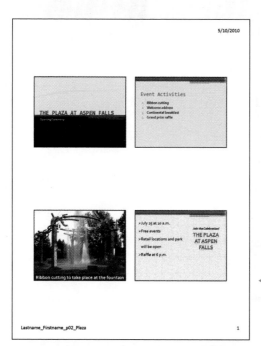

Figure 4

Assess Your Skills 1

To complete this presentation, you will need the following files:

- New blank presentation
- p02_AFD_Engines
- p02_AFD_Fireman

You will save your presentation as:

- Lastname_Firstname_p02_Station

1. **Start** PowerPoint and display a blank presentation. Apply the **Verve** theme. Change the theme color to **Aspect**, and the theme font to **Origin**. **Save** the file in your **PowerPoint Chapter 2** folder as Lastname_Firstname_p02_Station

2. In the title placeholder, type Aspen Falls Fire District and then in the subtitle placeholder, type New Station Proposal Change the subtitle **Font Size** to **36**, and the **Font Color** to **Orange, Accent 1, Darker 25%**.

3. Insert a **New Slide** with the **Title and Content** layout. In the content placeholder, type the following bullet points: Add 3 engines and 15 firefighters and Locate in southern area of city and Fund by municipal bonds

4. Display **Slide 1**. **Copy** the subtitle and **Paste** the selection to the title placeholder on **Slide 2**. Delete any extra blank lines.

5. Insert a **New Slide** with the **Blank** layout. On the slide background insert from your student files the picture **p02_AFD_Engines**. Hide background graphics.

6. Insert the third WordArt style—**Fill - White, Drop Shadow**—with the text Proposed Engine Additions Drag the WordArt to the upper left corner of the slide. Size the WordArt so that it extends from the left to the right edge of the slide. Change the shape fill color to **Black, Background 1**.

7. Insert a **New Slide** with the **Title and Content** layout. In the title placeholder, type Rationale In the text placeholder, type four bullet points: Reduced emergency response time and Increased population growth and Expanded city boundaries and Increased commercial density

8. To the **Slide 4** title, apply the fourth WordArt style—**Fill - White, Outline - Accent 1**. Use **Format Painter** to apply the same style to the **Slide 1** subtitle. Change the subtitle text **Font Size** to **36**. If necessary, Align Right the subtitle.

9. Display **Slide 4**, and then insert a **New Slide** with the **Picture with Caption** layout. Display **Slide 1**, and then **Copy** the title and **Paste** it in the **Slide 5** title. In the text placeholder, type Dedicated to serving our community **Center** the text, and change the **Font Size** to **32**. In the picture placeholder, from your student files, insert **p02_AFD_Fireman**. Apply the **Soft Edge Rectangle** picture style.

10. Insert a **Header & Footer** on the **Notes and Handouts**. Include the date, page number, and the footer Lastname_Firstname_p02_Station

11. Compare your presentation with **Figure 1**. **Save** and then submit the file as directed.

Done! You have completed Assess Your Skills 1

Figure 1

Assess Your Skills 3 and 4 can be found at
www.pearsonhighered.com/skills.

Assess Your Skills 2

To complete this presentation, you will need the following file:

- p02_Loans

You will save your presentation as:

- Lastname_Firstname_p02_Loans

Figure 1

1. **Start** PowerPoint. From your student files, open **p02_Loans**. Change the theme color to **Trek**, and change the theme font to **Verve**. Apply background **Style 12** to the entire presentation, and then **Save** the file in your **PowerPoint Chapter 2** folder as Lastname_Firstname_p02_Loans

2. On **Slide 1**, select the title, and then apply the last WordArt style—**Fill - Orange, Accent 1, Metal Bevel, Reflection**. Change the font size to **40**. Use **Format Painter** to apply the same formatting to the title on **Slide 4**.

3. Display **Slide 1**, and then select the subtitle. Apply **Bold**, and then expand the character spacing by **1** point. Use **Format Painter** to apply the same formatting to the subtitle on **Slide 4**.

4. Display **Slide 2**. Change the bullet style to **Star Bullets**, and then change the **Size** to 90 % of text. Move the last bullet point so that it is the first bullet point. Apply the **Rotated, White** picture style to the picture.

5. Display **Slide 3**, and then in the first bullet point, select the first word—*Apply*. Change the **Font Color** to the fifth color in the first row—**Orange, Accent 1**. Apply **Bold** and **Italic**, and then use **Format Painter** to apply the same formatting to the first word of each of the remaining bullet points. Convert the bullets to a numbered list, and change the **Color** of the numbers to **White, Text 1**.

6. Display **Slide 1**, and then format the slide background by applying the **Granite** texture. Apply the same background style to **Slide 4**.

7. With **Slide 4** displayed, apply the **Double Frame, Black** picture style to the picture.

8. Apply the **Wipe** transition to all of the slides in the presentation. View the slide show from the beginning.

9. Insert a **Header & Footer** on the **Notes and Handouts** that includes the page number and a footer with the text Lastname_Firstname_p02_Loans

10. Compare your completed presentation with **Figure 1**. **Save** your presentation, and then print or submit the file as directed by your instructor.

Done! You have completed Assess Your Skills 2

Assess Your Skills Visually

To complete this presentation, you will need the following files:

- New blank presentation
- p02_Natural_History_Museum

You will save your presentation as:

- Lastname_Firstname_p02_Museum

Start a new, blank presentation, and create the first two slides of a presentation as shown in **Figure 1**. To complete these two slides, apply the **Pushpin** theme. On **Slide 1**, change the title font size to **54**, and change the subtitle font size to **32**. On **Slide 2**, format the slide background by using the picture found in your student files— **p02_Natural_History_Museum**. Insert the appropriate WordArt style, type the text, and change the WordArt font size to **48**. Move and format the **Shape Fill** color as indicated in the figure. **Save** your presentation as Lastname_Firstname_p02_Museum and then insert the date, file name, and page number in the **Notes and Handouts** footer. **Save** the presentation, and then print or submit the file as directed by your instructor.

Done! You have completed Assess Your Skills Visually

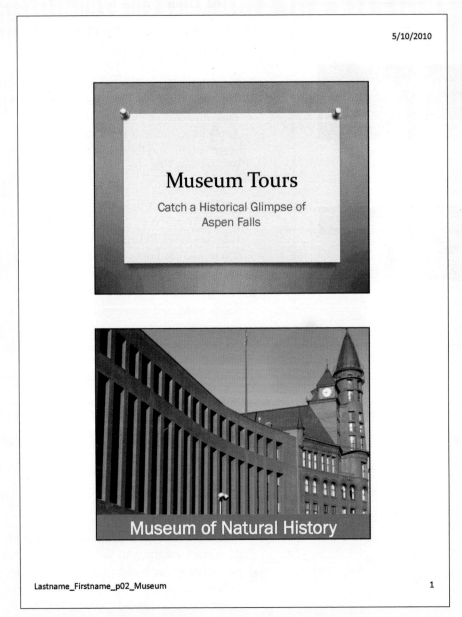

Figure 1

Skills in Context

To complete this presentation, you will need the following file:

- **New blank presentation**

You will save your presentation as:

- **Lastname_Firstname_p02_Celebration**

Each year the City of Aspen Falls hosts a Fourth of July celebration at the Aspen Falls Community Park. Using the skills you practiced in this chapter, create a presentation with five slides that describes the city's Fourth of July events, which include a parade, barbecue, games, arts and crafts fair, and fireworks. Create an appropriate title slide, and then on the second and third slides, provide a description of the event location and the celebration schedule. On the fourth slide, format the background with a picture that depicts the event, and include WordArt text that briefly describes the picture. On the fifth slide, provide a summary using the Section Header layout.

Apply an appropriate theme, and change fonts and colors as necessary. Save the presentation as Lastname_Firstname_p02_Celebration and then insert the file name and page number in the Notes and Handouts footer. Save the presentation, and then print or submit the file as directed by your instructor.

Done! You have completed Skills in Context

Skills and You

To complete this presentation, you will need the following file:

- **New blank presentation**

You will save your presentation as:

- **Lastname_Firstname_p02_City**

Using the skills you have practiced in this chapter, create a presentation with six slides describing a city that you would like to visit. Apply an appropriate theme, and change the fonts and colors themes. On at least one slide, format the slide background with a picture that depicts the city that you choose. On the first slide, format the slide title by using a WordArt style. Include in your presentation a numbered list that indicates at least four things that you would like to do or see in the city that you choose. The remaining slides may include information about the people, culture, and activities of the city.

Format the last slide with the Section Header layout, and enter text that briefly summarizes your presentation. Add a footer to the notes and handouts with the file name and page number, and then check spelling in the presentation. Save the presentation as Lastname_Firstname_p02_City and then print or submit electronically as directed by your instructor.

Done! You have completed Skills and You

CHAPTER 3

Enhance Presentations with Graphics

▶ Appropriate presentation graphics visually communicate your message and help your audience understand the points you want to convey.

▶ Review the graphics that you use, the text on your slides, and your spoken words to ensure that your presentation is coherent, precise, and accurate.

Your starting screen will look similar to this:

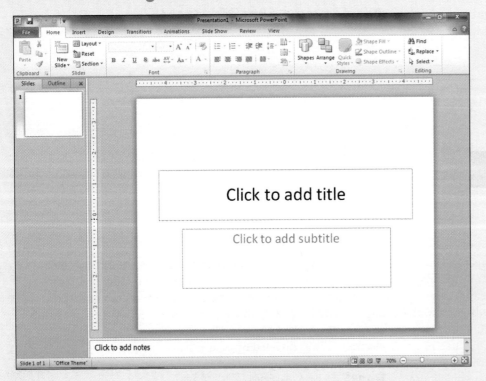

SKILLS

Skills 1-10 Training

At the end of this chapter, you will be able to:

Skill 1 Insert Slides from Other Presentations

Skill 2 Insert, Size, and Move Clip Art

Skill 3 Modify Picture Shapes, Borders, and Effects

Skill 4 Insert, Size, and Move Shapes

Skill 5 Add Text to Shapes and Insert Text Boxes

Skill 6 Apply Gradient Fills and Group and Align Graphics

Skill 7 Convert Text to SmartArt Graphics and Add Shapes

Skill 8 Modify SmartArt Layouts, Colors, and Styles

Skill 9 Insert Video Files

Skill 10 Apply Video Styles and Adjust Videos

MORE SKILLS

More Skills 11 Compress Pictures

More Skills 12 Save Groups as Picture Files

More Skills 13 Change Object Order

More Skills 14 Design Presentations Using Appropriate Graphics

Outcome

Using the skills listed to the left will enable you
to create a presentation like this:

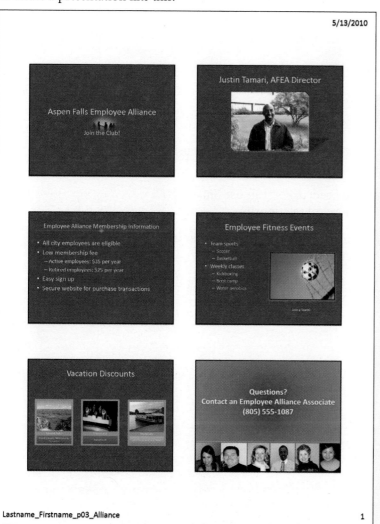

You will save this presentation as:
Lastname_Firstname_p03_Alliance

In this chapter, you will create presentations for the Aspen Falls City Hall, which provides essential services for the citizens and visitors of Aspen Falls, California.

Introduction

- In many organizations, team members commonly share presentations using slide libraries and file sharing procedures.

- When effective and illustrative diagrams are needed, you can use SmartArt graphics to list information and show process and relationships.

- When you have slides with many bullet points, consider inserting slides with SmartArt graphics to add interest and variety.

Time to complete all
10 skills – 60 minutes

Find your student data files here:

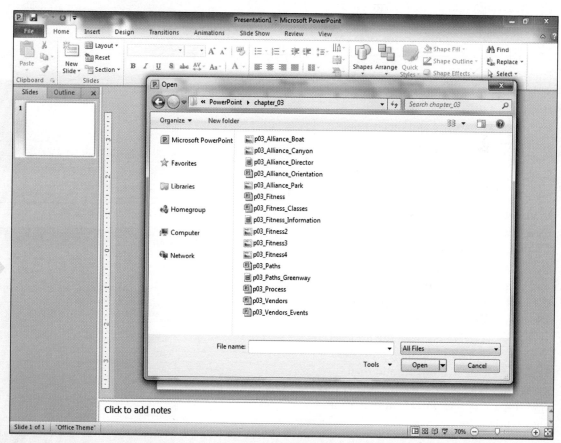

Student data files needed for this chapter:

- New blank presentation
- p03_Alliance_Orientation
- p03_Alliance_Canyon
- p03_Alliance_Director
- p03_Alliance_Boat
- p03_Alliance_Park

▶ Presentation slides can be shared using the Reuse Slides command so that frequently used content does not need to be recreated.

1. **Start** PowerPoint to display a new presentation. In the title placeholder, type Aspen Falls Employee Alliance and then in the subtitle placeholder, type Join the Club!

2. On the **Design tab**, in the **Background group**, click **Background Styles**. Click **Style 3**, and then compare your slide with **Figure 1**. ─────────

3. On the **Quick Access Toolbar**, click **Save**. Navigate to the location where you are saving your files, create a folder named PowerPoint Chapter 3 and then using your own name, save the document as Lastname_Firstname_p03_Alliance

4. On the **Home tab**, in the **Slides group**, click the **New Slide button arrow**, and then in the **Office Theme** gallery, click **Two Content**. In the title placeholder, type Employee Fitness Events

5. In the left placeholder, type Team sports and then press Enter. Press Tab to increase the list level. Type Soccer and then press Enter. Type Basketball and then press Enter.

6. Press Shift + Tab to decrease the list level. Type Weekly classes and then press Enter. Press Tab. Type Kickboxing and then press Enter. Type Boot camp and then press Enter. Type Water aerobics Compare your slide with **Figure 2**. ─────────

■ **Continue to the next page to complete the skill** ▶

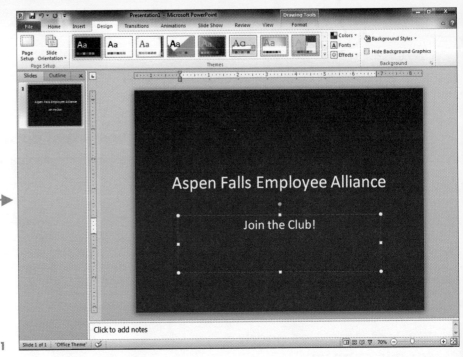

Figure 1

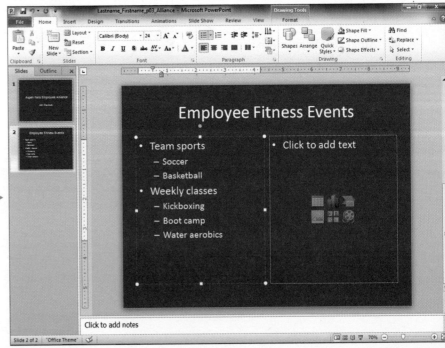

Figure 2

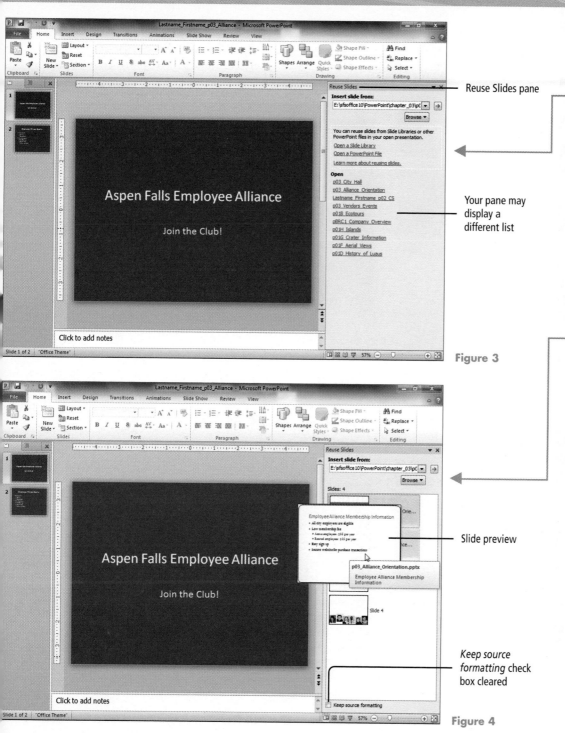

Reuse Slides pane

Your pane may display a different list

Figure 3

Slide preview

Keep source formatting check box cleared

Figure 4

7. Display **Slide 1**. On the **Home tab**, in the **Slides group**, click the **New Slide button arrow**. Below the gallery, click **Reuse Slides** to display the Reuse Slides pane as shown in **Figure 3**.

8. In the **Reuse Slides** pane, click **Browse**, and then click **Browse File**. Navigate to the location where your student files are stored, click **p03_Alliance_Orientation**, and then click **Open**.

   In the Reuse Slides pane, you can insert all of the slides from another presentation, or you can insert only the slides that you need.

9. At the bottom of the **Reuse Slides** pane, verify that the **Keep source formatting** check box is cleared. Point to the second slide thumbnail—*Employee Alliance Membership Information*—to preview the slide as shown in **Figure 4**.

10. Click the **Employee Alliance Membership Information** slide to insert it in the current presentation.

    With the *Keep source formatting* option cleared, the formatting of the current pre-sentation is applied to the inserted slide.

11. Display **Slide 3**. In the **Reuse Slides** pane, right-click the third slide—*Vacation Discounts*.

    On the shortcut menu, you have the option to insert only the selected slide or to insert all of the slides in the current presentation.

12. Click **Insert Slide**, and then in the upper right corner of the **Reuse Slides** pane, click the **Close** button ☒.

13. Save ⊟ the presentation.

   ■ **You have completed Skill 1 of 10**

► Recall that clip art refers to images included with Microsoft Office, whereas pictures are images that are saved as a file with an extension such as .jpg, .bmp, or .tif.

1. Display **Slide 3**. In the placeholder on the right, click the **Clip Art** button to display the Clip Art pane.

2. In the **Clip Art** pane, in the **Search for** box, replace any existing text with soccer sports equipment to search for images that contain the keywords *soccer*, *sports*, and *equipment*.

3. Click the **Results should be** arrow, and then clear or select the check boxes so that only **Photographs** is selected, as shown in **Figure 1**.

   When the Photographs check box is selected, only images that were created with a digital camera or a scanner will be searched.

4. Click the **Results should be arrow** to close the list, and then select the **Include Office.com content** check box.

5. In the **Clip Art** pane, click **Go** to display the pictures that match the search criteria.

6. In the **Clip Art** pane, scroll as necessary to locate and then click the picture of the soccer ball in the net with the blue sky background, shown in **Figure 2**. If you are unable to locate the picture, insert a similar picture.

■ **Continue to the next page to complete the skill**

soccer sports equipment keywords typed in *Search for* box

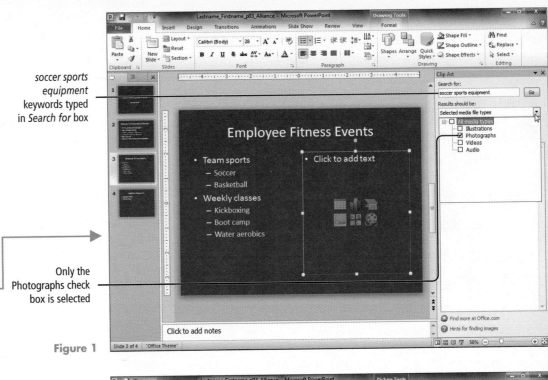

Only the Photographs check box is selected

Figure 1

Check box selected

Selected picture

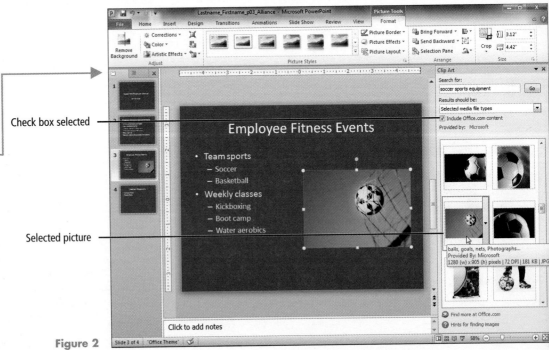

Figure 2

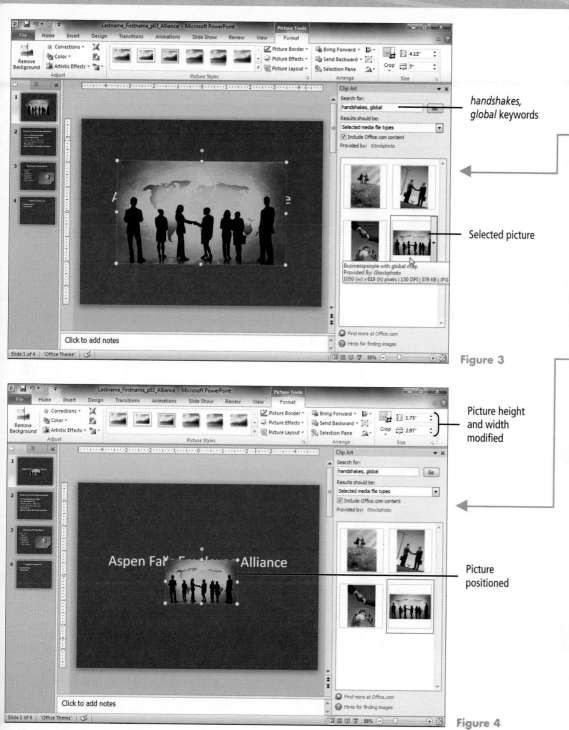

Figure 3

Figure 4

handshakes, global keywords

Selected picture

Picture height and width modified

Picture positioned

7. Display **Slide 1**. In the **Clip Art** pane, in the **Search for** box, replace the existing text with handshakes, global

8. Click the **Results should be** arrow, and if necessary, select only the **Photographs** check box. Click **Go**, and then locate and click the picture shown in **Figure 3**. If you are unable to locate the same picture, choose a similar picture.

9. On the **Format tab**, in the **Size group**, click in the **Shape Height** box 🔲 to select its displayed number. Type 1.75 and then press (Enter).

    When you change the height of a picture in this manner, the width is adjusted proportionately.

10. Point to the picture to display the 🔁 pointer. Drag the picture to the center of the slide so that the subtitle and part of the title are covered as shown in **Figure 4**.

11. **Close** ⊠ the **Clip Art** pane, and then **Save** 🔲 the presentation.

■ **You have completed Skill 2 of 10**

▶ Inserted pictures are usually rectangular, but they can be changed to a number of different shapes available in PowerPoint.

▶ *Picture effects* are picture styles that include shadows, reflections, glows, soft edges, bevels, and 3-D rotations.

1. On **Slide 1**, if necessary, select the picture.

2. On the **Format tab**, in the **Size group**, click the *lower* part of the Crop button— the **Crop button arrow**. Point to **Crop to Shape** to display the **Shape** gallery, and then compare your screen with **Figure 1**.

3. Under **Basic Shapes**, click the first shape—**Oval**—to change the shape of the picture from a rectangle to an oval.

4. In the **Picture Styles group**, click the **Picture Effects** button. Point to **Soft Edges**, and then point to each option and notice that the edges of the picture are blurred and softened.

5. Click **50 Point**, and then compare your screen with **Figure 2**. If necessary, point to the picture to display the 🔲 pointer, and drag to position the picture as shown in **Figure 2**.

6. Display **Slide 3**, and then select the picture. On the **Format tab**, in the **Picture Styles group**, click the **Picture Effects** button. Point to **Shadow**, and then point to, but do not click, several of the options to view the shadow effects on the picture.

■ **Continue to the next page to complete the skill**

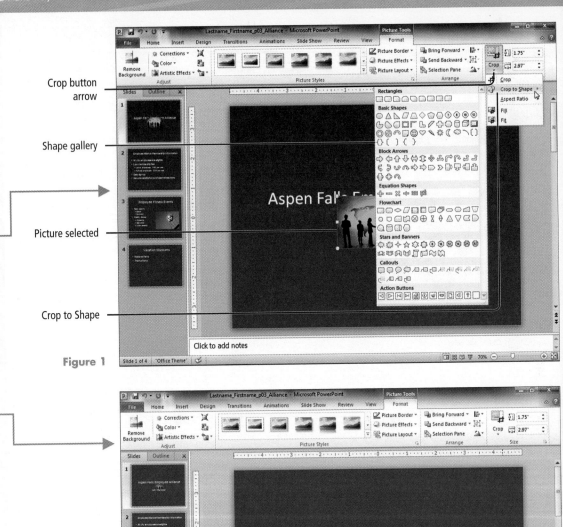

Crop button arrow

Shape gallery

Picture selected

Crop to Shape

Figure 1

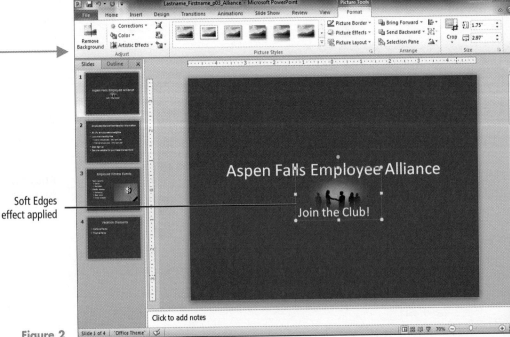

Soft Edges effect applied

Figure 2

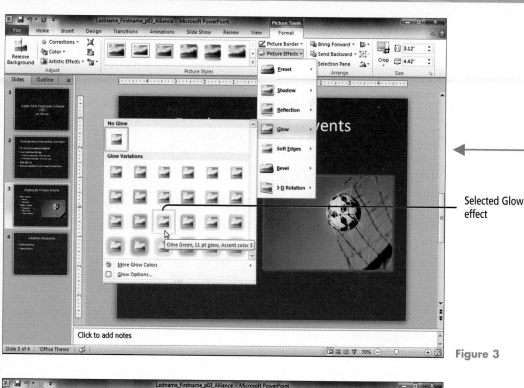

Selected Glow effect

Olive Green, 11 pt glow, Accent color 3

Figure 3

7. Point to **Reflection**, and then point to, but do not click, several of the options to view the reflection effects on the picture.

8. Point to **Glow** to display the gallery.

The Glow effect applies a diffused outline to the picture in varying intensities, using colors from the presentation theme.

9. In the third row, click the third glow variation—**Olive Green, 11 pt glow, Accent color 3**—as shown in **Figure 3**.

10. With the picture still selected, on the **Format tab**, in the **Picture Styles group**, click the **Picture Effects** button. Point to **Bevel**, and then under **Bevel**, click the first option—**Circle**.

When you apply multiple effects to a picture in this manner, choose effects that complement the picture and the presentation theme.

11. With the picture still selected, on the **Format tab**, in the **Picture Styles group**, click the **Picture Border** button. Under **Theme Colors**, click the first color—**Black, Background 1**.

A narrow border surrounds the picture between the bevel effect and the glow effect.

12. Click the **Picture Border** button again, and then point to **Weight**. Click **3 pt** to apply a thicker border.

13. Click a blank area on the slide so that nothing is selected, and then compare your slide with **Figure 4**.

14. **Save** 💾 the presentation.

■ **You have completed Skill 3 of 10**

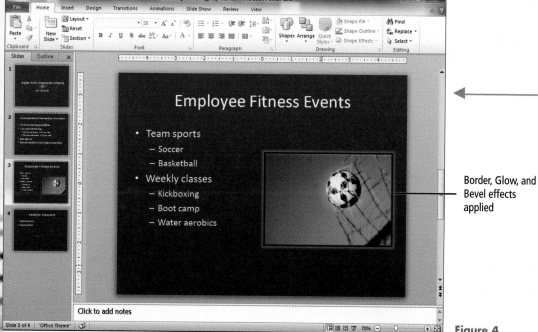

Border, Glow, and Bevel effects applied

Figure 4

► You can use shapes as design elements, particularly on slides with a simple background design.

1. Display **Slide 2**. On the **View tab**, in the **Show group**, if necessary, select the Ruler check box so that the rulers display in the Slide pane.

2. On the **Insert tab**, in the **Illustrations group**, click the **Shapes** button, and then under **Lines**, click the first shape—**Line**.

3. Align the ⊞ pointer with **4.5 inches** before zero on the horizontal ruler and **2.5 inches** above zero on the vertical ruler, as shown in **Figure 1**.

   As you position the pointer, the ruler displays *guides*—lines that display in the rulers to give you a visual indication of where the pointer is positioned.

4. Hold down Shift, and then drag to the right to **4.5 inches** after zero on the horizontal ruler. Release the mouse button.

   To draw a straight line, press Shift while dragging.

5. In the **Illustrations group**, click the **Shapes** button. Under **Basic Shapes**, in the first row, click **Diamond**. In the lower right corner of the slide, click one time to insert a one-inch-high diamond.

6. With the diamond selected, on the **Format tab**, in the **Size group**, click in the **Shape Height** box 🔲 to select the text *1"*. Type 0.25 and then click in the **Shape Width** box 🔲. Type 0.4 and then press Enter to resize the diamond. Compare your slide with **Figure 2**.

■ **Continue to the next page to complete the skill** ➤

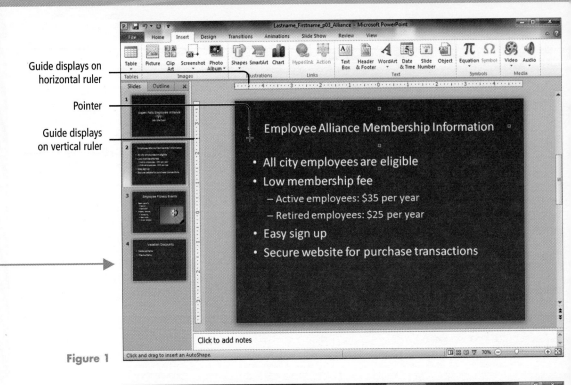

Guide displays on horizontal ruler

Pointer

Guide displays on vertical ruler

Figure 1

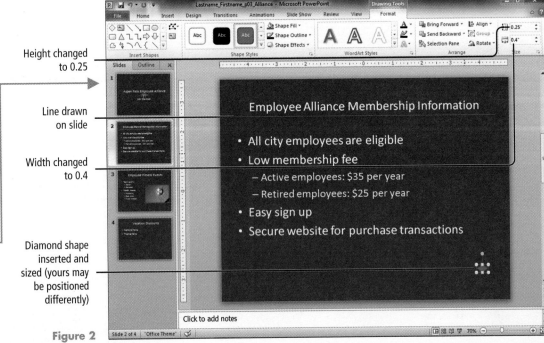

Height changed to 0.25

Line drawn on slide

Width changed to 0.4

Diamond shape inserted and sized (yours may be positioned differently)

Figure 2

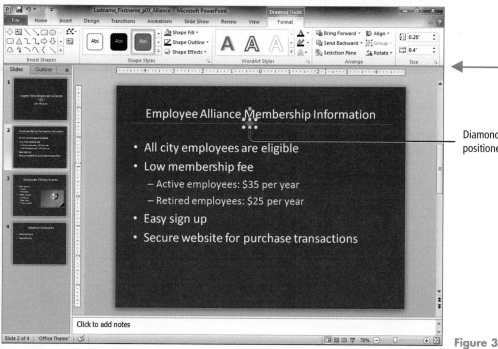

Diamond shape positioned

Figure 3

Height changed to 5.5

Width changed to 10

Rectangle positioned

Figure 4

7. Point to the diamond to display the pointer, and then drag the diamond so that it is positioned on the line below the *M* in *Membership* as shown in **Figure 3**.

8. Display **Slide 4**. On the **Home tab**, in the **Slides group**, click the **New Slide button arrow**, and then click **Reuse Slides** to display the **p03_Alliance_Orientation** slides in the Reuse Slides pane. If the slides from p03_Alliance_Orientation do not display in the Reuse Slides pane, click the Browse button, click Browse File, navigate to your student files, and then open p03_Alliance_Orientation.

9. In the **Reuse Slides** pane, click **Slide 4** to insert it in the presentation, and then **Close** ✖ the pane.

10. On the **Insert tab**, in the **Illustrations group**, click the **Shapes** button. Under **Rectangles**, click the first shape— **Rectangle**. With the ✚ pointer, drag from the upper left corner of the slide to the right edge of the slide and down to **2 inches** below zero on the vertical ruler.

11. With the rectangle selected, on the **Format tab**, in the **Size group**, change the **Shape Height** value to 5.5 and then in the **Shape Width** box, type 10 Press Enter to resize the rectangle.

12. Compare your slide with **Figure 4**, and if necessary, drag the rectangle so that it is positioned as shown in the figure.

   The rectangle will overlap some of the pictures.

13. **Save** 🖫 the presentation.

■ **You have completed Skill 4 of 10**

► A *text box* is an object used to position text anywhere on a slide.

► In addition to being used as design elements, shapes can be used as containers for text.

1. On **Slide 5**, if necessary, select the rectangle.

   To insert text in a shape, select the shape, and then begin to type.

2. Type Questions? Press Enter, and then type Contact an Employee Alliance Associate Press Enter, type (805) 555-1087 and then compare your slide with **Figure 1**.

   When you type text in a shape, it is centered both horizontally and vertically within the shape.

3. Select the three lines of text, and then change the **Font Size** to **40**.

4. With the three lines of text still selected, on the **Format tab**, in the **WordArt Styles group**, click the **More** button. Under **Applies to All Text in the Shape**, click the third thumbnail in the first row—**Fill - Red, Accent 2, Warm Matte Bevel**.

5. In the **WordArt Styles group**, click the **Text Fill button arrow** to display the gallery. Under **Theme Colors**, in the second column, click the first color—**White, Text 1**. Click in the gray area outside the slide so that nothing is selected, and then compare your slide with **Figure 2**.

   WordArt styles can be applied to the text in a shape.

■ **Continue to the next page to complete the skill**

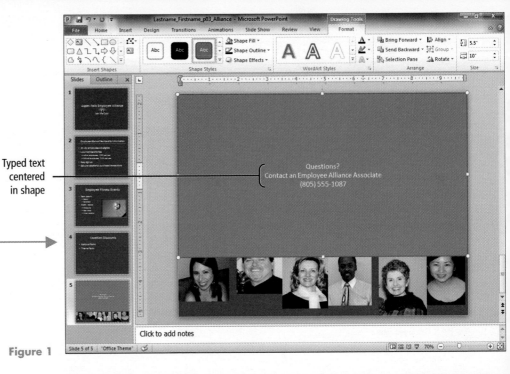

Typed text centered in shape

Figure 1

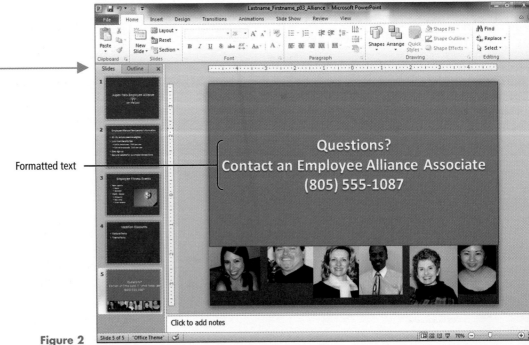

Formatted text

Figure 2

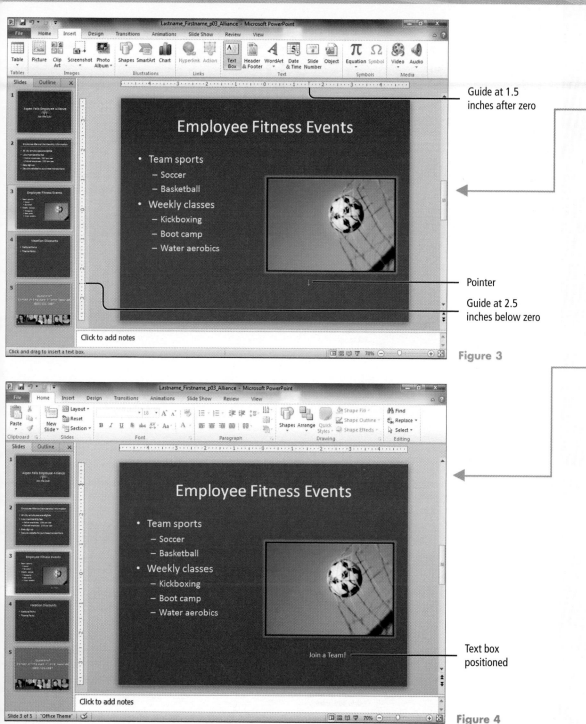

Guide at 1.5 inches after zero

Pointer

Guide at 2.5 inches below zero

Figure 3

Text box positioned

Figure 4

6. Display **Slide 3**. On the **Insert tab**, in the **Text group**, click the **Text Box** button. Position the pointer on the slide aligned at **1.5 inches** after zero on the horizontal ruler and at **2.5 inches** below zero on the vertical ruler as shown in **Figure 3**.

7. Without moving the pointer, click one time to insert a text box. Type Join a Team! If the text box displays one character at a time in a vertical line, on the Quick Access Toolbar, click Undo, and then repeat Steps 6 and 7.

8. Click anywhere on the slide so that the text box is not selected.

Unlike shapes, when a text box is inserted, it does not include borders or fill colors. Text inserted in a text box appears to be floating on the slide and is formatted in the same font as the body font used in content placeholders.

9. Compare your slide with **Figure 4**. If your text box is not positioned as shown in the figure, select the text box and then use the ↑, ↓, ←, or → keys on your keyboard to *nudge*—move an object in small increments using the directional arrow keys—the text box so that it is positioned as shown.

10. Save 🖫 the presentation.

■ **You have completed Skill 5 of 10**

► A *group* is a collection of multiple objects treated as one unit that can be copied, moved, or formatted.

1. Display **Slide 5**, and then select the rectangle. On the **Format tab**, in the **Shape Styles group**, click the **Shape Effects** button. Point to **Bevel**, and then click the second-to-last bevel—**Hard Edge**.

2. In the **Shape Styles group**, click the **Shape Fill** button. Point to **Gradient**, and then under **Dark Variations**, in the second row, click the second thumbnail—**From Center**—as shown in **Figure 1** to apply a gradient fill to the shape.

> A *gradient fill* is a gradual progression of colors and shades, usually from one color to another, or from one shade to another shade of the same color, to add a fill to a shape.

3. Display **Slide 2**. Select the diamond. Hold down Shift, and then click the line so that both objects are selected as shown in **Figure 2**. If you selected one of the placeholders, click anywhere on the slide to deselect the objects, and then try again.

4. On the **Format tab**, in the **Arrange group**, click the **Align** button, and then click **Align Center**. In the **Arrange group**, click the **Align** button, and then click **Align Middle** to align the shapes.

> The line and the diamond move so that their center points are aligned.

5. With the objects selected, on the **Format tab**, in the **Arrange group**, click the **Group** button, and then click **Group**. Sizing handles enclose the objects as one unit.

■ **Continue to the next page to complete the skill**

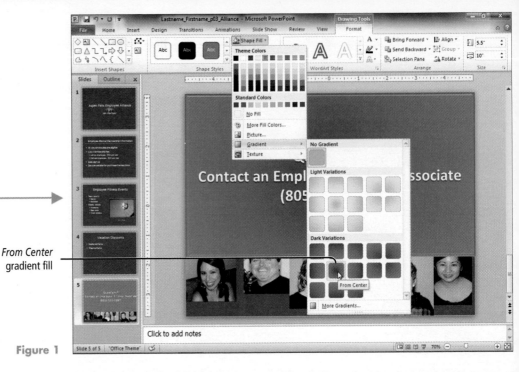

From Center
gradient fill

Figure 1

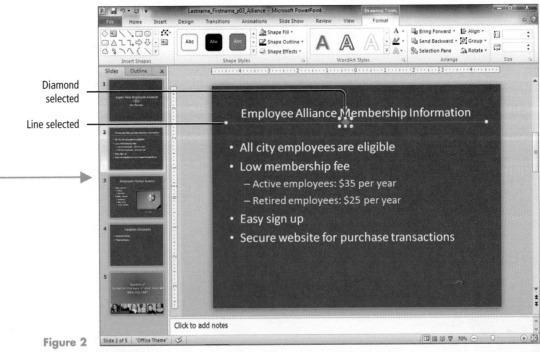

Diamond selected

Line selected

Figure 2

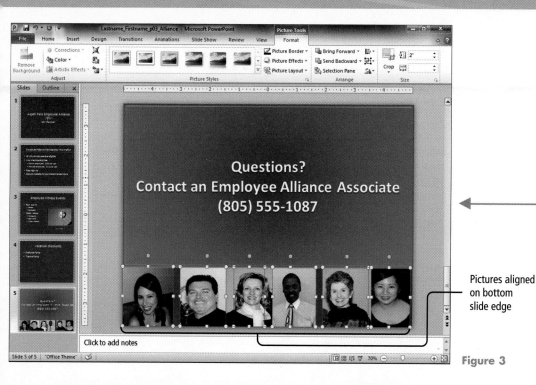

Figure 3

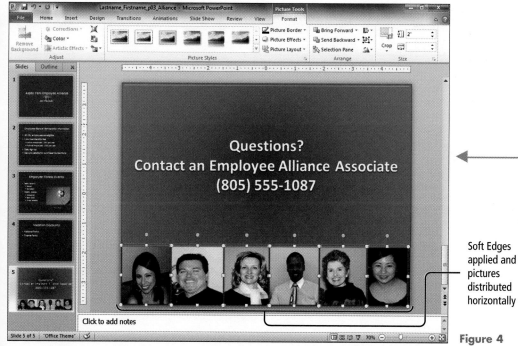

Figure 4

Pictures aligned on bottom slide edge

Soft Edges applied and pictures distributed horizontally

6. Display **Slide 5**. Hold down Shift, and then click each picture at the bottom of the slide so that all six of the pictures are selected. If you selected the rectangle, hold down Shift, and then click the rectangle so that it is not selected.

7. On the **Format tab**, in the **Arrange group**, click the **Align** button, and then click **Align to Slide**. Click the **Align** button, and then click **Align Bottom**. Compare your slide with **Figure 3**.

   The combination of the Align to Slide and Align Bottom options aligns the selected objects along the bottom of the slide.

8. With the pictures selected, on the **Format tab**, in the **Picture Styles group**, click the **Picture Effects** button. Point to **Soft Edges**, and then click **2.5 Point**.

9. With the pictures selected, on the **Format tab**, in the **Arrange group**, click the **Align** button. Click **Align Selected Objects**. Click the **Align** button, and then click **Distribute Horizontally**. Compare your slide with **Figure 4**.

   With Align Selected Objects selected, the pictures distribute evenly between the left edge of the left picture and the right edge of the right picture.

10. With the pictures selected, in the **Arrange group**, click the **Group** button, and then click **Group**. In the **Arrange group**, click the **Align** button. Click **Align Center** to center the group on the slide.

11. **Save** the presentation.

■ **You have completed Skill 6 of 10**

► A *SmartArt graphic* is a designer-quality visual representation of information that you can use to communicate your message or ideas effectively.

► You can include text and pictures in a SmartArt graphic, and you can apply colors, effects, and styles that coordinate with the presentation theme.

► You can convert text that you have already typed—such as a list—into a SmartArt graphic.

1. Display **Slide 4**, and then click anywhere in the bulleted list. On the **Home tab**, in the **Paragraph group**, click the **Convert to SmartArt Graphic** button 📷. Below the gallery, click **More SmartArt Graphics** to display the **Choose a SmartArt Graphic** dialog box. Compare your screen with **Figure 1**.

   The Choose a SmartArt Graphic dialog box is divided into three sections. The left section lists the SmartArt graphic types. The center section displays the layouts for the selected type. The third section displays a preview of the selected layout, along with a description of the layout.

2. On the left section of the dialog box, click each of the SmartArt graphic types to view the layouts in each category, and then in the center section of the dialog box, click several layouts to view their descriptions.

   The eight types of SmartArt graphics are summarized in **Figure 2**.

■ **Continue to the next page to complete the skill**

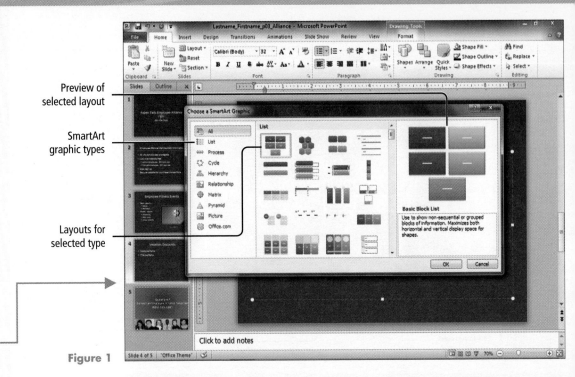

Preview of selected layout

SmartArt graphic types

Layouts for selected type

Figure 1

Microsoft PowerPoint SmartArt Layout Types	
Type	**Purpose**
List	Illustrates nonsequential information.
Process	Illustrates steps in a process or timeline.
Cycle	Illustrates a continual process.
Hierarchy	Illustrates a decision tree or creates an organization chart.
Relationship	Illustrates connections.
Matrix	Illustrates how parts relate to a whole.
Pyramid	Illustrates proportional relationships, with the largest component on the top or bottom.
Picture	Communicates messages and ideas using pictures in each layout.

Figure 2

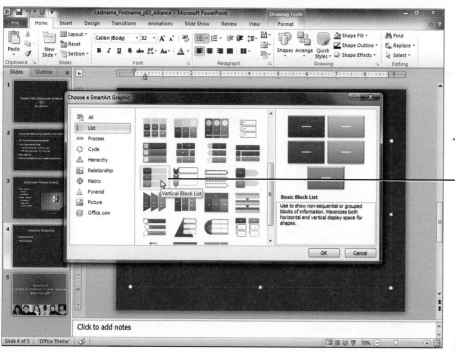

Selected layout

Figure 3

3. In the left section of the dialog box, click **List**, and then scroll the center section of the dialog box and use the ScreenTips to locate **Vertical Block List**. Compare your screen with **Figure 3**.

4. Click **Vertical Block List**, and then click **OK** to convert the bulleted list to a SmartArt graphic.

   The Text Pane button may be selected on the Ribbon, and the Text Pane may display to the left of the SmartArt graphic.

5. If the Text Pane displays, on the SmartArt Tools Design tab, in the Create Graphic group, click the Text Pane button so that the pane does not display.

6. Click anywhere in the text *National Parks*. On the **SmartArt Tools Design tab**, in the **Create Graphic group**, click the **Add Bullet** button to insert a shape to the right of *National Parks*. Type Grand Canyon, Yellowstone, Yosemite

7. Click in the *Theme Parks* shape, and then in the **Create Graphic group**, click the **Add Bullet** button. Type Nationwide

8. Click in the *Theme Parks* shape, and then in the **Create Graphic group**, click the **Add Shape** button to add a shape below *Theme Parks*. If you clicked the Add Shape button arrow and a menu displays, click Add Shape After.

9. Type Houseboats and then add a bullet. Type Lake Powell and Lake Mead

10. Compare your screen with **Figure 4**, and then **Save** 🖫 the presentation.

■ **You have completed Skill 7 of 10**

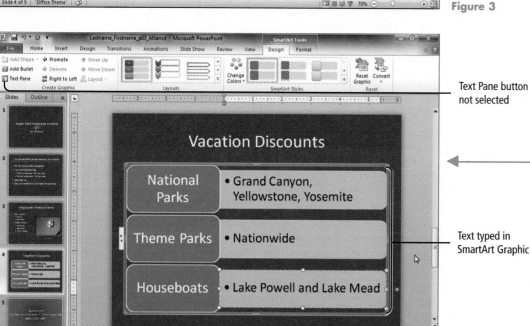

Text Pane button not selected

Text typed in SmartArt Graphic

Figure 4

▶ When you create a SmartArt graphic, choose a layout that provides the best visual representation of your information.

▶ The colors that you apply to a SmartArt graphic are coordinated with the presentation color theme.

▶ SmartArt styles include gradient fills and 3-D effects.

1. On **Slide 4**, if necessary, select the SmartArt graphic. Under **SmartArt Tools**, click the **Design tab**. In the **Layouts group**, click the **More** button ▾, and then click **More Layouts** to display the **Choose a SmartArt Graphic** dialog box. Click **Picture** scroll up or down as necessary, and then click **Captioned Pictures** as shown in **Figure 1**.

2. Click **OK** to convert the SmartArt to the Captioned Pictures layout.

3. In the SmartArt, in the first rectangle, click the **Insert Picture from File** button ▣. Navigate to the location where your student files are stored, click **p03_Alliance_Canyon**, and then click **Insert**.

4. In the middle rectangle, use the technique just practiced to insert **p03_Alliance_Park**, and then in the last rectangle, insert **p03_Alliance_Boat**. Compare your slide with **Figure 2**. If you moved the mouse when you clicked the Insert Picture from File button, the shape may have moved. If this happened, click Undo to reposition the shape, and then try again.

■ **Continue to the next page to complete the skill**

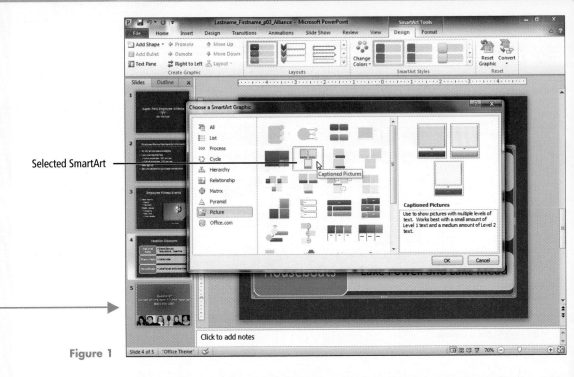

Selected SmartArt

Figure 1

Three pictures inserted

Figure 2

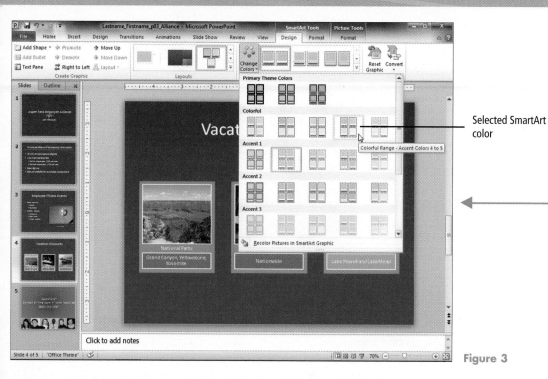

Selected SmartArt color

Figure 3

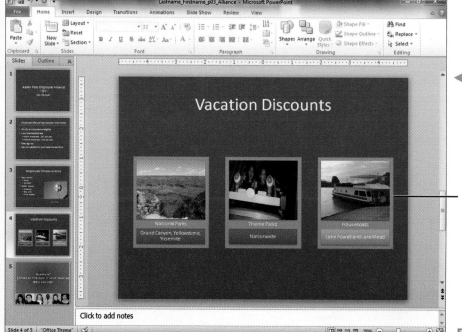

Color and SmartArt style applied

Figure 4

5. On the Ribbon, under **SmartArt Tools**, click the **Design tab**. In the **SmartArt Styles group**, click the **Change Colors** button to display the **Color** gallery.

   The colors that display in the gallery coordinate with the color theme.

6. Point to several of the color options to view the effect on the diagram. Then, under **Colorful**, point to the fourth style—**Colorful Range - Accent Colors 4 to 5**—as shown in Figure 3.

7. Click **Colorful Range - Accent Colors 4 to 5** to apply the color change to the SmartArt graphic.

8. On the **Design tab**, in the **SmartArt Styles group**, click the **More** button ⊡ to display the **SmartArt Styles** gallery. Point to several of the styles to view their effects on the diagram. Then, under **Best Match for Document**, click the fourth style—**Moderate Effect**. Click in a blank area of the slide, and then compare your screen with Figure 4.

9. **Save** 🖫 the presentation.

   ■ **You have completed Skill 8 of 10**

► You can insert, size, and move video files in a presentation, and you can control when the video will begin to play during a slide show.

1. Display **Slide 1**, and then insert a **New Slide** with the **Title and Content** layout. In the title placeholder, type Justin Tamari, AFEA Director

2. In the content placeholder, click the **Insert Media Clip** button 🖾, and then navigate to the location where your student files are stored. Click **p03_Alliance_Director**, and then click **Insert**. Alternately, on the Insert tab, in the Media group, click the Video button. Compare your screen with **Figure 1**.

   The video displays in the center of the slide, and playback and volume controls display in the control panel below the video. Video formatting and editing tools display on the Ribbon.

3. If speakers are available, be sure that they are on, or insert headphones into the computer. On the control panel below the video, point to the **Play/Pause** button ▶ so that it is highlighted as shown in **Figure 2**.

4. Click the **Play/Pause** button ▶ to view the video. Alternately, press ⟨Alt⟩ + ⟨P⟩. If necessary, on the control panel, click the Mute/Unmute button to adjust the volume on your system.

   As the video plays, the control panel displays the time that has elapsed since the start of the video.

■ **Continue to the next page to complete the skill** ➤

Video Tools

Mute/Unmute button

Video inserted

Move Forward 0.25 Seconds button

Move Back 0.25 Seconds button

Control panel

Play/Pause button

Figure 1

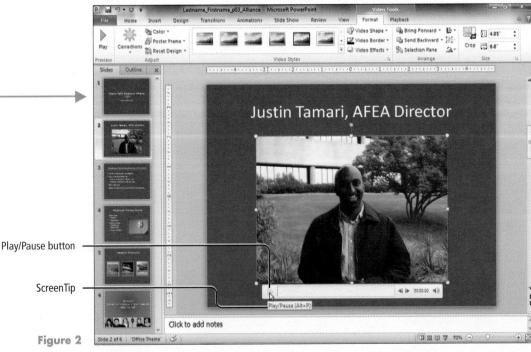

Play/Pause button

ScreenTip

Figure 2

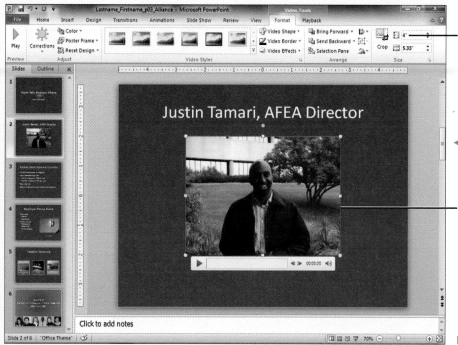

Video height
changed to 4

Video centered
horizontally on
the slide

Figure 3

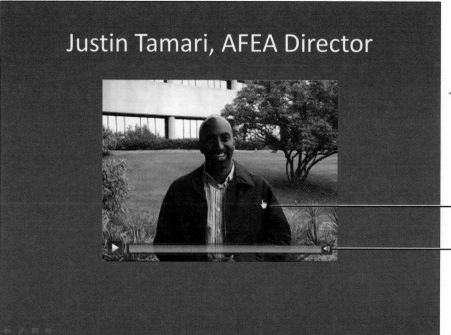

Link select
pointer displays

Control panel
displays

Figure 4

5. On the **Format tab**, in the **Size group**, click in the **Video Height** box. Type 4 and then press Enter. Notice that the video width adjusts proportionately. On the **Format tab**, in the **Arrange group**, click the **Align** button, and then click **Align Center** to center the video horizontally on the slide. Compare your screen with Figure 3.

6. On the right side of the status bar, in the **View** buttons, click the **Slide Show** button to display **Slide 2** in the slide show. Point to the video to display the pointer, and then compare your screen with Figure 4.

When you point to the video during the slide show, the control panel displays.

7. With the pointer displayed, click the mouse button to view the video. When the video is finished, press Esc to exit the slide show.

8. If necessary, select the video. On the **Playback tab**, in the **Video Options group**, click the **Start** arrow, and then click **Automatically**. In the **View** buttons, click the **Slide Show** button to display **Slide 2** in the slide show. When the video is finished, press Esc to exit the slide show.

The Start Automatically option begins the video when the slide displays in the slide show. You can use this option if you want the video to begin playing without clicking the mouse button.

9. **Save** the presentation.

■ **You have completed Skill 9 of 10**

▶ You can apply styles and effects to a video and change the video shape and border.

▶ You can recolor a video so that it coordinates with the presentation theme.

1. On **Slide 2**, if necessary, select the video. On the **Format tab**, in the **Video Styles group**, click the **More** button ⊡. In the **Video Styles** gallery, under **Moderate**, click the seventh style—**Snip Diagonal Corner, Gradient**. Click on a blank area of the slide, and then compare your screen with **Figure 1**.

2. Select the video. On the **Format tab**, in the **Video Styles group**, click the **Video Effects** button. Point to **Shadow**, and then if necessary, scroll down to display the **Perspective** options.

3. Under **Perspective**, click the second thumbnail—**Perspective Diagonal Upper Right**.

4. With the video selected, on the **Format tab**, in the **Adjust group**, click the **Color** button.

    The Recolor gallery displays colors from the presentation theme that you can apply to the video.

5. Point to several of the thumbnails to view the color change, and then click the second thumbnail—**Grayscale**—to change the color of the video. Compare your screen with **Figure 2**.

6. On the **Format tab**, in the **Adjust group**, click the **Color** button, and then click the first thumbnail—**No Recolor**—to change the video color back to the original.

■ **Continue to the next page to complete the skill** ▶

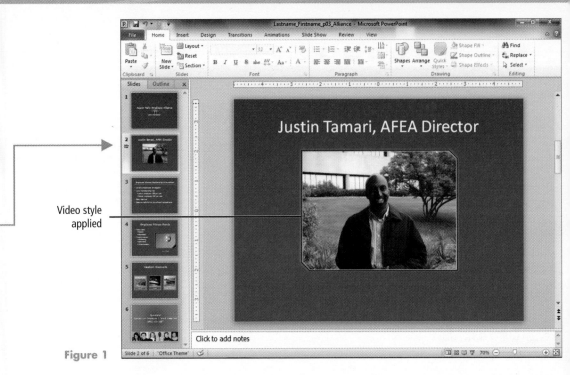

Video style applied

Figure 1

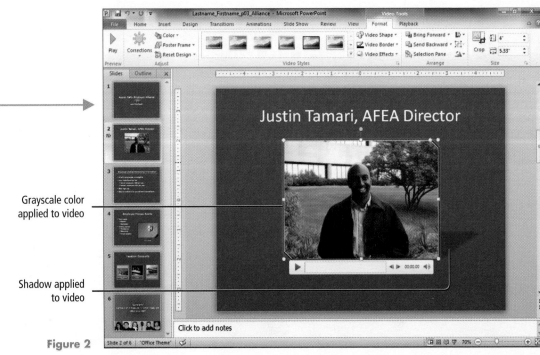

Grayscale color applied to video

Shadow applied to video

Figure 2

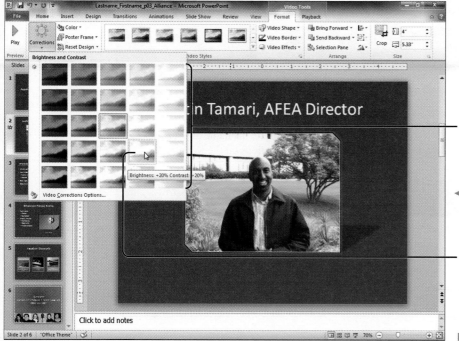

Brightness and Contrast gallery

Brightness and Contrast option selected

Figure 3

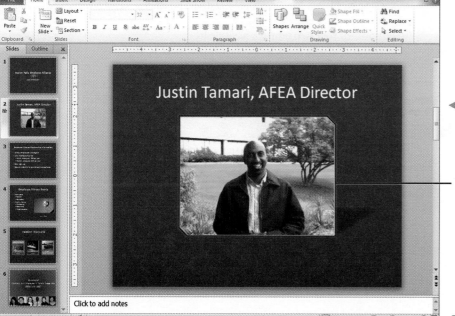

Brightness and Contrast applied to video

Figure 4

7. With the video selected, on the **Format tab**, in the **Adjust group**, click the **Corrections** button to display the **Brightness and Contrast** gallery.

   The Brightness and Contrast gallery displays combinations of brightness and contrast adjustments that you can apply to a video to improve color and visibility.

8. In the fourth column, point to the fourth thumbnail to display the ScreenTip **Brightness: +20% Contrast: +20%** as shown in **Figure 3**.

9. Click **Brightness: +20% Contrast: +20%** to apply the correction to the video, and then click anywhere on the slide so that the video is not selected. Compare your screen with **Figure 4**.

10. On the **Transitions tab**, in the **Transition to This Slide group**, click the **More** button ⏷. Under **Exciting**, click **Switch**. In the **Timing group**, click **Apply To All**. On the **Slide Show tab**, in the **Start Slide Show group**, click **From Beginning**, and then click the mouse button to advance the presentation. When the black slide displays, click one more time to return to your slides.

11. Insert a **Header & Footer** on the **Notes and Handouts** that includes the **Date and time**, a **Page number**, and the **Footer** Lastname_Firstname_p03_Alliance

12. **Save** 🖫 the presentation. Print your pre-sentation or submit the file, as directed by your instructor. **Exit** PowerPoint.

Done! You have completed Skill 10 of 10 and your presentation is complete!

The following More Skills are located at **www.pearsonhighered.com/skills**

More Skills ⑪ Compress Pictures

The large file sizes of pictures from digital cameras or scanners can slow the delivery of a presentation and make your presentation files large. You can compress the presentation pictures so that the file size is smaller.

In More Skills 11, you will open a presentation, view the file size, compress the pictures in the presentation, and then view the changes to the file size.

To begin, open your web browser, navigate to www.pearsonhighered.com/skills, locate the name of your textbook, and then follow the instructions on the website.

More Skills ⑫ Save Groups as Picture Files

A group can be saved as a picture file so that you can insert it on another slide, insert it in another presentation, or use it in other programs. In this way, saving a group as a picture facilitates easy sharing among presentations and applications.

In More Skills 12, you will open a presentation, create a group, and then save the group as a picture. You will then insert the picture into other slides in the presentation.

To begin, open your web browser, navigate to www.pearsonhighered.com/skills, locate the name of your textbook, and then follow the instructions on the website.

More Skills ⑬ Change Object Order

When objects such as shapes and pictures are inserted on a slide, they often overlap. The first object inserted is positioned at the bottom of the stack, and the next object inserted is above the first object. You can change the order in which objects overlap by moving them backward and forward in the stack.

In More Skills 13, you will open a presentation and change the order of inserted objects.

To begin, open your web browser, navigate to www.pearsonhighered.com/skills, locate the name of your textbook, and then follow the instructions on the website.

More Skills ⑭ Design Presentations Using Appropriate Graphics

When you are creating a presentation, the graphics that you choose affect how your message is perceived by your audience. Thus, it is important to choose appropriate graphics for every presentation that you create.

In More Skills 14, you will review design principles that will assist you in choosing appropriate graphics for your slides. You will view two slides and compare the different messages conveyed when different graphics are used.

To begin, open your web browser, navigate to www.pearsonhighered.com/skills, locate the name of your textbook, and then follow the instructions on the website.

Key Terms

Gradient fill 112

Group 112

Guides 108

Nudge 111

Picture effects 106

SmartArt graphic 114

Text box 110

Online Help Skills

1. **Start** 🌐 PowerPoint. In the upper right corner of the PowerPoint window, click the **Help** button 🔘. In the **Help** window, click the **Maximize** 🔲 button.

2. Click in the search box, type video play options and then click the **Search** button 🔍. In the search results, click **Turn your presentation into a video**.

3. Below **In this article**, click **Why turn your presentation into a video?** Compare your screen with **Figure 1**.

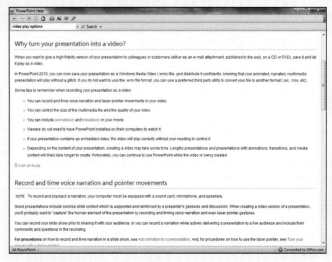

Figure 1

4. Read the entire article and then see if you can answer the following: What are some of the advantages of turning your presentation into a video?

Matching

Match each term in the second column with its correct definition in the first column by writing the letter of the term on the blank line in front of the correct definition.

____ **1.** A command used to insert slides from another presentation into an existing presentation so that content does not need to be recreated.

____ **2.** Formatting options applied to pictures that include shadows, reflections, glows, soft edges, bevels, and 3-D rotations.

____ **3.** Lines that display in the rulers to give you a visual indication of where the pointer is positioned.

____ **4.** Objects such as lines and circles that can be used as design elements on a slide.

____ **5.** An object used to position text anywhere on a slide.

____ **6.** The action of moving an object in small increments by using the directional arrow keys.

____ **7.** Multiple objects treated as one unit that can be copied, moved, or formatted.

____ **8.** A fill effect in which one color fades into another.

____ **9.** A designer-quality visual representation of information that you can use to communicate your message or ideas effectively by choosing from among many different layouts.

____ **10.** A command used to change a list into a SmartArt graphic.

A Convert to SmartArt Graphic

B Gradient fill

C Group

D Guides

E Nudge

F Picture effects

G Reuse Slides

H Shapes

I SmartArt graphic

J Text box

Multiple Choice

Choose the correct answer.

1. The task pane that is used to insert slides from another presentation.
   A. Insert Slides
   B. Browse Slides
   C. Reuse Slides

2. The name of the box in which the height of a picture can be changed.
   A. Height Size
   B. Shape Height
   C. Crop Height

3. The default alignment applied to text typed in a shape.
   A. Left
   B. Center
   C. Right

4. A SmartArt layout type that illustrates nonsequential information.
   A. Process
   B. Cycle
   C. List

5. A SmartArt layout type that illustrates a continual process.
   A. Hierarchy
   B. Cycle
   C. Process

6. A SmartArt layout type that illustrates a decision tree or creates an organization chart.
   A. Relationship
   B. Hierarchy
   C. Pyramid

7. A SmartArt layout type that illustrates connections.
   A. Relationship
   B. Hierarchy
   C. Pyramid

8. The tab in which video Start options are found.
   A. Format
   B. Playback
   C. Design

9. The button that displays video Brightness and Contrast options.
   A. Color
   B. Design
   C. Corrections

10. The button that displays the video Recolor gallery.
    A. Color
    B. Design
    C. Corrections

Topics for Discussion

1. Some PowerPoint presenters advocate using only slides that consist of a single statement and a graphic so that the presentation reads like a story. Other presenters advocate using slides that combine the "single statement and graphics" approach with slides that include detail in the form of bullet points, diagrams, and pictures. What is the advantage of each of these approaches? Which approach would you prefer to use?

2. Sharing presentation slides among employees in an organization is a common practice. What types of information and objects do you think should be included on slides that are shared within an organization?

Skill Check

To complete this presentation, you will need the following files:

- p03_Fitness
- p03_Fitness_Classes
- p03_Fitness_Information
- p03_Fitness2
- p03_Fitness3
- p03_Fitness4

You will save your presentation as:

- Lastname_Firstname_p03_Fitness

1. **Start** PowerPoint, open **p03_Fitness**, and then display **Slide 3**. On the **Home tab**, in the **Slides group**, click the **New Slide button arrow**. Click **Reuse Slides**.

2. In the **Reuse Slides** pane, click the **Browse** button, and then click **Browse File**. From your student files, click **p03_Fitness_Classes**, and then click **Open**. In the **Reuse Slides** pane, click **Slide 2** to insert it, and then **Close** the pane. **Save** your presentation in your **PowerPoint Chapter 3** folder as Lastname_Firstname_p03_Fitness

3. Display **Slide 2**. In the content placeholder, click the **Clip Art** button. In the **Clip Art** task pane, in the **Search for** box, type exercise bicycle Click the **Results should be arrow**, and then select only the **Photographs** check box. Click **Go**. Click the picture of several exercise bicycles in a row, and then **Close** the task pane. Compare your screen with **Figure 1**.

4. With the picture selected, on the **Format tab**, in the **Size group**, change the **Shape Height** to 3.75 and then press [Enter]. Drag the picture to center it within the blue rectangle on the right side of the slide.

5. On the **Format tab**, in the **Size group**, click the **Crop button arrow**, and then click **Crop to Shape**. Under **Rectangles**, click **Rounded Rectangle**. In the **Picture Styles group**, click the **Picture Effects button**, point to **Bevel**, and then under **Bevel**, click the first effect—**Circle**.

6. On the **Insert tab**, in the **Text group**, click **Text Box**. Align the pointer at **0.5 inches** after zero on the horizontal ruler and at **2 inches** below zero on the vertical ruler, and then click. Type Join a Class! Click in a blank area of the slide, and then compare your slide with **Figure 2**.

7. On **Slide 3**, in the content placeholder, click the **Insert Media Clip** button. From your student files, insert **p03_Fitness_Information**. On the **Format tab**, in the **Size group**, change the **Video Height** to 3.5 and then drag the video so that it is centered in the dark blue rectangle.

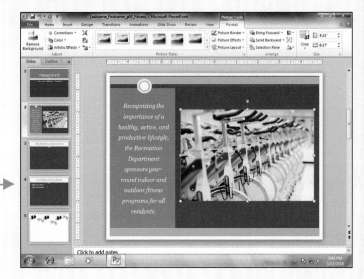

Figure 1

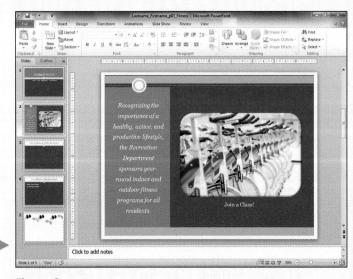

Figure 2

■ **Continue to the next page to complete this Skill Check**

8. On the **Playback tab**, in the **Video Options group**, click the **Start arrow**, and then click **Automatically**. On the **Format tab**, in the **Video Styles group**, click the **More** button, and then under **Subtle**, select **Glow Rectangle**.

9. On **Slide 4**, click the bulleted list. On the **Home tab**, in the **Paragraph group**, click the **Convert to SmartArt Graphic** button. Click **More SmartArt Graphics**, and then click **Picture**. Scroll the gallery, and then locate and click **Vertical Picture List**. Click **OK**.

10. On the **Design tab**, in the **Create Graphic group**, click the **Add Shape** button, and then type Water Wonders

11. In the first shape, click the **Insert Picture from File** button. From your student files, insert **p03_Fitness2**. In the second shape, insert **p03_Fitness3**. In the last shape, insert **p03_Fitness4**.

12. Change the SmartArt colors to **Colorful - Accent Colors**, and then apply the first 3-D SmartArt style—**Polished**. Compare your slide with **Figure 3**.

13. Display **Slide 5**. Hold down ⟨Shift⟩, and then click each picture. On the **Format tab**, in the **Arrange group**, click the **Align** button, and then click **Align to Slide**. Click the **Align** button, and then click **Align Top**.

14. With the pictures selected, click the **Align** button, and then click **Align Selected Objects**. Click the **Align** button, and then click **Distribute Horizontally**.

15. In the **Picture Styles group**, click the **Picture Effects** button. Point to **Soft Edges**, and then click **25 Point**. In the **Arrange group**, click the **Group** button, and then click **Group**.

16. On the **Insert tab**, in the **Illustrations group**, click **Shapes**. Under **Rectangles**, click **Rounded Rectangle**. Align the pointer with **4 inches** before zero on the horizontal ruler and with **2 inches** above zero on the vertical ruler. Drag to draw a rectangle that extends to **4 inches** after zero on the horizontal ruler and to **2 inches** below zero on the vertical ruler.

17. In the shape, type Contact the Aspen Falls Recreation Department and then press ⟨Enter⟩. Type (805) 555-7895 and then change the **Font Size** to **40** for all of the text in the shape. Apply the **Flip** transition to all of the slides.

18. View the slide show. Insert a **Header & Footer** on the **Notes and Handouts** with a **Page number** and the **Footer** Lastname_Firstname_p03_Fitness Compare your presentation with **Figure 4**, and then **Save**. Print or submit the file as directed.

Done! You have completed the Skill Check

Figure 3

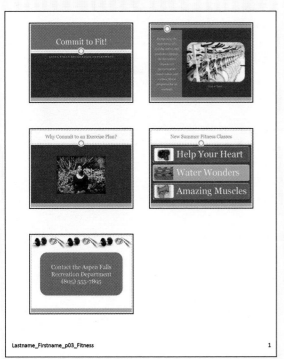

Figure 4

Assess Your Skills 1

To complete this presentation, you will need the following files:

- p03_Vendors
- p03_Vendors_Events

You will save your presentation as:

- Lastname_Firstname_p03_Vendors

1. **Start** PowerPoint, and then from your student files, open **p03_Vendors**. With **Slide 1** displayed, display the **Reuse Slides** pane, and then insert **Slide 3—Summer Events—**from the student data file **p03_Vendors_Events**. **Save** your presentation in your **PowerPoint Chapter 3** folder as Lastname_Firstname_p03_Vendors

2. On **Slide 2**, convert the text to a **Horizontal Bullet List** SmartArt. Change the SmartArt color to **Colorful Range - Accent Colors 4 to 5**, and then apply the **3-D Cartoon** SmartArt style.

3. On **Slide 4**, insert a **Bevel** basic shape. Draw the shape so that it extends from **4.5 inches** before zero on the horizontal ruler and **0 inches** on the vertical ruler to **4.5 inches** after zero on the horizontal ruler and **2.5 inches** below zero on the vertical ruler.

4. In the shape, type Summer events in Aspen Falls garner large tourist numbers. During the past five years, overall attendance has increased by 19 percent, and tourist spending has increased by 23 percent.

5. Increase the **Font Size** to **24**, and then change the **Font Color** to **Black, Text 1**. Apply a **Glow** shape effect—**Orange, 18 pt glow, Accent color 5**.

6. On **Slide 1**, insert a **Clip Art** by searching for a **Photograph** using keywords summer sun background Insert the picture of the yellow sun background. If you cannot locate the picture, choose another appropriate picture.

7. Change the **Height** of the picture to 3.5 and then change the shape to a **32-Point Star—**the last shape in the first row under **Stars and Banners**. Apply the **25 Point** Soft Edges picture effect. Using the **Align to Slide** option, change the alignment to **Align Center** and **Align Bottom**.

8. Insert a **Header & Footer** on the **Notes and Handouts**. Include a **Page number** and the **Footer** Lastname_Firstname_p03_Vendors **Save** the presentation, and print or submit as directed. Compare your completed presentation with **Figure 1**.

Done! You have completed Assess Your Skills 1

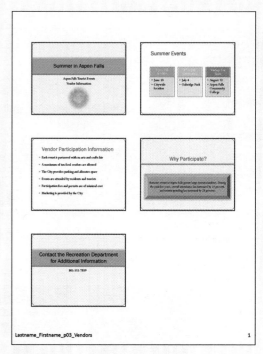

Figure 1

Assessment

Assess Your Skills 3 and 4 can be found at
www.pearsonhighered.com/skills.

Assess Your Skills 2

To complete this presentation, you will need the following files:

- p03_Paths
- p03_Paths_Greenway

You will save your presentation as:

- Lastname_Firstname_p03_Paths

Figure 1

1. **Start** PowerPoint, and then from your student files, open **p03_Paths**. Save your presentation in your **PowerPoint Chapter 3** folder as Lastname_Firstname_p03_Paths

2. Display **Slide 2**, and then change the picture shape to the last shape under **Rectangles—Rounded Diagonal Corner Rectangle**. Apply the first **Bevel** effect—**Circle**—and then apply an **Orange, 8 pt glow, Accent color 2** picture effect.

3. Insert a **Text Box** positioned just below the lower left corner of the picture. Type View from Hacienda Point and then change the **Font Size** to 24 and the **Font Color** to **Light Yellow, Text 2**. Select the slide title, the picture, and the text box, and then align the selected objects using the **Align Center** option.

4. Display **Slide 3**, and then in the content placeholder, from your student files, insert the video **p03_Paths_Greenway**. Apply the **Intense, Reflected Perspective Right** video style, and then change the **Video Options** so that the video starts **Automatically** during the slide show.

5. **Adjust** the video by changing the **Corrections** option to **Brightness: 0% (Normal) Contrast: +20%**.

6. Display **Slide 4**, and then convert the bulleted list to a SmartArt Graphic with the **Alternating Flow** layout located in the **Process** types. Change the SmartArt color to **Colored Outline - Accent 3**, and then apply the 3-D **Inset** SmartArt style.

7. On **Slide 5**, insert a **Wave** Stars and Banners shape that extends from **4 inches** before zero on the horizontal ruler and **2 inches** above zero on the vertical ruler to **4 inches** after zero on the horizontal ruler and **0** on the vertical ruler. Type Grand Opening on March 20 and then change the **Font Size** to **40**.

8. Apply a **Preset** shape effect—**Preset 8**—and then apply a **Bevel** shape effect—**Angle**.

9. Display **Slide 6**, and then align the four pictures by using the **Align Bottom** option. With the **Align to Slide** option selected, distribute the pictures horizontally. Apply a **50 Point Soft Edges** effect, and then **Group** the pictures. View the slide show from the beginning.

10. Insert a **Header & Footer** on the **Notes and Handouts**. Include a **Page number** and the **Footer** Lastname_Firstname_p03_Paths

11. Compare your completed presentation with Figure 1. **Save** the presentation, and then print or submit electronically.

Done! You have completed Assess Your Skills 2

Assess Your Skills Visually

To complete this presentation, you will need the following file:

- p03_Process

You will save your presentation as:

- Lastname_Firstname_p03_Process

Start PowerPoint, and then from your student files, open **p03_Process**. Format and edit the slide as shown in **Figure 1**. **Save** the file as Lastname_Firstname_p03_Process in your **PowerPoint Chapter 3** folder.

To complete this slide, apply the **Office** theme and apply the **Urban** theme colors. The content placeholder text is sized at **22** points. For the SmartArt graphic, use the **Repeating Bending Process** layout. After you create the SmartArt, drag the *Improve* shape so that it is centered as shown in **Figure 1**. Add a footer to the Notes and Handouts with the file name and page number, and then print or submit electronically, as directed by your instructor.

Done! You have completed Assess Your Skills Visually

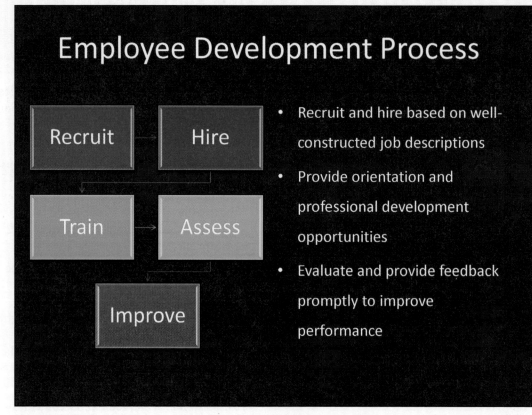

Figure 1

Skills in Context

To complete this presentation, you will need the following file:

- New blank PowerPoint presentation

You will save your presentation as:

- Lastname_Firstname_p03_Programs

Using the following information, create a presentation with an appropriate theme, and then create four slides that describe new programs offered to City employees. The presentation will be part of a larger presentation on employee benefits. On one slide, convert the text to a SmartArt graphic describing the programs, and then format the SmartArt appropriately. Insert and format at least one Clip Art image illustrating the programs.

To improve employee health and productivity, the City of Aspen Falls is offering several voluntary programs to City employees. The first program—*A City in Motion*—offers a free pedometer so that employees can record the number of steps taken each day. Human Resources will provide maps of walking routes adjacent to various city offices for those who want to walk with colleagues

before or after work or during lunch. The second program is *Fit in Aspen Falls*. All city employees are eligible to receive discounts on individual and family memberships at local fitness centers. The third program—*Wellness through the Week*—is a series of classes held during lunch hours or immediately after work, including yoga, preventive health care, stress reduction, health and nutrition, and more.

Save the presentation as Lastname_Firstname_p03_Programs Add a footer to the Notes and Handouts with the file name and page number, and then print or submit electronically as directed by your instructor.

Done! You have completed Skills in Context

Skills and You

To complete this presentation, you will need the following file:

- New blank PowerPoint presentation

You will save your presentation as:

- Lastname_Firstname_p03_Careers

Using the skills you have practiced in this chapter, create a presentation with an appropriate theme that includes four to six slides describing a career in which you are interested. On one slide, convert the text to a SmartArt graphic that either lists the credentials that you need or demonstrates the process that you must follow to be successful in this career. Insert and format pictures on at least two slides that illustrate people who have chosen this career.

Save the presentation as Lastname_Firstname_p03_Careers Add a footer to the Notes and Handouts with the file name and page number, and then check spelling in the presentation. Print or submit electronically, as directed by your instructor.

Done! You have completed Skills and You

CHAPTER 4

Present Data Using Tables, Charts, and Animation

▶ Tables and charts are used to present information in an organized manner that enables the audience to understand important data with ease.

▶ Animation effects enhance a presentation by drawing attention to important slide elements, particularly when the timing of animation effects is precisely controlled during a slide show.

Your starting screen will look like this:

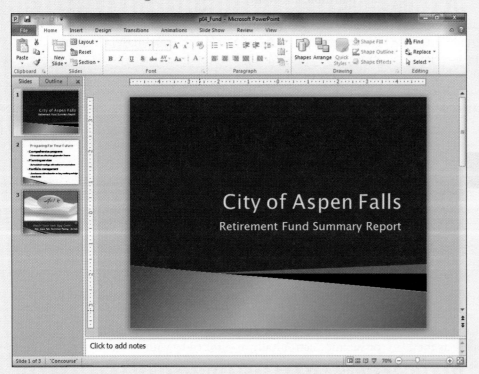

SKILLS

Skills 1-10 Training

At the end of this chapter, you will be able to:

Skill 1 Insert Tables

Skill 2 Modify Table Layouts

Skill 3 Apply Table Styles

Skill 4 Insert Column Charts

Skill 5 Edit and Format Charts

Skill 6 Insert Pie Charts

Skill 7 Apply Animation Entrance and Emphasis Effects

Skill 8 Modify Animation Timing and Use Animation Painter

Skill 9 Remove Animation and Modify Duration

Skill 10 Navigate Slide Shows

MORE SKILLS

More Skills 11 Prepare Presentations to Be Viewed Using Office PowerPoint Viewer

More Skills 12 Insert Hyperlinks in a Presentation

More Skills 13 Create Photo Albums

More Skills 14 Design Presentations with Appropriate Animation

Outcome

Using the skills listed to the left will enable you
to create a presentation like this:

You will save the presentation as:

Lastname_Firstname_p04_Fund

In this chapter, you will create presentations for the Aspen Falls City Hall, which provides essential services for the citizens and visitors of Aspen Falls, California.

Introduction

▶ Tables and charts can be used to present data in an organized manner. When possible, use charts to display numeric data, particularly when making comparisons between the data.

▶ Use chart and table styles to apply formatting in a manner that complements the presentation theme.

▶ Use animation in a manner that focuses audience attention on important slide information.

**Time to complete all
10 skills – 60 minutes**

Find your student data files here:

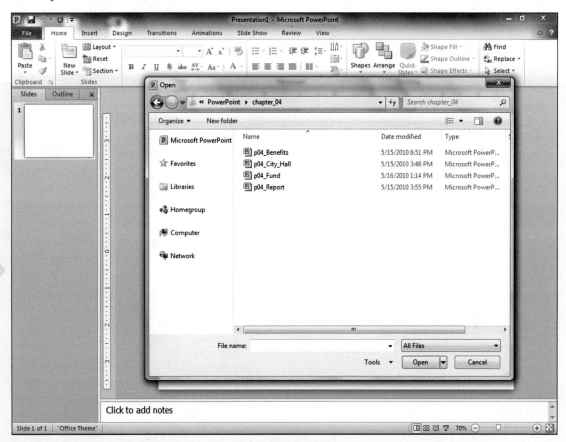

Student data files needed for this chapter:

- p04_Fund

▶ In a presentation, a *table* is used to organize and present information in columns and rows.

▶ In tables, text is typed into a *cell*—the intersection of a column and row.

1. **Start** PowerPoint. From your student files, **Open p04_Fund**. On the **File tab**, click **Save As**. Navigate to the location where you are saving your files, create a folder named PowerPoint Chapter 4 and then **Save** the presentation as Lastname_Firstname_p04_Fund

2. Display **Slide 2**, and then insert a **New Slide** with the **Title and Content** layout. In the title placeholder, type Active Membership and then **Center** ▤ the title.

3. In the content placeholder, click the **Insert Table** button ▦.

4. In the **Insert Table** dialog box, in the **Number of columns** box, type 3 and then press `Tab`. In the **Number of rows** box, type 2 and then compare your screen with **Figure 1**.

5. Click **OK** to create a table with three columns and two rows.

6. In the first row, click in the second cell. Type 2011 and then press `Tab`.

   Pressing `Tab` moves the insertion point to the next cell in the same row.

7. Type 2012 and then compare your table with **Figure 2**.

■ **Continue to the next page to complete the skill**

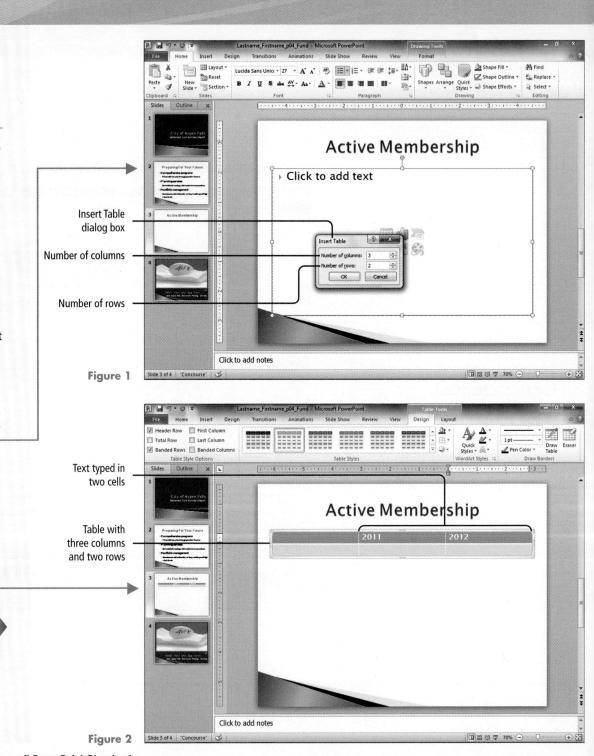

Insert Table dialog box

Number of columns

Number of rows

Figure 1

Text typed in two cells

Table with three columns and two rows

Figure 2

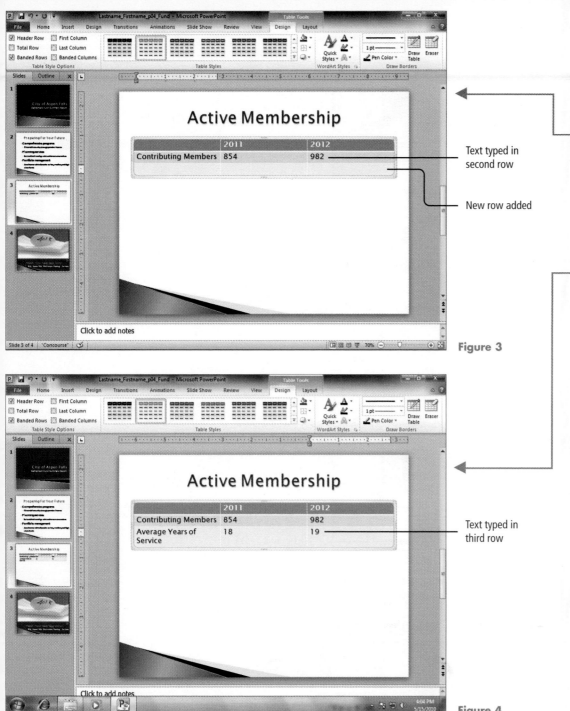

Text typed in second row

New row added

Figure 3

Text typed in third row

Figure 4

8. Press Tab to move the insertion point to the first cell in the second row. With the insertion point positioned in the first cell of the second row, type Contributing Members and then press Tab. Type 854 and then press Tab. Type 982 and then press Tab to insert a new blank row. Compare your table with **Figure 3**.

   When the insertion point is positioned in the last cell of a table, pressing Tab inserts a new blank row at the bottom of the table.

9. In the first cell of the third row, type Average Years of Service and then press Tab. Type 18 and then press Tab. Type 19 and then compare your screen with **Figure 4**. If you inadvertently inserted a blank row in the table by pressing Tab, on the Quick Access Toolbar, you can click Undo to remove it.

10. Save 🖫 the presentation.

   ▪ **You have completed Skill 1 of 10**

▶ You can modify the layout of a table by inserting or deleting rows and columns and by changing the height and width of rows and columns.

▶ The height and width of the entire table can also be modified.

1. Click in any cell in the second column, and then click the **Layout tab**. In the **Rows & Columns group**, click the **Insert Left** button.

   A new second column is inserted, and the width of every column is adjusted so that all four columns are the same width.

2. Click in the first cell in the second column. Type 2010 and then click in the second cell in the second column. Type 763 and then click in the last cell in the second column. Type 12 and then compare your table with **Figure 1**.

3. With the insertion point positioned in the third row, on the **Layout tab**, in the **Rows & Columns group**, click the **Insert Above** button to insert a new third row.

4. In the first cell of the row you inserted, type New Members and then press Tab. Type the remaining three entries, pressing Tab to move from cell to cell: 125 and 182 and 156 Compare your screen with **Figure 2**.

   When you need to delete a row or column, click in the row or column that you want to delete, and then in the Rows & Columns group, click Delete. A list will display with the option to delete columns, rows, or the entire table.

■ **Continue to the next page to complete the skill**

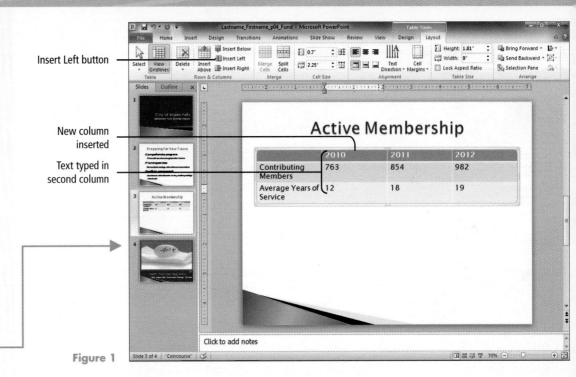

Insert Left button

New column inserted

Text typed in second column

Figure 1

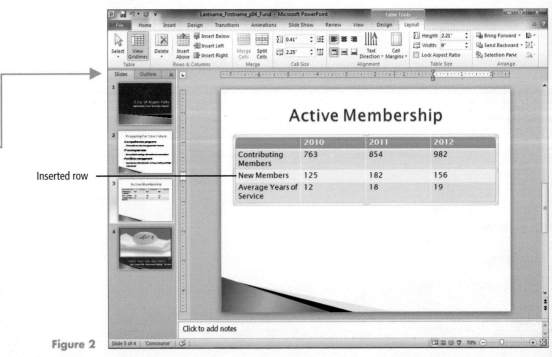

Inserted row

Figure 2

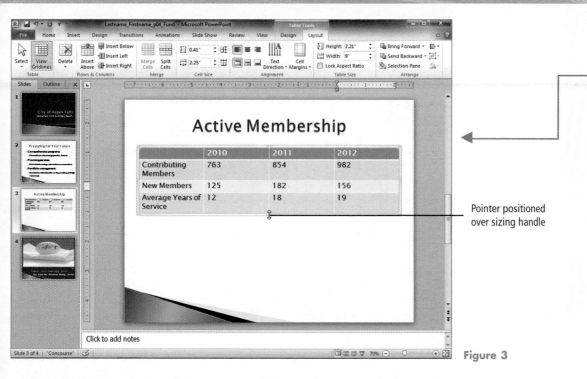

Pointer positioned over sizing handle

Figure 3

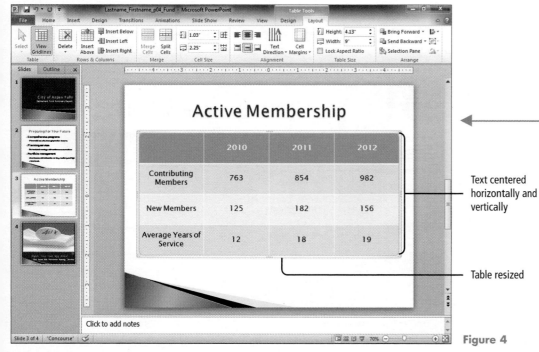

Text centered horizontally and vertically

Table resized

Figure 4

5. At the center of the lower border surrounding the table, point to the four dots—the sizing handle—to display the ⬍ pointer, as shown in **Figure 3**.

6. With the ⬍ pointer, drag down until the lower edge of the table extends to the **2 inch** mark below zero on the vertical ruler, and then release the mouse button to size the table.

7. Click in the first cell of the table. On the **Layout tab**, in the **Cell Size group**, click the **Distribute Rows** button ⊞.

   The Distribute Rows button adjusts the height of the rows in the table so that they are equal. If you do not select any rows, all of the table rows are adjusted. When you want to distribute certain table rows equally, select only the rows that you want to distribute. To distribute the width of columns equally, use the Distribute Columns button.

8. On the **Layout tab**, in the **Table group**, click the **Select** button, and then click **Select Table**. In the **Alignment group**, click the **Center** button ≡, and then click the **Center Vertically** button ▤.

   All of the text in the table is centered horizontally and vertically within the cells.

9. Compare your table with **Figure 4**, and then **Save** 💾 your presentation.

▪ **You have completed Skill 2 of 10**

▶ A *table style* applies borders and fill colors to the entire table in a manner consistent with the presentation theme.

▶ There are four color categories within the table styles—Best Match for Document, Light, Medium, and Dark.

1. Click in any cell in the table. Under the **Table Tools tab**, click the **Design tab**, and then in the **Table Styles group**, click the **More** button ⬇. In the **Table Styles** gallery, point to several styles and watch as Live Preview displays the table with the selected style.

2. Under **Medium**, in the third row, point to the second style—**Medium Style 3 - Accent 1**—as shown in **Figure 1**.

3. Click **Medium Style 3 - Accent 1**.

> The cells in the first table row are filled with a blue color. In the remaining rows, the fill color alternates between white and light gray.

4. On the **Design tab**, in the **Table Style Options group**, clear the **Banded Rows** check box.

> The Table Style Options group controls where table style formatting is applied. For example, when the Banded Rows check box is cleared, the alternating fill colors are cleared from the table rows, and only the header row contains a fill color.

5. In the **Table Style Options group**, select the **Banded Rows** check box to reapply the light gray fill color to alternating rows. Compare your slide with **Figure 2**.

■ **Continue to the next page to complete the skill**

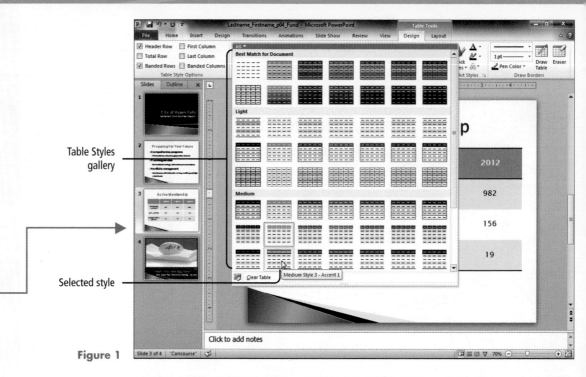

Table Styles gallery

Selected style

Figure 1

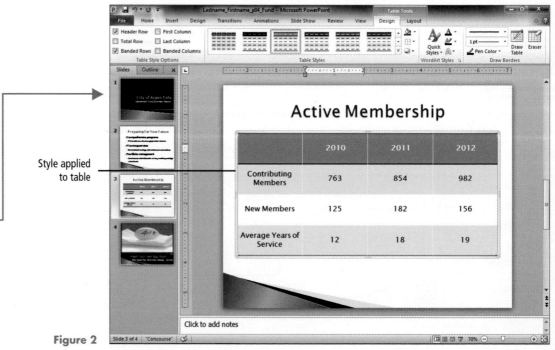

Style applied to table

Figure 2

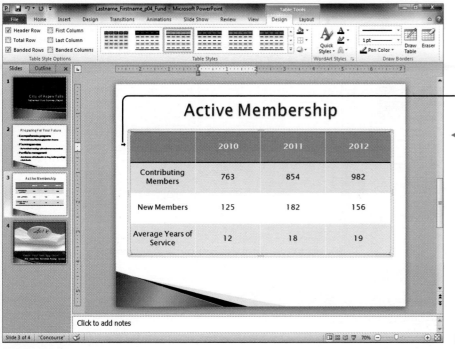

Right-pointing
Select Row pointer

Figure 3

Cell bevel applied
and font size
increased

Outside border
applied

Text formatted
with bold and
italic

Figure 4

6. Move the pointer to the left of the first row in the table to display the Select Row → pointer, as shown in **Figure 3**.

7. With the Select Row → pointer pointing to the first row in the table, right-click to select the entire row and to display the Mini toolbar and shortcut menu. On the Mini toolbar, change the **Font Size** to **24**.

8. With the first row still selected, under the **Table Tools tab**, on the **Design tab**, in the **Table Styles group**, click the **Effects** button. Point to **Cell Bevel**, and then under **Bevel**, click the first bevel—**Circle**—to apply the effect to the first table row.

9. In the first column, drag to select the second, third, and fourth cells. On the **Home tab**, in the **Font group**, apply **Bold** B, and then apply **Italic** I.

10. On the **Layout tab**, in the **Table group**, click **Select**, and then click **Select Table**. On the **Table Tools Design tab**, in the **Table Styles group**, click the **Borders button arrow**, and then click **Outside Borders**.

11. Click in a blank area of the slide, and then verify that a thin border displays on the outside edges of the table as shown in **Figure 4**. **Save** the presentation.

- **You have completed Skill 3 of 10**

- ► A **chart** is a graphic representation of numeric data.
- ► A **column chart** is useful for illustrating comparisons among related categories.

1. With **Slide 3** displayed, insert a **New Slide** with the **Title and Content** layout. In the title placeholder, type Fund Rate of Return by Risk Factor and then change the **Font Size** to **36**. **Center** the title.

2. In the content placeholder, click the **Insert Chart** button. On the left side of the **Insert Chart** dialog box, click several of the chart types to view the chart gallery. Then, click **Column**, as shown in **Figure 1**.

3. Click the first chart—**Clustered Column**—and then click **OK**. Compare your screen with **Figure 2**.

On the one side of your screen, the PowerPoint window displays a column chart. On the other side of your screen, an Excel worksheet displays columns and rows that intersect to form cells. A cell is identified by its column letter and row number.

The worksheet contains sample data in a data range outlined in blue, from which the chart in the PowerPoint window is generated. The column headings—*Series 1*, *Series 2*, and *Series 3*—display in the chart **legend**, which identifies the patterns or colors that are assigned to the data in the chart. The row headings—*Category 1*, *Category 2*, *Category 3*, and *Category 4*— display along the bottom of the chart as **category labels**—labels that identify the categories of data in a chart.

■ **Continue to the next page to complete the skill**

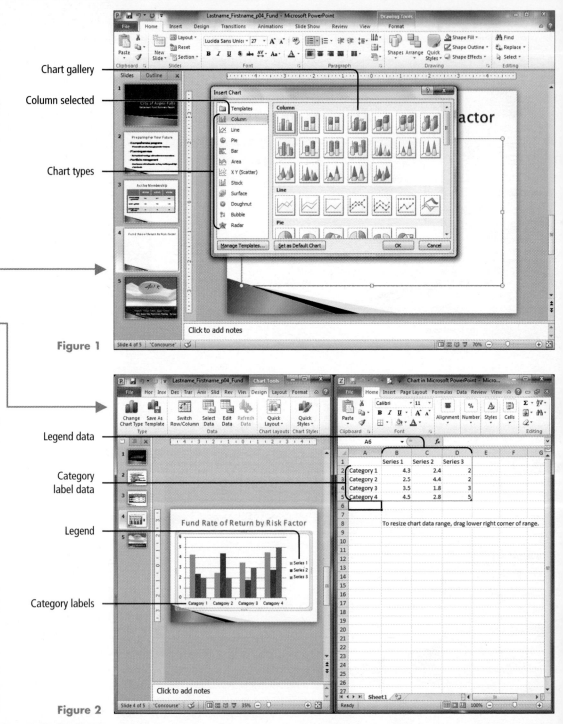

Chart gallery

Column selected

Chart types

Figure 1

Legend data

Category label data

Legend

Category labels

Figure 2

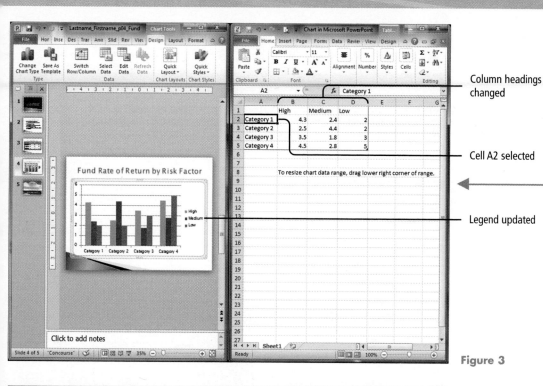

Column headings changed

Cell A2 selected

Legend updated

Figure 3

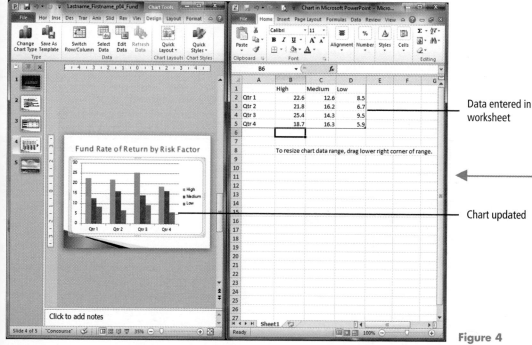

Data entered in worksheet

Chart updated

Figure 4

4. In the **Excel** window, click in cell **B1**, containing the text *Series 1*. Type High and then press Tab to move to cell **C1**. In the PowerPoint window, notice that the chart legend is updated to reflect the change in the Excel worksheet.

5. In cell **C1**, containing the text *Series 2*, type Medium Press Tab. In cell **D1**, type Low and then press Tab. Compare your screen with **Figure 3**, and verify that cell A2 is selected.

   When the rightmost cell in a blue, outlined range of data is selected, pressing Tab makes the first cell in the next row active.

6. Beginning in cell **A2**, type the following data, pressing Tab to move from cell to cell:

	High	Medium	Low
Qtr 1	22.6	12.6	8.5
Qtr 2	21.8	16.2	6.7
Qtr 3	25.4	14.3	9.5
Qtr 4	18.7	16.3	

7. In cell **D5**, which contains the number 5, type 5.9 and then press Enter. Compare your screen with **Figure 4**. If you have made any typing errors, click in the cell that you want to change, and then retype the data.

8. In the **Excel** window, click the **Close** button.

   You are not prompted to save the Excel worksheet because the worksheet data is part of the PowerPoint presentation. When you save the presentation, the Excel data is saved with it.

9. **Save** the presentation.

■ **You have completed Skill 4 of 10**

▶ After a chart is created, you can edit the data values in the Excel worksheet. Changes made in the Excel worksheet immediately display in the PowerPoint chart.

▶ Charts are formatted by applying predefined styles and by modifying chart elements.

1. On **Slide 4**, if necessary, click the chart so that it is selected. On the **Chart Tools Design tab**, in the **Data group**, click **Edit Data** to display the Excel worksheet.

   Each of the twelve cells containing the numeric data that you entered are *data points*—individual data plotted in a chart. Each data point is represented in the chart by a *data marker*—a column, bar, or other symbol that represents a single data point. Related data points form a *data series* and are assigned a unique color or pattern represented in the chart legend. Here there is a data series for *High*, one for *Medium*, and one for *Low*.

2. In the **Excel** worksheet, click cell **B2**, which contains the value *22.6*. Type 18.5 and then watch the chart as you press Enter. Compare your screen with **Figure 1**.

   In the chart, the first data marker in Qtr 1 is decreased to reflect the change to the data.

3. In the **Excel** worksheet, click cell **D5**, which contains the value *5.9*. Type 7.2 and then press Enter. Compare your screen with **Figure 2**.

4. In the **Excel** window, click the **Close** button ⊠.

■ **Continue to the next page to complete the skill**

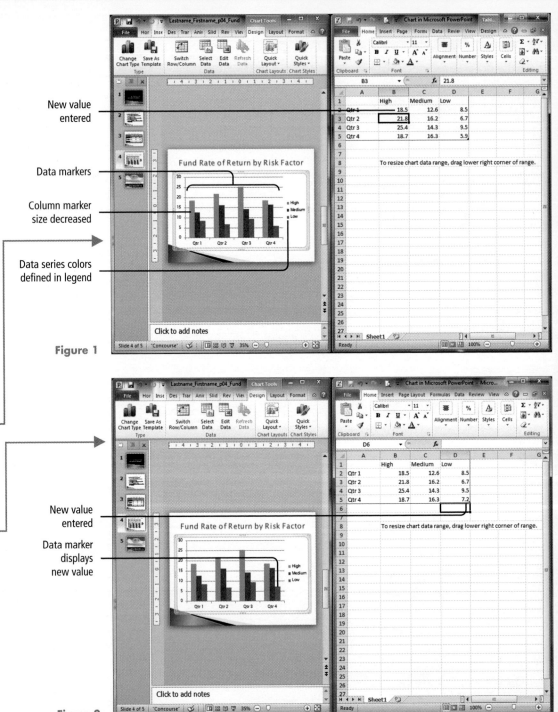

New value entered

Data markers

Column marker size decreased

Data series colors defined in legend

Figure 1

New value entered

Data marker displays new value

Figure 2

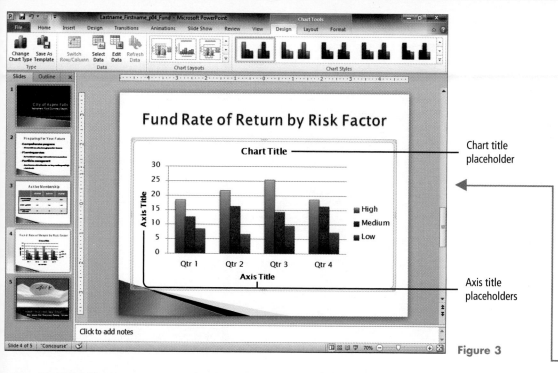

Chart title placeholder

Axis title placeholders

Figure 3

5. If necessary, click the chart so that it is selected. Under **Chart Tools**, on the **Design tab**, in the **Chart Styles group**, click the **More** button ⊡ to display the **Chart Styles** gallery.

> A *chart style* is a prebuilt set of effects, colors, and backgrounds designed to work with the presentation theme. For example, you can have flat or beveled columns, colors that are solid or transparent, and backgrounds that are dark or light.

6. The thumbnails in the **Chart Style** gallery are numbered sequentially. In the second column, locate and click **Style 26**.

7. On the **Design tab**, in the **Chart Layouts group**, click the **More** button ⊡ to display the **Chart Layout** gallery, which provides options for adding and positioning chart elements such as titles. Click the ninth layout—**Layout 9**—and then compare your screen with **Figure 3**.

> Placeholders for the chart title and axis titles display.

8. Click the **Chart Title** placeholder, and then type As of June 30, 2012 Below the chart, click the **Axis Title** placeholder, and the press Delete to remove the category axis title. To the left of the chart, click the **Axis Title** placeholder. Type Percent and then click on a blank area of the slide so that the chart is not selected. Compare your screen with **Figure 4**.

9. **Save** ⊟ the presentation.

■ **You have completed Skill 5 of 10**

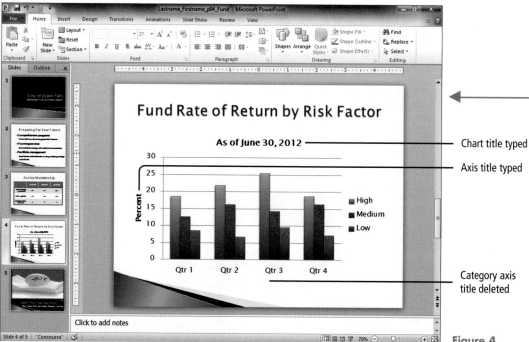

Chart title typed

Axis title typed

Category axis title deleted

Figure 4

▶ A *pie chart* is used to illustrate percentages or proportions and includes only one data series.

▶ When creating a chart, you may need to delete unwanted data from the Excel worksheet so that it does not display in the chart.

1. Display **Slide 3**, and then add a **New Slide** with the **Title and Content** layout. In the title placeholder, type Fund Allocation by Risk Factor and then **Center** ≣ the title.

2. In the content placeholder, click the **Insert Chart** button 📊. On the left side of the **Insert Chart** dialog box, click **Pie**. On the right side of the dialog box, under **Pie**, click the second chart—**Pie in 3-D**—and then click **OK**.

3. In the displayed **Excel** worksheet, click cell **B1**, which contains the word *Sales*. Type Amount and then press Tab. Type High and then press Tab. Type 293 and then press Tab. Type Medium and then press Tab. Type 562 and then press Tab. Type Low and then press Tab. Type 388 and then press Tab. Compare your screen with **Figure 1**.

   The sample data in the worksheet contains two columns and five rows as defined by the blue outline in the worksheet. In this chart, the 4th Qtr data in row 5 is unnecessary.

4. In the **Excel** worksheet, position the pointer over the row heading **5** so that the ➡ pointer displays as shown in **Figure 2**.

■ **Continue to the next page to complete the skill** ▶

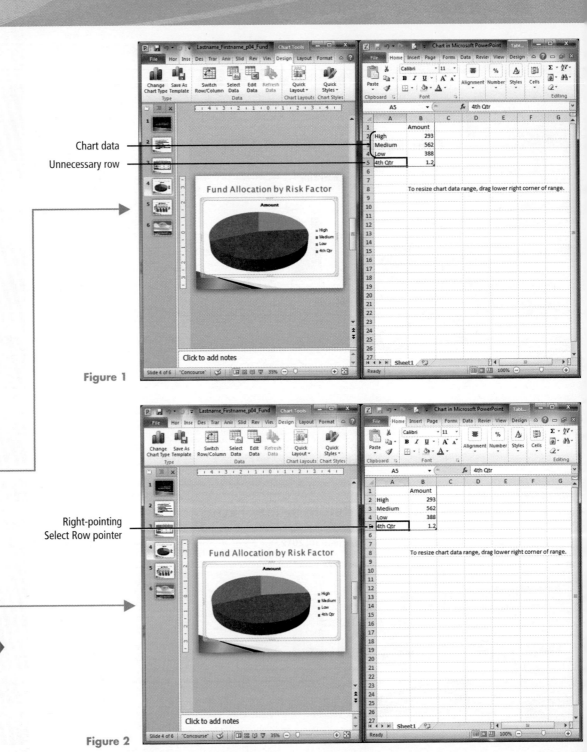

Chart data

Unnecessary row

Figure 1

Right-pointing
Select Row pointer

Figure 2

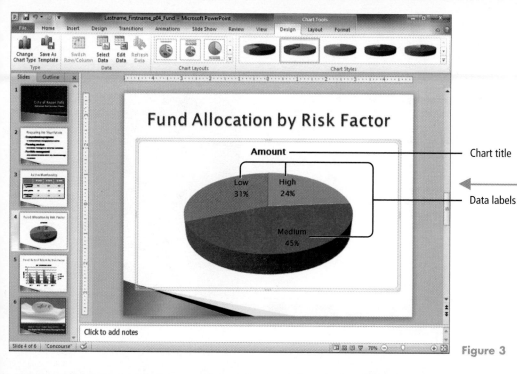

Chart title

Data labels

Figure 3

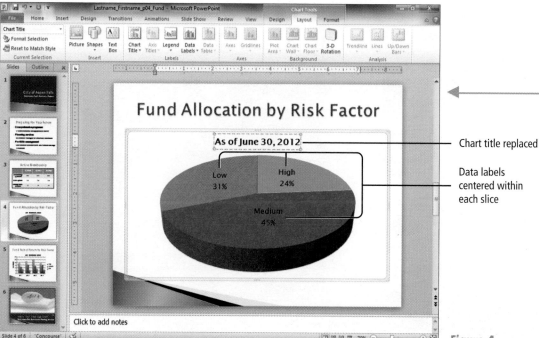

Chart title replaced

Data labels centered within each slice

Figure 4

5. With the → pointer displayed, click the right mouse button to select the row and to display the shortcut menu. In the shortcut menu, click **Delete** to delete the extra row from the worksheet.

6. **Close** the Excel window.

7. Under **Chart Tools**, click the **Design tab**, and then in the **Chart Layouts group**, click the first layout—**Layout 1**. Compare your screen with **Figure 3**.

   Recall that a pie chart includes one data series. Thus, the legend is usually omitted, and *data labels*—text that identifies data markers—are positioned on or outside of the pie slices. Layout 1 displays a title and the category names and the percentage that each slice represents of the total.

8. Click anywhere in the chart title—*Amount*—so that the title is selected. Type As of June 30, 2012 to replace the title.

9. On the **Layout tab**, in the **Labels group**, click **Data Labels**, and then click **Center**. Compare your screen with **Figure 4**.

   The data labels are centered within each pie slice.

10. On the **Chart Tools Design tab**, in the **Chart Styles group**, click the **More** button. In the second column, click **Style 10**, and then **Save** the presentation.

■ **You have completed Skill 6 of 10**

▶ *Animation* adds a special visual or sound effect to an object on a slide.

1. Display **Slide 1**. On the **Transitions tab**, in the **Transition to This Slide group**, click **Wipe**, and then in the **Timing group**, click the **Apply To All** button.

2. Click in the title. On the **Animations tab**, in the **Animation group**, click the **More** button ⊡ to display the **Animation** gallery. If necessary, scroll the Animation gallery to view the types of animation effects. Compare your screen with **Figure 1**.

   An *Entrance effect* is an animation that brings an object or text onto the screen. An *Emphasis effect* is an animation that emphasizes an object or text that is already displayed. An *Exit effect* is an animation that moves an object or text off the screen.

3. Under **Entrance**, point to several animations to view the effects, and then click **Split** to apply the effect. Compare your screen with **Figure 2**.

   The number 1 displays to the left of the title placeholder, indicating that the title is the first object in the slide animation sequence. The number will not display during the slide show.

4. On the **Animations tab**, in the **Animation group**, click the **Effect Options** button, and then click **Vertical Out**.

   The Effect Options control the direction and sequence in which the animation displays.

■ **Continue to the next page to complete the skill** ▶

Animation gallery

Title placeholder selected

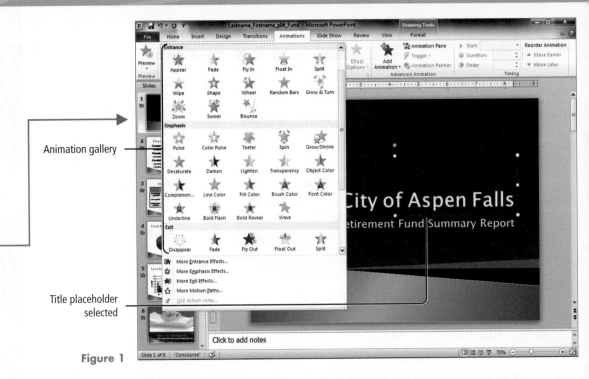

Figure 1

Split entrance effect selected

Animation number displays

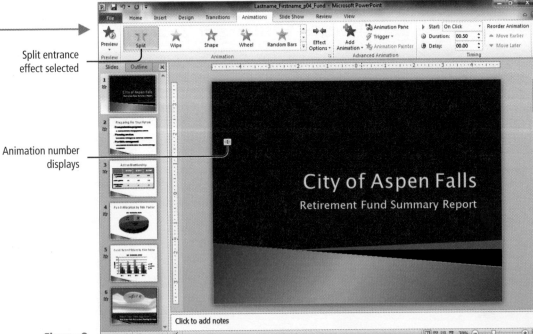

Figure 2

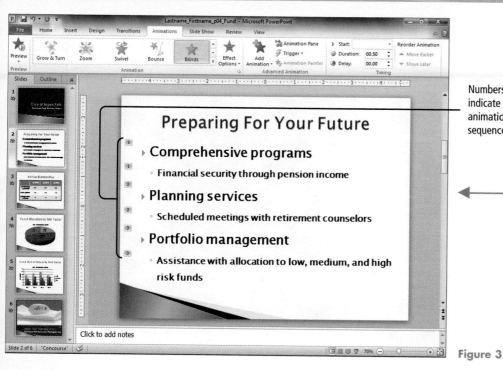

Numbers indicate animation sequence

Figure 3

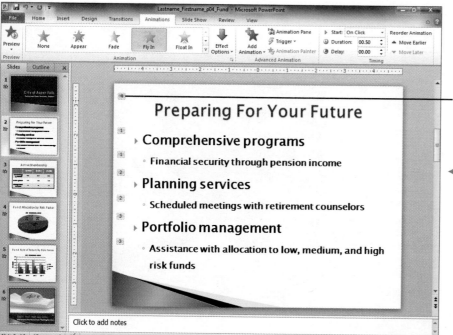

Title is fourth in animation sequence

Figure 4

5. Display **Slide 2**, and then click in the bulleted list. On the **Animations tab**, in the **Animation group**, click the **More** button ⊡. Below the gallery, click **More Entrance Effects**.

   The Change Entrance Effect dialog box displays additional entrance effects grouped in four categories: Basic, Subtle, Moderate, and Exciting.

6. Under **Basic**, click **Blinds**, and then click **OK**. Compare your screen with **Figure 3**.

   The numbers 1, 2, and 3 display to the left of the content placeholder, indicating the order in which the bullet points will display. For example, the first bullet point and its subordinate bullet are both numbered 1 and will display at the same time.

7. Click in the title. In the **Animation group**, click the **More** button ⊡, and then click **Fly In**. Click the **Effect Options** button, and then click **From Top**. Compare your screen with **Figure 4**.

   The number 4 displays next to the title text placeholder, indicating that the title is the fourth item in the animation sequence.

8. Display **Slide 6**, and then select the blue title. In the **Animation group**, click the **More** button ⊡. Under **Emphasis**, click **Grow/Shrink**.

9. On the status bar, on the **View** buttons, click the **Slide Show** button 🖵, and then click the mouse button to view the emphasis effect. Press (Esc) to exit the slide show.

10. Save 🖫 the presentation.

   ■ **You have completed Skill 7 of 10**

▶ Timing options control when animated items display in the animation sequence.

▶ *Animation Painter* is used to copy animation settings from one object to another.

1. Display **Slide 1**, and then select the title placeholder. Recall that the number 1 displayed to the left of the placeholder indicates that the title is first in the slide animation sequence.

2. On the **Animations tab**, in the **Timing group**, click the **Start** arrow to display three options—*On Click, With Previous,* and *After Previous.* Compare your screen with **Figure 1.**

    On Click begins the animation sequence when the mouse button is clicked or the [Spacebar] is pressed. **With Previous** begins the animation sequence at the same time as any animation preceding it or, if it is the first animation, with the slide transition. **After Previous** begins the animation sequence immediately after the completion of the previous animation.

3. Click **After Previous**.

    The number 1 is changed to 0, indicating that the animation will begin immediately after the slide transition; the presenter need not click the mouse button or press [Spacebar] to display the title.

4. With the title selected, on the **Animations tab**, in the **Advanced Animation group**, click the **Animation Painter** button. Point to the subtitle to display the [pointer icon] pointer as shown in **Figure 2.**

▪ **Continue to the next page to complete the skill**

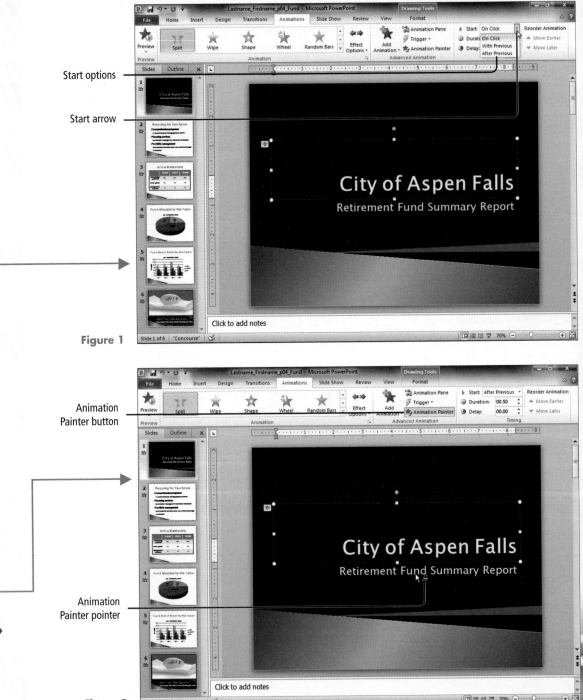

Start options

Start arrow

Figure 1

Animation Painter button

Animation Painter pointer

Figure 2

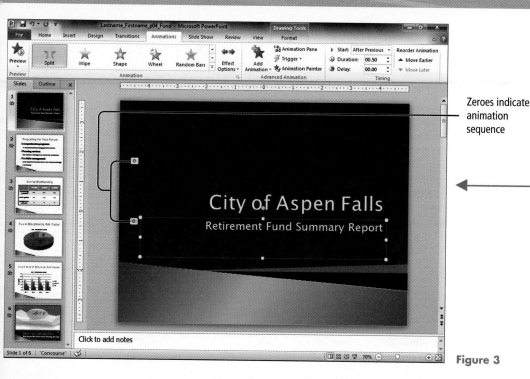

Zeroes indicate animation sequence

Figure 3

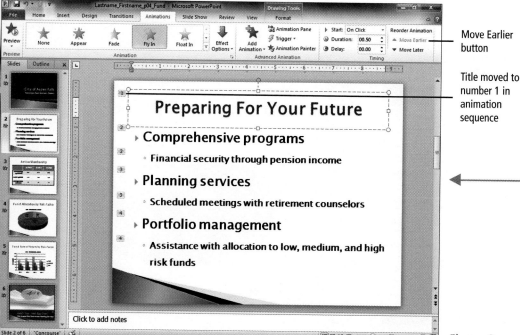

Move Earlier button

Title moved to number 1 in animation sequence

Figure 4

5. Click the subtitle to copy the animation from the title to the subtitle, and then compare your screen with **Figure 3**.

> The title and the subtitle display zeroes, indicating that each begins immediately upon completion of the previous animation.

6. On your keyboard, press F5 to view the slide show. Notice that the title displays immediately after the slide transition, and the subtitle animations display immediately after the title animation is completed.

7. Click the mouse button to display **Slide 2**. Continue to click the mouse button to display each of the first-level points and their associated second-level points. Click the mouse button one more time and notice that the title displays after the list text. Press Esc to return to Normal view.

8. On **Slide 2**, select the title, and notice that the number 4 is highlighted. On the **Animations tab**, in the **Timing group**, click the **Move Earlier** button, and then compare your screen with **Figure 4**.

> The title animation number changes to 1, indicating that it is the first animated object on the slide. You can use the Move Earlier and Move Later buttons to change the animation order of selected objects.

9. With the title selected, in the **Timing group**, click the **Start** arrow, and then click **After Previous** so that the title displays immediately after the slide transition.

10. **Save** 🖫 the presentation.

■ **You have completed Skill 8 of 10**

► You can change the duration of an animation effect by making it longer or shorter.

► When an animation effect interferes with the flow of the presentation, you can remove the effect.

1. Display **Slide 3**. Click anywhere in the table to select it. On the **Animations tab**, in the **Animation group**, click **Fade** to apply the animation to the table.

2. With the table selected, on the **Animations tab**, in the **Animation group**, click the first thumbnail—**None**. Compare your screen with **Figure 1**.

> It is not necessary to animate every object on every slide. In this slide, the slide transition provides sufficient animation to draw attention to the table.

3. Display **Slide 4**, and then select the pie chart. On the **Animations tab**, in the **Animation group**, click the **More** button ⮟, and then under **Entrance**, click **Wipe** to apply the animation to the chart. In the **Animation group**, click the **Effect Options** button, and then under **Direction**, click **From Top**.

4. At the left of the **Animation tab**, click the **Preview** button, and notice that the Wipe effect is a rapid animation. In the **Timing group**, click the **Duration up spin arrow** two times to increase the **Duration** to **01.00**—1 second. Compare your screen with **Figure 2**.

> You can set the duration of an animation by typing a value in the Duration box, or you can use the up and down spin arrows to increase and decrease the duration in increments.

■ **Continue to the next page to complete the skill**

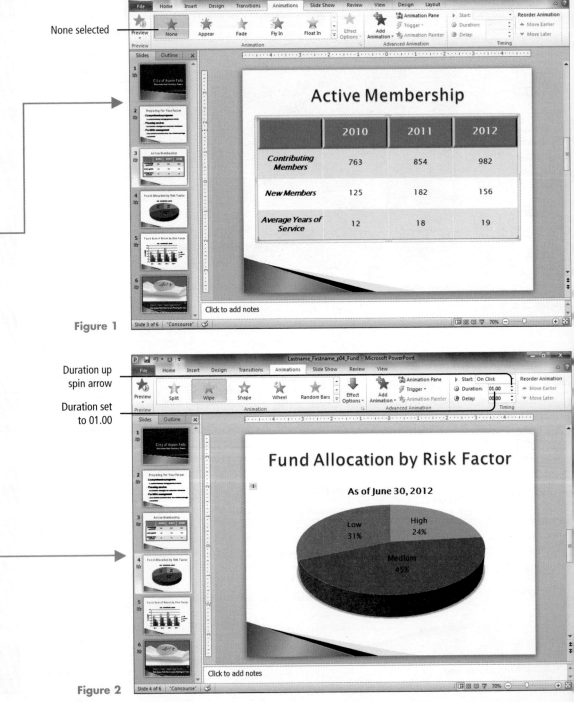

Figure 1

Figure 2

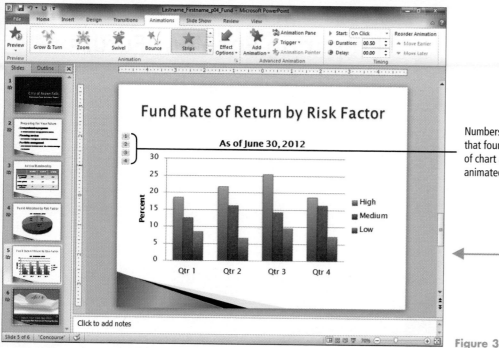

Numbers indicate that four parts of chart are animated

Figure 3

Start option set to After Previous

Delay up spin arrow

Delay set to 00.50

Figure 4

5. On the **Animations tab**, click the **Preview** button to view the longer duration of the Wipe effect.

6. Display **Slide 5**, and then select the chart. On the **Animations tab**, in the **Animation group**, click the **More** button 🔽, and then click **More Entrance Effects**. Under **Basic**, click **Strips**, and then click **OK**.

7. In the **Animation group**, click the **Effect Options** button, and then under **Sequence**, click **By Series**. Notice that the animation first displays the chart plot area, then the High series, then the Medium series, and last, the Low series. Compare your screen with **Figure 3**.

   The numbers 1 through 4 correspond to the four parts of the chart that are animated when the By Series option is selected.

8. Display **Slide 6**, and then select the slide title. Recall that the Grow/Shrink entrance effect has been applied to the slide title.

9. On the **Animations tab**, in the **Timing group**, click the **Start arrow**, and then click **After Previous**. In the **Timing group**, click the **Delay up spin arrow** two times to display **00.50**. Compare your screen with **Figure 4**.

   You can use Delay to begin a selected animation after a specified amount of time has elapsed.

10. View the slide show from the beginning, clicking the mouse button to advance through the slides.

11. Save 🔲 the presentation.

   ■ **You have completed Skill 9 of 10**

▶ During a slide show, a *navigation toolbar* displays in the lower left corner of the slide. You can use the navigation toolbar to go to any slide while the slide show is running.

1. On the **Slide Show tab**, in the **Start Slide Show group**, click the **From Beginning** button. Click the mouse button to display **Slide 2**.

2. Point to the lower left corner of the slide, and notice that a left-pointing arrow displays, as shown in **Figure 1.**

   The left-pointing arrow is a navigation tool that, when clicked, displays the previous slide.

3. Move the pointer slightly to the right, and notice that a pen displays.

   The pen can be used to *annotate*—write on the slide while the slide show is running.

4. Move the pointer to the right, and notice that a slide displays.

5. Click the **Slide** button to display a menu. Point to **Go to Slide**, and notice that the slide numbers and titles display as shown in **Figure 2.**

   You can navigate to any slide in the presentation by using the Go to Slide option. Thus, if an audience member has a question that is relevant to another slide, you can easily display the slide without exiting the presentation.

6. In the list of slides, click **4 Fund Allocation by Risk Factor** to display the fourth slide. Click the mouse button so that the pie chart displays.

■ **Continue to the next page to complete the skill**

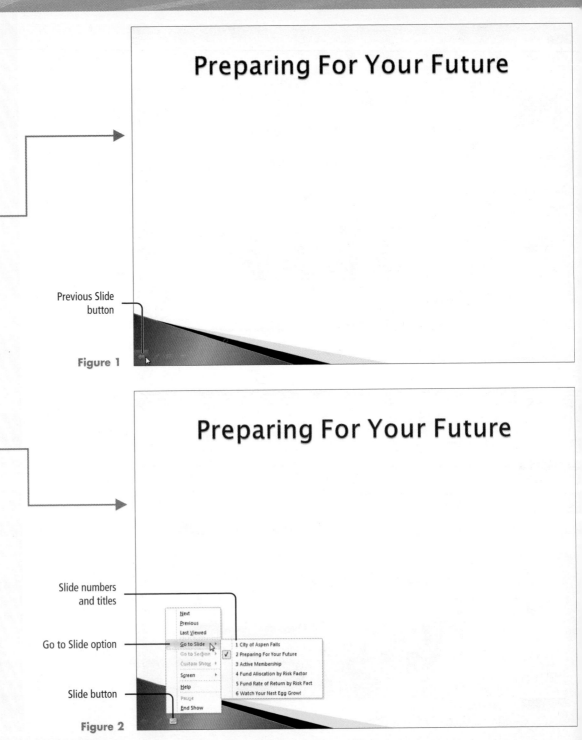

Previous Slide button

Figure 1

Slide numbers and titles

Go to Slide option

Slide button

Figure 2

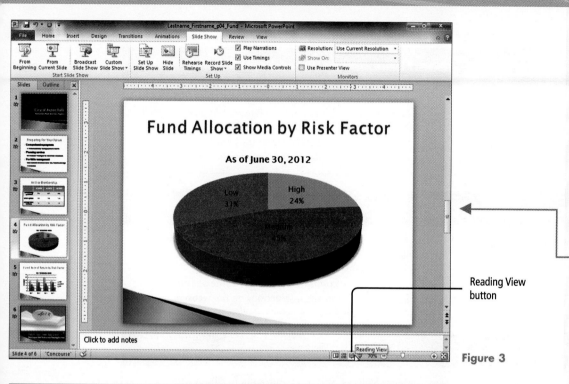

Reading View button

Figure 3

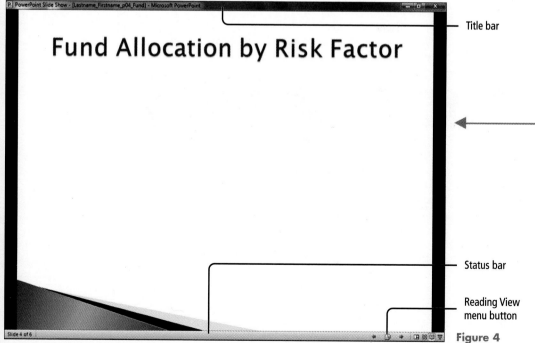

Title bar

Status bar

Reading View menu button

Figure 4

7. On your keyboard, press B.

The B key is a toggle key that displays a black screen. During a slide show, it may be desirable to pause a presentation so that a discussion can be held without the distraction of the presentation visuals. Rather than turning off the projection system or ending the slide show, you can display the slide as a black screen and then redisplay the same slide when you are ready to resume the presentation.

8. On your keyboard, press B to redisplay **Slide 4**. Press Esc to end the slide show.

9. On the **View** buttons, locate the **Reading View** button ▦, as shown in **Figure 3**.

Recall that you can use Reading View to display a presentation in a manner similar to a slide show, except that the taskbar, title bar, and status bar remain available in the presentation window. This view is useful when you are making a presentation during a web conference.

10. Click the **Reading View** button ▦, and then compare your screen with **Figure 4**.

11. Press Esc to return to Normal view, and then insert a **Header & Footer** on the **Notes and Handouts**. Include the **Page number** and the **Footer** Lastname_Firstname_p04_Fund

12. **Save** ▦ the presentation. Print or submit the file, as directed by your instructor. **Exit** PowerPoint.

Done! You have completed Skill 10 of 10 and your presentation is complete!

The following More Skills are located at **www.pearsonhighered.com/skills**

More Skills (11) Prepare Presentations to Be Viewed Using Office PowerPoint Viewer

When you are delivering a presentation, it is not always possible to use your own computer equipment and software. When PowerPoint 2010 is not available on the system that you will use for your presentation, you can prepare the presentation to be viewed using the Office PowerPoint Viewer.

In More Skills 11, you will prepare a presentation to be viewed on a system that does not have PowerPoint 2010 installed.

To begin, open your web browser, navigate to www.pearsonhighered.com/skills, locate the name of your textbook, and then follow the instructions on the website.

More Skills (12) Insert Hyperlinks in a Presentation

Hyperlinks include text, buttons, and images that when clicked during a slide show, activate another slide or a website.

In More Skills 12, you will open a presentation and insert a hyperlink to a website.

To begin, open your web browser, navigate to www.pearsonhighered.com/skills, locate the name of your textbook, and then follow the instructions on the website.

More Skills (13) Create Photo Albums

You can use PowerPoint 2010 to create a photo album presentation that is composed primarily of pictures.

In More Skills 13, you will create a photo album with several pictures.

To begin, open your web browser, navigate to www.pearsonhighered.com/skills, locate the name of your textbook, and then follow the instructions on the website.

More Skills (14) Design Presentations with Appropriate Animation

Animation effects, when used properly, can emphasize important presentation information and provide a method for improving presentation pace and timing.

In More Skills 14, you will review design concepts for applying appropriate animation in a presentation.

To begin, open your web browser, navigate to www.pearsonhighered.com/skills, locate the name of your textbook, and then follow the instructions on the website.

Key Terms

After Previous 150

Animation 148

Animation Painter. 150

Annotate 154

Category label 142

Cell. 136

Chart 142

Chart style 145

Column chart. 142

Data label 147

Data marker 144

Data point. 144

Data series 144

Emphasis effect 148

Entrance effect 148

Exit effect 148

Legend. 142

Navigation toolbar 154

On Click 150

Pie chart 146

Table 136

Table style 140

With Previous 150

Online Help Skills

1. **Start** ⊙ PowerPoint. In the upper right corner of the PowerPoint window, click the **Help** button ⊙. In the **Help** window, click the **Maximize** ▭ button.

2. Click in the search box, type animate text or objects and then click the **Search** button ⊙. In the search results, click **Animate text or objects**.

3. Read the introductory text, and then below **In this article**, click **View a list of animations currently on the slide**. Compare your screen with **Figure 1**.

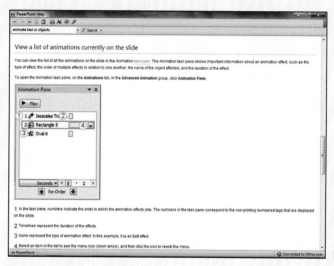

Figure 1

4. Read the entire article and then see if you can answer the following: What animation effect information can be viewed in the Animation task pane?

Matching

Match each term in the second column with its correct definition in the first column by writing the letter of the term on the blank line in front of the correct definition.

____ **1.** In a table or worksheet, the rectangular box formed by the intersection of a column and row.

____ **2.** A format used to organize and present information in columns and rows.

____ **3.** Predefined formatting that applies borders and fill colors to a table so that it is consistent with the presentation theme.

____ **4.** A graphic representation of numeric data.

____ **5.** A chart type useful for illustrating comparisons among related categories.

____ **6.** Text that identifies the categories of data in a chart.

____ **7.** Text that identifies a data marker in a chart.

____ **8.** A column, bar, area, dot, pie slice, or other symbol that represents a single data point.

____ **9.** Individual data plotted in a chart.

____ **10.** Visual or sound effects added to an object on a slide.

A Animation

B Cell

C Chart

D Column chart

E Category label

F Data label

G Data marker

H Data point

I Table

J Table style

Multiple Choice

Choose the correct answer.

1. A prebuilt set of effects, colors, and backgrounds applied to a chart that is designed to work with the presentation theme.
   A. Chart layout
   B. Chart style
   C. Chart effect

2. A group of related data points.
   A. Data series
   B. Data label
   C. Data marker

3. A chart element that identifies the patterns or colors that are assigned to the data in the chart.
   A. Data series
   B. Data label
   C. Legend

4. A type of chart used to illustrate percentages or proportions using only one series of data.
   A. Column chart
   B. Line chart
   C. Pie chart

5. A type of animation that brings a slide element onto the screen.
   A. Entrance effect
   B. Emphasis effect
   C. Exit effect

6. Animation that emphasizes an object or text that is already displayed.
   A. Entrance effect
   B. Emphasis effect
   C. Exit effect

7. Animation that moves an object or text off the screen.
   A. Entrance effect
   B. Emphasis effect
   C. Exit effect

8. A feature that copies animation settings from one object to another.
   A. Format Painter
   B. Animation Painter
   C. Copy and Paste

9. The action of writing on a slide while the slide show is running.
   A. Annotate
   B. Edit
   C. Navigation

10. A toolbar used to go to any slide while the slide show is running.
   A. Animation toolbar
   B. Slide Show toolbar
   C. Navigation toolbar

Topics for Discussion

1. When you apply animation to a slide, you can also apply sound effects. Do you think that using sound in a presentation is an effective technique for keeping the audience focused? Why or why not?

2. Recall that a column chart is used to compare data, and a pie chart is used to illustrate percentages or proportions. Give examples of the types of data that an organization such as the City of Aspen Falls might use in a column or a pie chart.

Skill Check

To complete this presentation, you will need the following file:

- p04_Report

You will save your presentation as:

- **Lastname_Firstname_p04_Report**

Comments
Increased revenue from sales and property tax
Increased facilities capital expenditures
Increased revenue from bond issue

Figure 1

1. **Start** PowerPoint. From your student files, **Open p04_Report. Save** the presentation in your **PowerPoint Chapter 4** folder as Lastname_Firstname_p04_Report

2. Display **Slide 3**. In the content placeholder, click the **Insert Table** button. In the **Insert Table** dialog box, in the **Number of columns** box, type 2 and then click **OK**.

3. In the first table cell, type Month and then press [Tab]. Type Ending Cash Balance and then press [Tab]. Type January and then press [Tab]. Type 33,713,918 and then press [Tab] to create a new row. Type February and then press [Tab]. Type 28,688,318 and then press [Tab]. Type March and then press [Tab]. Type 35,987,156

4. With the insertion point positioned in the last column, on the **Layout tab**, in the **Rows & Columns group**, click the **Insert Right** button. In the new column, type the text shown in the table in **Figure 1**.

5. Point to the table's bottom center sizing handle—the four dots. Drag down until the lower edge of the table extends to the **3 inch** mark below zero on the vertical ruler.

6. Click in the table, and then on the **Layout tab**, in the **Table group**, click **Select**, and then click **Select Table**. In the **Cell Size group**, click the **Distribute Rows** button. In the **Alignment group**, click the **Center** button, and then click the **Center Vertically** button.

7. Under **Table Tools**, click the **Design tab**, and then in the **Table Styles group**, click the **More** button. Under **Medium**, in the third row, click **Medium Style 3 - Accent 2**. Select the first table row, and then change the **Font Size** to **24**. Select the remaining table text, and then change the **Font Size** to **20**. Click in a blank area of the slide, and then compare your slide with **Figure 2**.

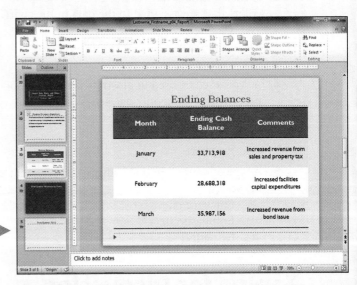

Figure 2

- Continue to the next page to complete this Skill Check

8. Display **Slide 4**. In the content placeholder, click the **Insert Chart** button. With the first chart—**Clustered Column**—selected, click **OK**. In the **Excel** window, click cell **B1**, containing the text *Series 1*. Type General and then type the remaining data shown in **Figure 3**, pressing [Tab] to move from cell to cell.

9. In the **Excel** worksheet, point to row heading **5**, and then right-click. In the shortcut menu, click **Delete**. **Close** Excel.

	General	Utilities	Assessments
January	2568700	1698470	1875020
February	3258694	1833241	1221900
March	2794127	2057964	2384005

Figure 3

10. With the chart selected, on the **Chart Tools Design tab**, in the **Chart Styles group**, click the **More** button. Click **Style 26**.

11. Display **Slide 5**. In the content placeholder, click the **Insert Chart** button. Insert a **Pie in 3-D**. In the **Excel** worksheet, click cell **B1**. Type Expenditures and then press [Tab]. Type January and then press [Tab]. Type 2287769 and then press [Tab]. Type February and then press [Tab]. Type 4589760 and then press [Tab]. Type March and then press [Tab]. Type 3200336 and then press [Tab]. Position the pointer over row heading **5**, right-click, and then on the shortcut menu, click **Delete**. **Close** Excel.

12. On the **Chart Tools Design tab**, in the **Chart Layouts group**, click **Layout 1**. On the **Layout tab**, in the **Labels group**, click **Data Labels**, and then click **Center**.

13. Display **Slide 2**, and then click the bulleted list. On the **Animations tab**, in the **Animation group**, click **Fly In**. Click the **Effect Options** button, and then click **From Left**. In the **Timing group**, click the **Duration up arrow** to change the duration to **00.75**. Select the title. In the **Animation group**, click the **More** button, and then click **None**.

14. Display **Slide 4**, and then select the chart. On the **Animations tab**, in the **Animation group**, click the **More** button, and then under **Emphasis**, click **Transparency**. In the **Timing group**, click the **Duration up arrow** three times to display **00.50**. Click the **Start arrow**, and then click **With Previous**.

15. Display **Slide 1**, and then select the title. On the **Animations tab**, in the **Timing group**, click the **Start arrow**. Select **After Previous**. With the title selected, in the **Advanced Animation group**, click **Animation Painter**, and then click the subtitle. View the slide show from the beginning, and then display the presentation in **Reading View**. Return to **Normal** view.

16. Insert a **Header & Footer** on the **Notes and Handouts**. Include a **Page number** and the **Footer** Lastname_Firstname_p04_Report

17. **Save**, and then compare your presentation with **Figure 4**. Submit as directed, and then **Exit** PowerPoint.

Done! You have completed the Skill Check

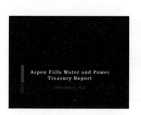

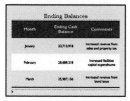

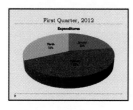

Lastname_Firstname_p04_Report   1

Figure 4

Assess Your Skills 1

To complete this presentation, you will need the following file:

■ p04_City_Hall

You will save your presentation as:

■ **Lastname_Firstname_p04_City_Hall**

1. **Start** PowerPoint. From your student files, open **p04_City_Hall**. Save the presentation in your **PowerPoint Chapter 4** folder as Lastname_Firstname_p04_City_Hall

2. Display **Slide 3**. In the content placeholder, insert a table with 2 columns and 5 rows. In the five cells of the first column, type the following headings: Project and Exterior and Interior and Parking and Landscape In the second column, type the following: Percent Complete and 85% and 45% and 20% and 0%

3. Insert a third column to the right of the *Percent Complete* column. Type the following: Completion Date and November 2013 and January 2014 and June 2014 and July 2014 Size the table so that its lower edge aligns at the **3 inch** mark below zero on the vertical ruler. If necessary, distribute the rows, and then apply the **Medium Style 3 - Accent 1** table style. Center the text horizontally and vertically within the cells. Animate the table by applying the **Wipe** entrance effect.

4. Display **Slide 4**. Insert a **Pie in 3-D** chart. In the **Excel** worksheet, in cell **B1**, type Cost Beginning in cell **A2**, enter the following data:

Exterior	1257500
Interior	1258650
Parking	750000

5. In the **Excel** window, delete row **5**, and then **Close** Excel. Change the chart layout to **Layout 1**, and then delete the chart title. Apply the **Style 10** chart style, and change the **Data Labels** placement to **Center**.

6. Display **Slide 2**, and then remove the animation effect from the title placeholder.

7. With **Slide 2** displayed, select the content placeholder, and then apply the **Split** entrance effect and change the **Effect Options** to **Vertical Out**.

8. Display **Slide 5**, and then apply the **Dissolve In** entrance effect to the picture. Change the **Duration** to **00.75** and the **Delay** to **00.25**. Apply the **Darken** emphasis effect to the caption. For both the caption and the picture, modify the **Start** option to **After Previous**.

9. View the slide show from the beginning, and use the navigation toolbar to display **Slide 4** after you display **Slide 1**. Return to **Slide 1**, and then view the presentation in the correct order.

10. Insert a **Header & Footer** on the **Notes and Handouts**. Include a **Page number** and the **Footer** Lastname_Firstname_p04_City_Hall

11. **Save**, and then compare your presentation with **Figure 1**. Print your presentation or submit the file, as directed by your instructor. **Exit** PowerPoint.

Done! You have completed Assess Your Skills 1

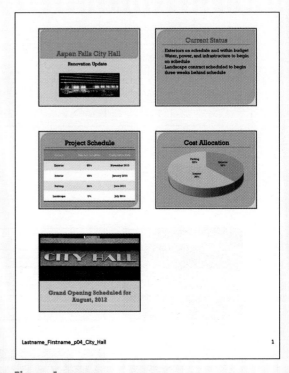

Figure 1

Assess Your Skills 2

Assess Your Skills 3 and 4 can be found at **www.pearsonhighered.com/skills**.

To complete this presentation, you will need the following file:

- p04_Benefits

You will save your presentation as:

- Lastname_Firstname_p04_Benefits

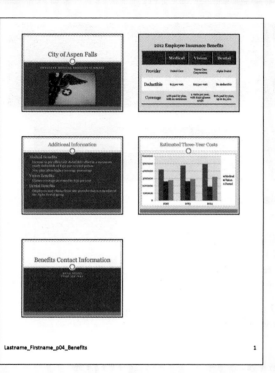

Lastname_Firstname_p04_Benefits   1

Figure 1

1. **Start** PowerPoint. From your student files, **Open p04_Benefits**. **Save** the presentation in your **PowerPoint Chapter 4** folder as Lastname_Firstname_p04_Benefits

2. Display **Slide 2**. In the content placeholder, insert a table with 3 columns and 4 rows. In the first row, type the following headings: Medical and Vision and Dental In the second row, type United Care and Vision Care Corporation and Alpha Dental In the third row type $15 per visit and $25 per visit and No deductible In the fourth row, type 90% paid by plan, with no maximum and 2 visits per year, with $250 glasses credit and 80% paid by plan, up to $2,000

3. Insert a column to the left of the first column. Beginning in the second row, type the following headings: Provider and Deductible and Coverage

4. Size the table so that its lower edge aligns at the **3 inch** mark below zero on the vertical ruler. Distribute the rows, and then apply the **Medium Style 3 - Accent 1** table style. Center the table text horizontally and vertically. Change the first row and first column **Font Size** to **28**, and then apply the **Circle** cell bevel effect to the first row. **Animate** the table by applying the **Wipe** effect.

5. Display **Slide 4**, and then insert a **Clustered Column** chart. In the **Excel** worksheet, in cell **B1**, type Medical In cell **C1** type Vision

and in cell **D1** type Dental Beginning in cell **A2** enter the following data:

2012	4228550	2586430	2758490
2013	4752280	2687500	2896430
2014	4967870	1889480	3198560

6. In the **Excel** worksheet, delete row **5**, and then **Close** Excel. Apply the **Style 34** chart style, and then use **Animation Painter** to copy the animation from the table on **Slide 2** to the chart on **Slide 4**.

7. Edit the chart data by changing the *2013 Vision* data in cell **C3** to 2622330

8. On **Slide 3**, apply the **Float In** entrance effect to the content placeholder.

9. On **Slide 5**, apply the **Fly In** entrance effect to the title. Change the **Effect Options** to **From Top**. Use the **Reorder Animation** options to move the title animation earlier so that it displays before the subtitle. Set the title and subtitle animations to start **After Previous**. View the slide show from the beginning.

10. Insert a **Header & Footer** on the **Notes and Handouts**. Include a **Page number** and the **Footer** Lastname_Firstname_p04_Benefits

11. **Save**, and then compare your presentation with Figure 1. Print your presentation or submit the file, as directed by your instructor. **Exit** PowerPoint.

Done! You have completed Assess Your Skills 2

Assess Your Skills Visually

To complete this presentation, you will need the following file:

- New blank PowerPoint presentation

You will save your presentation as:

- Lastname_Firstname_p04_Accounts

Start PowerPoint. Create the table as shown in **Figure 1**. **Save** the file as Lastname_Firstname_p04_Accounts in your **PowerPoint Chapter 4** folder. To complete this presentation, use the **Module** design theme. Type and align the text as shown in the figure, and apply the **Light Style 2 - Accent 1** table style. In the first table row, change the **Font Size** to **24**, and apply a **Circle** bevel effect. Add a footer to the **Notes and Handouts** with the file name and page number, and then print or submit the file, as directed by your instructor.

Done! You have completed Assess Your Skills Visually

Account Type	Description	Rate
Savings Account	Traditional account for short-term needs	1%
Savings Certificate	Competitive rates Guaranteed return	1.5% to 3.5%
Money Market Account	Minimum $2,500 balance Unlimited withdrawals	1.25% to 1.75%
Individual Retirement Account	Invest after-tax dollars	2.25% to 4.5%

Savings Account Comparison

Figure 1

Skills in Context

To complete this presentation, you will need the following file:

- New blank PowerPoint presentation

You will save your presentation as:

- Lastname_Firstname_p04_Power

Using the information provided, create a presentation in which the first slide title is Aspen Falls Utilities Division and the subtitle is Power Distribution and Usage Apply a design theme. Create two more slides, one with a table and one with a pie chart, that include information about the types of power that the city uses and its distribution to customers. The city's power supply is composed of 52% hydroelectric power, 28% natural gas, 15% renewable energy sources, and 5% coal. On a monthly basis, the average distribution of power in megawatt hours is 705,500 for residential customers, 1,322,600 for commercial customers, and 587,900 for industrial customers.

Format the chart and table with styles, and apply animation to each. Insert a footer with the file name on the **Notes and Handouts**. Print or submit electronically, as directed by your instructor.

Done! You have completed Skills in Context

Skills and You

To complete this presentation, you will need the following file:

- New blank PowerPoint presentation

You will save your presentation as:

- Lastname_Firstname_p04_Cars

Using the skills you have practiced in this chapter, create a presentation with four slides in which you compare three cars that you would be interested in purchasing. Apply an appropriate presentation theme. On one slide, insert a table with three columns that includes the vehicle name, price range, and description of important features. On another slide, insert a column chart that compares the prices of the three vehicles. On

the last slide, insert a picture of the car that you would like to purchase, and include at least three bullet points indicating why you chose the vehicle. Apply animation to the slides, and insert an appropriate footer. Print or submit electronically, as directed by your instructor.

Done! You have completed Skills and You

CHAPTER 5

Enhance PowerPoint Presentations

▶ You can gather content for presentations by using PowerPoint's research tools, duplicating slides from other presentations, or copying and pasting information from files created with other programs.

▶ Increase the impact of your presentations by changing the space between characters, altering the direction in which text displays, and placing text in columns.

Your starting screen will look like this:

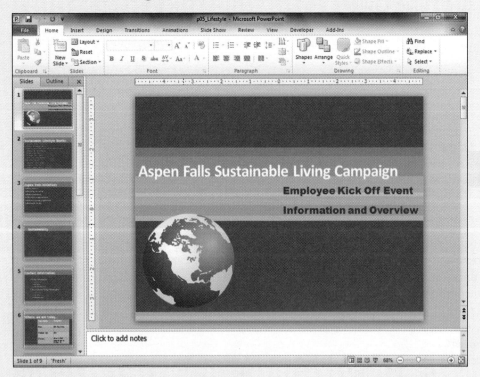

SKILLS

Skills 1-10 Training

At the end of this chapter, you will be able to:

Skill 1 Use the Research Task Pane

Skill 2 Copy and Paste Between Programs

Skill 3 Customize Character Spacing

Skill 4 Clear Formatting

Skill 5 Adjust Line Spacing

Skill 6 Change Text Direction and Case

Skill 7 Divide Text into Columns

Skill 8 Align Text and Shapes

Skill 9 Duplicate Slides

Skill 10 Replace Fonts

MORE SKILLS

More Skills 11 Create Custom Slide Shows and Add Sections

More Skills 12 Change and Reset Pictures

More Skills 13 Equalize Character Height

More Skills 14 Format Title Backgrounds

Outcome

Using the skills listed to the left will enable you to create a presentation like this:

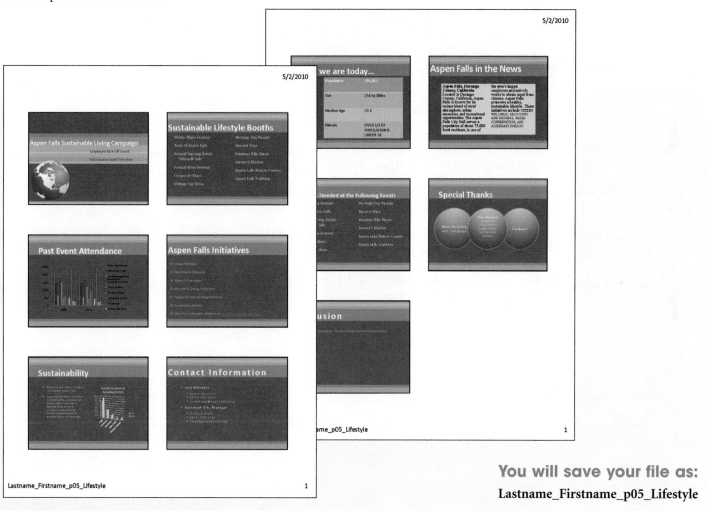

In this chapter, you will create presentations for the Aspen Falls City Hall, which provides essential services for the citizens and visitors of Aspen Falls, California.

Introduction

▶ You can add content to your presentation by using the Research pane or by copying and pasting objects from other applications.

▶ You can enhance the appearance of text by adjusting the space between characters and changing the direction of the text.

▶ You can replace fonts in a presentation, adapt individual sentences by changing case, and clear formatting from a presentation.

▶ Text and objects can be aligned, moved, or divided into columns.

Time to complete all
10 skills – 50 to 90 minutes

Find your student data files here:

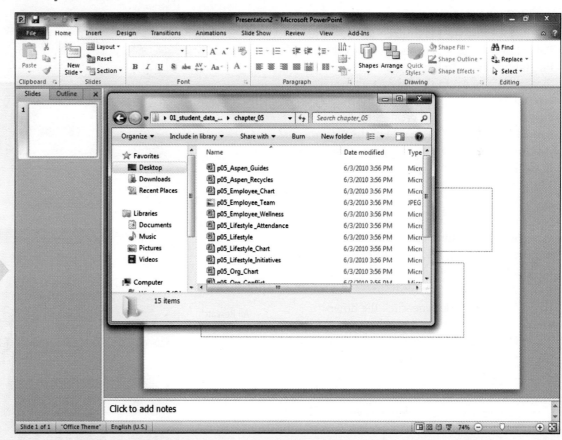

Student data files needed for this chapter:

- p05_Lifestyle
- p05_Lifestyle_Initiatives
- p05_Lifestyle_Chart
- p05_Lifestyle_Attendance

► The ***Research task pane*** enables you to select specific words or phrases in your presentation and begin researching using Internet resources.

► Hyperlinks can be inserted into your presentation to link it to online content such as articles found using the Research task pane.

1. **Start** PowerPoint. From your student files, open **p05_Lifestyle**. **Maximize** the PowerPoint window if necessary. Click the **File tab** to switch to **Backstage** view, and then click **Save As**. In the **Save As** dialog box, navigate to the location where you are saving your files, and create a folder named PowerPoint Chapter 5 Substituting your own name for *Lastname_Firstname*, in the **File Name** box, type Lastname_Firstname_p05_Lifestyle and then press Enter.

2. Navigate to **Slide 3**, and then select the word *Sustainable*. On the **Review tab**, in the **Proofing group**, click the **Research** button. Compare your screen with **Figure 1**.

3. In the **Research** task pane, click the **down arrow** in the second box and select *All Research Sites* as shown in **Figure 2**. If a list of research sites does not appear automatically, click the green Start searching arrow.

> Information about the word *sustainable* displays in the Research task pane. The ***Research task pane*** provides online dictionaries, resources, and related websites. The Research options command at the bottom of the task pane is used to select sources and set Parental Controls.

■ **Continue to the next page to complete the skill** ➡

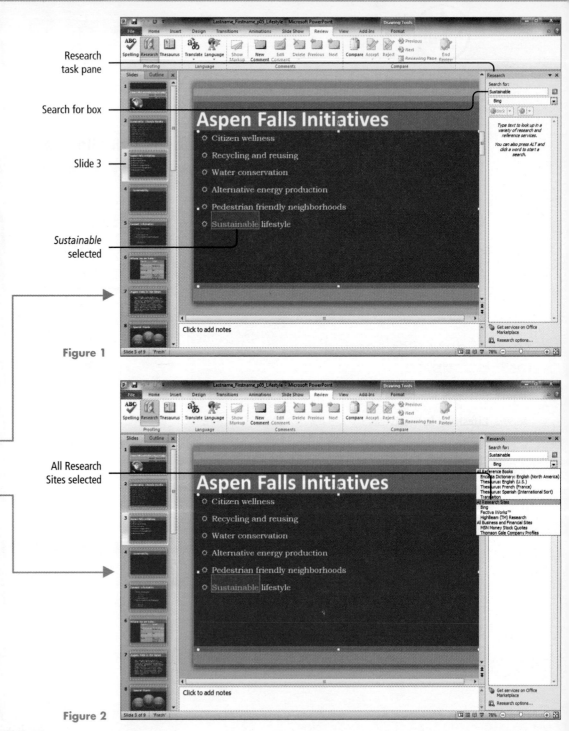

Research task pane

Search for box

Slide 3

Sustainable selected

Figure 1

All Research Sites selected

Figure 2

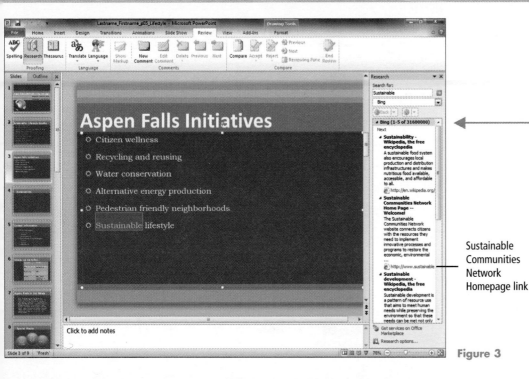

Sustainable
Communities
Network
Homepage link

Figure 3

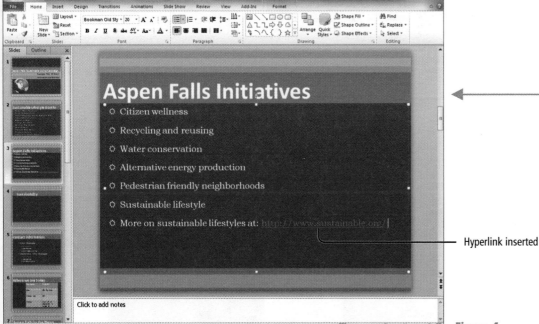

Hyperlink inserted

Figure 4

4. In the **Research** task pane, view all of the text under the heading *Sustainable Communities Network Home Page -- Welcome*. Click the link under the heading, as shown in **Figure 3**. If this link is not displayed in your search results, click another similar link.

5. **Maximize** the browser window.

   Clicking the linked sidebar article opens a web browser with the *Sustainable Communities Network Home Page* displayed. Here, you can continue to search for information using your browser, or you can return to PowerPoint.

6. In the **Address Bar** of your browser window, right-click the web address, and then click **Copy**. **Close** ⊠ the browser window and return to PowerPoint.

7. On **Slide 3**, place the insertion point after *Sustainable lifestyle*, and then press Enter. Type More on sustainable lifestyles at: and then press Spacebar one time.

8. On the **Home tab**, in the **Clipboard group**, click the **Paste** button to place the web address at the end of the line. Press the Spacebar, and then notice that the text changes to a hyperlink. Compare your screen with **Figure 4**.

9. **Close** ⊠ the **Research** task pane, and then **Save** 🖫 the presentation.

■ **You have completed Skill 1 of 10**

- ► Information can be copied from other Office programs and pasted into PowerPoint presentations.

- ► You can use the Office Clipboard to collect information from other Office files—text, pictures, and charts—and paste them into your presentation.

- ► When pasting text, the formatting from either the source document or the destination file can be applied.

1. On the **Home tab**, in the **Clipboard group**, click the **Clipboard Dialog Box Launcher** 🔲 to open the **Clipboard** task pane, and then click **Clear All** to remove any items that were previously copied. Compare your screen with **Figure 1**. ——————

    The *Office Clipboard*—which is accessed in the Clipboard task pane—stores up to 24 items copied from any type of Office document.

2. Click the **Start** button ⊕, locate and then start Microsoft Word. Click the **File tab** to switch to **Backstage** view, and then click **Open**. From your student files, open the document **p05_Lifestyle_Initiatives**. On the **Home tab**, in the **Clipboard group**, click the **Dialog Box Launcher** to display the Clipboard task pane.

3. Select the entire first paragraph beginning with *Aspen Falls City Hall is committed*. On the **Home tab**, in the **Clipboard group**, click **Copy**.

4. Using the technique just practiced, copy the last paragraph, *Everyone can help create a sustainable Aspen Falls*, and compare your screen with **Figure 2**. ——————

■ **Continue to the next page to complete the skill**

Home tab

Clipboard Dialog Box Launcher button

Clipboard task pane

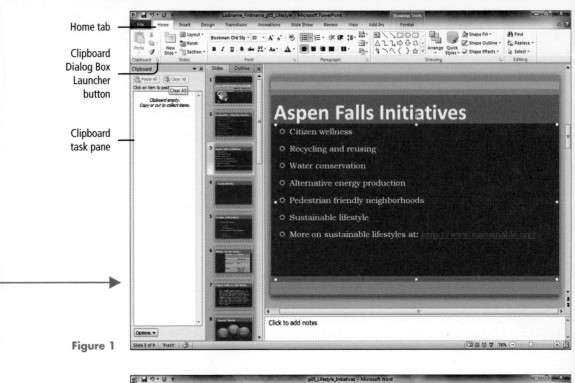

Figure 1

Word document

Items copied

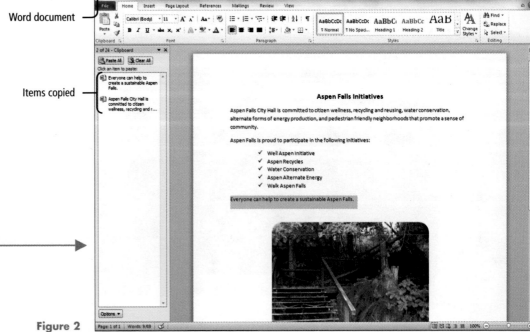

Figure 2

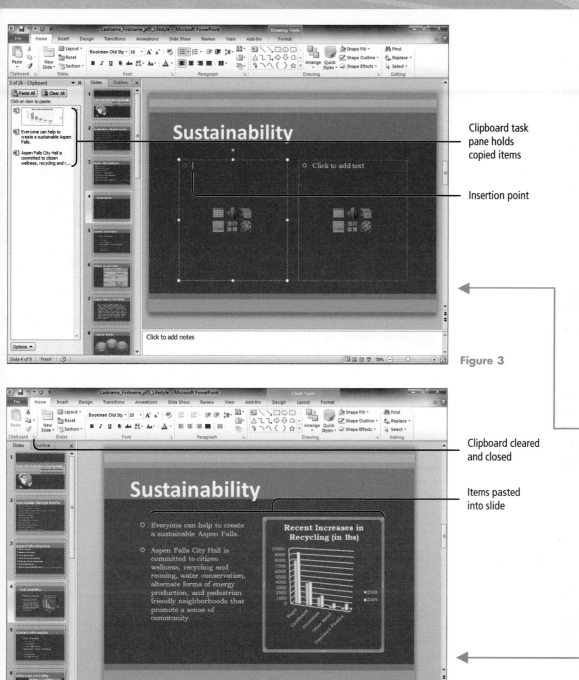

Clipboard task pane holds copied items

Insertion point

Figure 3

Clipboard cleared and closed

Items pasted into slide

Figure 4

5. **Exit** Word. Click the Start button ⊕, and then start Excel. Click the **File tab** to switch to **Backstage** view, and then click **Open**. Navigate to your student files, and then open the workbook **p05_Lifestyle_ Chart**.

6. Display the **Clipboard** task pane. Click a blank space on the column chart to select it. On the **Home tab**, in the **Clipboard group**, click the **Copy** button to copy the chart, and then **Exit** Excel.

   As you copy items, a message temporarily displays in the notification area, indicating the number of items stored on the Office Clipboard.

7. In PowerPoint, verify that the two sentences from the Word document and the Excel chart display in the **Clipboard** task pane.

8. Navigate to **Slide 4**, and then click the left content placeholder. Be sure that the insertion point is positioned to the right of the first bullet point, as shown in **Figure 3**.

9. In the **Clipboard** task pane, click the sentence beginning with *Everyone can* to paste it in the content placeholder, and then click the sentence beginning with *Aspen Falls* to paste it into the content placeholder.

10. Click the border of the right content placeholder to select it. In the **Clipboard** task pane, click the chart to paste it into the placeholder.

11. On the **Clipboard** task pane, click **Clear All**. **Close** ☒ the Clipboard and compare your screen with **Figure 4**. **Save** ▣ the presentation.

■ **You have completed Skill 2 of 10**

► *Character spacing*—the spaces between the letters in titles or bullet points—can be increased or decreased as a visual effect or to make text fill a desired space.

► You can use a built-in setting—for example, the Tight setting moves letters closer together—or type your own value by which text should be condensed or expanded.

1. On **Slide 4**, select the sentence *Everyone can help to create a sustainable Aspen Falls*.

2. On the **Home tab**, in the **Font group**, click the **Character Spacing** button, and then click **More Spacing** as shown in **Figure 1**.

3. In the **Font** dialog box, click the **Spacing box arrow**, and then click **Expanded**. Click the **By box up spin arrow** until it displays **1.2**.

4. Clear the **Kerning for fonts** check box. Compare your screen with **Figure 2**. Click the **Font tab**, and under **Font style**, click **Italic**. Click **OK** to close the **Font** dialog box.

   Kerning is adjustment of the spacing between characters. It is the amount of overlap between certain pairs of letters such as *T* and *o*. For example, the letter *o* can be moved slightly beneath the top of the letter *T* by applying kerning.

5. On **Slide 5**, select the title *Contact Information*. In the **Font group**, click the **Character Spacing** button, and then click **More Spacing**. In the **Font** dialog box, on the **Character Spacing** tab, click the **Spacing box arrow**, and then click **Expanded**. In the **By** box, type 7.5 and click **OK**.

■ **Continue to the next page to complete the skill** ➤

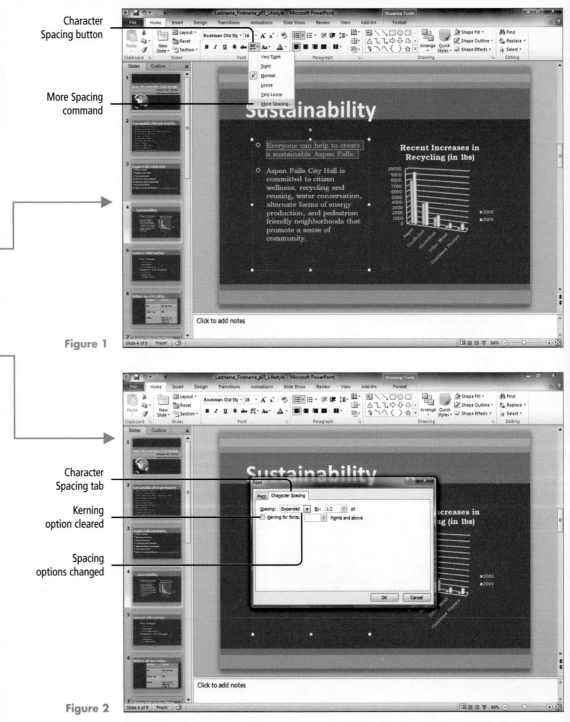

Character Spacing button

More Spacing command

Figure 1

Character Spacing tab

Kerning option cleared

Spacing options changed

Figure 2

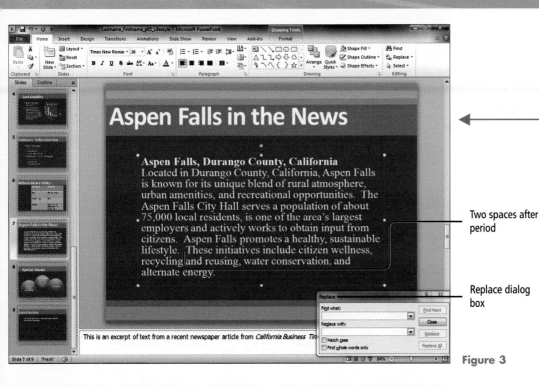

Two spaces after period

Replace dialog box

Figure 3

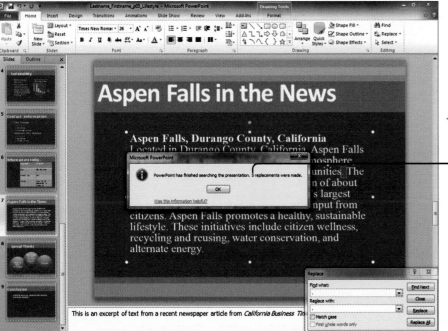

Five replacements found

Figure 4

6. On **Slide 7**, select the title *Aspen Falls in the News*. On the **Home tab**, in the **Font group**, click the **Character Spacing** button, and then click **Tight**.

7. Display **Slide 9**, and then select the title *Conclusion*. On the **Home tab**, in the **Font group**, click the **Character Spacing** button, and then click **Very Loose**.

8. Display **Slide 7**, and click the content placeholder. On the **Home tab**, in the **Editing group**, click **Replace**, and then compare your screen with **Figure 3**.

   The text in the content placeholder is formatted with two spaces after each period, but it should be formatted with only one space after the period.

9. In the **Replace** dialog box, in the **Find what** box, type . and press Spacebar two times. In the **Replace with** box, type . and then press Spacebar one time. Click the **Replace All** button. Read the message, as shown in **Figure 4**.

   In the presentation, five instances of periods followed by two spaces are found and replaced.

10. In the message, click **OK**, and then **Close** the **Replace** dialog box. **Save** the presentation.

- **You have completed Skill 3 of 10**

► With text that has several formatting styles applied, it is efficient to clear all formatting and then apply new formatting.

► The formatting applied to text can be removed in a single step without deleting the text itself.

► Formatting can be cleared on Notes pages and on slides.

1. On **Slide 5**, select all of the bulleted text beginning with *City Manager* and ending with *rmack@aspenfalls.org*

2. On the **Home tab**, in the **Font group**, click the **Clear All Formatting** button 🔲, and compare your screen with **Figure 1**. ⎯⎯⎯⎯⎯⎯⎯⎯⎯⎯

   All formatting is removed from the selection—color, bold, size, and italic. When you have pasted information from another presentation or from the Internet, you can remove unwanted formatting this way.

3. With the bulleted text still selected, in the **Font group**, click the **Character Spacing** 🔲 button, and then click **Loose**.

4. Select the text *City Manager*. Press and hold Ctrl, and then select the text *Assistant City Manager*. Release Ctrl. In the **Font group**, click the **Bold** 🔲 button.

5. On the **View tab**, in the **Presentation Views group**, click the **Notes Page** button to view the slide and speaker's notes. Click the speaker's notes shown below the slide and then compare your screen with **Figure 2**. ⎯⎯⎯⎯⎯⎯⎯⎯⎯

■ **Continue to the next page to complete the skill**

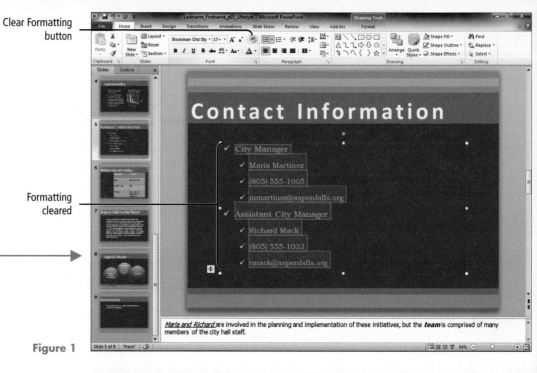

Clear Formatting button

Formatting cleared

Figure 1

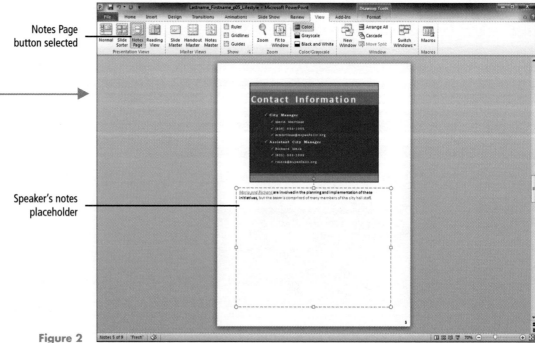

Notes Page button selected

Speaker's notes placeholder

Figure 2

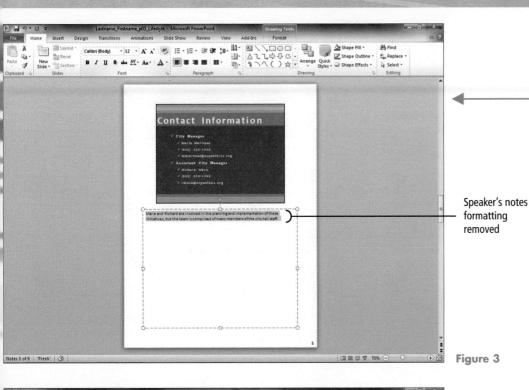

Speaker's notes formatting removed

Figure 3

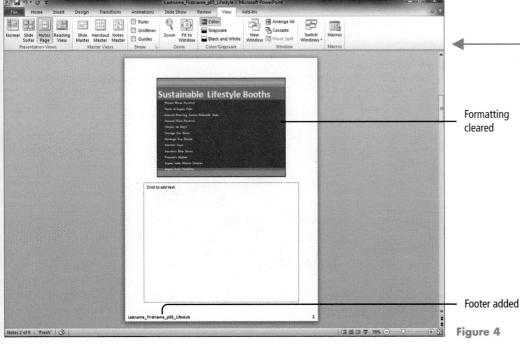

Formatting cleared

Footer added

Figure 4

6. Select all of the text in the speaker's notes placeholder.

7. On the **Home tab**, in the **Font group**, click the **Clear All Formatting** button 🗛. Compare your screen with **Figure 3**.

   The formatting is removed from the speaker's notes.

8. On the **View tab**, in the **Presentation Views group**, click the **Normal** button to switch back to Normal view.

9. On **Slide 2**, select all events, beginning with *Winter Blues Festival* and ending with *Aspen Falls Triathlon*. Use the technique practiced earlier to clear the formatting.

10. On the **Insert tab**, in the **Text group**, click the **Header & Footer** button. Click the **Notes and Handouts tab**. Click to select the **Footer** check box, and then type Lastname_Firstname_p05_Lifestyle and click **Apply to All**.

11. On the **View tab**, in the **Presentation Views group**, click **Notes Page** to view the changes you made, and compare your screen with **Figure 4**.

12. Return to **Normal** view. Change the spelling of *Cinquo* to *Cinco*. **Save** 🖫 the presentation.

■ **You have completed Skill 4 of 10**

► The amount of space between lines of text can be changed to balance slide elements.

► Increasing the line spacing for the speaker's notes makes them easier to read, navigate, and annotate.

1. On **Slide 5**, select the three bullet points under *City Manager*. On the **Home tab**, in the **Paragraph group**, click the **Line Spacing** button, and then click **Line Spacing Options**.

2. In the **Paragraph** dialog box, under **Spacing**, replace the value in the **Before** box with 1 pt as shown in **Figure 1**.

3. Click **OK** to close the dialog box. With the bulleted points still selected, on the **Home tab**, in the **Clipboard group**, click the **Format Painter** button. With the mouse pointer, select the three bullet points under *Assistant City Manager*. Compare your screen with **Figure 2**.

The Format Painter is used to apply the same formatting to the selected text as previously.

■ **Continue to the next page to complete the skill**

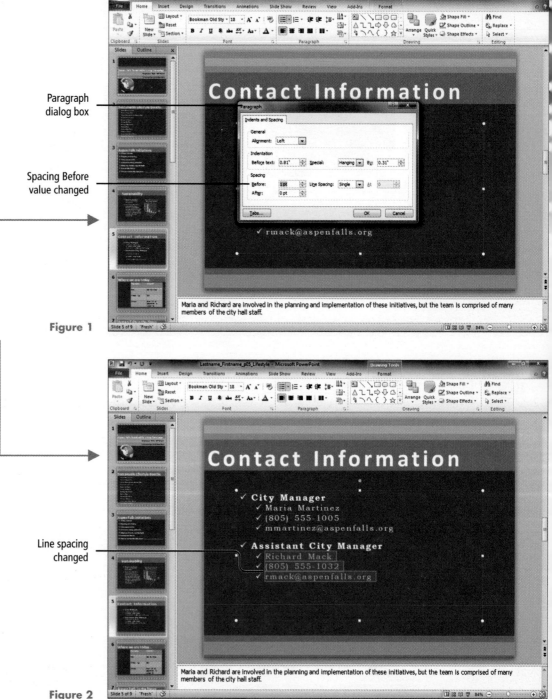

Paragraph dialog box

Spacing Before value changed

Figure 1

Line spacing changed

Figure 2

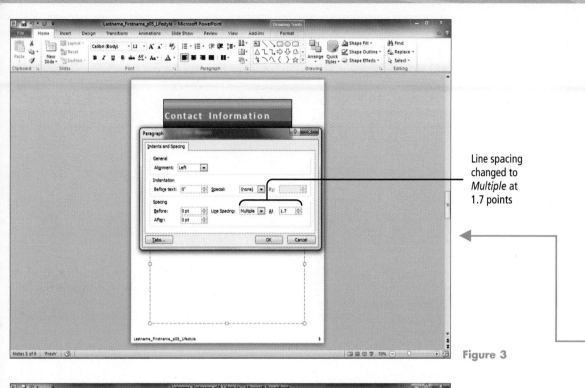

Line spacing
changed to
Multiple at
1.7 points

Figure 3

4. Select the text *City Manager*. Press and hold Ctrl, and then select *Assistant City Manager*. Release Ctrl.

5. In the **Paragraph group**, click the **Line Spacing** button, and then click **Line Spacing Options**. Under **Spacing**, replace the values in the **Before** and **After** boxes with 12 pt and then click **OK**.

6. Switch to **Notes Page** view, and then select all of the text in the speaker's notes placeholder.

7. On the **Home tab**, in the **Paragraph group**, click the **Line Spacing** button, and then click **Line Spacing Options**. Under **Spacing**, click the **Line Spacing box arrow**, and then click **Multiple**. To the right of the **Line Spacing** box, replace the value in the **At** box with 1.7 Compare your screen with **Figure 3**.

8. Click **OK** to close the dialog box, and then switch to **Normal** view. On **Slide 3**, select all of the bulleted points, by clicking the Content placeholder border. Using the technique you just practiced, reduce the **Spacing Before** to **0** points, and then change the **Line Spacing** to **Double**. Click **OK**, click a blank area to deselect the text, and then compare your screen with **Figure 4**.

   The text is AutoFit to the placeholder.

9. **Save** the presentation.

■ **You have completed Skill 5 of 10**

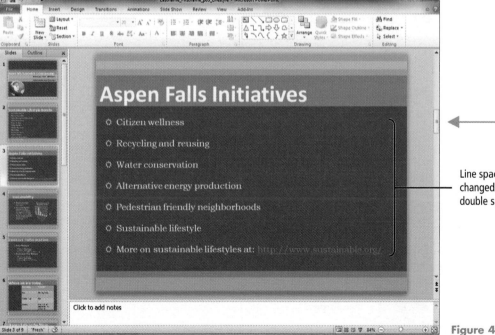

Line spacing
changed to
double spacing

Figure 4

▶ The direction of text can be changed. For example, text can display in a vertical stack with each letter displaying directly below the previous letter.

▶ The *Change Case* tool changes the selected text to uppercase, lowercase, title case, or sentence case.

1. Display **Slide 6**, and then on the **Insert tab**, in the **Text group**, click **Text Box**. With the mouse pointer ↧ near the left edge of the slide and aligned vertically with the word *Population*, click to insert a text box and type Census Data

2. Make sure the text box is still selected. On the **Home tab**, in the **Paragraph group**, click the **Text Direction** button ⬚, and then click **Stacked**.

3. If necessary, point to the lower right sizing handle of the selected text box, and then with the mouse ↖ pointer, drag left and downward so that the text box is approximately as wide as one letter.

4. Position the text box so that its top is aligned with the top of the table and each letter displays on one line, as shown in **Figure 1.**

5. On the **Home tab**, in the **Font group**, click the **Dialog Box Launcher** ⬚. In the **Font** dialog box, change the **Size** to **24**, change the **Font Style** to **Bold**, select the **Small Caps** and **Equalize Character Height** check boxes, and then click **OK**. Compare your screen with **Figure 2.**

■ **Continue to the next page to complete the skill** ➡

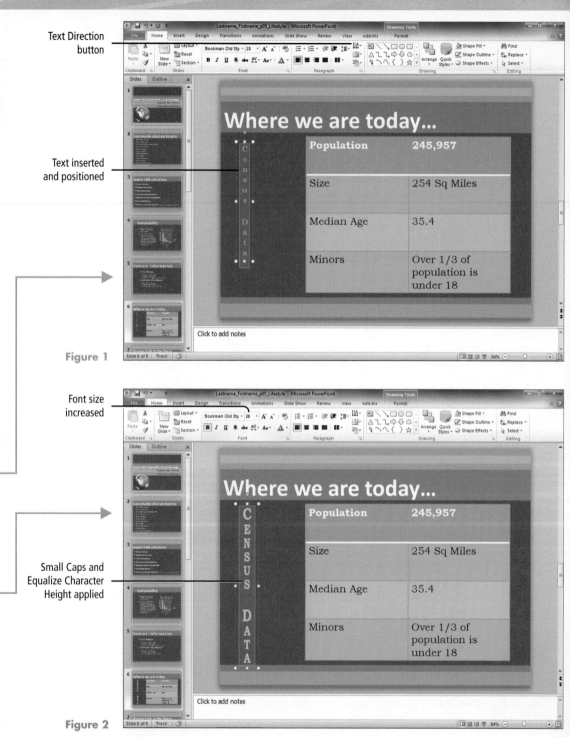

Text Direction button

Text inserted and positioned

Figure 1

Font size increased

Small Caps and Equalize Character Height applied

Figure 2

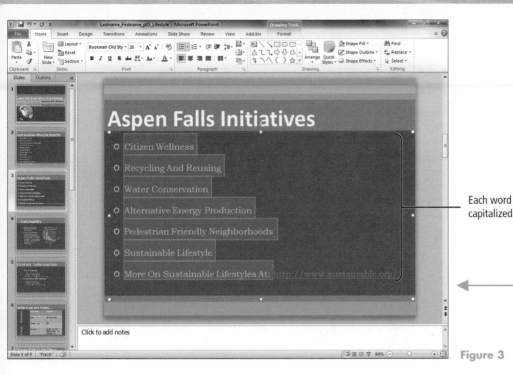

Each word capitalized

Figure 3

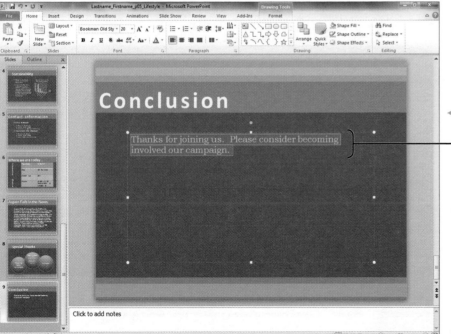

Sentence case applied

Figure 4

6. On **Slide 6**, in the last cell of the table, select the text *Over 1/3 of population is under 18.*

7. On the **Home tab**, in the **Font group**, click the **Font Dialog Box Launcher** ⬚. In the **Font** dialog box, under **Effects**, select the **All Caps** check box, and then click **OK**.

8. Navigate to **Slide 3**, select the text starting with *Citizen wellness* and ending with *More on sustainable lifestyles at:* Do not select the hyperlink.

9. On the **Home tab**, in the **Font group**, click the **Change Case** button ⎰Aa⎱, and then click **Capitalize Each Word**. Compare your screen with **Figure 3**.

10. On **Slide 7**, at the end of the content placeholder, select the phrase *Citizen Wellness, Recycling and Reusing, Water Conservation, and Alternate Energy*. On the **Home tab**, in the **Font group**, click the **Font Dialog Box Launcher** ⬚, and then select **Small Caps**.

11. On **Slide 9**, select all of the text in the content placeholder. On the **Home tab**, in the **Font group**, click the **Change Case** button ⎰Aa⎱. Change the case to **Sentence case**. Compare your screen with **Figure 4**.

12. **Save** ⬚ the presentation.

- **You have completed Skill 6 of 10**

► Long lists can be divided into columns to create a more reader-friendly format.

1. Navigate to **Slide 2**, and then click anywhere in the content placeholder.

2. On the **Home tab**, in the **Paragraph group**, click the **Columns** button ▦▾, and then click **More Columns**. In the **Columns** dialog box, change the **Number** box value to 2, and then change the **Spacing** box value to 1.3", and then click **OK**. Change the spelling of *Cinquo* to *Cinco*.

   The text is divided into two columns, with a 1.3-inch space between the columns.

3. Click the **View tab**, and in the **Show group**, select the **Ruler** check box if it is not already selected. Drag the bottom center sizing handle up to the 2.5 inch mark on the vertical ruler—the measurements on the ruler will change as you begin to resize. Compare your screen with **Figure 1**.

4. On the **Home tab**, in the **Font group**, click the **Font Size** box (not the down arrow), type 25 and then press Enter.

5. Navigate to **Slide 7**, and then click anywhere in the content placeholder.

6. On the **Home tab**, in the **Paragraph group**, click the **Columns** button, and then click **More Columns**. Change the **Number** of columns to 2 and increase the **Line Spacing** to 0.5" Click **OK**, and then compare your screen with **Figure 2**.

▪ **Continue to the next page to complete the skill**

Ruler is displayed

Text in two columns with 1.3" of space between

Content placeholder resized to 2.5" mark on vertical ruler

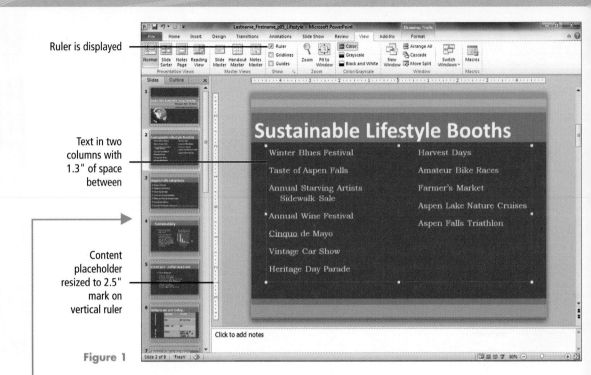

Figure 1

Text in two columns with .5" of space between

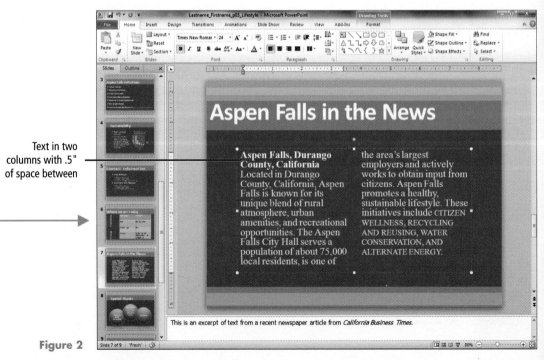

Figure 2

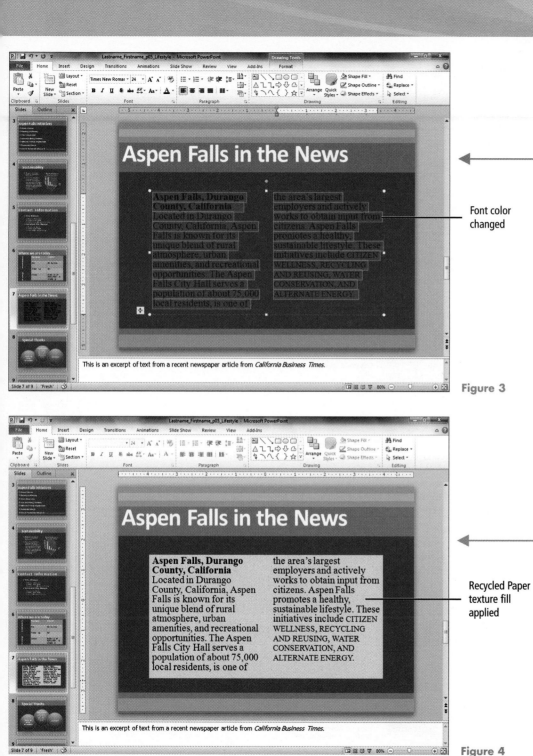

Font color
changed

Figure 3

Recycled Paper
texture fill
applied

Figure 4

7. Select all of the text in the content placeholder. On the **Home tab**, in the **Font group**, click the **Font Color down arrow** [A▾] and click **Brown, Background 1, Darker 50%**—the first choice in the last row under **Theme Colors**. Compare your screen with **Figure 3**.

8. Right-click anywhere in the content placeholder, and then in the displayed shortcut menu, click **Format Shape**. In the left pane of the displayed **Format Shape** dialog box, verify that **Fill** is selected. On the right, click the **Picture or texture fill** option button.

9. Click the **Texture** button, and then in the displayed gallery, click **Recycled Paper**— the fourth option in the third row. Click the **Close** button and then click a blank area of the slide to deselect the text. Compare your screen with **Figure 4**.

> A newspaper-like look is applied to the newspaper article shown on this slide.

10. Save [💾] the presentation.

■ **You have completed Skill 7 of 10**

▶ Text in an object or shape can be aligned vertically or horizontally or can be evenly distributed in the shape's boundaries.

▶ Shapes can be aligned with each other, so that their edges display along a straight line.

1. Navigate to **Slide 3**, and then click anywhere in the content placeholder.

2. On the **Home tab**, in the **Paragraph group**, click the **Align Text** button 📊, and then click **More Options**. Click the title bar of the **Format Text Effects** dialog box and drag to move the dialog box to the upper right corner of the screen.

   With the dialog box moved, you can view effects as you apply them.

3. In the **Format Text Effects** dialog box, click the **Vertical alignment box arrow**, and then click **Middle**. Compare your screen with **Figure 1**.

   The middle vertical alignment centers the text vertically in the content placeholder.

4. With the **Format Text Effects** dialog box open, navigate to **Slide 5**, and then click anywhere in the content placeholder.

5. In the **Format Text Effects** dialog box, click the **Vertical alignment box arrow**, and then click **Middle Centered**. In the **Format Text Effects** dialog box, click the **Close** button, and then compare your screen with **Figure 2**.

   The text is centered horizontally and vertically in the content placeholder.

■ **Continue to the next page to complete the skill**

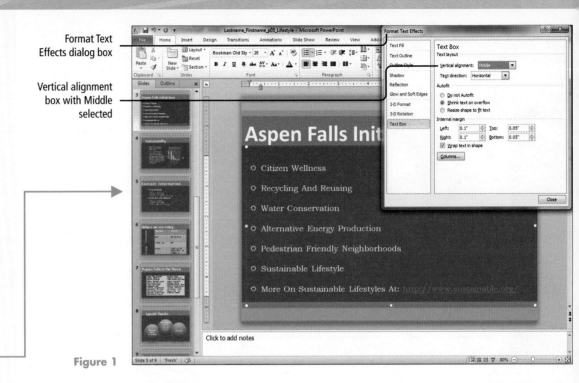

Format Text Effects dialog box

Vertical alignment box with Middle selected

Figure 1

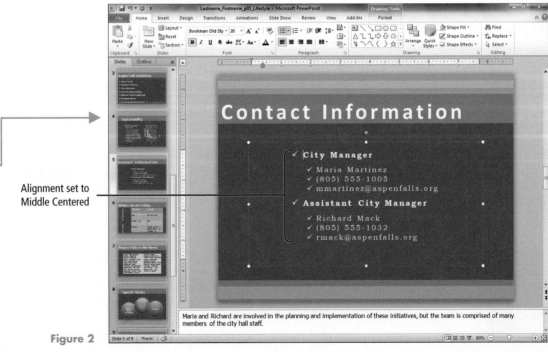

Alignment set to Middle Centered

Figure 2

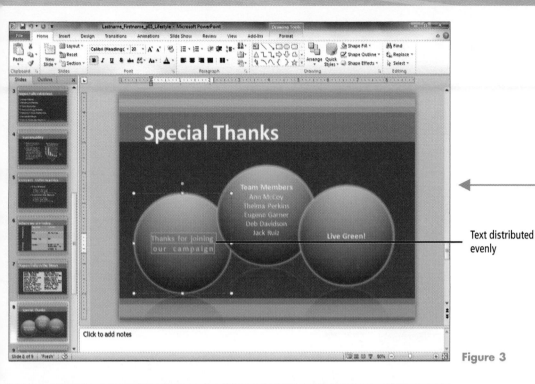

Text distributed
evenly

Figure 3

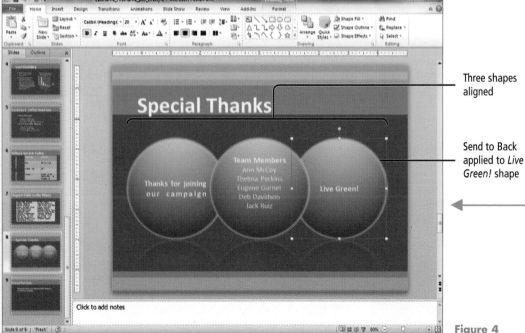

Three shapes
aligned

Send to Back
applied to *Live
Green!* shape

Figure 4

6. Navigate to **Slide 8**, and in the left **Circle** shape, select all of the text, beginning with *Thanks* and ending with *campaign*.

7. Right-click the selected text, and then from the displayed shortcut menu, click **Paragraph**.

8. In the **Paragraph** dialog box, under **General**, click the **Alignment box arrow**, and then click **Distributed**. Click **OK**, and then compare your screen with **Figure 3**.

   The text spreads out to fill the shape.

9. With the first **Circle** shape still selected, press and hold Ctrl, and then click a blank area in the **Circle** shape in the middle of the screen. Continue to hold Ctrl, and then click a blank area in the right **Circle** shape. Release Ctrl.

10. With all three shapes selected, on the **Home tab**, in the **Drawing group**, click the **Arrange** button, point to **Align**, and then click **Align Top**.

    The top edges of the three shapes align along a straight line.

11. Click a blank area of the slide to deselect the text, and then select the right **Circle** shape. On the **Home tab**, in the **Drawing group**, click **Arrange**, and then click **Send to Back**. Compare your screen with **Figure 4**.

    The *Live Green!* shape now displays behind the *Team Members* shape.

12. Save 🖫 the presentation.

■ **You have completed Skill 8 of 10**

► A *duplicate slide* is a slide that has been created by making a copy of, or duplicating, an original slide. Sometimes it is faster to modify a duplicate instead of creating a new slide from scratch.

1. Display **Slide 2**. On the **Home tab**, in the **Slides group**, click the *lower* half of the **New Slide** button—the **New Slide button arrow**—and then compare your screen with **Figure 1**.

2. In the displayed gallery, click **Duplicate Selected Slides**. Alternatively, in the Slide pane, right-click a thumbnail, and then click Duplicate Slide.

   The duplicated slide displays immediately below the original slide.

3. In the **Slides/Outline pane**, point to the new duplicate slide—**Slide 3**. Drag the slide to move it below the current **Slide 8**.

4. On Lifestyle **Slide 8**, select the title text *Sustainable Lifestyles Booths*, and then replace it with Volunteers Needed at the Following Events

5. Reduce the title font size to 35 so that the title fits on one line. Compare your screen with **Figure 2**.

6. Click **Save** 🖫. Display **Slide 2**. On the **Home tab**, in the **Slides group**, click the **New Slide button arrow**, and then click **Reuse Slides**.

   On the right of the screen, the Reuse Slides task pane displays. The *Reuse Slides task pane* displays slide thumbnails from other presentations; they can be inserted into the current presentation.

■ **Continue to the next page to complete the skill** ▶

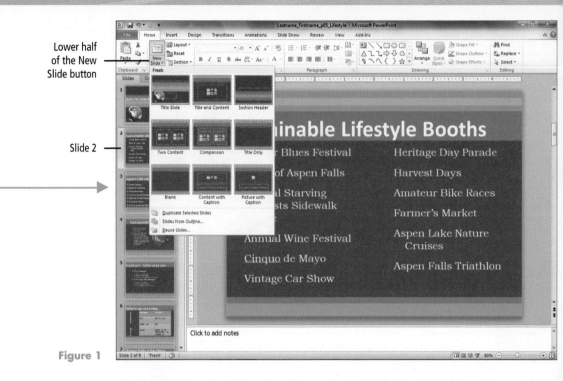

Lower half of the New Slide button

Slide 2

Figure 1

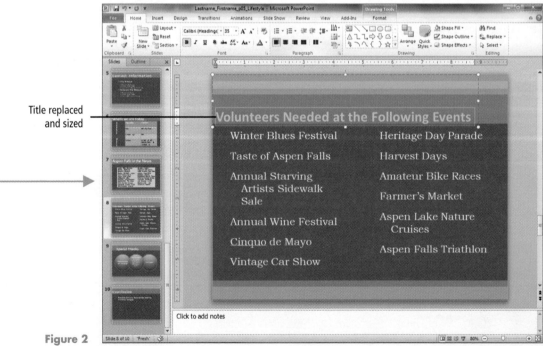

Title replaced and sized

Figure 2

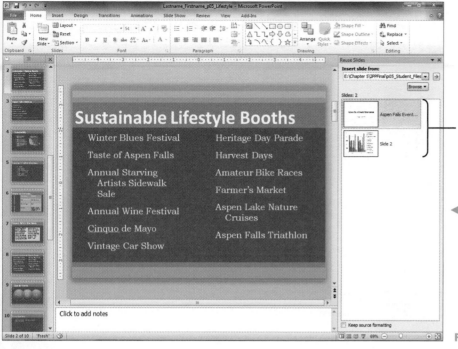

7. In the **Reuse Slides** task pane, click the **Open a PowerPoint File** link. In the **Browse** dialog box, navigate to your student files, and then double-click **p05_Lifestyle_Attendance**. Compare your screen with **Figure 3**.

Slides from the other presentation are shown in thumbnail previews. Thumbnails can be clicked to add the corresponding slide to the current presentation.

8. In the **Reuse Slides** task pane, click the **Slide 2** thumbnail.

Slide 2 from *p05_Lifestyle_Attendance* is inserted as Slide 3. The original slide remains in the original presentation. The new duplicate slide is formatted using the current presentation theme.

9. Close ⊠ the **Reuse Slides** task pane. With the new **Slide 3** still selected, on the **Home tab**, in the **Slides group**, click **Layout**, and then click the **Title and Content** thumbnail.

10. In the title placeholder, type Past Event Attendance and then compare your screen with **Figure 4**.

11. Save 🖫 the presentation.

■ **You have completed Skill 9 of 10**

Slides from *p05_Lifestyle_Attendance* in Reuse Slides task pane

Figure 3

Title added

Slide layout changed

Figure 4

▶ You can replace all fonts throughout your presentation in a single step by using the Replace Fonts command.

▶ You can use the *Replace Fonts command* to replace one font for another without having to search for and select text on individuals slides.

1. Display **Slide 1**. Click the **Slide Show** button on the lower right side of the window. As you move through the presentation, note the various fonts used. View each slide and then end the presentation.

2. On **Slide 1**, click the title placeholder, if necessary. On the **Home tab**, in the **Editing group**, click the **Replace button arrow**, and then point to **Replace Fonts** as shown in **Figure 1**.

3. Click **Replace Fonts**. In the displayed **Replace Font** dialog box, be sure that the **Replace** box displays **Arial Black**. Click the **With box arrow**, scroll down to click **Calibri**, and then click **Replace**. Click **Close**, and then compare your screen with **Figure 2**.

   Throughout the presentation, all occurrences of Arial Black are now formatted with the Calibri font.

■ **Continue to the next page to complete the skill** ▶

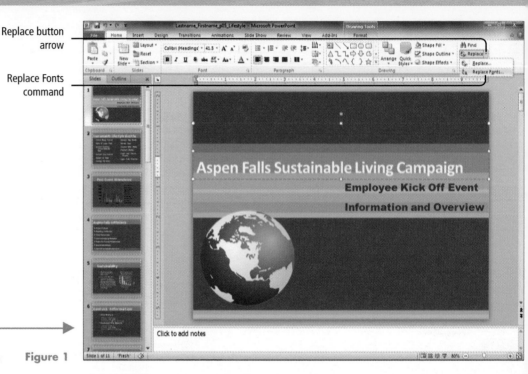

Replace button arrow

Replace Fonts command

Figure 1

Font changed to Calibri

Figure 2

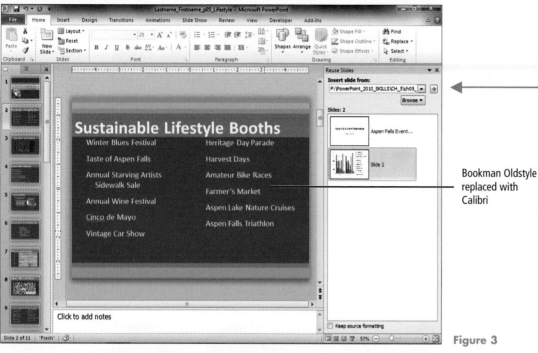

Bookman Oldstyle replaced with Calibri

Figure 3

Fonts replaced with Calibri for a consistent appearance

Figure 4

4. Select **Slide 2**. On the **Home tab**, in the **Editing group**, click the **Replace button arrow**, and then click **Replace Fonts**. Using the technique just practiced, replace all occurrences of **Bookman Oldstyle** with **Calibri**, **Close** the **Replace Font** dialog box, and then compare your screen with **Figure 3**.

   Positioning your insertion point on the font you want to replace causes this font to appear in the Replace box. Alternatively, you could scroll through the Replace list to select the font to be replaced.

5. Press F5 to view the presentation from the beginning. Compare your screen with **Figure 4**.

   As you click through the slide show, note that the fonts are consistent. However, the text copied from Word has remained in a Times New Roman font.

6. End the slide show and then **Save** 🖫 the presentation. Submit your presentation as directed by your instructor. **Exit** PowerPoint.

Done! You have completed Skill 10 of 10 and your presentation is complete!

The following More Skills are located at **www.pearsonhighered.com/skills**

More Skills Create Custom Slide Shows and Add Sections

You might want to create a slide show that displays only certain slides from your presentation. By creating a custom slide show, you can present specific slides without having to delete the other slides.

You might want to further organize your presentation by breaking it into sections, allowing you to format or print only the selected sections.

In More Skills 11, you will open an existing presentation, add sections, and create a new, custom show that contains specific slides from the original slide show. To begin, open your web browser, navigate to www.pearsonhighered.com/skills, locate the name of your book, and follow the instructions on the website.

More Skills Change and Reset Pictures

Often you may have reason to replace one picture in your presentation with another. Other times you may alter an image, only to decide later that you would like to change the image back to its original settings.

In More Skills 12, you will open a presentation and then reset and change images. To begin, open your web browser, navigate to www.pearsonhighered.com/skills, locate the name of your book, and follow the instructions on the website.

More Skills Equalize Character Height

Equalizing the character height of a font transforms the font so that all characters—uppercase and lowercase—are the same height. The effect can make text stand out on a slide, but because it decreases readability, it should not be used on large amounts of text.

In More Skills 13, you will open a presentation and equalize the font character height of text. To begin, open your web browser, navigate to www.pearsonhighered.com/skills, locate the name of your book, and follow the instructions on the website.

More Skills Format Slide Title Backgrounds

Slide title placeholders can be formatted with different fill effects, shape outlines, and shape effects so that they stand out and customize your presentation.

In More Skills 14, you will open a presentation and add formatting to the background of slide titles. To begin, open your web browser, navigate to www.pearsonhighered.com/skills, locate the name of your book, and follow the instructions on the website.

Key Terms

Character spacing 174

Duplicate slide 186

Kerning 174

Office Clipboard 172

Replace Fonts command. 188

Research task pane 170

Reuse Slides task pane 186

Online Help Skills

1. **Start** PowerPoint. In the upper right corner of the PowerPoint window, click the **Help** ⊙ button. In the **Help** window, click the **Maximize** button.

2. Click in the search box, type Select individual slide components and then click the Search ⌕ button. In the search results, click Select individual slide components that are stacked. Compare your screen with **Figure 1**.

Figure 1

3. Read the section, and then see if you can answer the following question: In what instances might you need to select one object from a group of stacked objects?

Matching

Match each term in the second column with its correct definition in the first column by writing the letter of the term on the blank line in front of the correct definition.

____ **1.** This task pane provides several online dictionaries and reference websites.

____ **2.** This feature stores multiple items copied from any Office program.

____ **3.** This is clicked to display the Office Clipboard.

____ **4.** The adjustment of the spacing between two characters.

____ **5.** The amount of room between two letters can be set to Loose, Tight, and more.

____ **6.** A task pane that displays slides from other presentations and stores them for placement into the current presentation.

____ **7.** A button that removes formatting that has been applied to text.

____ **8.** The view that shows the speaker notes as they will look when they are printed.

____ **9.** A slide that has been created by making a copy of an original slide.

____ **10.** A tool used to replace all occurrences of one font with a different font.

A Character spacing

B Clear Formatting

C Dialog Box Launcher

D Duplicate slide

E Kerning

F Notes view

G Office Clipboard

H Replace Fonts

I Research

J Reuse Slides

Multiple Choice

Circle the correct choice.

1. To copy the URL of a website, which of the following do you right-click before you click Copy?
   A. Address bar
   B. Search box
   C. Hyperlink

2. To insert a web address that has been copied from an Web browser into a presentation, click this button.
   A. Format Painter
   B. Paste
   C. Bullets

3. How many items can the Office Clipboard store?
   A. 24
   B. 36
   C. 64

4. To make the speaker's notes easier to read, navigate, and annotate, increase this.
   A. Line spacing
   B. Right margin
   C. Character spacing

5. To increase the amount of space before a line in a presentation, in the Paragraph dialog box, increase this value.
   A. Top margin
   B. Font size
   C. Spacing before

6. Large paragraphs of text may be divided into two or more of these with adjustable space between.
   A. Slides
   B. Columns
   C. Rows

7. To make text appear in a vertical line, with characters appearing directly above or on top of the other, change the text direction to this.
   A. Stacked
   B. Justified
   C. Horizontal

8. To select more than one object at a time, press this key while clicking.
   A. Alt
   B. Ctrl
   C. Spacebar

9. To copy a slide, use this command.
   A. New Slide
   B. Paste Special
   C. Duplicate Slide

10. You can change all instances of a specified font throughout a presentation by using which of the following commands?
   A. Find and Replace
   B. Font dialog box
   C. Replace Fonts

Topics for Discussion

1. What tips in this chapter will help you save time?

2. Why should you review your presentation's fonts, design, and content? Include comments on fonts, design, and information presented.

Skill Check

To complete this project, you will need the following files:

- p05_Aspen_Recycles
- p05_Aspen_Guides

You will save your file as:

- Lastname_Firstname_p05_Aspen_Recycles

1. **Start** PowerPoint, and then open **p05_Aspen_Recycles**. **Save** the file in your **PowerPoint Chapter 5** folder as Lastname_Firstname_p05_Aspen_Recycles

2. On **Slide 2**, select the word *recycling*. On the **Review tab**, in the **Proofing group**, click **Research**. In the **Research** task pane, select **All Reference Books**. In the **Research** task pane, select and then **Copy** the first definition, which begins with the phrase *the processing of*. **Close** the **Research** task pane.

3. Add a second bullet point, and then type Recycling Defined: followed by a space.

4. On the **Home tab**, in the **Clipboard group**, click **Paste**.

5. Press Enter, press Tab, type Source: and then type the name of the source listed: Encarta Dictionary: English (North America) Select *Source:* and the name of the source you entered, and then change the **Font Size** to **24**. Compare your screen with **Figure 1**. ─────

6. On the **Home tab**, in the **Clipboard group**, click the **Clipboard Dialog Box Launcher**, and then click the **Clear All** button.

7. **Start** Word, and then open the document **p05_Aspen_Guides**. Select the entire paragraph beginning with *Aspen Falls guidelines for*. On the **Home tab**, in the **Clipboard group**, click **Copy**.

8. Select the picture of the recycling bins. On the **Home tab**, in the **Clipboard group**, click **Copy**. **Exit** Word and return to PowerPoint.

9. Display **Slide 4**, and click the first bullet point. In the **Clipboard** task pane, click the sentence beginning with *Aspen Falls* to paste it onto the slide.

10. In the **Clipboard** task pane, click the picture of recycling bins to insert it. Drag the picture below the text on the slide. On the **Clipboard** task pane, click **Clear All** and **Close** it. Compare your screen with **Figure 2**. ─────

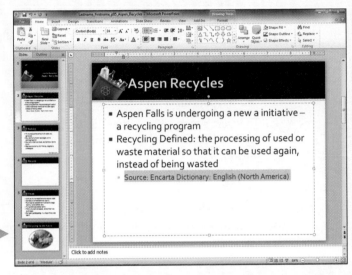

Figure 1

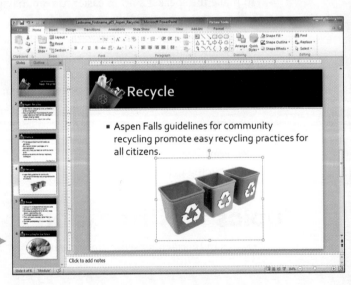

Figure 2

■ Continue to the next page to complete this Skill Check

11. Display **Slide 2**, and then click inside the content placeholder. On the **Home tab**, in the **Paragraph group**, click the **Align Text** button, and then click **More Options**. Change the **Vertical Alignment** to **Middle Centered** and then click **Close**.

12. On **Slide 2**, select the words *Recycling Defined*. On the **Home tab**, in the **Font group**, click the **Character Spacing** button, and then click **More Spacing**. Change the **Spacing** box to **Expanded**, increase the **By** value to 2.5 pt, and then click **OK**.

13. With *Recycling Defined* still selected, on the **Home tab**, in the **Font group**, click the **Change Case** button. Click **UPPERCASE**. Compare your screen with Figure 3.

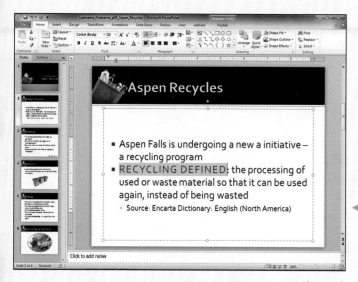

14. On **Slide 5**, select all of the bullet points. On the **Home tab**, in the **Font group**, use the **Clear All Formatting** button to remove all formatting from the text.

15. With the text still selected, on the **Home tab**, in the **Paragraph group**, click the **Line Spacing** button, and then click **Line Spacing Options**. Change the **Line Spacing** box to **Multiple**, and in the **At** box, type 1.2 In the **After** box, type 1 and then click **OK**.

16. With the bullets still selected, on the **Home tab**, in the **Paragraph group**, click the **Columns** button, and then click **Two Columns**. Click a blank area of the slide and then compare your screen with Figure 4.

17. On the **Home tab**, in the **Editing group**, click the **Replace button arrow**, and then click **Replace Fonts**. In the **Replace** box, click **Corbel**, and then in the **With** box, click **Eras Light ITC**. Click **Replace** and then click **Close**.

18. Display **Slide 6**. On the **Home tab**, in the **Slides group**, click the **New Slide button arrow**, and then click **Duplicate Selected Slides**. On the new duplicate slide, replace the title with Questions?

19. Type the file name in the **Notes and Handouts** footer. **Save** the presentation, and then print or submit electronically as directed.

Done! You have completed the Skill Check

Figure 3

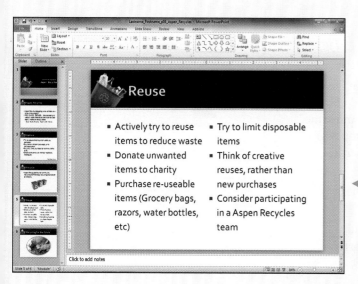

Figure 4

Assess Your Skills 1

To complete this project, you will need the following files:

- p05_Org_Chart
- p05_Org_Conflict

You will save your file as:

- Lastname_Firstname_p05_Org_Chart

1. **Start** PowerPoint, and then open **p05_Org_Chart**. **Save** the file in your **PowerPoint Chapter 5** folder as Lastname_Firstname_p05_Org_Chart

2. On **Slide 1**, select the word *Leadership*. Use the **Research** task pane to find definitions of leadership. **Copy** the first definition.

3. Click to the right of *Leadership*, add a colon and a space, and then **Paste** the definition. Select the paragraph beginning with *Leadership*, and change the **Font Size** to **14**. At the end of the paragraph, press Enter twice, and cite the source of the definition. Change the **Font Color** for the cited source to **Black**, and change the **Font Size** to **12**. **Close** the **Research** task pane.

4. At the end of the presentation, **Insert** a new slide with the **Title and Content** layout. Add the title Conflict Resolution

5. Select the title and adjust the **Character Spacing** to **Expanded** by **2.6 pt**.

6. With the title still selected, change the **Case** to **Sentence case**.

7. **Start** Word, and then open **p05_Org_Conflict**. Open the **Clipboard** task pane. **Copy** the first paragraph, beginning with *At first conflict*, and then **Copy** the photo.

8. **Exit** Word and return to **Slide 3**. Click in the content placeholder, and then **Paste** the sentence that begins with *At first conflict*.

9. Select the sentence just pasted, and then change the **Character Spacing** to **Condensed** by **1.5 pt**. Change the **Line Spacing** to **Multiple** at **1.3 lines**.

10. **Paste** the picture into the content placeholder. Position the photo below the bulleted sentence. **Clear** and **Close** the **Clipboard**.

11. Replace all occurrences of the font **Book Antiqua** with **Calibri**.

12. Duplicate **Slide 1**, and move the new duplicate so that it is the last slide.

13. On **Slide 4**, select the title, *City Clerk's Office*, and replace it with Conflict Resolution Team

14. Still on **Slide 4**, delete the subtitle. In the subtitle placeholder, **Align** the **Text** to **Middle**. Type Ann McCoy - Team Lead and move the subtitle placeholder up so that the top edge is even with the 0-inch mark on the vertical ruler.

15. Select the subtitle and adjust the **Character Spacing** to **Tight**.

16. Insert the file name in the **Notes and Handouts** footer. Click the **Slide Sorter View**, and **compare** your presentation with Figure 1. **Save** and submit as directed.

Done! You have completed Assess Your Skills 1

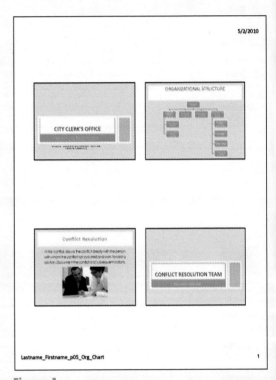

Figure 1

Assess Your Skills 2

To complete this project, you will need the following files:

- p05_Tourist
- p05_Tourist_Inns
- p05_Tourist_Information

You will save your file as:

- Lastname_Firstname_p05_Tourist

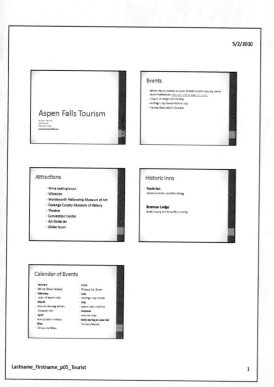

Figure 1

1. **Start** PowerPoint, and then open **p05_Tourist**. Save the file in your **PowerPoint Chapter 5** folder as Lastname_Firstname_p05_Tourist

2. On **Slide 1**, select the text *Visit Aspen Falls*. Change the **Text Direction** using the **Rotate all text 270°** command.

3. With *Visit Aspen Falls* still selected, change the **Character Spacing** to **Expanded** by **3 pt**.

4. Resize the text box so that all letters appear on one vertical line, and then position the text box in the lower right corner of the slide.

5. Display **Slide 2**, select all of the bulleted text, and then **Clear All Formatting**. Change the spelling of *Cinquo* to *Cinco*.

6. Select the text *Blues Festival*. Use the **Research** task pane to locate an article about blues music on the Internet. Position your pointer at the end of the first bullet point, type a period and Spacebar, and then type More Blues Festivals at **Create a hyperlink to** the article. **Close** the **Research** task pane.

7. Display **Slide 3**, and then apply **Middle Centered** text alignment to the content placeholder.

8. After **Slide 3**, insert **Slide 2** from the file **p05_Tourist_Inns**.

9. At the end of the presentation, insert a new slide with the **Title and Content Layout**. In the title, type Calendar of Events and then display the Clipboard task pane.

10. **Start** Word, and then open **p05_Tourist_Information**. **Copy** the list of events under the heading *Aspen Falls Calendar of Events*, and then **Close** Word. In the **Slide 5** content placeholder, **Paste** the list of events. For the text just pasted, change the **Spacing Before** to **0 pt**, and then change the **Line Spacing** to **Single**.

11. For the list just pasted, apply **2 columns** with **1 inch** of spacing between the two columns. Select *January*, and apply **Bold**. Use the **Format Painter** to duplicate this formatting to the remaining months and the text *Early Spring to Late Fall*.

12. Use the **Replace Fonts** command to replace all occurrences of the font **Cambria** with **Calibri**.

13. Insert the file name in the **Notes and Handouts** footer. Compare your presentation with Figure 1. **Save** the presentation, and then print it or submit it electronically, as directed.

Done! You have completed Assess Your Skills 2

Assess Your Skills Visually

To complete this project, you will need the following files:

- p05_Employee_Wellness
- p05_Employee Chart

You will save your file as:

- Lastname_Firstname_p05_Employee_Wellness

Open **p05_Employee_Wellness**, and then save the file as Lastname_Firstname_p05_Employee_Wellness in your **Chapter 5** folder. Replace all occurrences of the **Times New Roman** font with the **Candara** font. On **Slide 2**, expand the character spacing in the title to **4 pts**. Still on **Slide 2**, adjust the line spacing in the content placeholder to **1.5** lines. Use the **Arrange** button to align the three shapes vertically to the right, as shown in **Figure 1**. Insert a new **Slide 3** with a **Blank** layout, and then, using the Clipboard, copy and paste the chart from the Excel file **p05_Employee_Chart**, and then resize and position it as shown in **Figure 1**.

Insert the file name in the **Notes and Handouts** footer. **Save** and submit the file as directed.

Done! You have completed Assess Your Skills Visually

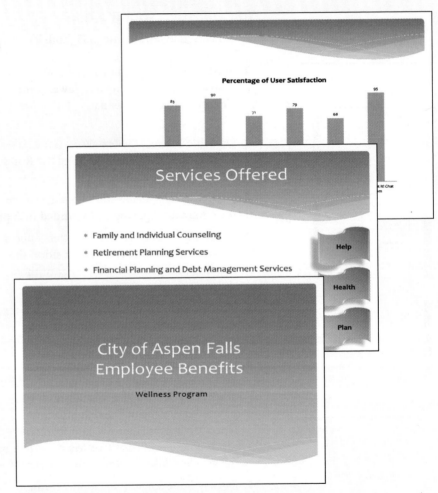

Figure 1

Skills in Context

To complete this project, you will need the following file:

- New blank presentation

You will save your file as:

- Lastname_Firstname_p05_Community_Services

Use the **Research** task pane to research sustainable housing. Copy and paste appropriate information to create a presentation with at least six slides. For each item that you paste into your presentation, copy and paste the related web address on the bottom of the slide. Jack Ruiz, the community services director, will use this presentation when he visits agencies that are interested in background information and research on the sustainable community movement. Jack's contact information should display in the footer of each slide—Jack Ruiz (805) 555-1010, jruiz@aspenfalls.org.

Modify the fonts by changing line and character spacing, alignment, and text direction. Apply columns on at least one slide. **Save** your presentation as Lastname_Firstname_p05_Community_Services in your **PowerPoint Chapter 5** folder. Add the file name to the footer on the **Notes and Handouts** page, and **Save**.

Done! You have completed Skills in Context

Skills and You

To complete this project, you will need the following files:

- New blank PowerPoint Presentation
- p05_Vacation_Goals

You will save your file as:

- Lastname_Firstname_p05_Vacation

Create a presentation that showcases a vacation destination. The first slide should list the destination as the title and your name and course name as the subtitle. For the second slide, paste the paragraph from the Word document **p05_Vacation_Goals**. Use the **Research** task pane to research your destination. Add a third slide that describes the destination in bullet points. Add a text box to the presentation that lists the name of your destination. Format the presentation by using the skills you practiced in this chapter. Add the file name to the footer on the Notes and Handouts page. Name the presentation Lastname_Firstname_p05_Vacation and then **Save** it to your **PowerPoint Chapter 5** folder. Submit as directed.

Done! You have completed Skills and You

CHAPTER 6

Add Multimedia Objects to a Presentation

▶ *Multimedia objects*, including sounds and motion videos, can be added to presentations to better communicate your message to your audience.

▶ Charts, hyperlinks, and action buttons add visual interest and interactivity to your presentations.

Your starting screen will look like this:

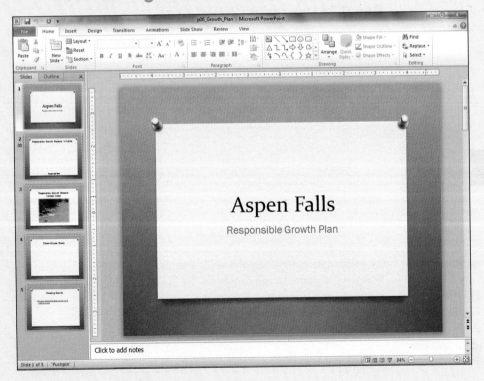

SKILLS
Skills 1-10 Training

At the end of this chapter, you will be able to:

Skill 1 Edit Videos

Skill 2 Change Video Options

Skill 3 Insert Hyperlinks

Skill 4 Insert and Edit Excel Charts

Skill 5 Link Files with Paste Special

Skill 6 Add Action Settings to Shapes

Skill 7 Create Slides with Timed Breaks

Skill 8 Insert Sound Effects

Skill 9 Insert Watermarks

Skill 10 Create SmartArt Organization Charts

MORE SKILLS

More Skills 11 Record and Play Narrations

More Skills 12 Add Rehearsal Timings

More Skills 13 Insert Songs

More Skills 14 Download and Apply Microsoft Office Templates

Outcome

Using the skills listed to the left will enable you to create a presentation like this:

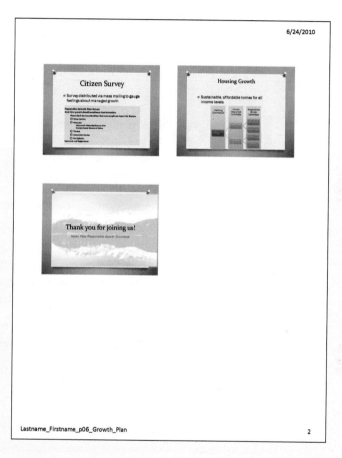

In this chapter, you will create presentations for the Aspen Falls City Hall, which provides essential services for the citizens and visitors of Aspen Falls, California.

Introduction

- ► An effective method to communicate with an audience is to add multimedia such as video and sound to a presentation.

- ► Video and sound files can be linked to a presentation or embedded into the presentation files. After the files are inserted, PowerPoint provides many options for playing the media—for example, a movie can be set to play when clicked or a sound can play automatically when the slide displays.

- ► Hyperlinks and action settings direct your presentation to websites, files on your computer, or other slides within the presentation.

- ► Charts can be copied from other programs, such as Excel, or they can be created in PowerPoint using the Chart tool.

- ► Watermarks are nearly transparent pictures used to add interest to a slide background without distracting the audience. They are placed in the slide background or behind slide placeholders by using the Send to Back feature.

Time to complete all
10 skills – 50 to 90 minutes

Find your student data files here:

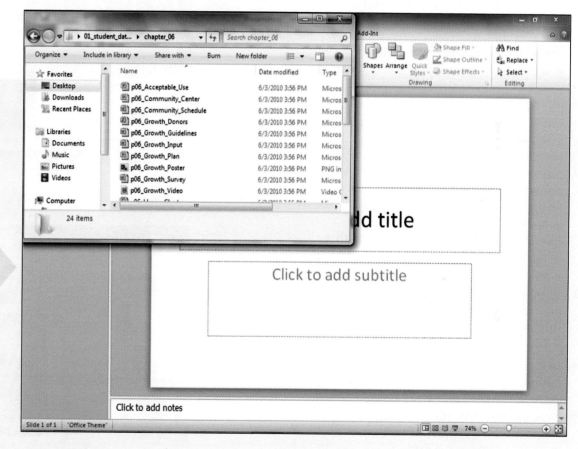

Student data files needed for this chapter:

- p06_Growth_Plan
- p06_Growth_Video
- p06_Growth_Guidelines
- p06_Growth_Donors
- p06_Growth_Survey

▶ *Multimedia* is the presentation of information using a variety of computer-based content such as text, images, sound, and video.

▶ *Trimming* a video reduces the length and can be used to remove unwanted portions of video.

1. **Start** PowerPoint. From your student files, open **p06_Growth_Plan**. Click **File**, and then click **Save As**. Navigate to the location where you are saving your files, create a folder named PowerPoint Chapter 6 and then **Save** the presentation as Lastname_ Firstname_p06_Growth_Plan

2. Display **Slide 2**. Click the **Insert tab**, and in the **Media group**, click the **Video button arrow**, and then click **Video from File**. In the **Insert Video** dialog box, navigate to your student files, and then double-click **p06_Growth_Video** to insert it. Under the video, click the **Play/Pause** ▶ button and note the length of the video—00:16.40. Compare your screen with **Figure 1**.

3. When the video has finished playing, on the **Video Tools contextual tab**, click the **Playback tab**. In the **Editing group**, click the **Trim Video** button.

4. In the **Trim Video** dialog box, in the **End Time** box, type 00:10 to trim the video length to 10 seconds.

5. Click the **Play** ▶ button to view the newly adjusted video. Compare your screen with **Figure 2**, and then click **OK**.

■ **Continue to the next page to complete the skill**

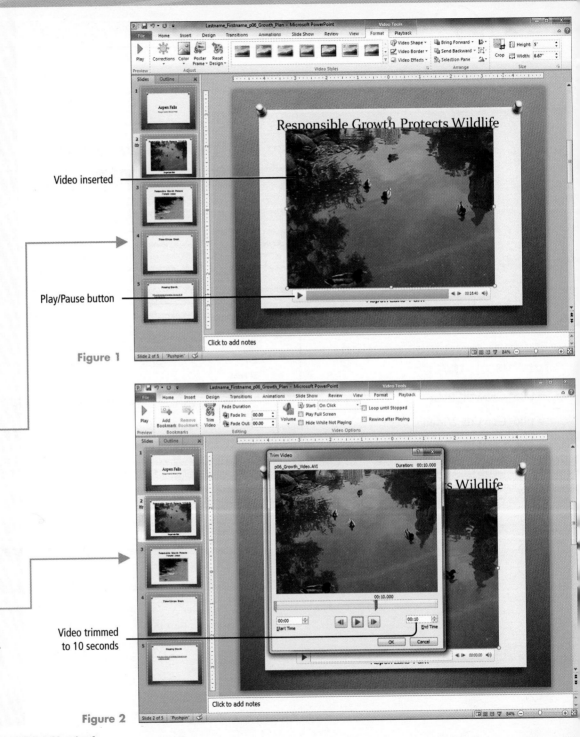

Video inserted

Play/Pause button

Figure 1

Video trimmed to 10 seconds

Figure 2

Poster Frame added

Video aligned Center and Middle

Figure 3

6. With the video still selected, on the **Video Tools Playback tab**, in the **Size group**, adjust the **Shape Height** to 4.5". In the **Arrange group**, click the **Align** button, and then click **Align Center**. Click the **Align** button again, and then click **Align Middle**.

7. On the **Video Tools Playback tab**, in the **Adjust group**, click **Poster Frame**, and then click **Image from File**. From your student files, select **p06_Growth_Poster**. Click **Insert**, and then compare your screen with **Figure 3**.

> The *Poster Frame* is an introductory frame that displays before the video begins playing.

8. In the **Video Styles group**, click **Simple Beveled Rectangle**—the first option. Click the **Slide Show** button. Point to the video, compare your screen with **Figure 4**, and then click **Play/Pause** button to view the video.

> *Video styles* are enhancements—frames and effects—that can be applied to add interest and a finished look to the video you have included in your presentation.

9. While in **Slide Show** view, right-click anywhere over the slide and then, on the displayed shortcut menu, click **End Show**.

10. **Save** the presentation.

■ **You have completed Skill 1 of 10**

Play/Pause button visible when pointing to video

Figure 4

► Video options can be changed so that the video plays in a full-screen format, begins playing automatically, is rewound after playing, and fades in and out.

1. If necessary, display **Slide 2**, and then select the video. On the **Video Tools Playback tab**, in the **Editing group**, under **Fade Duration**, adjust the **Fade In** to 2.50 and the **Fade Out** to 2.00 Compare your screen with **Figure 1**.

2. Click the **Slide Show** 🖵 button and view the effect that you just added. After the video has played, right-click the slide, and then click **End Show**.

3. Display **Slide 3**. Select the video. Click the **Play/Pause** ▶ button under the video—already inserted—to view it.

4. With the video still selected, on the **Playback tab**, in the **Video Options group**, click the **Start list arrow**. Click **Automatically**.

5. On the **Playback tab**, in the **Video Options group**, click to select **Rewind after Playing**. Compare your screen with **Figure 2**.

> The presenter will not need to click the video to begin playing. When it has completed playing, it will be rewound to the beginning.

6. Click the **Slide Show** 🖵 button and view the video. When the video is done playing, right-click the slide, and then click **End Show** to return to Normal view.

■ **Continue to the next page to complete the skill** ➤

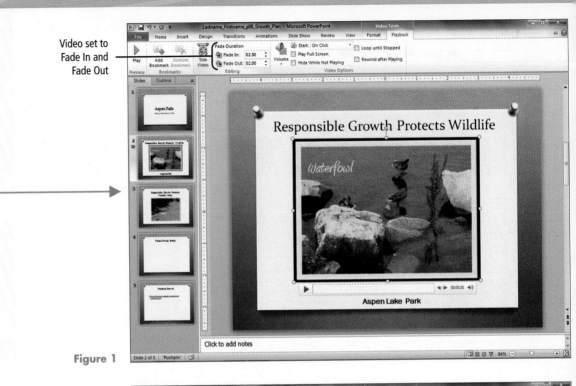

Video set to Fade In and Fade Out

Figure 1

Start Automatically selected

Rewind after Playing selected

Figure 2

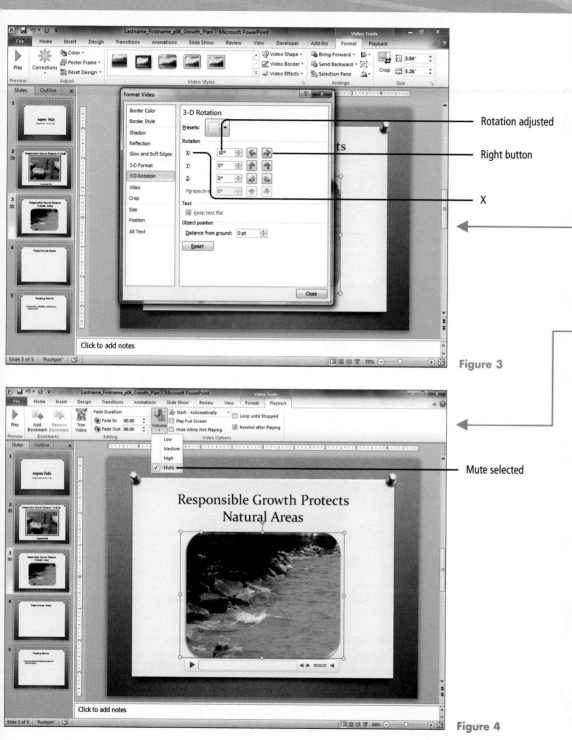

Figure 3

Figure 4

7. With the video selected, click the **Format tab**, and then in the **Video Styles group**, click the **More** button.

8. Under **Intense**, click **Bevel Rectangle**—the second choice in the third row.

9. Click the **Video Effects** button, point to **Preset**, and then click **3-D Options**. In the **Format Video** dialog box, in the left pane, click **3-D Rotation**. Under **Rotation**, for **X** click the **Right** button two times to adjust the rotation to **10**. Compare your screen with **Figure 3**, and then in the **Video Format** dialog box, click the **Close** button.

10. To eliminate sound from the video, on the **Playback tab**, in the **Video Options group**, click the **Volume** button, and then click **Mute**, as shown in **Figure 4**.

11. Press [F5] and then preview all of the options you applied to the videos. Right-click and end the show after **Slide 3**.

12. **Save** the presentation.

■ **You have completed Skill 2 of 10**

Labels on figures: "Rotation adjusted", "Right button", "X", "Mute selected"

▶ *Hyperlinks* connect your presentation to other files, websites, or other slides in the same presentation.

▶ Hyperlinks can include a *ScreenTip*—a box that contains information about an image or a hyperlink that displays when you point to the hyperlink.

1. Display **Slide 1**, and then select *Aspen Falls*. On the **Insert tab**, in the **Links group**, click the **Hyperlink** button.

2. In the **Insert Hyperlink** dialog box, under **Link to**, verify that **Existing File or Web Page** is selected. In the **Address** box, type http://www.ca.gov/HomeFamily/Housing.html and then compare your screen with **Figure 1**.

3. Click the **ScreenTip** button, and then in the displayed **Set Hyperlink ScreenTip** dialog box, in the **ScreenTip** box, type Growth rates in California Click **OK** two times to close both dialog boxes.

   The text displays with an underline and alternate color to indicate that the text is a hyperlink.

4. On **Slide 1**, select *Responsible Growth Plan*. On the **Insert tab**, in the **Links group**, click the **Hyperlink** button.

5. With **Existing File or Web Page** selected, click the **Look In arrow** to display files on your computer. Navigate to your student files, and then locate the Word document named **p06_Growth_Guidelines**. Click **p06_Growth_Guidelines**.

6. Click the **ScreenTip** button. Type Growth Plan document and then click **OK** in each dialog box. Click a blank area of the slide to deselect the text and compare your screen with **Figure 2**.

■ **Continue to the next page to complete the skill**

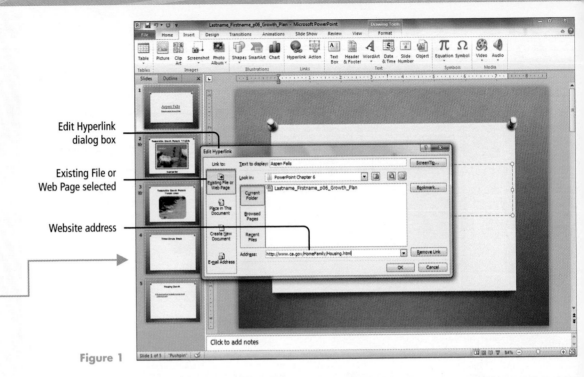

Edit Hyperlink dialog box

Existing File or Web Page selected

Website address

Figure 1

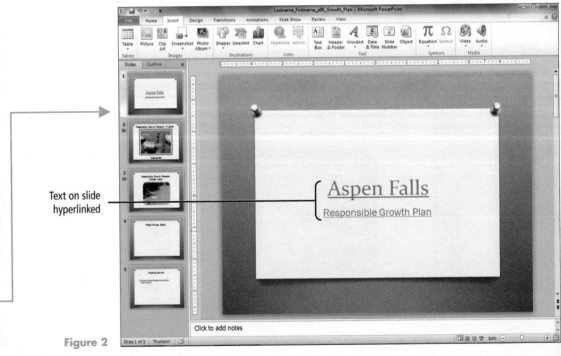

Text on slide hyperlinked

Figure 2

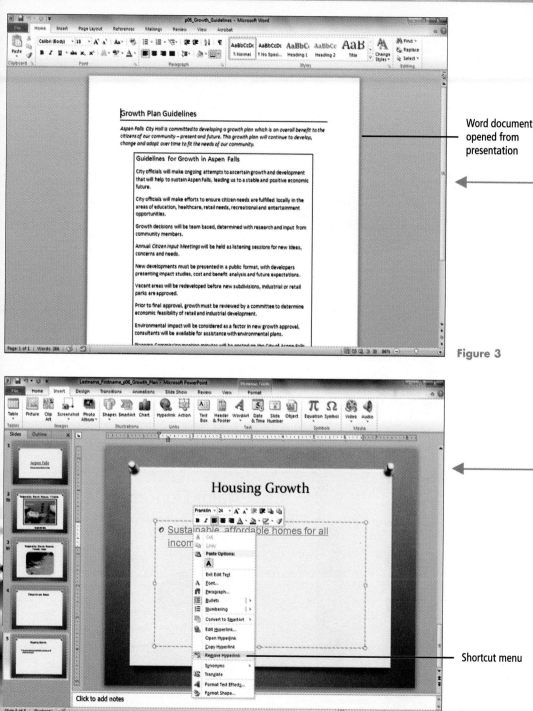

Word document opened from presentation

Figure 3

Shortcut menu

Figure 4

7. **Save** 💾 your presentation, and then click the **Slide Show** 🖵 button. On **Slide 1**, move your mouse over the title *Aspen Falls*. When the mouse pointer 👆 displays, click to open the linked webpage. View the webpage, and then **Close** ✖ the browser window.

8. Click the subtitle *Responsible Growth Plan*. Wait a few moments for the Word document to display, as shown in **Figure 3**.

9. **Close** ✖ Word to return to the slide show. Right-click anywhere in the background of **Slide 1**, and then from the displayed shortcut menu, click **End Show**.

10. Display **Slide 5**. Right-click the hyperlink with the text *Sustainable, affordable homes for all income levels*. Compare your screen with **Figure 4**, and then from the shortcut menu, click **Remove Hyperlink**.

    The text remains, but the hyperlink is removed because the information was outdated. It is important to regularly check and maintain hyperlinks. Outdated hyperlinks should be updated or deleted.

11. **Save** 💾 the presentation.

    ■ **You have completed Skill 3 of 10**

▶ Excel charts and items from other programs can be placed into a PowerPoint presentation.

▶ Excel charts can be modified in PowerPoint so they display effectively during a presentation.

1. Display **Slide 3**, and then insert a new **Slide 4** with the **Title Only** layout. In the title placeholder, type Major Donors

2. Click the **Start** button ⊙, locate and **Open** Excel. Click **File**, and then click **Open**. Navigate to your student·files for this chapter, click **p06_Growth_Donors**, and then click **Open**.

3. If necessary, **Maximize** the window. Click the upper left corner of the chart to select it, as shown in **Figure 1**.

4. On the **Home tab**, in the **Clipboard group**, click the **Copy** 📋 button, and then **Close** ⊠ Excel.

   The chart is stored in the system clipboard.

5. Make PowerPoint the active window. On **Slide 4**, click a blank area below the title placeholder so that nothing is selected. On the **Home tab**, in the **Clipboard group**, click the **Paste** button.

   The chart style now matches the presentation color scheme.

6. In the **Chart Tools Format** tab, increase the **Shape Height** to 4.6". Compare your screen with **Figure 2**.

■ **Continue to the next page to complete the skill**

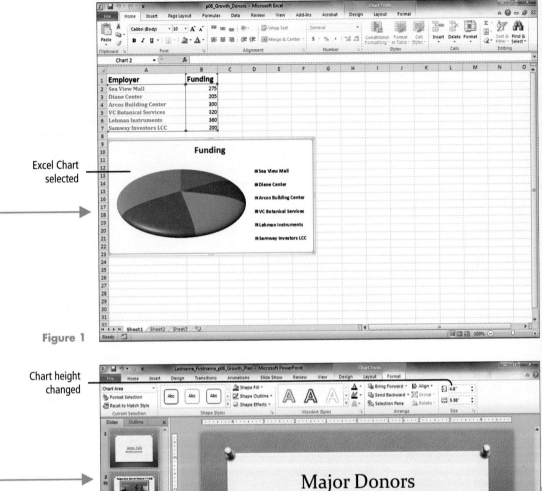

Excel Chart selected

Figure 1

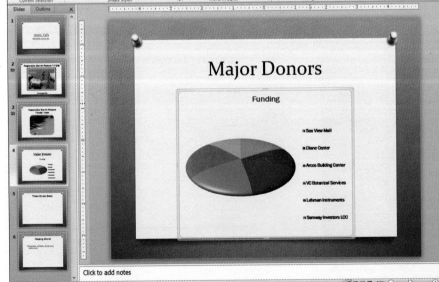

Chart height changed

Figure 2

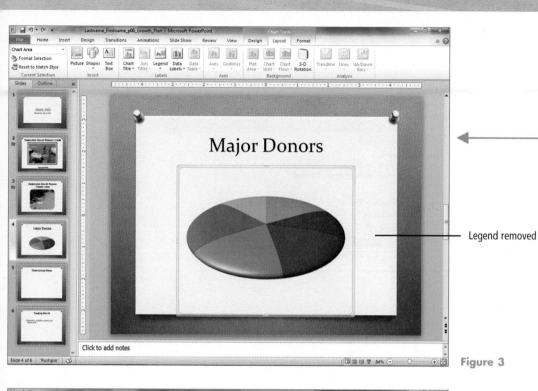

Legend removed

Figure 3

Lehman
Instruments
slice exploded

Figure 4

7. Click one time on the chart title *Funding* to select it, and then press Delete to remove the title.

8. Click the **Layout tab**, and in the **Labels group**, click **Legend**. Click **None Turn off Legend**. Compare your screen with **Figure 3**.

9. With the chart still selected, on the **Layout tab**, in the **Labels group**, click the **Data Labels** button, and then click **More Data Label Options**.

10. In the **Format Data Labels** dialog box, under **Label Contains**, select **Category Name** and **Percentage**, and then deselect—remove the check mark from—**Value**.

11. In the **Format Data Labels** dialog box, under **Label Position**, click **Center**, and then click **Close**. Click a blank area of slide to deselect chart.

12. Over the **Lehman Instruments** slice of the pie chart, click one time to select the slice. Drag the slice directly left to explode this slice. Compare your screen with **Figure 4**.

   The Lehman Instruments slice stands out.

13. **Save** 🖫 the presentation.

   ■ **You have completed Skill 4 of 10**

▶ Items pasted into presentations from other Office applications can be linked so that when the original file is changed, the same changes will be reflected in the presentation.

▶ The *source file* refers to the original file from which the items are copied, and the *destination file* refers to the file in which the items are pasted.

1. Display **Slide 5**. On the **Home tab**, in the **Slides group**, click the **New Slide** button to insert a new **Slide 6** with the **Title and Content** layout.

2. In the title placeholder, type Citizen Survey

3. In the content placeholder, type Survey distributed via mass mailing to gauge feelings about managed growth

4. **Start** Microsoft Word. Click the **File tab** and in **Backstage** view, click **Open**. Navigate to your student files, and then open **p06_Growth_Survey**. Click the **File tab** and in **Backstage** view, click **Save As**. Name the file Lastname_Firstname_ p06_Growth_Survey and then **Save** it in your **PowerPoint Chapter 6** folder.

5. On the **Home tab**, in the **Editing group**, click the **Select** button, and then click **Select All**. Alternately, press Ctrl + A. On the **Home tab**, in the **Clipboard group**, click the **Copy** 🔾 button. Compare your screen with **Figure 1**.

6. Switch to the PowerPoint window. On the **Home tab**, in the **Clipboard group**, click the **Paste button arrow**, and then click **Paste Special**. Select **Paste link** as shown in **Figure 2**, and then click **OK**.

    Paste Special pastes items as HTML, device-independent bitmap images, or links into a specified file. It creates an updateable link between a source and destination file.

■ **Continue to the next page to complete the skill**

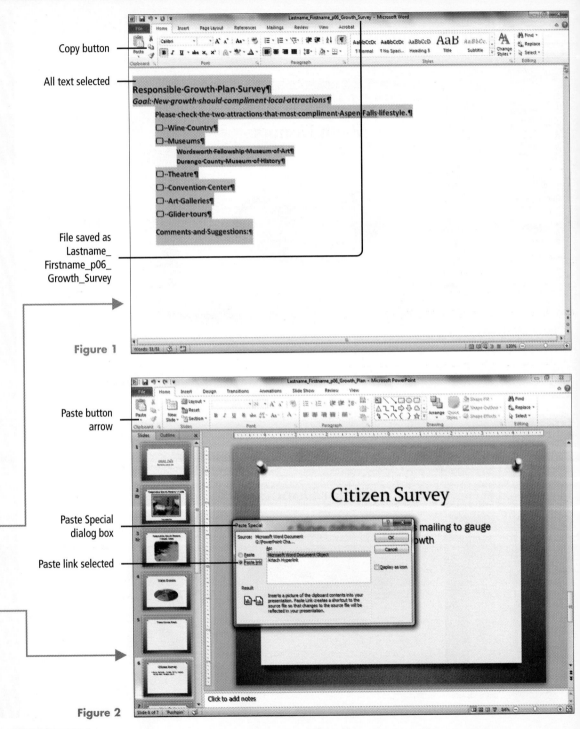

Copy button

All text selected

File saved as Lastname_ Firstname_p06_ Growth_Survey

Figure 1

Paste button arrow

Paste Special dialog box

Paste link selected

Figure 2

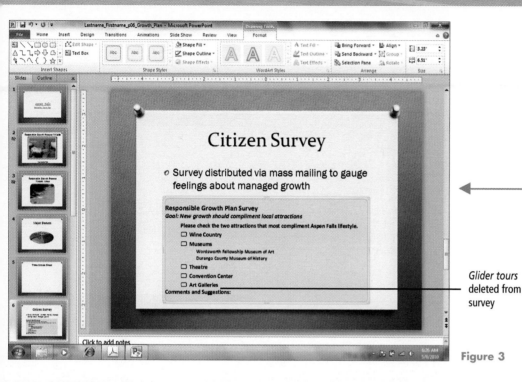

Glider tours deleted from survey

Figure 3

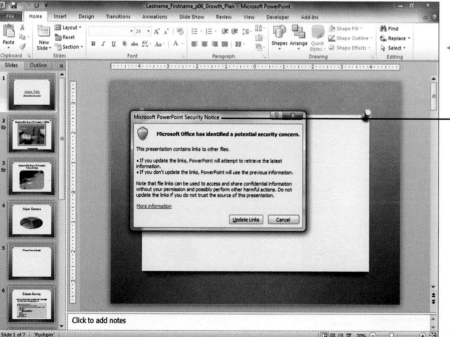

Microsoft PowerPoint Security Notice dialog box

Figure 4

7. With the mouse pointer 🖑, drag the pasted item below the text already on the slide.

8. On the **Drawing Tools Contextual tab**, click the **Format tab**. In the **Shape Styles group**, click **Shape Fill**, and then under **Theme Colors**, select **Ice Blue, Background 2**—the third color in the top row.

9. Notice that the last item in the survey is *Glider tours*. Switch to the Word document **Lastname_Firstname_p06_Growth_Survey**. Select the entire bullet point with the text *Glider tours*, and then press Delete. Click **Save** 🔲 and then **Close** ☒ Word.

10. Switch to the PowerPoint window, and then verify that *Glider tours* was deleted as shown in **Figure 3**.

    When items are linked and saved, changes to the source document are also made in the destination file.

11. **Save** 🔲, and then **Close** ☒ the presentation. **Start** PowerPoint, click the **File tab**, point to **Recent**, and then click to open **Lastname_Firstname_p06_Growth_Plan**. Compare your screen with **Figure 4**.

    The Microsoft Office PowerPoint Security Notice informs you that the file contains links to other files. You should update the links only when you are sure the source file can be trusted. Trust source files only if you are sure the file's original source is credible; otherwise, scan the file for viruses before updating.

12. Click **Update Links**.

    When the Update Links button is clicked, PowerPoint checks the source file for changes and applies those changes to the presentation.

▪ **You have completed Skill 5 of 10**

► *Action settings* are settings applied to objects—buttons, shapes, pictures, or clip art—so you can navigate to a specific slide, open a webpage, or play a sound by clicking.

1. Display **Slide 1**. On the **Insert tab**, in the **Illustrations group**, click **Shapes**, and then under **Action Buttons**, click **Action Button: Home**, as shown in **Figure 1**.

2. Place the mouse pointer ⊞ under the center of the subtitle, and then click one time to insert the **Action Button Home** shape.

3. In the **Action Settings** dialog box, click the **Hyperlink to: list arrow**. Click **Last Slide**.

> When an action button shape is inserted, the Action Settings dialog box displays with settings common for that shape. The Home shape fits the theme of the presentation, and while this shape is sometimes used to indicate a "home" location, it can be linked to any slide.

4. Select the **Play Sound** check box, and then click the **list arrow**. Select **Click**, and then click **OK**.

> When the presenter clicks the Home Action Button, a click sound will play, and the presentation will move to the last slide.

5. On the **Format tab**, in the **Shape Styles group**, click the **More** ⋥ **arrow**, and then click **Subtle Effect – Black, Dark 1**—the first choice in the fourth row. Compare your screen with **Figure 2**.

■ **Continue to the next page to complete the skill**

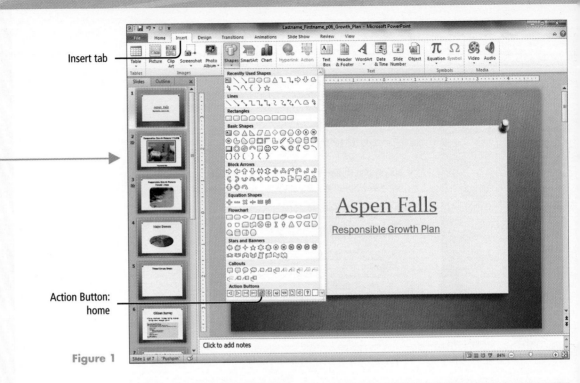

Insert tab

Action Button: home

Figure 1

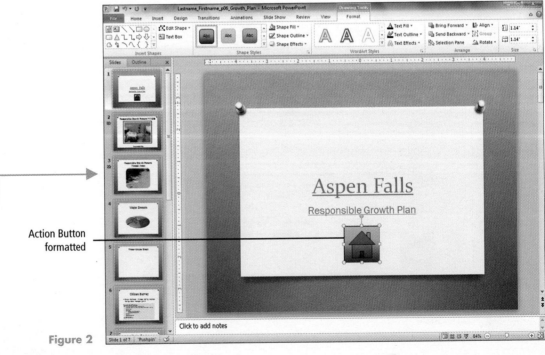

Action Button formatted

Figure 2

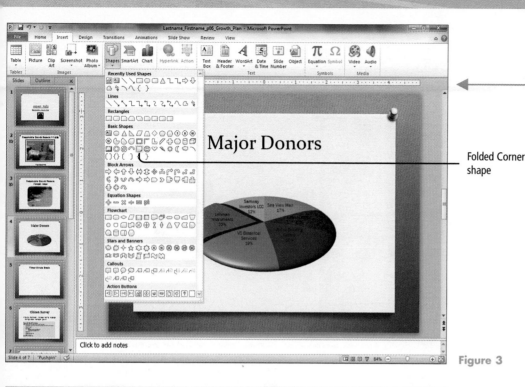

Folded Corner shape

Figure 3

6. Display **Slide 4**. On the **Insert tab**, in the **Illustrations group**, click **Shapes**.

7. Under **Basic Shapes**, click **Folded Corner**, as shown in **Figure 3**.

8. Point to the lower right corner of the slide, and then click to insert the **Folded Corner** shape. Using the mouse pointer, if necessary, move the shape to the lower corner of the paper graphic on the slide. With the shape selected, type Survey

9. With the shape still selected, on the **Format tab**, in the **Shape Styles Gallery**, click **Subtle Effect – Black, Dark 1**—the same theme you applied to the shape on **Slide 1**.

10. With the shape still selected, on the **Insert tab**, in the **Links group**, click **Action**.

11. In the **Action Settings** dialog box, click **Hyperlink to**, and then click the **list arrow**. Scroll down and click **Slide**.

12. In the **Hyperlink to Slide** dialog box, click **6. Citizen Survey** as shown in **Figure 4**.

13. Click **OK**, and then in the displayed **Action Settings** dialog box, click **OK**.

14. If you have speakers, turn them on, or insert headphones into the computer. Press F5 to start the slide show from the beginning. View the slide show, and then click the action button on **Slide 4**. End the show, and then **Save** the presentation.

■ **You have completed Skill 6 of 10**

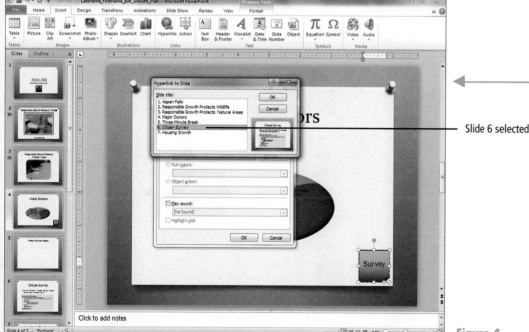

Slide 6 selected

Figure 4

► Presentations often include timed breaks—breaks given during a presentation. ***Timed break slides*** are used to plan and control the length of breaks in a presentation.

1. Display **Slide 5**, and then in the speaker's notes, type Give participants a three-minute break. When the spinner turns red, ask them to find their seats.

2. In Normal view, on the **Insert tab**, in the **Illustrations group**, click the **Shapes** button. Under **Stars and Banners**, click the **12-Point Star**.

3. In the center of the slide, click to insert a **Star** shape. On the **Format tab**, in the **Size group**, adjust the **Shape Height** to 3" and the **Shape Width** to 3" and then drag the shape to the center of the slide.

4. With the **Star** shape still selected, type Take a short break!

5. On the **Format tab**, in the **Shape Styles group**, click the **Shape Effects** button. Point to **Bevel**, and then click **Art Deco**—the last shape in the gallery. Click **Shape Fill**, and then click **Indigo, Text 2, Darker 50%**—the last choice in the fourth column. Compare your screen with **Figure 1**.

6. On the **Animations tab**, in the **Advanced Animation group**, click **Add Animation**. Under **Emphasis**, click **Spin**.

7. In the **Timing group**, click the **Start box arrow**, and then click **With Previous**.

    The With Previous option sets the effect to begin with the mouse click that advanced the presentation to the current slide.

8. In the **Duration** box, type 5 and then press Enter to adjust the spin speed, and then compare your screen with **Figure 2**.

■ **Continue to the next page to complete the skill**

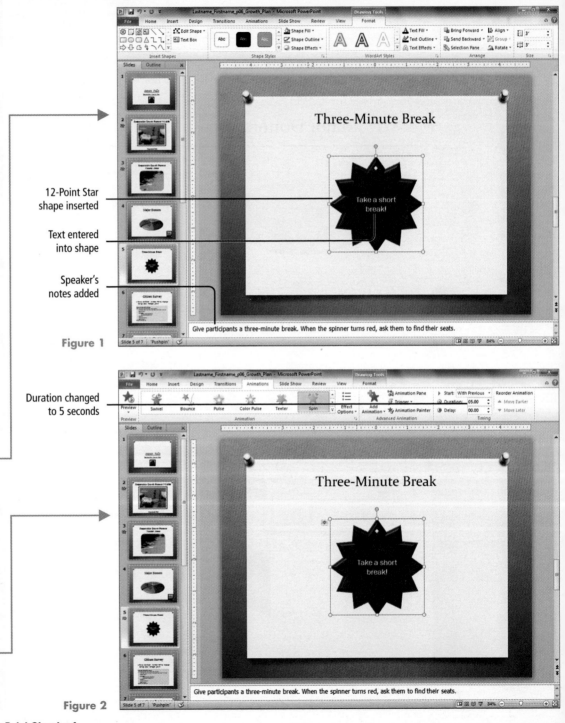

12-Point Star shape inserted

Text entered into shape

Speaker's notes added

Figure 1

Duration changed to 5 seconds

Figure 2

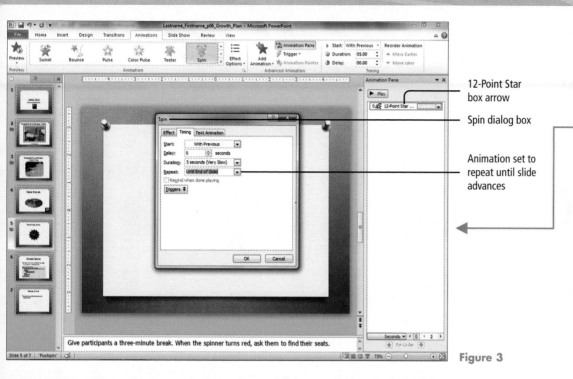

12-Point Star
box arrow

Spin dialog box

Animation set to
repeat until slide
advances

Give participants a three-minute break. When the spinner turns red, ask them to find their seats.

Figure 3

9. In the **Advanced Animation group**, click the **Animation Pane** button. In the **Animation Pane**, click the **12-Point Star box arrow**, and then click **Timing**. In the **Spin** dialog box, click the **Repeat** arrow, and then click **Until End of Slide**. Compare your screen with **Figure 3**.

> The Until End of Slide option repeats the animation—in this case, spinning—until the presentation is advanced to the next slide.

10. Click **OK** to close the **Spin** dialog box. On the **Transitions tab**, in the **Timing group**, select the **After** check box, and then type 02:30.00 Leave **On Mouse Click** selected.

11. On the **Home tab**, in the **Slides group**, click the **New Slide button arrow**, and then click **Duplicate Selected Slides**.

12. On the new slide, replace the shape's text with Back to work On the **Format tab**, in the **Shape Styles group**, click the **Shape Fill** button, and then click **Red, Accent 2, Darker 50%**—the last option in the sixth column.

13. On the **Transitions tab**, in the **Timing group**, under **Advance Slide**, adjust the **After** box to 0:30.00

14. Click **Save** 🖫. Press F5 to view the presentation from the beginning. When you come to the three-minute break slide, notice the animation. Compare your screen with **Figure 4**.

15. Click to advance to the next slide. Verify that the second animation runs for 30 seconds and the presentation advances to the next slide. End the show, and then **Close** ☒ the **Animation Pane**.

■ **You have completed Skill 7 of 10**

Three-Minute Break

Take a short break!

Timed break slide

Figure 4

▶ *Sound effects* are prebuilt sounds that play for specific events such as a slide transition or when clicking an object that has action settings applied.

▶ Sound effects should enhance—not detract—from the presentation.

1. Navigate to **Slide 5**. On the **Insert tab**, in the **Media group**, click the **Audio button arrow**, and then click **Clip Art Audio**.

2. In the **Clip Art** task pane, type Thankful People in the **Search for** box and click **Go** to insert the file. Compare your screen with **Figure 1**.

    A sound icon displays in the middle of the slide.

3. **Close** ☒ the Clip Art task pane.

4. On the **Playback tab**, in the **Audio Options group**, select the **Loop until Stopped** option.

    The sound clip will play during the break, until the slide is advanced either by clicking or automatically.

5. Drag the speaker icon to the lower right corner of the slide. Click the **Play/Pause** ▶ button to hear the audio clip. Click a blank area of the slide to stop playing the clip. Compare your screen with **Figure 2**.

6. Display **Slide 8**. On the **Home tab**, in the **Slides group**, click the **New Slide button arrow**, and then click the **Section Header** thumbnail.

■ **Continue to the next page to complete the skill**

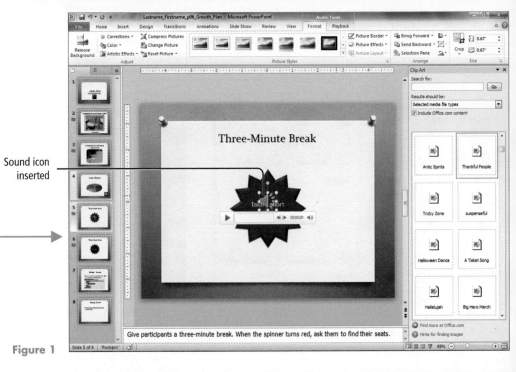

Sound icon inserted

Figure 1

Speaker icon moved

Figure 2

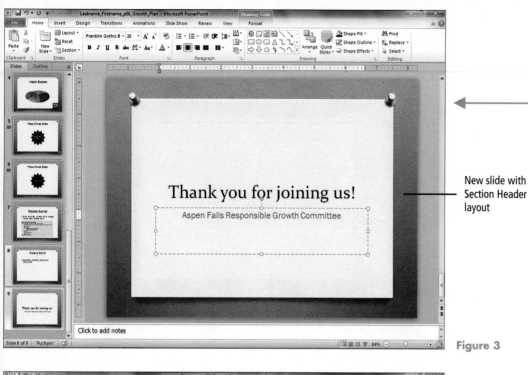

New slide with
Section Header
layout

Figure 3

Sound added
to transition

Duration adjusted

Glitter transition
applied

Figure 4

7. On the slide just inserted, in the title placeholder, type Thank you for joining us!

8. In the content placeholder, type Aspen Falls Responsible Growth Committee and then compare your screen with **Figure 3**.

9. On **Slide 9**, on the **Transitions tab**, in the **Transition to this Slide group**, click the **More** arrow, and then, under **Exciting**, click **Glitter**.

10. On the **Transitions tab**, in the **Timing group**, click the **Sound box arrow**, click **Chime**, and then adjust the **Duration** to 02.50. Compare your screen with **Figure 4**.

11. Be sure that speakers are on, or insert headphones. Display **Slide 5**, and then click the **Slide Show** 🖳 button. During the slide show, click the sound icon in the lower right corner to begin playing the audio track. Click to move through the slides and listen to the sound effects and view the transition just applied.

12. End the show, and then **Save** 🖬 the presentation.

■ **You have completed Skill 8 of 10**

▶ Pictures can be added to your entire slide as background or to just part of your slide as a *watermark*.

▶ Adding a *washout effect* to a picture increases brightness and decreases contrast so that the image does not detract from other slide objects.

1. Navigate to **Slide 9**.

2. On the **Insert tab**, in the **Images group**, click the **Clip Art** button. In the **Clip Art** task pane, in the **Search for** box, type Lake

3. Under **Results should be**, click the **box arrow**, and then select only **Photographs**. Compare your screen with **Figure 1**.

4. Click the **Go** button. If no results display, be sure that the *Include Office.com content* box is selected. Click to insert the photo shown, and then **Close** ☒ the **Clip Art** task pane. If necessary, substitute a similar photo of a nature setting. Compare your screen with **Figure 2**.

5. With the picture still selected, on the Format tab, in the Size group, adjust Shape Height and Width so that the picture covers the paper.

6. With the mouse pointer 🔩, drag the picture to center it on the paper in the middle of the slide.

■ **Continue to the next page to complete the skill**

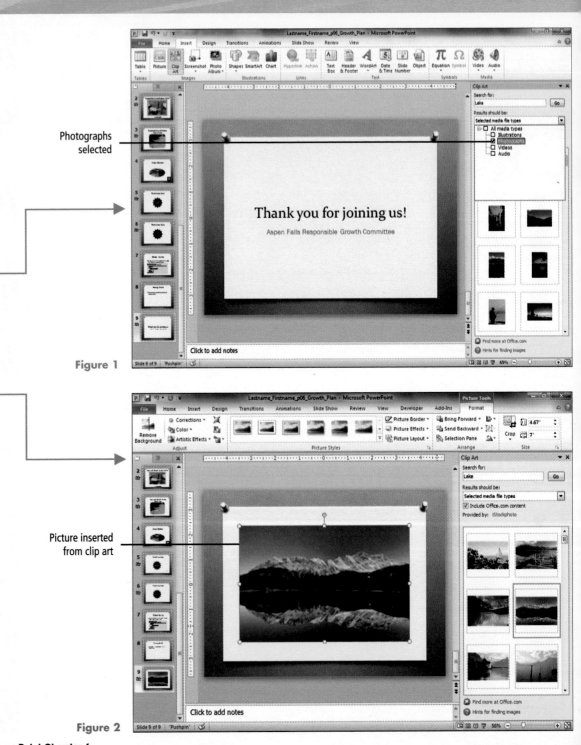

Photographs selected

Figure 1

Picture inserted from clip art

Figure 2

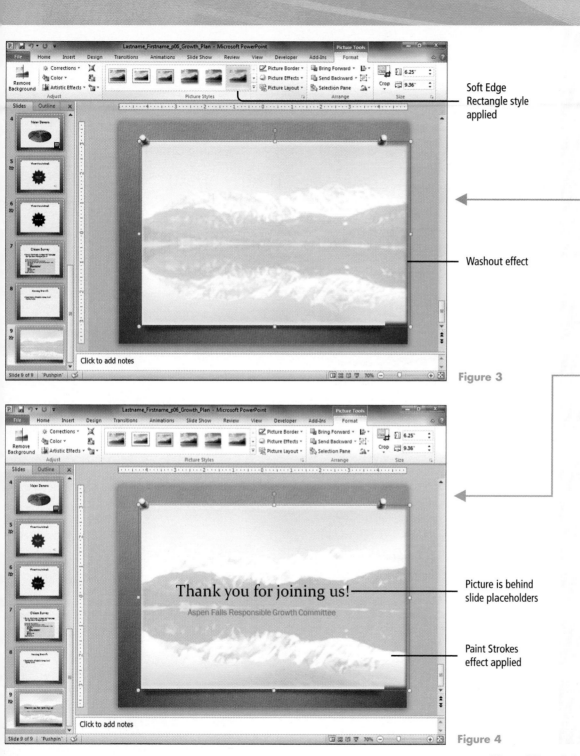

Soft Edge
Rectangle style
applied

Washout effect

Figure 3

Picture is behind
slide placeholders

Paint Strokes
effect applied

Figure 4

7. With the picture still selected, on the **Format tab**, in the **Adjust group**, click **Color**. In the displayed gallery, under **Recolor**, click the fourth thumbnail in the first row—**Washout**.

8. With the picture still selected, on the **Format tab**, in the **Picture Styles group**, click **Soft Edge Rectangle**—the sixth choice in the **Picture Styles Gallery**. Compare your screen with **Figure 3**.

9. On the **Format tab**, in the **Arrange group**, click the **Send Backward arrow**, and then click **Send to Back**.

   The picture now moves behind the slide's content placeholder text. In this manner, images can be placed behind other objects.

10. On the **Format tab**, in the **Adjust group**, click **Artistic Effects**. Click **Paint Strokes**—the second choice in the second row. Compare your screen with **Figure 4**.

11. Click the **Slide Show** button to view the slide. End the show, and then **Save** the presentation.

■ **You have completed Skill 9 of 10**

► ***Organization charts*** are used to show the hierarchy within an organization or process.

► Organization chart layouts, like other SmartArt graphics that provide predesigned layouts, can be customized.

1. Display **Slide 8**. On the **Insert tab**, in the **Illustrations group**, click the **SmartArt** button.

2. In the left pane of the displayed **Choose A SmartArt Graphic** dialog box, click **Hierarchy**. In the right pane, click **Horizontal Labeled Hierarchy**—the first choice in the fourth row. Click **OK**, and then compare your screen with **Figure 1**.

3. Click the up arrow on the left border of graphic to display the **Type your text here** pane. In the **Type your text here** pane, enter the text in the order shown in **Figure 2**, using the arrow keys or clicking to move to a new line.

■ **Continue to the next page to complete the skill**

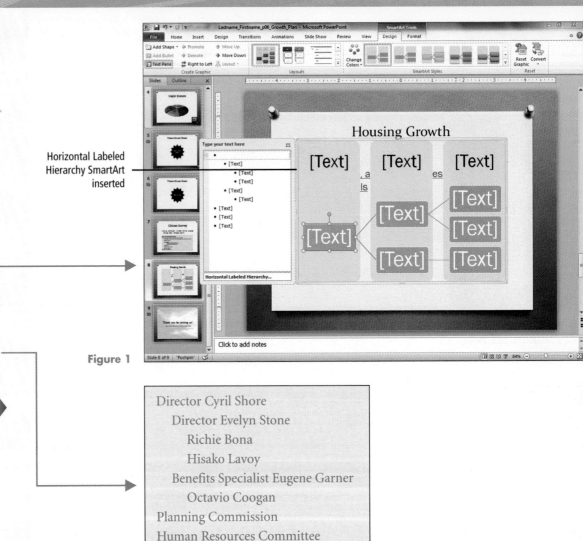

Horizontal Labeled Hierarchy SmartArt inserted

Figure 1

Director Cyril Shore
  Director Evelyn Stone
    Richie Bona
    Hisako Lavoy
  Benefits Specialist Eugene Garner
    Octavio Coogan
Planning Commission
Human Resources Committee
Responsible Growth Committee

Figure 2

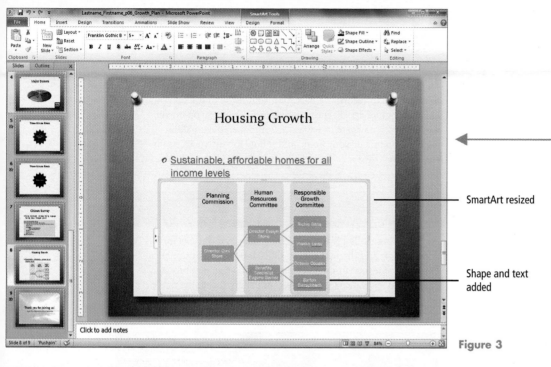

SmartArt resized

Shape and text added

Figure 3

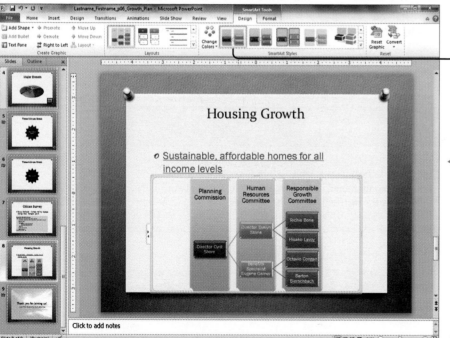

Polished SmartArt style selected

Figure 4

4. **Close** the **Type your text here** pane. Click the **Octavio Coogan** shape to select it. Under the **SmartArt Tools contextual tab**, on the **Design tab**, in the **Create Graphic group**, click the **Add Shape** button, and then type Barton Bierschbach

5. Select the entire SmartArt shape, point to the border, and then with the mouse pointer ⟦⟧, drag to extend the bottom edge of the SmartArt border even with the bottom edge of the paper image on slide.

6. Point to the top center sizing handle. With the mouse pointer ⟦⟧, drag the top edge of the SmartArt graphic so that it displays under the bulleted text. Compare your screen with **Figure 3**.

7. With the chart still selected, on the **Design tab**, in the **SmartArt Styles group**, click the **Change Colors** button. Under **Colorful**, click the third thumbnail—**Colorful Range - Accent Colors 3 to 4**.

8. With the chart still selected, on the **Design tab**, in the **SmartArt Styles group**, click the **More** ⊡ button, and then under **3D**, click the first choice—**Polished**. Compare your screen with **Figure 4**.

9. On the **Insert tab**, in the **Text group**, click the **Header & Footer** button. In the **Header and Footer** dialog box, on the **Notes and Handouts tab**, select **Footer**. In the **Footer** box, type Lastname_Firstname_p06_Growth_Plan and then click **Apply to All**.

10. **Save** 🖫, and then **Close** ☒ PowerPoint. Print or submit as directed by your instructor.

Done! You have completed Skill 10 of 10 and your presentation is complete!

The following More Skills are located at **www.pearsonhighered.com/skills**

More Skills Record and Play Narrations

Narrations can be recorded to accompany a presentation. This is useful for presentations that run at public events such as trade shows or that are presented over the Internet.

In More Skills 11, you will rehearse a presentation, use a microphone to record the narration, and listen to the presentation using computer speakers or headphones. To begin, open your web browser, navigate to www.pearsonhighered.com/skills, locate the name of your book, and follow the instructions on the website.

More Skills Add Rehearsal Timings

Rehearsal timings provide the elapsed time for each slide and the total time for the entire presentation so that you can judge the length of your presentation. You can also use rehearsal timings to play a slide show automatically—a slide advances automatically when the elapsed time for that slide expires.

In More Skills 12, you will create rehearsal timings for a presentation and then set up the slide show to run automatically using the rehearsal timings. To begin, open your web browser, navigate to www.pearsonhighered.com/skills, locate the name of your book, and follow the instructions on the website.

More Skills Insert Songs

Music from your personal collecion can be linked to a slide and played during the presentation. Including music during key parts of a presentation adds emotional impact. Choose music that conveys the feelings you want your audience to experience during your presentation.

In More Skills 13, you will link your presentation to a song from your personal collection or one provided by your instructor. To begin, open your web browser, navigate to www.pearsonhighered.com/skills, locate the name of your book, and follow the instructions on the website.

More Skills Download and Apply Microsoft Office Templates

Microsoft Office 2010 includes built-in templates and themes that can be applied to any Word document, Excel worksheet, or PowerPoint presentation. Additional templates and themes can be downloaded from the Internet and then applied to your Office 2010 files.

In More Skills 14, you will download and apply a new template. To begin, open your web browser, navigate to www.pearsonhighered.com/skills, locate the name of your book, and follow the instructions on the website.

Key Terms

Action setting. 214

Destination file 212

Hyperlink 208

Multimedia. 204

Multimedia object 200

Organization chart 222

Paste Special. 212

Poster Frame 205

ScreenTip 208

Sound effect 218

Source file. 212

Timed break slide 216

Trimming 204

Video style 205

Watermark 220

Washout effect 220

Online Help Skills

1. **Start** PowerPoint. In the upper right corner of the PowerPoint window, click the **Help** 🔘 button. In the **Help** window, click the **Maximize** 🔲 button.

2. Click in the search box, type Optimize the media in your presentation and then click the **Search** 🔍 button. In the search results, click **Optimize the media in your presentation for compatibility**. Compare your screen with Figure 1.

Figure 1

3. Read the article and then see if you can answer the following question: What are some of the compatibility issues that might occur in a presentation that contains media clips? How can you avoid these issues?

Matching

Match each term in the second column with its correct definition in the first column by writing the letter of the term on the blank line in front of the correct definition.

____ **1.** A method of connecting a presentation with other files, webpages, or slides.

____ **2.** A box that displays information about a hyperlink when you point to the hyperlink.

____ **3.** An event—moving to another slide or opening a file, for example—that occurs in response to a click.

____ **4.** Slides used to plan and control the length of pauses in a presentation.

____ **5.** Option that sets the effect to begin with the mouse click that advanced the presentation to the current slide.

____ **6.** A color effect that increases a picture's brightness and decreases its contrast.

____ **7.** A picture that can be added to your entire slide as background or to just part of your slide.

____ **8.** A predesigned layout such as a list, process, cycle, hierarchy, or relationship.

____ **9.** An introductory frame that displays before the video begins playing.

____ **10.** A SmartArt layout that illustrates the hierarchy within an organization.

A Action

B Hyperlink

C Organization chart

D Poster Frame

E ScreenTip

F SmartArt

G Timed break slides

H Washout

I Watermark

J With Previous

Multiple Choice

Choose the correct answer.

1. To reduce the length of a video, on the Playback tab, in the Editing group, click this button.
   A. Trim Video
   B. Clip Art
   C. Reduce Length

2. Enhancements—frames and effects—that can be applied to add interest and a finished look to the video you have included in your presentation are called these.
   A. Page colors
   B. Video effects
   C. Video styles

3. To delete a hyperlink, right-click the hyperlink, and then from the shortcut menu, click this option.
   A. Remove Hyperlink
   B. Insert Hyperlink
   C. Edit Hyperlink

4. To drag one slice of a pie chart outward, so that it stands out, is to do this to that section.
   A. Explode
   B. Resize
   C. Increase

5. The location or file to which the source data is copied or linked is called this type of file.
   A. Source
   B. Original
   C. Destination

6. The file from which an object is copied is referred to as this type of file.
   A. Destination
   B. Source
   C. Linked

7. A shape that automatically opens the Action Settings dialog box when the shape is inserted into a slide is called this.
   A. Action Button
   B. Enhanced Shape
   C. Animation Setting

8. To decrease clutter and at the same time increase functionality, add this to a slide.
   A. WordArt
   B. Sounds
   C. Hyperlinks

9. To animate a single shape inserted into a slide, on the Animations tab, click this button.
   A. Add Animation
   B. Rehearse Timings
   C. Transition Speed

10. A speaker icon on a slide indicates that this has been inserted.
    A. Transition
    B. Timing
    C. Sound

Topics for Discussion

1. What are the benefits of adding multimedia objects—including movies, sounds, and actions—to a presentation? Discuss the advantages and disadvantages of adding multimedia objects.

2. What are three things important to consider when linking slides to other files?

Skill Check

To complete this project, you will need the following files:

- p06_Home_Sales
- p06_Home_Video
- p06_Home_Relocate
- p06_Home_Park
- p06_Home_Chart

You will save your files as:

- Lastname_Firstname_p06_Home_Sales
- Lastname_Firstname_p06_Home_Relocate

1. **Start** PowerPoint, and then open **p06_Home_Sales**. **Save** the file in your **PowerPoint Chapter 6** folder as Lastname_Firstname_p06_Home_Sales

2. Display **Slide 1**, and then select the title *Home Sales*. On the **Insert tab**, in the **Links group**, click **Hyperlink**. In the **Insert Hyperlink** dialog box, in the **Address** box, type http://www.hcd.ca.gov Click the **ScreenTip** button, and then in the **ScreenTip** text box, type California housing information and resources Click **OK**, and then click **OK** in the **Insert Hyperlink** dialog box.

3. Display **Slide 2**. On the **Insert tab**, in the **Media group**, click the **Video button arrow**. Click **Video from File**. In the **Insert Video** dialog box, navigate to the student files for this chapter, click **p06_Home_Video**, and then click **Insert**. On the **Playback tab**, in the **Video Options group**, verify that **On Click** displays in the **Start** box, and then compare your screen with **Figure 1**. ─────

Figure 1

4. Display **Slide 3**. On the **Transitions tab**, in the **Timing group**, click **After**, and then type 03:00.00 in the box.

5. **Start** Word, and then open **p06_Home_Relocate**. **Save** the file in your **PowerPoint Chapter 6** folder as Lastname_Firstname_p06_Home_Relocate

6. Select the first group of bullet points, from *Housing for all income levels* through *Citizen driven city government*. On the **Home tab**, in the **Clipboard group**, click **Copy**.

7. In PowerPoint, display **Slide 4**. In the content placeholder, type New citizens enjoy and then press [Enter].

8. On the **Home tab**, in the **Clipboard group**, click the **Paste button arrow**, and then click **Paste Special**. Select the **Paste link** option button, and then click **OK**.

9. On the **Format tab**, in the **Size group**, change the **Shape Width** box to 8.5" Drag the linked object's border so that the bullets display under the *N* in *New*. Compare your screen with **Figure 2**. ─────

Figure 2

- **Continue to the next page to complete this Skill Check**

Figure 3

Figure 4

10. Switch to the Word document. Select the first bullet, *Housing for all income levels*, and then press Delete. **Save** the document, and then **Close** Word.

11. On **Slide 4**, on the **Insert tab**, in the **Media group**, click the **Audio button arrow**, and then click **Clip Art Audio**.

12. In the **Clip Art** task pane, click **Claps Cheers** or another appropriate sound clip.

13. Drag the sound icon to the upper right corner of the slide. Deselect the sound icon. **Close** the **Clip Art** task pane. Compare your screen with **Figure 3**.

14. On **Slide 4**, select the picture. On the **Insert tab**, in the **Links group**, click the **Action** button. Click the **Hyperlink to** option button. In the **Action Settings** dialog box, click the **Hyperlink to box arrow**, scroll down and select **Last Slide**, and then click **OK**.

15. **Start** Excel, and then open **p06_Home_Chart**. Click one time to select the chart, and then click **Copy**. **Close** Excel.

16. Display **Slide 5**. On the **Home tab**, in the **Clipboard group**, click **Paste**. On the **Format tab**, in the **Size group**, change the **Shape Height** to 5" and the **Shape Width** to 7" With the chart selected, on the **Home tab**, in the **Font group**, change the **Font Size** to **18**. Drag the chart to center it on the slide.

17. Display **Slide 6**. Select the diagram. On the **SmartArt Tools contextual tab**, on the **Design tab**, in the **Create Graphic group**, click **Add Shape**. In the newly inserted shape, type Firstname Lastname, Land Trust Inc.

18. Display **Slide 7**. On the **Insert tab**, in the **Images group**, click the **Picture** button. From your student files, double-click **p06_Home_Park** to insert the picture.

19. With the picture selected, on the **Format tab**, in the **Adjust group**, click the **Color** button. Under **Recolor**, click the fourth thumbnail—**Washout**. In the **Arrange group**, click the **Send Backward arrow**, and then click **Send to Back**. Compare your screen with **Figure 4**.

20. On the **Insert tab**, in the **Text group**, click the **Header & Footer** button. On the **Notes and Handouts tab**, select the footer box, and in the **Footer** box, type Lastname_Firstname_p06_Home_Sales Click **Apply to All**. **Save** the presentation. **Exit** PowerPoint, and then submit your presentation as directed.

Done! You have completed the Skill Check

Assess Your Skills 1

To complete this project, you will need the following files:

- p06_Neighborhood_Watch
- p06_Neighborhood_Worksheet
- p06_Neighborhood_Pic

You will save your file as:

- Lastname_Firstname_p06_Neighborhood_Watch

1. **Start** PowerPoint, open **p06_Neighborhood_Watch**. **Save** the presentation in your **PowerPoint Chapter 6** folder as Lastname_Firstname_p06_Neighborhood_Watch

2. Display **Slide 1**, and then from the **Shape** gallery, insert the **Action Button: Home** shape. Set the shape to hyperlink to the last slide, and resize it to 1" in height and 1" in width. Move the shape to the lower right corner of the slide.

3. Display **Slide 2**. Select the word *Safety* and then insert a hyperlink that opens http://www.california.gov/HomeFamily/Safety.html

4. On **Slide 2**, add an **Action** setting to the picture so that when it is clicked, the last slide displays and the **Chime** sound plays.

5. On **Slide 3**, use the **Transitions tab** to set a timing of **5** minutes to create a Timed break slide. Use the **Animations tab** to add a **Spin** effect to the circle shape, and use the **Animation pane** to set the **Timing** for the animation to **Repeat Until End of Slide**.

6. Display **Slide 4**. From your student files, insert the picture **p06_Neighborhood_Pic**. Recolor the picture using **Washout**, and then send it to the back.

7. Display **Slide 5**. **Start** Excel, and then open **p06_Neighborhood_Worksheet**. In the Excel worksheet, **Copy** the range **A1:I25**. In PowerPoint, use **Paste Special** to **Link** the Excel worksheet to **Slide 5**.

8. Resize the pasted worksheet to approximately 4.7" in height and 7.13" in width, and then move the worksheet below the bullet point so that the left edge of the worksheet appears directly under the *D* in *Distribute*.

9. Display **Slide 6**. Use **SmartArt** to create a **Horizontal Labeled Hierarchy** with the following information entered into the shapes:

   Block Watch Captain
       Block Secretary
           Volunteer Liaisons
           Security Patrol
       Block Recruiter
           Police Liaisons
   Block Organizer
   Block Reporters
   Block Members

13. Add the file name to the **Notes and Handouts** footer. **Save** the presentation, and then print or submit as directed.

   Done! You have completed Assess Your Skills 1

Figure 1

Assess Your Skills 2

To complete this project, you will need the following files:

- p06_Park_Acquisition
- p06_Park_Visits
- p06_Park_River
- p06_Park_Questionnaire
- p06_Park_Development

You will save your files as:

- Lastname_Firstname_p06_Park_Acquisition
- Lastname_Firstname_p06_Park_Quesitonnaire

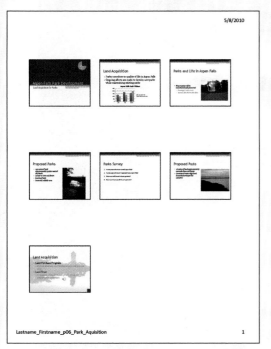

5/8/2010

Lastname_Firstname_p06_Park_Aquisition   1

Figure 1

1. **Start** PowerPoint, and then from your student files, open **p06_Park _Acquisition**. **Save** your presentation in your **PowerPoint Chapter 6** folder as Lastname_Firstname_p06_ Park_Acquisition

2. Display **Slide 1**. To the pie shape in the upper right corner of the slide, add a **Spin** animation effect. Adjust the timing to **Start with Previous**, and set the animation to **Repeat until the end** of the slide. Set the slide timing to advance automatically after one minute.

3. **Start** Excel, and then open **p06_Park_Visits**. **Copy** the chart titled *Number of Visitors per Month*, and then **Exit** Excel.

4. Display **Slide 2**, and below the bulleted text, **Paste** the chart, and center it on the slide. Size it 3" in height and 6" in width. Change the chart title to Aspen Falls Park Visitors

5. On **Slide 3**, add a hyperlink to the picture so that it opens **http://parks.ca.gov**.

6. **Start** Word, and then open **p06_Park_ Questionnaire**. Save the document in your **PowerPoint Chapter 6** folder as Lastname_ Firstname_p06_Park_Questionnaire **Copy** questions 1 through 5.

7. In PowerPoint, display **Slide 5**. In the title placeholder, type Parks Survey **Paste** the

questions so that they are linked to the Word document. Size the hyperlinked text box to 2.9" in height, and center it on the slide.

8. In Word, **Delete** question 5. **Save**, and then **Exit** Word.

9. Display **Slide 6**. In the right content placeholder, insert the video **p06_Park_ Development** with the option to play **On Click**. Size the video to 3.5" in height and 4.67" in width. **Trim** the video to 10 seconds in length, and click **Mute**.

10. Move the video clip so that the top border is even with the top line of text in the left content pane.

11. Display **Slide 7**, and then insert the picture named **p06_Park_River**. Recolor the picture using **Washout**. **Send to Back** so that the picture appears behind the placeholders.

12. On **Slide 7**, insert the **Claps Cheers**—or similar—sound from the **Clip Organizer**. Set the sound to play **On Click**. Place the sound icon to the right of *easement*.

13. Add the file name to the **Notes and Handouts** footer. **Save** the presentation, and **Print** or submit it as directed.

Done! You have completed Assess Your Skills 2

Assess Your Skills Visually

To complete this project, you will need the following files:

- p06_Community_Center
- p06_Community_Schedule

You will save your file as:

- Lastname_Firstname_p06_Community_Center

Start PowerPoint. Open **p06_Community_Center**. **Save** the file in your **PowerPoint Chapter 6** folder as Lastname_Firstname_p06_Community_Center Use the Word document **p06_Community_Schedule** as a resource to insert an **Horizontal Labeled Hierarchy chart** on **Slide 2**, as shown in **Figure 1**. After creating the organization chart, apply the **Polished** SmartArt style, and then change the color to **Colorful Range – Accent Colors 5 to 6**. Resize the SmartArt graphic as shown in **Figure 1**. **Hyperlink** the title *Upcoming Art Classes* to http://www.cac.ca.gov the California Arts Council website.

Add the file name to the **Notes and Handouts** footer, and print or submit the presentation electronically as directed.

Done! You have completed Assess Your Skills Visually

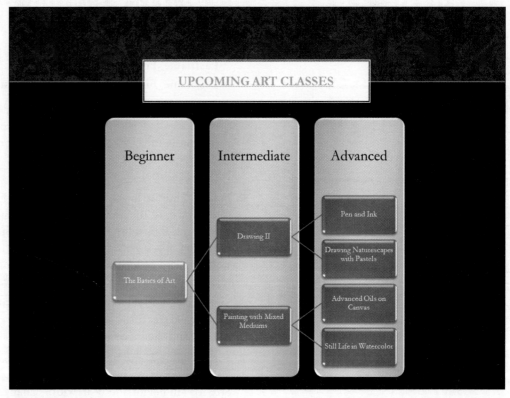

Figure 1

Skills in Context

To complete this project, you will need the following file:

- **p06_Acceptable_Use**

You will save your file as:

- **Lastname_Firstname_p06_Acceptable_Use**

From your student files, open **p06_Acceptable_Use**. In your **PowerPoint Chapter 6** folder, **Save** the presentation as Lastname_Firstname_p06_Acceptable_Use On the **View tab**, in the **Master Views group**, click the **Slide Master** button, and then click on the **Slide Master**, the top slide thumbnail in the left pane. Create a navigation bar by inserting the following action buttons: **Action Button: Beginning, Action Button: Forward or Next**, and **Action Button: End**. Size the buttons to 0.3" by 0.3". Align the buttons side by side, in a single row in the upper right corner of the screen. Be sure that the navigation bar displays on each slide, except on the Title slide, regardless of slide layout.

Add the file name to the **Notes and Handouts** footer. **Save** the presentation and submit as directed.

Done! You have completed Skills in Context

Skills and You

To complete this project, you will need the following file:

- **New blank PowerPoint presentation**

You will save your file as:

- **Lastname_Firstname_p06_Writing**

Using the skills you have practiced in this chapter, create a presentation with six to eight slides that would provide a useful overview for an introductory college writing course. Use one slide to describe the writing course. Use your college's course catalog to locate a description for an introductory writing course, if needed. Use at least two slides to describe the need for writing skills in your field. Add an organization chart to one slide, and use the organization chart to show either your college's management structure or the management structure in your program area, including deans, instructors, students, and tutors. On one slide, include a hyperlink to your college's website. Add at least one sound and at least one action button to the presentation.

Save the presentation as Lastname_Firstname_p06_Writing Add the file name to the **Notes and Handouts** footer. **Save**, and then submit as directed.

Done! You have completed Skills and You

CHAPTER 7

Customize Graphics and Draw on Slides

▶ You can combine pictures and text boxes to create a single custom graphic—a logo, for example—or provide pictures with captions.

▶ You can customize your presentation by inserting symbols, modifying Notes and Handouts pages, and animating objects so that they move on a custom path.

Your starting screen will look like this:

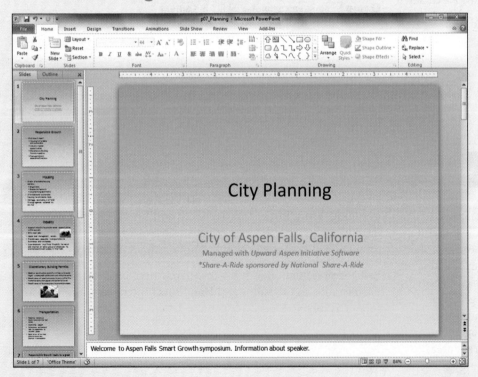

SKILLS
Skills 1-10 Training

At the end of this chapter, you will be able to:

Skill 1 Create Custom Shapes
Skill 2 Group Objects and Export Custom Shapes
Skill 3 Use the Ruler to Apply Indents and Align Objects
Skill 4 Animate Graphics Using Motion Paths
Skill 5 Recolor and Customize Pictures
Skill 6 Modify and Link to Photo Albums
Skill 7 Add Captions and Convert Text to SmartArt
Skill 8 Modify Graphics to Reduce Presentation File Sizes
Skill 9 Insert Symbols
Skill 10 Edit Notes and Handouts Masters

MORE SKILLS

More Skills 11 Save Slides as Image Files
More Skills 12 Export Customized SmartArt as a Picture
More Skills 13 Create SmartArt with the Nested Target Layout
More Skills 14 Create Text Effects by Combining WordArt and Shapes

Outcome

Using the skills listed will enable you to create a presentation like this:

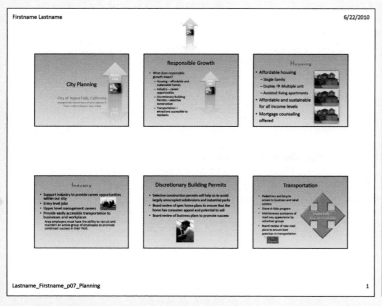

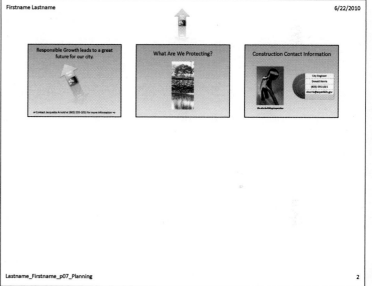

You will save your files as:

Lastname_Firstname_p07_Planning
Lastname_Firstname_p07_Planning_Logo
Lastname_Firstname_p07_Planning_Album

In this chapter, you will create presentations for the Aspen Falls City Hall, which provides essential services for the citizens and visitors of Aspen Falls, California.

Introduction

- ▶ Shapes can be drawn on slides and customized by adding pictures, applying styles, and adding text, and then grouping them as a single object.

- ▶ You can recolor, remove unwanted edges, and link images to photo albums.

- ▶ To reduce the size of a presentation file, you can alter images in several ways.

- ▶ Rulers can be used to position objects and to change the indentation in bulleted lists.

- ▶ To add visual interest, an object can move along a path during a presentation.

- ▶ Notes and Handouts pages can be customized with a logo.

**Time to complete all
10 skills – 50 to 90 minutes**

Find your student data files here:

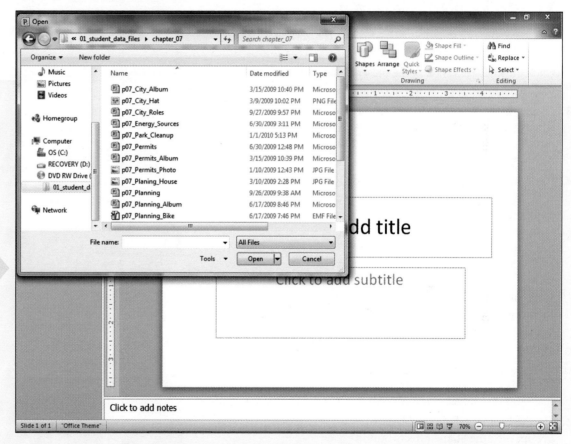

**Student data files needed
for this chapter:**

- p07_Planning
- p07_Planning_Park
- p07_Planning_Hammer
- p07_Planning_House
- p07_Planning_Album
- p07_Planning_Shovel
- p07_Planning_Bike
- p07_Planning_Durango_Park

▶ You can customize shapes by adding text and pictures to them.

▶ Shapes and objects can be stacked, one on top another, to create a logo.

1. **Start** PowerPoint. From your student files, open **p07_Planning**. Click **File**, and then click **Save As**. Navigate to the location where you are saving your files, create a folder named PowerPoint Chapter 7 and then **Save** the presentation as Lastname_ Firstname_p07_Planning

2. Click through each slide in the presentation to familiarize yourself with the content.

3. Display **Slide 1**. On the **Insert tab**, in the **Illustrations group**, click the **Shapes** button. In the **Shapes** gallery, under **Block Arrows**, click the **Up Arrow** shape.

4. Position your mouse pointer over a blank area on the left side of the slide, and click to insert an **Up Arrow** shape. Under **Drawing Tools**, on the **Format tab**, in the **Size group**, use the **Shape Height** and **Shape Width** boxes to adjust the size to 3.25" in height and 2.83" in width. Compare your screen with **Figure 1**, and then move the arrow, if necessary, to match the location shown.

5. On the **Format tab**, in the **Shape Styles group**, click the **More** ⊡ button, and then in the sixth row, click the fourth thumbnail—**Intense Effect - Lime, Accent 3**.

6. On the **Format tab**, in the **Shape Styles group**, click the **Shape Effects** button. Point to **Reflection**, and then click the last thumbnail—**Full Reflection, 8 pt offset**.

7. Click a blank area to deselect the arrow, and then compare your screen with **Figure 2**.

■ **Continue to the next page to complete the skill**

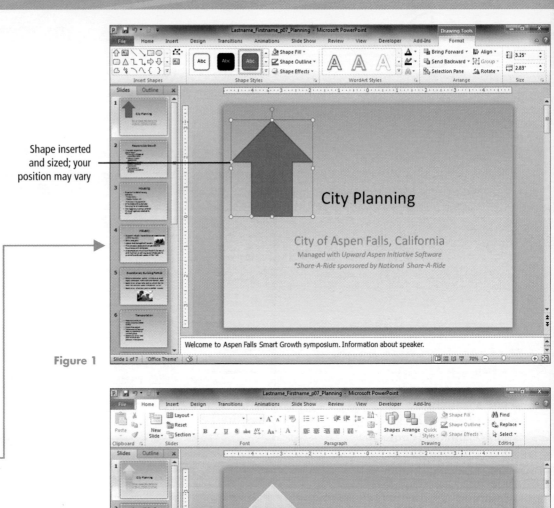

Shape inserted and sized; your position may vary

Figure 1

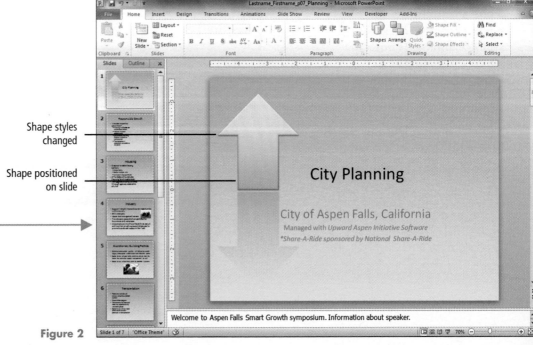

Shape styles changed

Shape positioned on slide

Figure 2

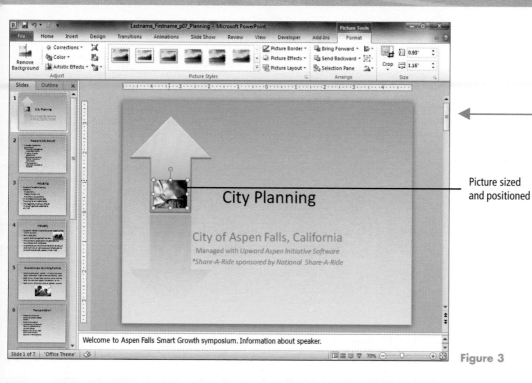

Figure 3

8. On the **Insert tab**, in the **Images group**, click **Picture**. In the displayed **Insert Picture** dialog box, locate your student files, and then double-click **p07_ Planning_Shovel** to insert the picture.

9. On the **Format tab**, in the **Size group**, adjust the height to 0.93" and then press Enter. The width should adjust automatically to 1.16".

10. Position the shovel picture toward the bottom of the arrow shape, as shown in **Figure 3**.

11. With the shovel image still selected, on the **Format tab**, in the **Picture Styles group**, click **Drop Shadow Rectangle**—the fourth option.

12. Click the arrow shape one time to select it.

13. Type Aspen Falls and then press Enter three times. Select the text just inserted. On the **Home tab**, in the **Font group**, click in the **Font Size** box, and then type 24 Change the **Font** to **Impact**. Click a blank area of the slide to deselect the arrow. Compare your screen with **Figure 4**.

14. On the **Insert tab**, in the **Text group**, click the **Header & Footer** button. In the **Header and Footer** dialog box, click the **Notes and Handouts tab**. Select the **Footer** check box, type Lastname_ Firstname_p07_Planning and then click **Apply to All**.

15. Click **Save** 🖫.

- **You have completed Skill 1 of 10**

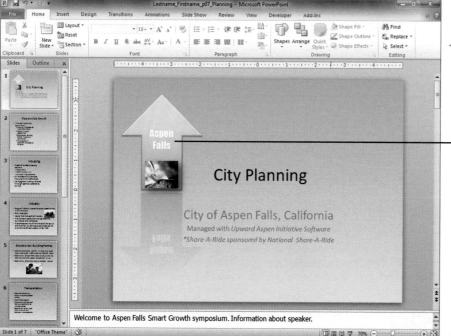

Picture sized and positioned

Text inserted and modified

► A *grouped object*—a single object originally made up of several different images and text—can be copied, moved, or formatted as a single item.

► Grouped objects can be *exported*—saved in a different file format—so that they can be inserted into other documents or viewed with other programs. Grouped objects are often exported as image files so they can be shared with others.

1. Click the arrow shape one time to select it. Press and hold Ctrl while clicking the shovel picture. Release Ctrl and verify that both objects are selected.

2. With both objects selected, under the **Drawing Tools contextual tab**, on the **Format tab**, in the **Arrange group**, click the **Group** button, and then click **Group**.

   The selection border indicates that the objects are now a single item. It can be moved as a single shape rather than individually.

3. Move your pointer over an outer border of the grouped object, drag it to the right side of the slide, and position it as shown in **Figure 1**.

4. Right-click over the picture on the new custom logo—the grouped arrow, shovel, and text—and from the displayed shortcut menu, click **Save as Picture**.

5. In the displayed **Save As Picture** dialog box, navigate to your **PowerPoint Chapter 7** folder. Name the file Lastname_Firstname_p07_Planning_Logo Click the **Save as type box arrow**, click **TIFF Tag Image File Format**, and then click **Save**.

   Common graphic file formats are summarized in the table in **Figure 2**.

■ **Continue to the next page to complete the skill** ►

Grouped arrow object moved as a single item to right slide of slide

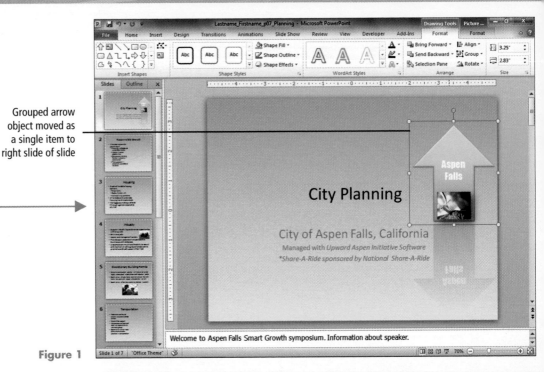

Figure 1

Common Graphic File Types

Name	Extension	Description
Microsoft Windows Metafile Format	.wmf	Common clip art format. Developed for use for use with PCs. Generally not used for high-definition printing.
Bitmap	.bmp	Picture made of a series of pixels; each pixel contains one color, creates a large file size.
Graphics Interchange Format	.gif	Format often used on webpages. Supports up to 256 colors. No image data is lost when compressed.
Joint Photographic Experts Group	.jpg or .jpeg	Format often used on webpages. Developed for compressing and storing images. Used for graphics with many colors. Format often used with digital cameras.
Portable Network Graphics	.png	Format often used for webpages. Supports image transparency and control of image brightness on different systems.
Tagged Image File Format	.tif or .tiff	High resolution, tag-based format. Often used in the publishing industry.

Figure 2

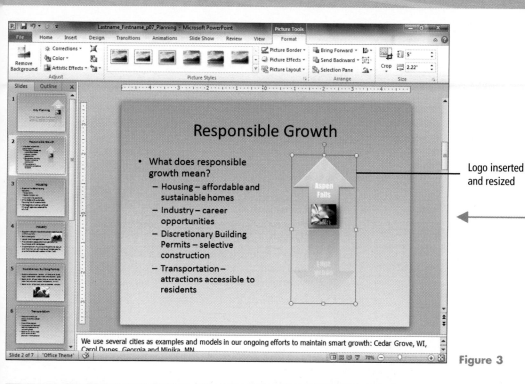

Figure 3

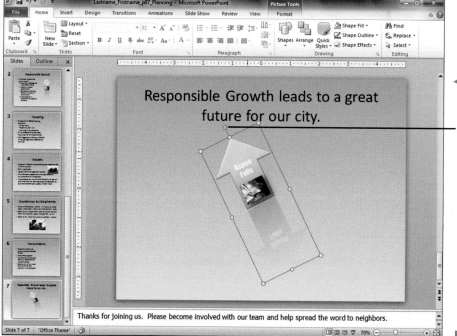

Figure 4

6. Display **Slide 2**. On the **Insert tab**, in the **Images group**, click **Picture**. Navigate to your **PowerPoint Chapter 7** folder. Click Lastname_Firstname_p07_Planning_Logo and then click **Insert** to place the logo on the slide.

7. With the newly inserted logo selected, on the **Format tab**, in the **Size group**, change the **Shape Height** to 5" and then move the shape so the tip of the arrow is directly under the *t* in *Growth*. Compare your screen with **Figure 3** and reposition the logo as needed.

8. Display **Slide 7**, and then in the content placeholder, click the **Insert Picture from File** button. Select Lastname_Firstname_p07_Planning_Logo, and then click **Insert**.

9. Point to the rotate handle—the green circle above the selected graphic—and then with the pointer, drag to the left so that the arrow shape points to the second *u* in the word *future*. Compare your screen with **Figure 4**.

10. **Save** your presentation.

■ **You have completed Skill 2 of 10**

▶ In PowerPoint, the horizontal ruler is used to set *indents*—the amount of space between the placeholder margin and the text.

1. Display **Slide 4**, and then click a blank area in the content placeholder. Verify that your rulers display as shown in **Figure 1**. If necessary, on the View tab, in the Show group, select the Ruler check box.

   The horizontal ruler displays three markers: the first line indent marker, the hanging indent marker, and the left indent marker.

2. In the last bullet, place the insertion point to the left of *Area employers*. On the **Home tab**, in the **Paragraph group**, click the **Bullets** ☰▾ button.

3. On the horizontal ruler, drag the left indent marker ▨ to the **.5 inch** mark.

4. Select the sentence beginning with *Area employers*. On the **Home tab**, in the **Font group**, click the **Italic** 🇮 button. Click the **Decrease Font Size** 🇦▾ button to change the **Font Size** to 28 Click anywhere to deselect the text, and then compare your screen with **Figure 2**.

■ Continue to the next page to complete the skill ▶

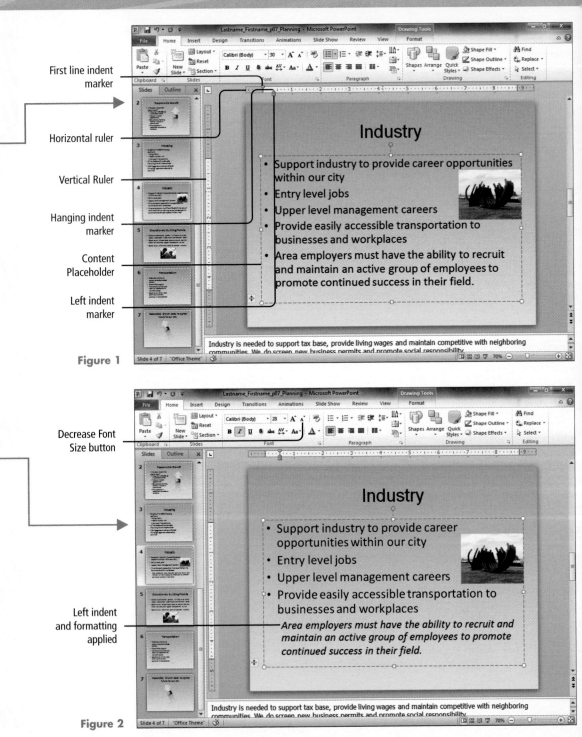

First line indent marker

Horizontal ruler

Vertical Ruler

Hanging indent marker

Content Placeholder

Left indent marker

Figure 1

Decrease Font Size button

Left indent and formatting applied

Figure 2

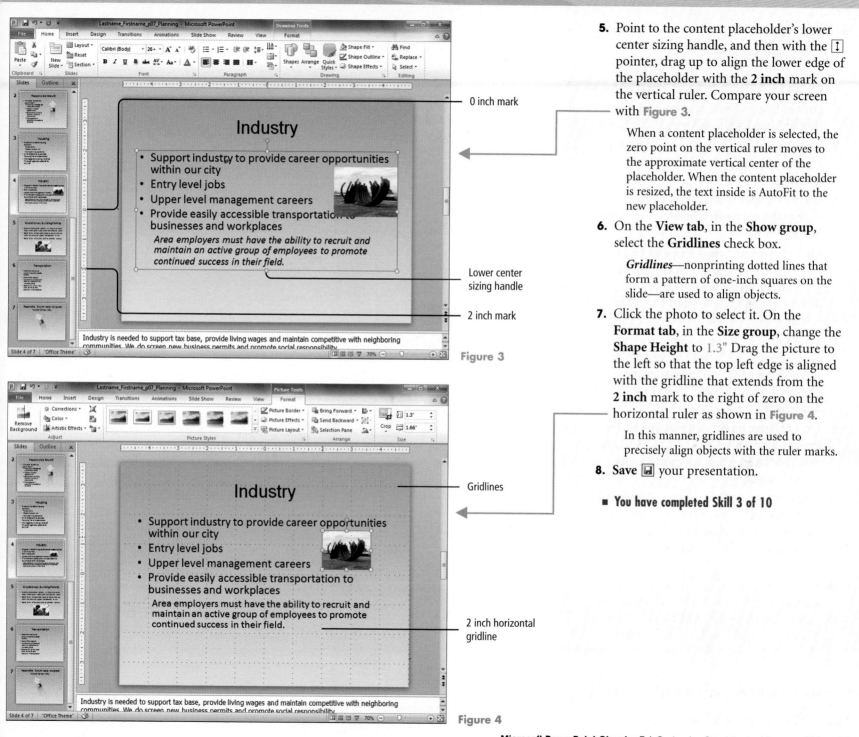

Figure 3

Figure 4

5. Point to the content placeholder's lower center sizing handle, and then with the ⬍ pointer, drag up to align the lower edge of the placeholder with the **2 inch** mark on the vertical ruler. Compare your screen with **Figure 3**.

When a content placeholder is selected, the zero point on the vertical ruler moves to the approximate vertical center of the placeholder. When the content placeholder is resized, the text inside is AutoFit to the new placeholder.

6. On the **View tab**, in the **Show group**, select the **Gridlines** check box.

Gridlines—nonprinting dotted lines that form a pattern of one-inch squares on the slide—are used to align objects.

7. Click the photo to select it. On the **Format tab**, in the **Size group**, change the **Shape Height** to 1.3" Drag the picture to the left so that the top left edge is aligned with the gridline that extends from the **2 inch** mark to the right of zero on the horizontal ruler as shown in **Figure 4**.

In this manner, gridlines are used to precisely align objects with the ruler marks.

8. **Save** 🖫 your presentation.

■ **You have completed Skill 3 of 10**

► A *motion path* is an animation effect that moves an object along a line or curve.

1. Display **Slide 6**. On the **Insert tab**, in the **Illustrations group**, click the **Shapes** button. Under **Block Arrows**, click the seventh shape—**Quad Arrow**.

2. Position the ⊞ pointer on the right side of the slide, and then click to insert a **Quad Arrow** shape.

3. On the **Format tab**, in the **Size group**, change the **Shape Height** to 4.7" and the **Shape Width** to 4.7"

4. Move the **Quad Arrow** shape so that the top border is on the **2 inch** horizontal gridline and the left border is on the **0 inch** vertical gridline. Compare your screen with **Figure 1**.

5. Type Aspen Falls = press Enter, and type Easy Accessibility Select the text, and then on the **Home tab**, in the **Font group**, change the **Font Size** to 28 and apply **Text Shadow** ⑤.

6. On the **Format tab**, in the **Shape Styles group**, click **Shape Fill**. Point to **Texture**, and click **Sand**—the last choice in the second row.

7. Under **Drawing Tools**, on the **Format tab**, in the **Shape Styles group**, click **Shape Effects**. Point to **Bevel**, and then under **Bevel**, click the fourth thumbnail—**Cool Slant**.

8. On the **Format tab**, in the **Shape Styles group**, click **Shape Outline**. Click the last color in the first **Theme Colors** column—**White, Background 1, Darker 50%** as shown in **Figure 2**.

■ **Continue to the next page to complete the skill**

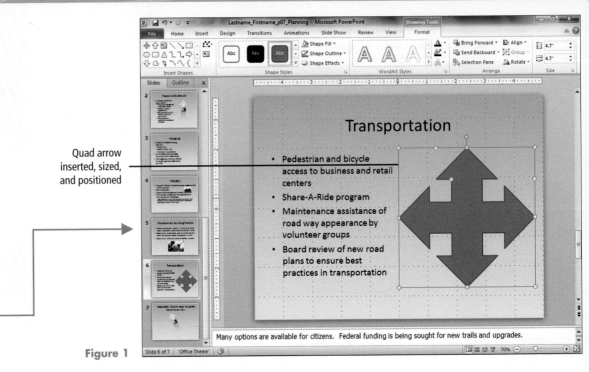

Quad arrow inserted, sized, and positioned

Figure 1

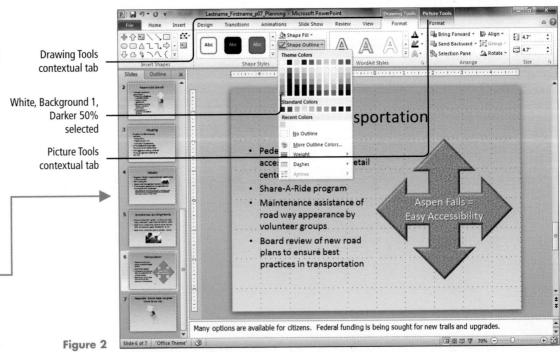

Drawing Tools contextual tab

White, Background 1, Darker 50% selected

Picture Tools contextual tab

Figure 2

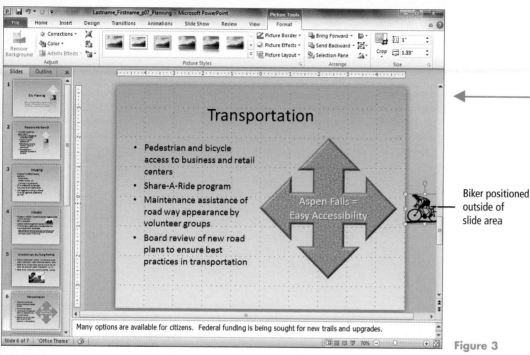

Figure 3

Biker positioned outside of slide area

Motion path

Figure 4

9. Click a blank area on the slide. On the **Insert tab**, in the **Images group**, click the **Picture** button. Navigate to your student files, and then double-click to insert the image file **p07_Planning_Bike**.

10. On the **Picture Tools Format tab**, and in the **Size group**, adjust the **Shape Height** to 1".

11. Drag the biker image off the slide area as shown in **Figure 3**.

   Objects inserted outside of the slide area will not display during the presentation.

12. With the biker still selected, on the **Animations tab**, in the **Animation group**, click the **More** arrow. Scroll all the way to end of the list, and then under **Motion Paths**, click **Custom Path**.

13. With the ⊞ pointer, draw a path from the front bicycle tire to the middle of the **Quad Arrow** shape, and then, without releasing the mouse button, turn and draw straight down to the **2 inch** mark gridline, as shown in **Figure 4**. Double-click to stop drawing.

14. On the **Animations tab**, in the **Preview group**, click the **Preview** button and verify that the biker moves across and down the screen and stops at the bottom of the **Quad Arrow** shape. If necessary, click Undo and try again.

15. Save 🔙 the presentation.

   ■ **You have completed Skill 4 of 10**

► The mood or tone of an image can be changed by *recoloring*—applying a stylized color or hue, such as sepia—or converting the image to black and white.

1. Display **Slide 3**. On the **Insert tab**, in the **Images group**, click **Picture**. From your student files, double-click **p07_Planning_House** to insert it.

2. On the **Format tab**, in the **Size group**, adjust the size of the picture to 1.7" by 2.54"

3. Position the top edge of the picture on the **2 inch** horizontal gridline, and position the right edge on the **4 inch** vertical gridline as shown in **Figure 1**. ──────

4. With the house picture selected, on the **Format tab**, in the **Adjust group**, click **Color**. Under **Recolor**, click the third option in the first row—**Sepia**.

5. While pressing and holding Ctrl, drag the picture down to create a copy of the picture. Repeat this step to create a total of three pictures.

>   Dragging an object or selected text while pressing Ctrl creates a copy of the object or text.

6. Click the middle picture, and then on the **Format tab**, in the **Adjust group**, click **Color**. Under **Recolor**, click the third option in the second row—**Ice Blue, Accent color 2 Dark**. Repeat this technique to recolor the bottom picture with **Lime, Accent color 3 Dark**—the fourth option in the second row under **Recolor**.

7. Compare your screen with **Figure 2**. If necessary, position the pictures as shown.

■ **Continue to the next page to complete the skill**

Picture aligned with gridlines

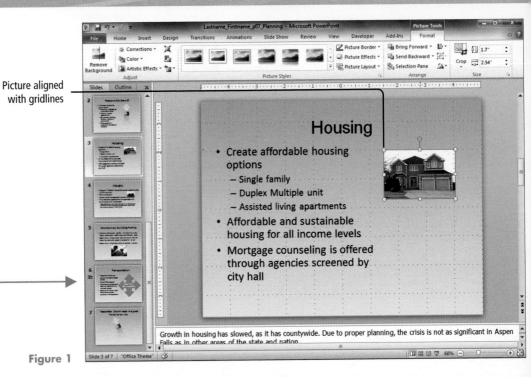

Figure 1

Images copied and recolored

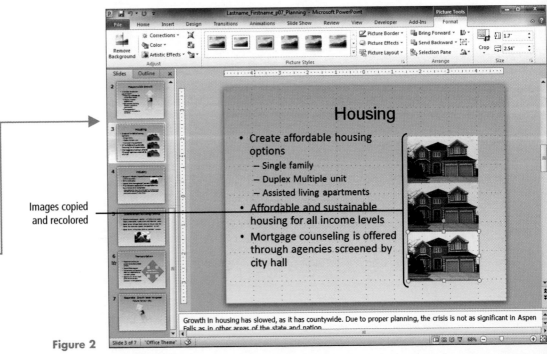

Figure 2

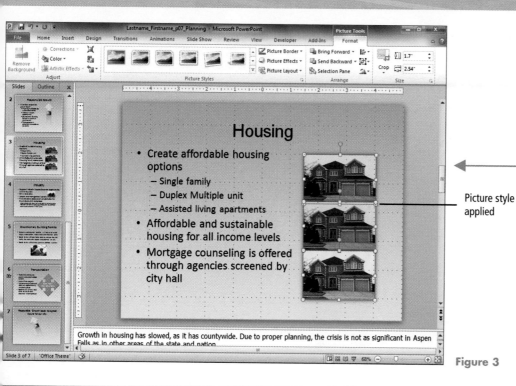

Figure 3

Figure 4

8. Select the top picture. Press and hold Ctrl, and then click the second and third pictures. With the three pictures selected, on the **Format tab**, in the **Picture Styles group**, click the **More** button. In the displayed **Picture Styles** gallery, click the first option in the third row—**Center Shadow Rectangle**. Compare your screen with **Figure 3**.

9. Display **Slide 6**. On the **Insert tab**, in the **Illustrations group**, click **Shapes**, and then under **Callouts**, click the sixth shape—**Line Callout 2**. Position the + pointer below the last bullet point, under the word *practices*, and then click to insert the shape.

10. Change the **Shape Height** to 0.7" Change the **Shape Width** to 1.2" and then insert the text City Engineer

11. With the callout selected, on the **Format tab**, in the **Shape Styles group**, click the **More** button, and then apply the second style in the fifth row—**Moderate Effect - Blue-Gray, Accent 1**.

12. In the **Shape Styles group**, click **Shape Fill**. In the displayed list, point to **Gradient**, and then under **Variations**, click **From Center**—the second option in the second row.

13. With the callout selected, point to the callout line handle—the yellow diamond at the top end of the callout line, and then with the pointer, drag so that the callout points to *practices* as shown in **Figure 4**.

14. **Save** your presentation.

- **You have completed Skill 5 of 10**

Picture style applied

Callout line handle

▶ *Photo Albums*—presentations composed of pictures—can be created and stored separately and then linked to other presentations.

1. Display **Slide 7**. Press Ctrl + M to insert a new **Slide 8**.

2. In the title placeholder, type What Are We Protecting? and then compare your screen with **Figure 1**.

3. In the content placeholder, click the **Insert Picture from File** 🖼 button, and then from the student files for this chapter, insert **p07_Planning_Durango_Park**.

4. Click **Save** 🖫. From your student files, open the PowerPoint presentation **p07_Planning_Album**. View all of the slides.

5. In the Planning Album presentation, display **Slide 1**. On the **Transitions tab**, in the **Transition to This Slide group**, click the **More** ▾ button. In the **Transitions** gallery, under **Dynamic Content**, click the second thumbnail—**Ferris Wheel**. In the **Timing group**, click **Apply To All**, and then compare your screen with **Figure 2**.

6. **Save** the Planning Album presentation in your **PowerPoint Chapter 7** folder as Lastname_Firstname_p07_Planning_Album Insert the file name as a footer on the **Notes and Handouts** pages.

■ **Continue to the next page to complete the skill**

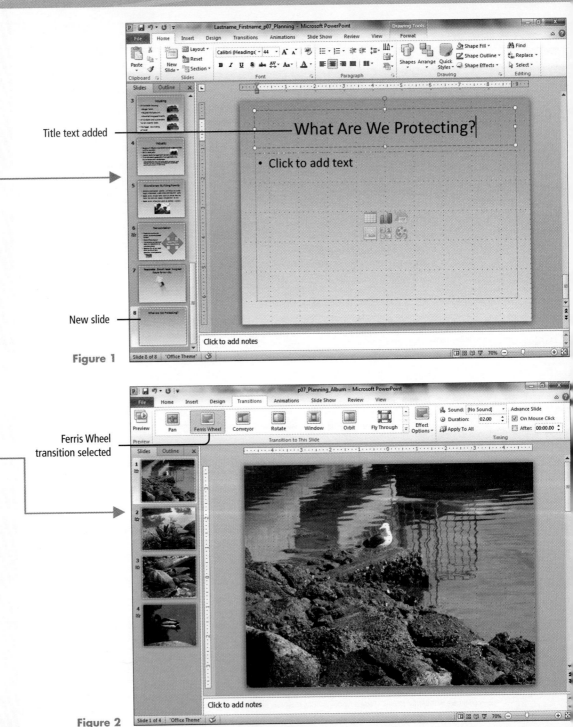

Title text added

New slide

Figure 1

Ferris Wheel transition selected

Figure 2

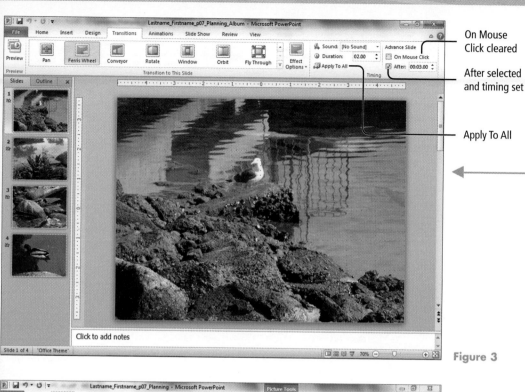

On Mouse
Click cleared

After selected
and timing set

Apply To All

Figure 3

7. On the **Transitions tab**, in the **Timing group**, deselect **On Mouse Click**. Select **After**, and then click the **After up spin arrow** to display **00:03.00**.

8. In the **Timing group**, click **Apply to All**. Compare your screen with **Figure 3**.

   With *On Mouse Click* disabled and *After* enabled, the presentation will advance to the next slide at the assigned time interval instead of when the mouse is clicked.

9. **Save** 🖫, and then **Close** ❎ the Planning Album presentation.

10. In **Lastname_Firstname_p07_Planning**, on **Slide 8**, select the picture. On the **Insert tab**, in the **Links group**, click **Hyperlink**.

11. In the displayed **Insert Hyperlink** dialog box, verify that your **PowerPoint Chapter 7** folder displays. If necessary, click the **Look in box arrow**, and then navigate to your folder. Select **Lastname_Firstname_p07_Planning_Album**. Compare your screen with **Figure 4**, and then click **OK**.

12. **Save** 🖫 your presentation. Press ⌊F5⌋ to start the presentation from **Slide 1**. Click through your presentation, and when you reach **Slide 8**, click the Durango Park picture.

13. In the displayed Photo Album presentation, verify that each slide advances every three seconds. When the black slide displays at the end of the presentation, click to exit and return to **Slide 8** in the original presentation.

■ **You have completed Skill 6 of 10**

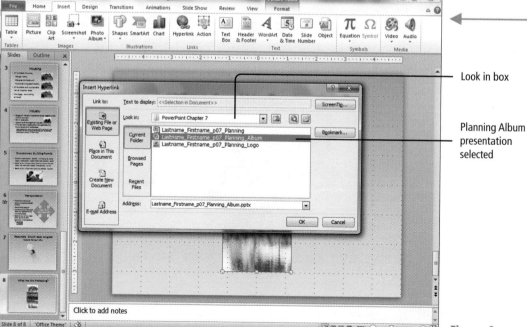

Look in box

Planning Album
presentation
selected

Figure 4

▶ *Captions* are text boxes added to pictures to clarify their purpose or add meaning to the images.

▶ Text boxes can be formatted and positioned to match the width of an image or to complement the slide design.

1. Display **Slide 8**. On the **Home tab**, in the **Slides group**, click the **New Slide button arrow**, and then click the **Two Content** thumbnail to insert a new **Slide 9**.

2. In the title placeholder, type Construction Contact Information

3. In the left content placeholder, click the **Insert Picture from File** ⬚ button, and then from your student files, insert **p07_Planning_Hammer**. Compare your screen with **Figure 1**.

4. On the **Insert tab**, in the **Text group**, click **Text Box**. Click once below the lower left corner of the hammer to insert a text box.

5. On the **Home tab**, in the **Font group**, verify that the **Font Size** is **18** points, apply **Bold** Ⓑ, and then apply **Italic** Ⓘ.

6. In the text box, type On-site building inspection

7. Select the picture. On the **Format tab**, in the **Picture Styles group**, click the **More** ⬇ button, and then click the fifth thumbnail—**Reflected Rounded Rectangle**. Compare your screen with **Figure 2**.

■ **Continue to the next page to complete the skill**

Picture inserted

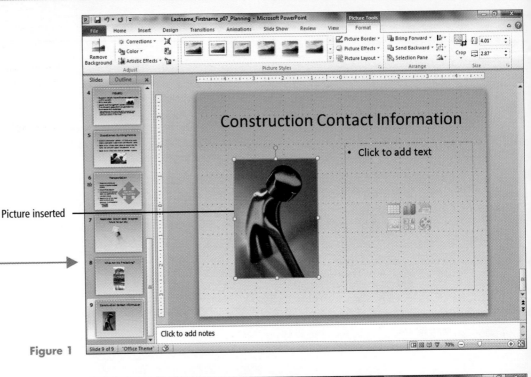

Figure 1

Picture style applied

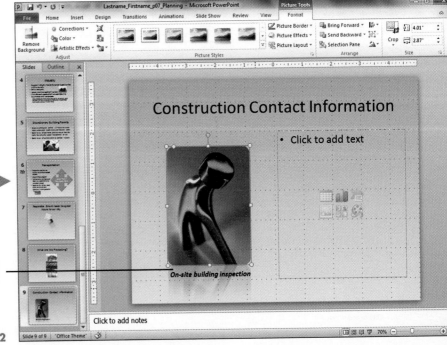

Figure 2

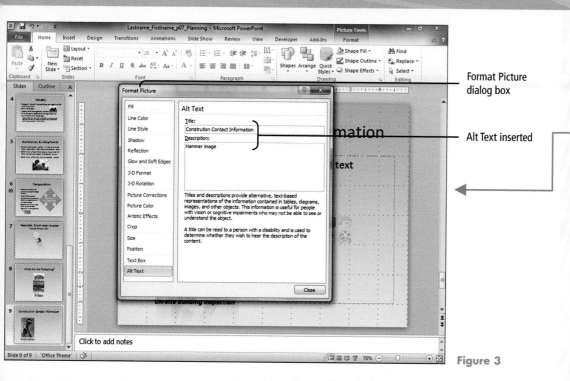

Format Picture dialog box

Alt Text inserted

Figure 3

Bulleted text converted to SmartArt

Construction Contact Information

Figure 4

8. Right-click the hammer picture, and then click **Size and Position**. In the **Format Picture** dialog box, click **Alt Text**. In the **Title** box, type Construction Contact Information In the **Description** box, type Hammer image Compare your screen with **Figure 3**, and then click **Close**.

   Alternative text appears if a graphic does not display correctly and is useful for screen-reading software.

9. In the right content placeholder, type the following four bullets:

   City Engineer
   Donald Norris
   (805) 555-1021
   dnorris@aspenfalls.gov

10. On the **Home tab**, in the **Paragraph group**, click the **Convert to SmartArt Graphic** button. In the displayed gallery, click **Target List**—the fourth layout in the first row.

11. On the **SmartArt Tools Design tab**, in the **SmartArt Styles group**, click the fifth style—**Intense Effect**—and then compare your screen with **Figure 4**.

12. Click the SmartArt border so that the entire graphic is selected. Right-click a blank area of the SmartArt, and in the displayed shortcut menu, click **Size and Position**. Repeat the technique practiced to change the **Alternative text** title to Donald Norris, (805) 555-1021 Leave the description blank, and then **Close** the dialog box.

13. Save the presentation.

■ **You have completed Skill 7 of 10**

▶ Graphics can use a large amount of storage space, which may cause a presentation to open slowly, cause transitions between slides to appear sluggish, or prevent sending the presentation as an e-mail attachment.

▶ Presentation images can be *compressed*—changing the information stored in a file in order to reduce the size of the file.

1. Display **Slide 1**. Click the **File tab**, and in Backstage view, in the far right pane, view the **Properties**. Compare your screen with **Figure 1**, and note the size of your presentation.

   The presentation's file size is currently between about 850 and 900 kilobytes. File sizes vary depending on the system you are using.

2. Click the **Home tab** to return to the presentation, and then display **Slide 5**. Click to select the picture of the men reviewing blueprints. On the **Format tab**, in the **Size group**, click the **Crop** button. Point to the right middle crop handle, and then with the pointer, drag to the left so that the man with the white hat does not display, as shown in **Figure 2**. Click the **Crop** button to turn it off.

   To *crop* is to remove unwanted areas along the edges of a graphic or picture. Cropping a picture does not permanently delete the unused parts of the picture.

■ **Continue to the next page to complete the skill**

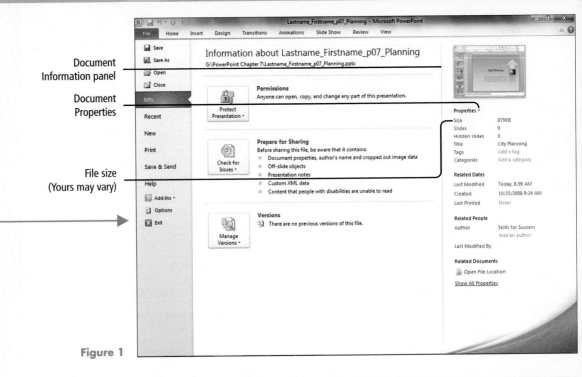

Document Information panel

Document Properties

File size (Yours may vary)

Figure 1

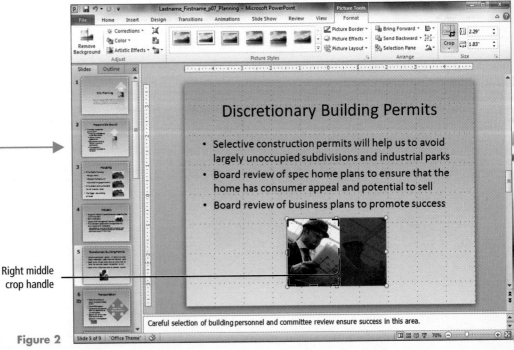

Right middle crop handle

Figure 2

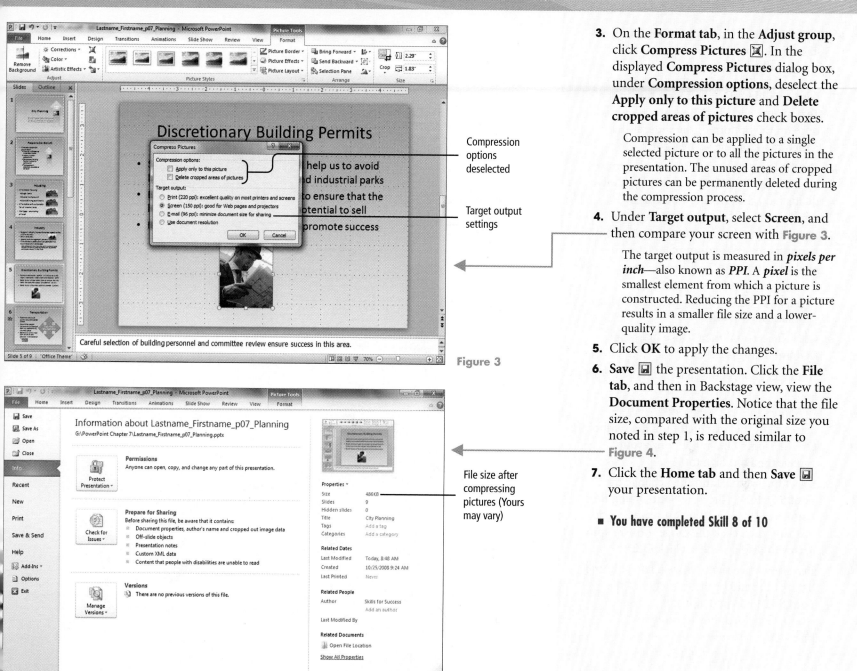

Compression options deselected

Target output settings

Figure 3

File size after compressing pictures (Yours may vary)

Figure 4

3. On the **Format tab**, in the **Adjust group**, click **Compress Pictures** 🖾. In the displayed **Compress Pictures** dialog box, under **Compression options**, deselect the **Apply only to this picture** and **Delete cropped areas of pictures** check boxes.

   Compression can be applied to a single selected picture or to all the pictures in the presentation. The unused areas of cropped pictures can be permanently deleted during the compression process.

4. Under **Target output**, select **Screen**, and then compare your screen with **Figure 3**.

   The target output is measured in *pixels per inch*—also known as *PPI*. A *pixel* is the smallest element from which a picture is constructed. Reducing the PPI for a picture results in a smaller file size and a lower-quality image.

5. Click **OK** to apply the changes.

6. **Save** 🖫 the presentation. Click the **File tab**, and then in Backstage view, view the **Document Properties**. Notice that the file size, compared with the original size you noted in step 1, is reduced similar to **Figure 4**.

7. Click the **Home tab** and then **Save** 🖫 your presentation.

   ■ **You have completed Skill 8 of 10**

▶ Many characters and symbols not found on a standard keyboard can be found in the Symbol dialog box.

1. Display **Slide 7**. On the **Insert tab**, in the **Text group**, click **Text Box**, and then click once on the bottom of the slide, at the **3 inch** mark on the vertical ruler.

2. On the **Insert tab**, in the **Symbols group**, click the **Symbol** button. In the **Symbol** dialog box, click the **Font box arrow**, scroll down, and then click **Wingdings**. In the third row, click the right-pointing hand figure—**Wingdings** character **70**—as shown in **Figure 1**. ─────

   Wingdings is a font with ***character graphics***—small graphic characters that can be formatted as text.

3. Click **Insert**, and then **Close** ☒ the **Symbol** dialog box.

4. In the text box, add a space, and then type Contact Jacquetta Arnold at (805) 555-1031 for more information

5. Select all of the text, including the symbol. On the **Home tab**, in the **Font group**, change the **Font Size** to 22

6. Select the symbol, and then change the **Font Size** to 36 Click the **Font Dialog Box Launcher** . Select the **Subscript** check box, and then click the **Offset box up spin arrow** to display −12%. Click **OK**.

7. Repeat this process to place a left-pointing hand at the end of the line, change the **Font Size** to 36 and adjust the offset to −12%. Compare your screen with **Figure 2**. ─────

■ **Continue to the next page to complete the skill** ▶

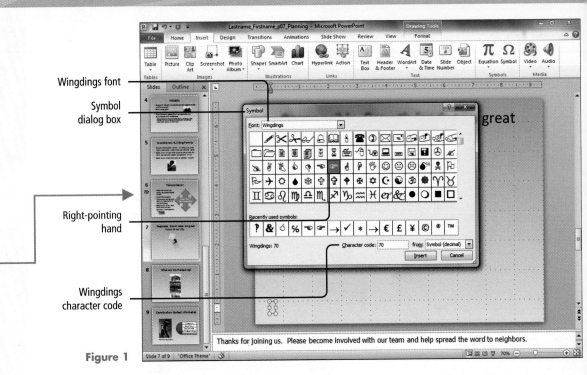

Wingdings font

Symbol dialog box

Right-pointing hand

Wingdings character code

Figure 1

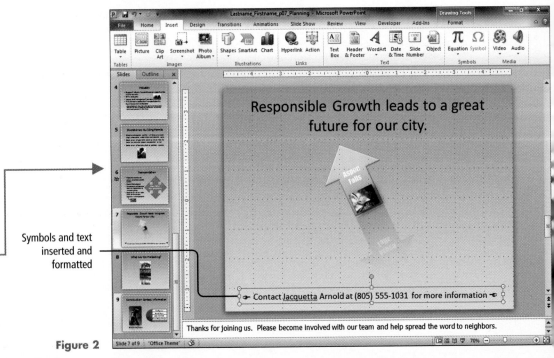

Symbols and text inserted and formatted

Figure 2

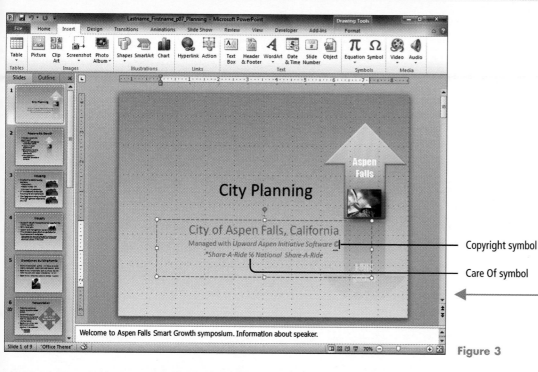

Copyright symbol

Care Of symbol

Figure 3

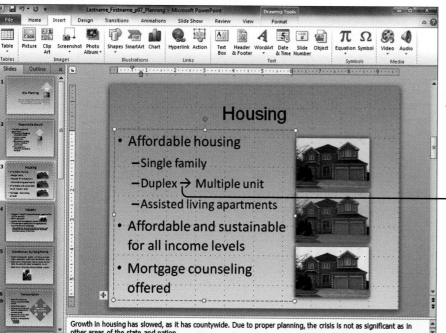

Rightwards arrow

Figure 4

8. Display **Slide 1**. Select the phrase *sponsored by*. On the **Insert tab**, in the **Symbols group**, click **Symbol**. In the displayed **Symbol** dialog box, verify the **Font box** shows (**normal text**). In the **Character code** box, replace the existing value with 2105 Verify that the ℅ symbol is selected, and then click **Insert**. **Close** the dialog box.

> You can find characters by entering their code into the Insert dialog box.

9. Place the insertion point to the right of *Upward Aspen Initiative Software*. Add a Space, and then type (c)—an opening parenthesis, the letter *c*, and a closing parenthesis, with no spaces. Compare your screen with **Figure 3**.

> Autocorrect changes the keystroke sequence to ©—the copyright symbol. If Autocorrect is disabled on your computer, you can insert the same symbol by using the Symbol dialog box.

10. Display **Slide 3**. Place your insertion point directly after the *x* in *Duplex*. Type a Space and then type --> (two hyphens followed by the greater-than symbol). Verify that Autocorrect inserted the arrow as shown in **Figure 4**. If necessary, use the Symbol dialog box to insert character code 2192 from the (**normal text**) font group.

11. **Save** your presentation.

- **You have completed Skill 9 of 10**

▶ The **Notes and Handouts Masters** can be edited so that information and images are added to all the **Notes and Handouts** pages.

1. Display **Slide 1**. On the **View tab**, in the **Master Views group**, click the **Notes Master** button.

2. In the **Page Setup group**, click **Notes Page Orientation**, click **Landscape**, and then compare your screen with **Figure 1**.

3. On the **Insert tab**, in the **Images group**, click **Picture**. From your **PowerPoint Chapter 7** folder, insert the picture **Lastname_Firstname_p07_Planning_Logo**.

4. With the logo selected, on the **Format tab**, in the **Size group**, change the **Shape Height** to 2"

5. Move the logo to the left of the slide placeholder as shown in **Figure 2**.

6. In the top left corner of the Notes Page, click the Header placeholder, and then type Firstname Lastname

7. On the **Notes Master tab**, click **Close Master View**. On the **View tab**, click the **Handout Master** button.

8. On the **Insert tab**, in the **Images group**, click **Picture**, and then from your **PowerPoint Chapter 7** folder, insert **Lastname_Firstname_p07_Planning_Logo**.

9. With the logo still selected, on the **Format tab**, in the **Size group**, change the **Shape Height** to 1"

▪ **Continue to the next page to complete the skill**

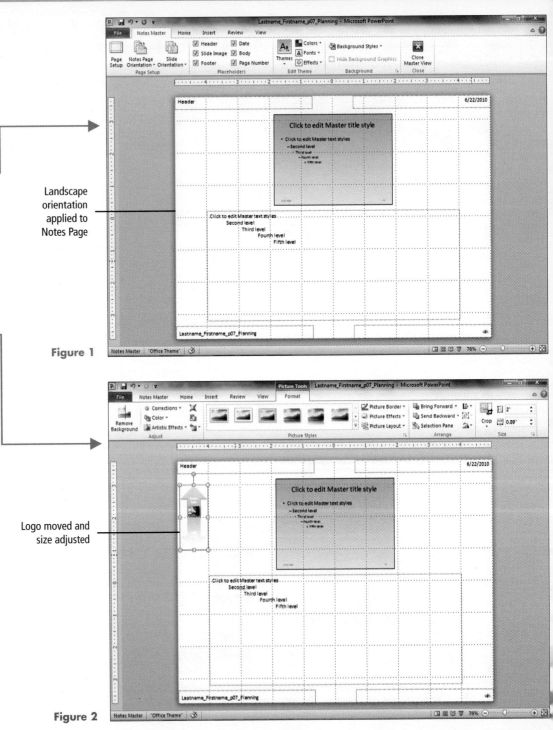

Landscape orientation applied to Notes Page

Figure 1

Logo moved and size adjusted

Figure 2

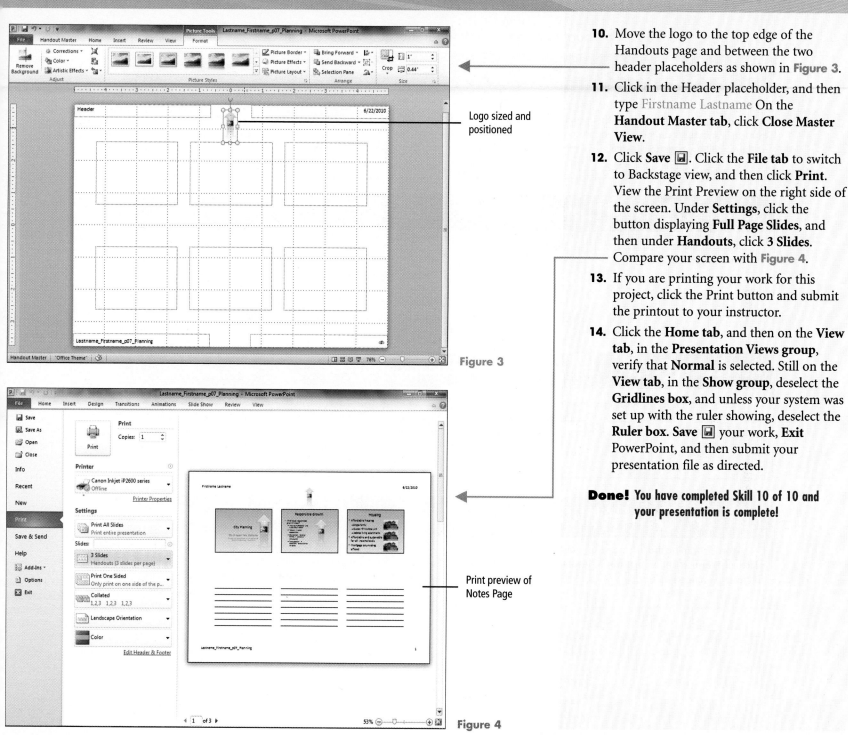

Logo sized and positioned

Figure 3

Print preview of Notes Page

Figure 4

10. Move the logo to the top edge of the Handouts page and between the two header placeholders as shown in **Figure 3**.

11. Click in the Header placeholder, and then type Firstname Lastname On the **Handout Master tab**, click **Close Master View**.

12. Click **Save** 🔲. Click the **File tab** to switch to Backstage view, and then click **Print**. View the Print Preview on the right side of the screen. Under **Settings**, click the button displaying **Full Page Slides**, and then under **Handouts**, click **3 Slides**. Compare your screen with **Figure 4**.

13. If you are printing your work for this project, click the Print button and submit the printout to your instructor.

14. Click the **Home tab**, and then on the **View tab**, in the **Presentation Views group**, verify that **Normal** is selected. Still on the **View tab**, in the **Show group**, deselect the **Gridlines box**, and unless your system was set up with the ruler showing, deselect the **Ruler box**. **Save** 🔲 your work, **Exit** PowerPoint, and then submit your presentation file as directed.

Done! You have completed Skill 10 of 10 and your presentation is complete!

The following More Skills are located at **www.pearsonhighered.com/skills**

More Skills ⑪ Save Slides as Image Files

Slides can be saved as individual image files so that they can be shared as pictures or used by other programs. Individual slides exported as pictures can be inserted into publications as graphics or thumbnail previews to provide visual reinforcement and add interest.

In More Skills 11, you will save the slides in a presentation as separate image files and then insert them into a Word document. To begin, open your web browser, navigate to www.pearsonhighered.com/skills, locate the name of your book, and follow the instructions on the website.

More Skills ⑫ Export Customized SmartArt as a Picture

SmartArt can be saved as a picture so that it can be inserted into other programs, including non-Microsoft programs.

In More Skills 12, you will create a customized piece of SmartArt, using photographs as backgrounds for the shapes in a Process Diagram. You will then export the custom diagram as a picture. To begin, open your web browser, navigate to www.pearsonhighered.com/skills, locate the name of your book, and follow the instructions on the website.

More Skills ⑬ Create SmartArt with the Nested Target Layout

The Nested Target layout is used to show relationships that occur within other relationships, such as a department that is part of—or nested within—another department.

In More Skills 13, you will create SmartArt with the Nested Target layout to illustrate relationships within departments in a city government. To begin, open your web browser, navigate to www.pearsonhighered.com/skills, locate the name of your book, and follow the instructions on the website.

More Skills ⑭ Create Text Effects by Combining WordArt and Shapes

WordArt can be used to create unique text effects. Multiple pieces of WordArt and shapes can be arranged and then grouped to create a single text effect.

In More Skills 14, you will combine WordArt effects and shapes to create a subtitle on a slide. To begin, open your web browser, navigate to www.pearsonhighered.com/skills, locate the name of your book, and follow the instructions on the website.

Key Terms

Alternative text 251

Character graphic 254

Compress 252

Crop. 252

Export 240

Gridlines. 243

Grouped object 240

Indent 242

Motion path 244

Photo Album 248

Pixel. 253

Pixels per inch 253

PPI. 253

Recolor 246

Online Help Skills

1. **Start** PowerPoint. In the upper right corner of the PowerPoint window, click the **Help** ⑨ button. In the **Help** window, click the **Maximize** 🔲 button.

2. Click in the search box, type Apply animation effects and then click the **Search** 🔍 button. In the search results, click **Apply PowerPoint animation effects with one click**. Compare your screen with **Figure 1**.

Figure 1

3. Read the pages and/or video, and then see if you can answer the following question: What is the advantage of using the Animation Painter? When might you use this feature?

Matching

Match each term in the second column with its correct definition in the first column by writing the letter of the term on the blank line in front of the correct definition.

____ **1.** A picture file format supported by web browsers and used in most digital cameras.

____ **2.** The top indent marker on the horizontal ruler.

____ **3.** An animation effect that moves objects along a line or curve.

____ **4.** Nonprinting dotted lines that form a pattern of one-inch squares on the slide, used for alignment.

____ **5.** The application of a stylized color or hue to a picture.

____ **6.** To remove unwanted areas from the edges of a picture.

____ **7.** Presentations composed of pictures.

____ **8.** Feature that changes a set of keystrokes to a common character, such as ©.

____ **9.** The smallest element from which a picture is constructed.

____ **10.** You can view the size of a presentation by clicking the File tab and then viewing these.

A Autocorrect

B Crop

C Properties

D First line indent marker

E Gridlines

F Joint Photographic Experts Group, or .jpg, file

G Motion path

H Photo Albums

I Pixel

J Recolor

Multiple Choice

Choose the correct answer.

1. To create a custom logo, you can do this to shapes, images, and text.
   A. Stack
   B. Superimpose
   C. Compress

2. Individual objects can be combined into a single object by doing this to them.
   A. Grouping
   B. Selecting
   C. Clicking

3. The process of saving a presentation picture as a separate graphic file.
   A. Compressing
   B. Exporting
   C. Zipping

4. The process of reducing a presentation's file size by changing the information stored about each picture in the presentation.
   A. Saving
   B. Minimizing
   C. Compressing

5. The text that displays when a graphic will not.
   A. Alternative text
   B. Broken graphic
   C. Picture caption

6. Text placed beneath a picture.
   A. Bio
   B. Tag
   C. Caption

7. Existing text can be changed to SmartArt by doing the following.
   A. Clicking the Convert to SmartArt Graphic button
   B. Copying and pasting information into SmartArt
   C. Clicking the Insert tab and then clicking SmartArt

8. Wingdings is an example of a font that contains these.
   A. Font style
   B. Character graphics
   C. Bit maps

9. The tool that converts a series of keystrokes into a symbol such as →.
   A. Autocomplete
   B. Autocharacter
   C. Autocorrect

10. Characters in the Symbol dialog box can be found using their character.
    A. Name
    B. Code
    C. Map

Topics for Discussion

1. Name some of the advantages and disadvantages of using images and graphics in presentations.

2. When you are designing a logo in PowerPoint, what things should you take into consideration?

Skill Check

To complete this project, you will need the following files:

- p07_City_Roles
- p07_City_Hat
- p07_City_Album

You will save your files as:

- Lastname_Firstname_p07_City_Roles
- Lastname_Firstname_p07_City_Logo

1. **Start** PowerPoint, and from your student files, open **p07_City_Roles**. **Save** it as Lastname_Firstname_p07_City_Roles in your **PowerPoint Chapter 7** folder.

2. On the **Insert tab**, in the **Illustrations group**, click **Shapes**, and then under **Basic Shapes**, click **Oval**. Draw a circle approximately 3" by 3" and then move the shape to the center of the slide, below the words *Aspen Falls, California*.

3. With the shape selected, on the **Format tab**, in the **Shape Styles group**, apply the **Subtle Effect - Black, Dark 1** shape style—the first effect in the fourth row of the gallery. Click **Shape Effects**, point to **Bevel**, and then click **Soft Round**—the second effect in the second row. Compare your screen with **Figure 1**.

4. On **Insert tab**, in the **Images group**, click **Picture**. From your student files, insert **p07_City_Hat**. Place the hat picture inside of the circle shape, centering it toward the top of the circle.

5. Select the circle shape, press **Enter** six times, and then type Aspen Falls On the **Home tab**, in the **Font group**, change the **Font Color** to **Blue**—located under **Standard Colors**.

6. With the circle shape still selected, press and hold **Ctrl**, and then click the hat picture. Release **Ctrl**. On the **Home tab**, in the **Drawing group**, click **Arrange**, and then click **Group**.

7. Right-click the grouped graphic, and then click **Save As Picture**. Navigate to your **PowerPoint Chapter 7** folder, and save the logo with the name Lastname_Firstname_p07_City_Logo in .jpg format.

8. With the logo selected, on the **Animations tab**, in the **Animation group**, click the **More** arrow. Scroll down, and under **Motion Paths**, click **Shapes**. Compare your screen with **Figure 2**.

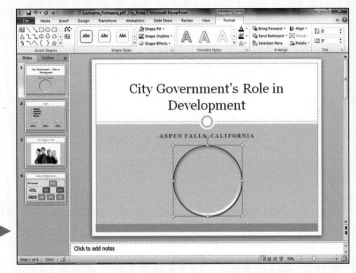

Figure 1

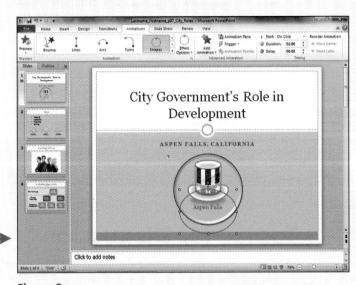

Figure 2

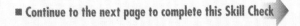
■ Continue to the next page to complete this Skill Check

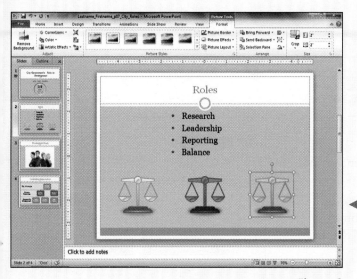

Figure 3

Figure 4

9. Display **Slide 2**, and select all of the bulleted text. If necessary, click the View tab, and select Ruler. On the horizontal ruler, move the left indent marker to the **3.5 inch** mark.

10. Select the center justice scale image. On the **Format tab**, in the **Adjust group**, click **Color**. Under **Recolor**, click **Red, Accent color 1 Dark**. Select the right image, and then recolor it with **Green, Accent color 5 Dark**. Compare your screen with **Figure 3**.

11. Display **Slide 3**. Select the photo, and then on the **Insert tab**, in the **Links group**, click **Hyperlink**. In the **Hyperlink** dialog box, navigate to your student files and click **p07_City_Album**.

12. On the **Insert tab**, in the **Text group**, click **Text Box**. Below the team picture, draw a text box that matches the width of the picture.

13. In the text box, add the text Aspen Falls City Management Team Photo Album and then change the **Font Size** to 20 and **Center** the text.

14. In the title placeholder, click to the left of the word *Development*. On the **Insert tab**, in the **Symbols group**, click **Symbol**. In the **Symbol** dialog box, change the **Font** to **Wingdings 2**, and then click the thumbs-up symbol—**Character code 60**. Click the **Insert** button, and then click the **Close** button.

15. On the **View tab**, in the **Master Views group**, click **Handout Master**.

16. On the **Insert tab**, in the **Images group**, click **Picture**. From your **PowerPoint Chapter 7** folder, insert **Lastname_Firstname_p07_City_Logo**.

17. With the logo still selected, on the **Format tab**, in the **Size group**, adjust both the height and width to 1" Move the logo to the upper center of the page. Click the left **Footer** placeholder, and then type Lastname_Firstname_p07_City_Roles Click **Close Master View**.

18. Click the **Home tab**, display **Slide 3**, and then select the picture. On the **Format tab**, in the **Adjust group**, click **Compress Pictures**. Verify that the **Screen** option button is selected, and then click **OK**. **Save** the presentation, and then click the **File tab** and compare your screen with **Figure 4**.

19. Submit your presentation as directed.

Done! You have completed the Skill Check

Assess Your Skills 1

To complete this project, you will need the following files:

- p07_Permits
- p07_Permits_Photo
- p07_Permits_Album

You will save your files as:

- Lastname_Firstname_p07_Permits
- Lastname_Firstname_p07_Permits_Logo

1. **Start** PowerPoint, and from your student files, open **p07_Permits**. **Save** the file in your **PowerPoint Chapter 7** folder as Lastname_Firstname_p07_Permits

2. Display **Slide 1**, and then insert a **Striped Right Arrow** shape—the fifth shape in the second row under **Block Arrows**. Change shape's height to 1.5" and then change its width to 3.3" In the shape, add the text Managed Growth

3. Turn on **Gridlines** and then drag to align the right edge of the arrow shape to the **1** inch mark on the horizontal ruler and align the top edge with the **2** inch mark on the vertical ruler.

4. Still on **Slide 1**, insert the picture **p07_Permits_Photo**. Change the picture's height to 0.75" and place it to the left of the arrow shape, so that the border of the picture touches the border of the arrow. **Group** the arrow shape and the picture. **Save** the grouped shape as a .tiff file with the name Lastname_Firstname_p07_Permits_Logo

5. For the grouped shape, add a **Motion Path** in the **Arcs** format.

6. Display **Slide 2**. Place your insertion point in the last bullet point, *Appeal process at city meeting*. With the **Ruler** displayed, drag the first line indent marker to the **1.5** inch mark on the horizontal ruler.

7. On **Slide 2**, select the image, and insert a hyperlink that opens the Photo Album located in your student files—**p07_Permits_Album**.

8. Below the image on **Slide 2**, insert the caption Building permit approval and size it to fit under the image.

9. On **Slide 3**, convert the bulleted text to SmartArt, with the **Continuous Block Process** layout. With the SmartArt shape selected, and under **SmartArt Tools**, use the **Design tab** and **SmartArt Styles group** to change the style to **Polished**.

10. On **Slide 3**, click to the left of the title, and using Wingdings 3, insert the Character 103. Click to the right of the title, and then insert the Character 102. Compare with **Figure 1**.

11. Edit the **Handout Master** to include the file name in the left footer. Place the logo you created, **Lastname_Firstname_p07_Permits_Logo**, in the upper left corner. Size the logo approximately to a **Shape Height** of 1" and a **Shape Width** of 2.83"

12. **Save**, and then submit your presentation as directed.

Done! You have completed Assess Your Skills 1

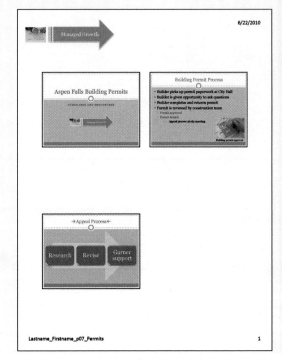

Figure 1

Assess Your Skills 2

To complete this project, you will need the following files:

- p07_Training
- p07_Training_Photo

You will save your presentation as:

- Lastname_Firstname_p07_Training

7/3/2010

Lastname_firstname_p07_Training   1

Figure 1

1. **Start** PowerPoint, and then open **p07_Training**. **Save** the presentation in your **PowerPoint Chapter 7** folder as Lastname_Firstname_p07_Training

2. On **Slide 1**, insert a **Curved Up Ribbon** shape, found under **Stars and Banners**. Change the **Size** to 1.7" height and 3.25" width. Add the text State Growth Award Winner and then change the **Shape Style** to **Moderate Effect - Blue-Gray, Accent 1**.

3. Move the Training Award shape to the lower right corner of the slide.

4. For all of the bulleted text on **Slide 2**, apply a left indent of **1 inch**.

5. On **Slide 3**, insert the picture named **p07_Training_Photo** from your student files, and move it below the text on the slide. Recolor the picture as **Grayscale**, and then apply the **Reflected Rounded Rectangle** picture style.

6. Below the picture, insert a text box that matches the width of the picture. Insert the text One-on-one training opportunities **Center** the text, and then apply **Italic**.

7. On **Slide 4**, to the left of the title, insert the question mark character graphic ?—**Wingdings 2**, character code **95**—and then add a space. To the right of the title, insert a space and the same character graphic.

8. **Compress** all of the presentation images by using the **Screen** target output.

9. On **Slide 4**, for the image, add the **Motion Path, Arcs**.

10. Edit the **Handout Master** by adding Lastname_Firstname_p07_Training to the footer.

11. **Save** the presentation, and then submit it as directed.

Done! You have completed Assess Your Skills 2

Assess Your Skills Visually

To complete this project, you will need the following file:

- p07_Energy_Sources

You will save your files as:

- Lastname_Firstname_p07_Energy_Sources
- Lastname_Firstname_p07_Energy_Logo

Start PowerPoint. Create a presentation as shown in **Figure 1**. **Save** the file as Lastname_Firstname_p07_Energy_Sources in your **PowerPoint Chapter 7** folder.

To complete this slide, insert a rectangle shape above the clip art on the slide. Size the rectangle to a **Height** of 2.6" and a **Width** of 1" Center the shape above the clip art. Type Aspen Falls in the rectangle, and change the font to **Calibri**. Apply **Bold** and change the font color to **Light Green**—the fifth choice under **Standard Colors**. Change the **Shape Style** of the rectangle to **Intense Effect - Black, Dark 1**—the first option in the last row of the **Shape Styles** gallery. **Group** the rectangle and the clip art. **Save** the newly grouped image as Lastname_Firstname_p07_Energy_Logo Add Lastname_Firstname_p07_Energy_Logo to the upper left header of the Handout Master, and then change the shape **Height** to 2"—the width will automatically adjust. Add the file name to the lower left footer of the Handout Master. **Save** and submit your presentation as directed by your instructor.

Done! You have completed Assess Your Skills Visually

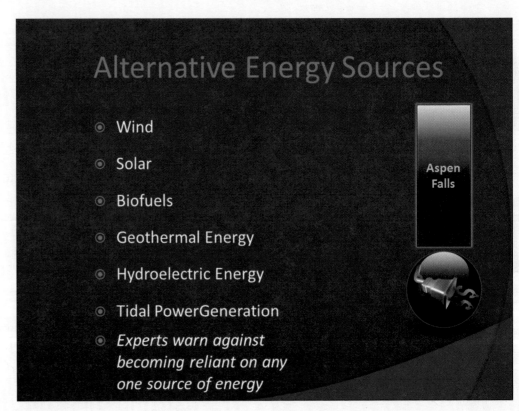

Figure 1

Skills in Context

To complete this project, you will need the following file:

- p07_Park_Cleanup

You will save your files as:

- Lastname_Firstname_p07_Park_Cleanup
- Lastname_Firstname_p07_Park_Logo

Using your student data files, open the file **p07_Park_Cleanup** to create a presentation for Maria Martinez, City Manager, for use at upcoming community events. On the first slide, create a logo for Park Cleanup Days composed of at least three objects—shapes, clip art, text, or pictures—and then group the objects. Save the newly created logo as Lastname_Firstname_ p07_Park_Logo Insert the **Trademark symbol, Character code 2122**—™—to the right of the title on **Slide 1**. On **Slide 2**, **Recolor** the picture in the lower right corner of the slide, and then **Compress** the image for a **Target output** for **Screen** to reduce its file size. Insert the following caption beneath the image on **Slide 2**: Parks impact

quality of life On **Slide 3**, insert a piece of related clip art, and then animate it by using a **Motion Path** of your choice. On **Slide 4**, convert the text in the right content placeholder to any style of **SmartArt**. **Save** the presentation in your **PowerPoint Chapter 7** folder as Lastname_Firstname_p07_Park_Cleanup Add the file name to the **Notes and Handouts** footer, and then **Apply to All** and click **Save**. Print or submit electronically, as directed by your instructor.

Done! You have completed Skills in Context

Skills and You

To complete this project, you will need the following file:

- New blank PowerPoint presentation

You will save your presentation as:

- Lastname_Firstname_p07_Photo_Album

Using the skills you have practiced in this chapter, create a Photo Album presentation about a topic of your choice. Include at least six slides. Insert images of your choice into the presentation. Add a caption to at least two images. Apply picture styles, slide transitions, and animations as appropriate. Add at least one motion path. Insert a shape and then add an image to the shape,

and group the objects into a logo. Compress all images in the presentation. Save the presentation in your **PowerPoint Chapter 7** folder as Lastname_Firstname_p07_Photo_Album

Done! You have completed Skills and You

CHAPTER 8

Create Custom Templates

▶ You can create your own custom templates and then use them to create new presentations with custom designs and content.

▶ Custom templates save time and promote a consistent look and feel for all of your presentations.

Your starting screen will look like this:

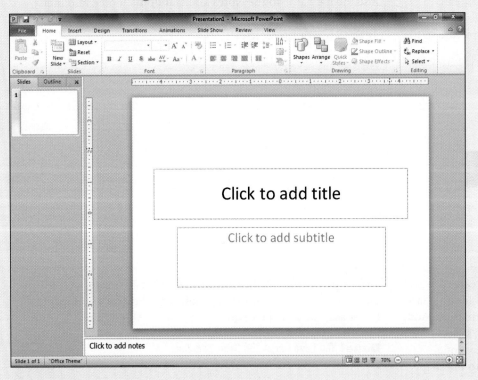

SKILLS

Skills 1-10 Training

At the end of this chapter, you will be able to:

Skill 1 Create Custom Templates

Skill 2 Customize Slide Layouts

Skill 3 Set Transparent Colors and Organize Slide Masters and Layouts

Skill 4 Customize Slide Master Elements

Skill 5 Create Custom Layouts

Skill 6 Add Custom SmartArt Placeholders

Skill 7 Work with Multiple Slide Masters

Skill 8 Use Templates to Create New Presentations

Skill 9 Insert Slides from Multiple Slide Masters

Skill 10 Organize Slide Elements Using the Selection and Visibility Task Pane

MORE SKILLS

More Skills 11 Create Photo Albums from Templates

More Skills 12 Create Quiz Shows from Templates

More Skills 13 Add Online Templates to Existing Presentations

More Skills 14 Customize the Quick Access Toolbar

Outcome

Using the skills listed to the left will enable you to create a presentation like this:

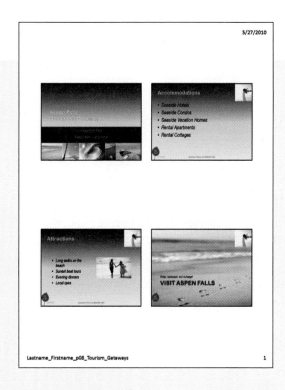

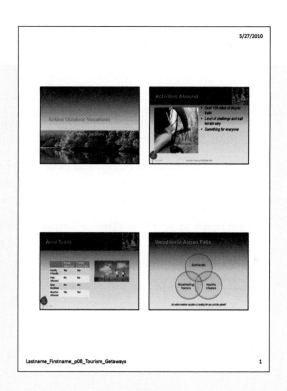

You will save your files as:

Lastname_Firstname_p08_Tourism_Template
Lastname_Firstname_p08_Tourism_Getaways

In this chapter, you will create presentations for the Aspen Falls City Hall, which provides essential services for the citizens and visitors of Aspen Falls, California.

Introduction

- ► Templates are PowerPoint files with prebuilt layouts, theme colors, theme fonts, background styles, and slide content.

- ► Template files can be opened to create new presentations. When you share your template files, others can use the templates to create their own presentations that contain your custom design elements.

- ► When you need the same information or objects on all slides, you can place them in a slide master. You can then edit them in the slide master instead of on each individual slide.

- ► You can modify or add placeholders on existing slide layouts or create new layouts in which you insert your own placeholders.

Time to complete all
10 skills – 50 to 90 minutes

Find your student data files here:

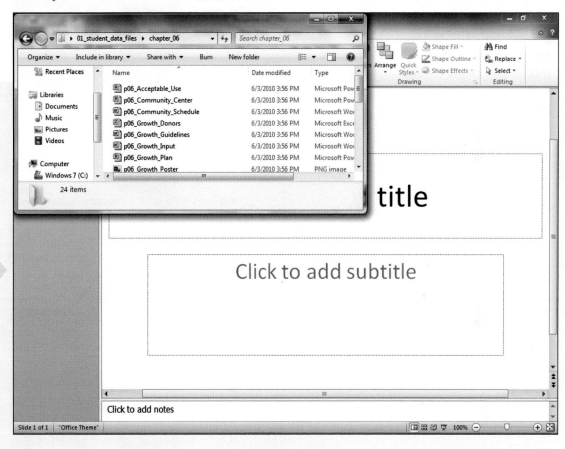

Student data files needed for this chapter:

- p08_Tourism_Logo
- p08_Tourism1
- p08_Tourism2
- p08_Tourism3
- p08_Tourism4
- p08_Tourism5
- p08_Tourism6
- p08_Tourism7
- p08_Tourism8
- p08_Tourism9
- p08_Tourism10
- p08_Tourism11

▸ A *template* is a prebuilt slide, or group of slides, that is saved in the template file format, with the .potx file extension.

▸ PowerPoint designers often create *custom templates*—slides with prebuilt backgrounds, images, logos, and colors designed for a specific organization.

1. **Start** PowerPoint to display a new, blank presentation.

2. On the **View tab**, in the **Master Views group**, click **Slide Master**. Alternately, press [Shift], and then click the Normal View 🔲 button.

3. On the **Slide Master tab**, in the **Background group**, click **Background Styles**. In the **Background Styles** gallery, click **Format Background**.

4. Select the **Gradient fill** option, and then click the **Color button arrow**. Under **Standard Colors**, click **Dark Blue**. Click **Apply to All**, and then click **Close**. Compare your screen with **Figure 1**.

5. Click the **File tab**, and click **Save As**. In the **Save As** dialog box, click the **Save as type box arrow**, and in the list, click **PowerPoint Template**.

6. In the **Save As** dialog box, navigate to the location where you are saving your files, and create a new folder named PowerPoint Chapter 8 Name the file Lastname_Firstname_p08_Tourism_Template and then click **Save**. Compare your screen with **Figure 2**.

7. Select the top slide thumbnail, the **Office Theme Slide Master**. On the **Insert tab**, in the **Illustrations group**, click the **Shapes** button. Under **Rectangles**, click the first choice—**Rectangle**.

■ **Continue to the next page to complete the skill**

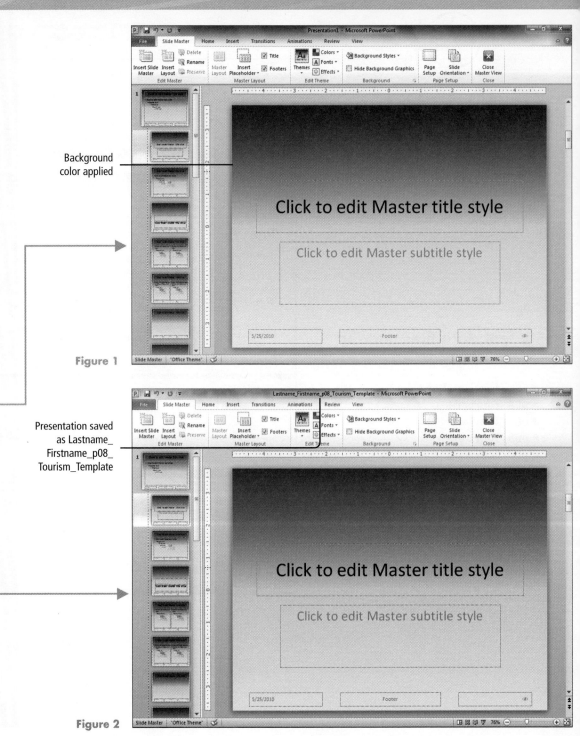

Background color applied

Figure 1

Presentation saved as Lastname_Firstname_p08_Tourism_Template

Figure 2

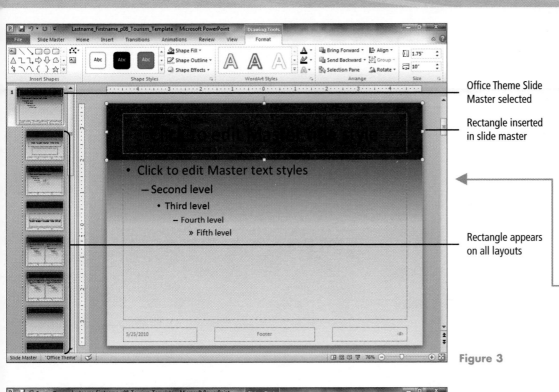

Office Theme Slide Master selected

Rectangle inserted in slide master

Rectangle appears on all layouts

Figure 3

Master title color and alignment edited

Picture added

Figure 4

8. On the slide, draw a rectangle starting at the top left corner and ending at the right edge of the slide, even with the top of the content placeholder.

9. On the **Drawing Tools Format tab**, in the **Shape Styles group**, click the **Shape Fill** button. Under **Standard Colors**, click **Dark Blue**. In the **Shape Styles group**, click the **Shape Outline** button, and then click **No Outline**. In the **Arrange group**, click the **Send Backward button arrow**, and then click **Send to Back**.

10. On the **Format tab**, in the **Size group**, adjust the height of the rectangle to 1.75 and the width to 10 Move the rectangle as necessary to match **Figure 3**.

Because the Slide Master is selected, the format is applied to all associated *slide layouts*—the arrangement of objects—like titles and placeholders—on a slide.

11. In the title placeholder, select the text *Click to edit Master title style*. On the **Home tab**, change the **Font Color** to **White, Background 1**. Click the **Align Text Left** button.

12. On the **Insert tab**, in the **Images group**, click **Picture**. From your student files, insert **p08_Tourism1**. Move the picture to the upper right corner of the slide as shown in **Figure 4**.

13. Save the template. If you are continuing to Skill 2, no further action is necessary. If you are exiting PowerPoint and working on Skill 2 later, you will need to reopen the file as a template. To do this, open PowerPoint, click the **File tab**, click **Open**, locate the file, and then click **Open**.

■ **You have completed Skill 1 of 10**

► A *slide master* stores the master layout and theme for the slides contained in a presentation. All presentations contain a master; some contain more than one master.

1. Still in Slide Master view, select the second thumbnail—**Title Slide Layout**. On the **Slide Master tab**, in the **Background group**, select the **Hide Background Graphics** check box.

   The smaller thumbnails below the slide master are the various slide layouts associated with the slide master.

2. Be sure that your ruler is displayed. On the **Insert tab**, in the **Illustrations group**, click the **Shapes** button, and then click **Rectangle**. Draw a rectangle starting at the left edge of the slide and the **.5** inch mark below zero on the vertical ruler and ending at the lower right corner.

3. Apply the same **Dark Blue** shape fill used in Skill 1, and remove the shape outline. In the **Arrange group**, click the **Send Backward button arrow**, and then click **Send to Back**.

4. Delete the three footer placeholders, and compare your screen with **Figure 1**.

5. On the **Insert tab**, in the **Images group**, click **Picture**, and then from your student files, insert the file **p08_Tourism2**. Position the picture in the lower left corner of the slide. Repeat this technique to insert **p08_Tourism3**, **p08_Tourism4**, **p08_Tourism5**, and **p08_Tourism6**. Position the pictures from left to right, aligning their edges as shown in **Figure 2**.

■ **Continue to the next page to complete the skill** ➤

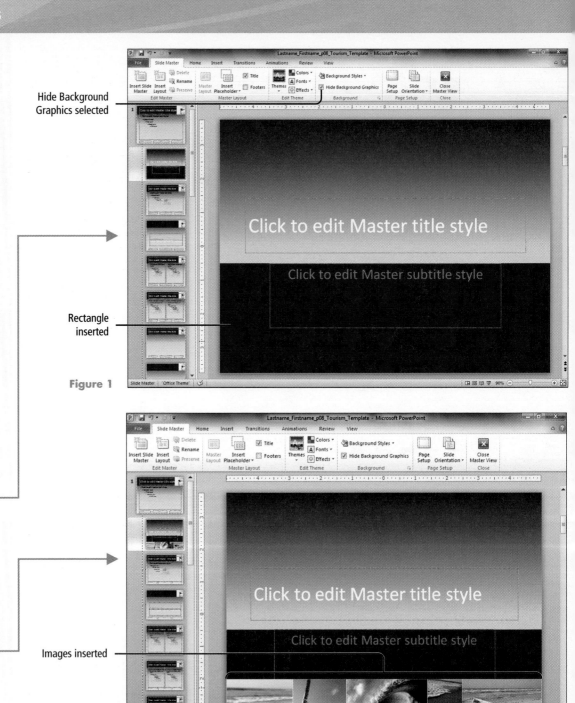

Hide Background Graphics selected

Rectangle inserted

Figure 1

Images inserted

Figure 2

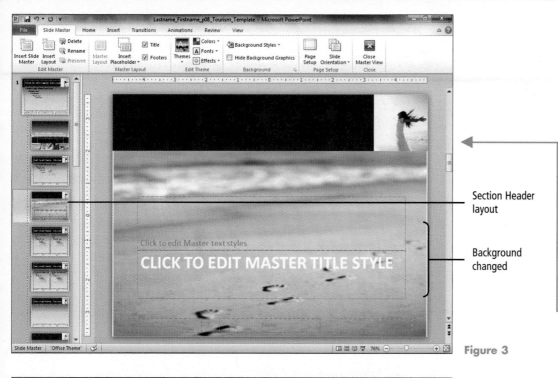

Figure 3

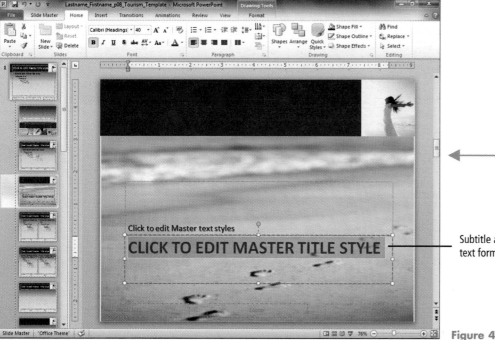

Figure 4

6. Click anywhere on the top of the slide to deselect the picture, and then select the subtitle placeholder. Point to the lower middle sizing handle, and then with the ⬍ pointer, drag up so the lower edge is aligned just above the top of the pictures.

7. Select the fourth thumbnail—**Section Header Layout**. On the **Slide Master tab**, in the **Background group**, click the **Background Styles** button, and then click **Format Background**.

8. In the **Format Background** dialog box, select the **Picture or texture fill** option button, and then under **Insert from**, click **File**. From your student files, insert **p08_Tourism2**. **Close** the dialog box, and compare your screen with **Figure 3**.

   The background is changed for the Section Header layout only. This design will appear on all new slides assigned the Section Header layout.

9. In the subtitle placeholder, select the text *Click to edit Master text styles*, and then on the **Home tab**, change the font color to **Dark Blue**. In the **Font group**, click the **Text Shadow** button ⬜.

10. In the title placeholder, select the text *Click to edit Master title style*, and then change the font color to **Dark Blue**. Compare with **Figure 4**.

11. On the **View tab**, in the **Presentation Views group**, click **Normal**. Press F5 to preview the design of the title slide, press Esc to end the show, and then switch back to Slide Master view. **Save** 💾 your template.

- **You have completed Skill 2 of 10**

► Slide masters and layouts can be renamed to help users identify their purpose.

1. In Slide Master view, select the first thumbnail—the slide master.

2. On the **Insert tab**, in the **Images group**, click **Picture**, and then from your student data files, insert **p08_Tourism_Logo**.

   The thumbnails reflect that the logo is inserted into all slide layout backgrounds. Recall that the Title Slide layout has the background graphics hidden.

3. Right-click the selected image. On the displayed shortcut menu, change the picture's **Shape Height** value to 1.4 and align the logo with the lower left corner of the slide.

4. On the **Format tab**, in the **Adjust group**, click the **Color** button, and then click **Set Transparent Color**. Point to a white area in the background of the logo, and click one time. Compare your screen with **Figure 1**.

   Transparent color can be applied to certain graphic formats to remove unwanted color from areas of the image.

5. With the slide master still selected in the pane containing the slide thumbnails, on the **Slide Master tab**, in the **Edit Master group**, click **Rename**.

6. In the **Rename Layout** dialog box, in the **Layout name** box, type General Tourism Click **Rename**. Point to the slide master thumbnail, and compare your screen with **Figure 2**.

   The status bar displays the name of the slide master. Naming a slide master is helpful when there are multiple slide masters.

■ **Continue to the next page to complete the skill**

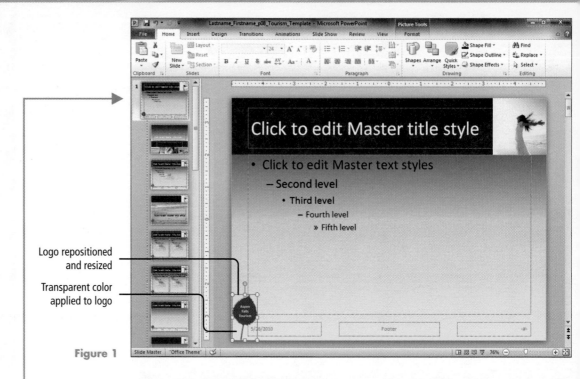

Logo repositioned and resized

Transparent color applied to logo

Figure 1

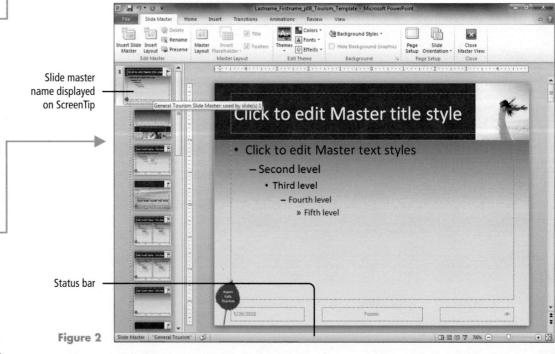

Slide master name displayed on ScreenTip

Status bar

Figure 2

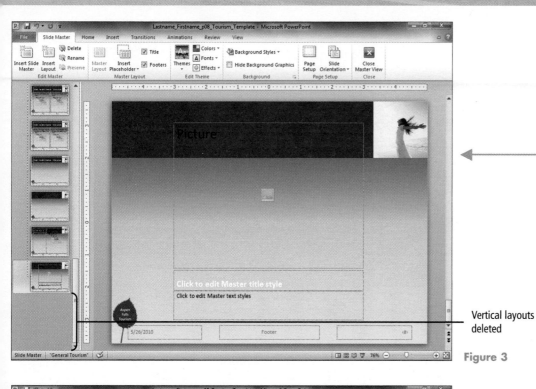

Vertical layouts deleted

Figure 3

Preserved slide master

Figure 4

7. In the pane that contains the thumbnails, right-click the second thumbnail—**Title Slide** layout. In the shortcut menu, click **Rename Layout**. In the **Rename Layout** dialog box, type Opening Slide and then click **Rename**.

The slide layout is renamed.

8. Using the technique just practiced, change the name of the **Section Header** layout to Tourism Section Title

9. Scroll to the bottom of the pane that contains the thumbnails. Click the second-to-last thumbnail—**Title and Vertical Text** layout—and then on the **Slide Master tab**, in the **Edit Master group**, click **Delete** to remove the slide layout from the slide master group.

10. Repeat the technique just practiced to delete the last thumbnail—**Vertical Title and Text** layout. Compare your screen with **Figure 3**.

The two vertical layouts are deleted and will not be available when you use this template to create presentations.

11. In the pane that contains the thumbnails, select the slide master—**General Tourism**. On the **Slide Master tab**, in the **Edit Master group**, click **Preserve**. Compare your screen with **Figure 4**.

The pushpin indicates that the slide master has been *preserved*—a slide master setting that prevents the slide master from accidentally being deleted.

12. Save 🖫 the template.

■ **You have completed Skill 3 of 10**

▶ If you make formatting changes to the slide master, they will be made to all slides in the presentation.

▶ Shapes can be added to the slide master so that they display on each slide in the presentation.

1. In Slide Master view, select the **General Tourism** slide master. On the slide, select the text *Click to edit Master title style*. On the **Home tab**, in the **Font group**, decrease the **Font Size** to **36**.

2. Click the **Font** arrow, and then click **Arial Rounded MT Bold**.

3. On the **Format tab**, in the **WordArt Styles group**, click the **Text Effects** button. Point to **Bevel**, and then click **Riblet**, the second option in the third row. Compare your screen with **Figure 1**.

4. In the slide master content placeholder, select all of the text from *Click to edit Master text styles* to *Fifth level*.

5. On the **Home tab**, in the **Font group**, click the **Font** arrow, and then click **Arial Narrow**.

6. In the content placeholder, select the text beginning with *Second level* and ending with *Fifth level*.

7. In the **Font group**, click the **Italic** button, and then compare your screen with **Figure 2**.

■ **Continue to the next page to complete the skill**

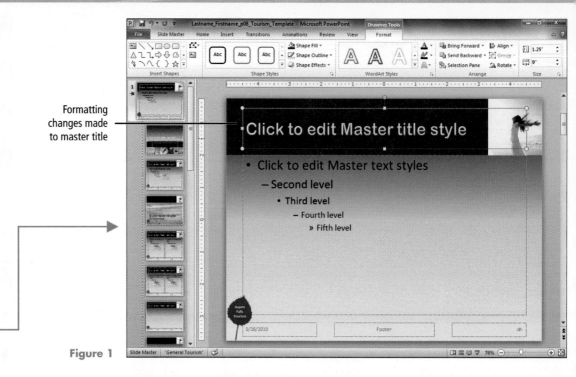

Formatting changes made to master title

Figure 1

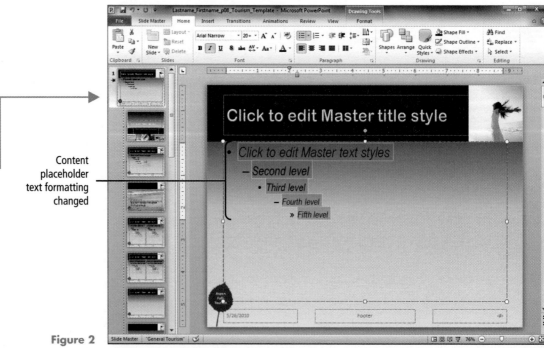

Content placeholder text formatting changed

Figure 2

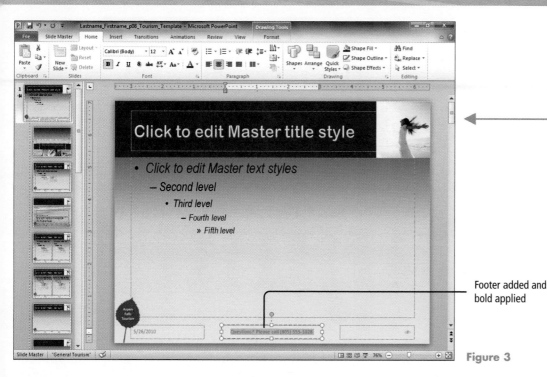

Footer added and
bold applied

Figure 3

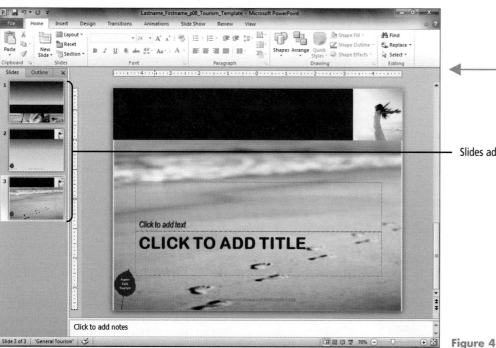

Slides added

Figure 4

8. With the slide master still selected, click the center box that says **Footer**.

9. Type Questions? Please call (805) 555-1028

10. Select the text, and then on the **Home tab**, in the **Font group**, click the **Bold** button. Compare your screen with Figure 3.

11. On the **Insert tab**, in the **Text group**, click **Header & Footer**. In the **Header and Footer** dialog box, select the **Date and time** check box. Verify that **Update Automatically** is selected.

12. Select the **Footer** check box.

    The text entered in the footer on the slide displays in the Header and Footer dialog box. When the Footer option is selected, this information will display automatically on all slides.

13. Click **Apply to All**.

14. Click the **Normal View** button . On the **Home tab**, in the **Slides group**, click the lower half of the **New Slide** button, and then click **Title and Content** to insert a new slide. Insert another new slide with the **Tourism Section Title** layout, and then compare your screen with Figure 4.

    Recall that the New Slide gallery displays the available layouts for new slides. Here, the changes made to the slide master and Section Header layouts are reflected in each thumbnail in the gallery.

15. **Save** and then press and hold Shift while clicking the **Normal View** button to return to Slide Master view.

■ **You have completed Skill 4 of 10**

► When built-in slide layouts do not meet your needs, you can build a *custom slide layout*—a reusable layout in which you insert your own placeholders, backgrounds, and theme sets.

1. In Slide Master view, select the fourth thumbnail—**Tourism Section Title** layout. On the **Slide Master tab**, in the **Edit Master group**, click the **Insert Layout** button.

2. In the **Edit Master group**, click the **Rename** button. In the **Rename Layout** dialog box, in the **Layout name** box, type Tourism Comparison and then click **Rename**.

3. On the **View tab**, in the **Show group**, select the **Gridlines** check box.

4. On the **Slide Master tab**, in the **Master Layout group**, click the **Insert Placeholder button arrow**, and then compare your screen with **Figure 1**.

Placeholders can be inserted into a custom layout.

5. Click **Table**. With the ⊞ pointer, use the gridlines—each square represents an inch—to draw a placeholder that is 3" in **Height** and 4" in **Width**. Use the **Format tab** and the **Size group** to adjust the size if necessary.

6. Point to the placeholder's border, and then with the ⌖ pointer, drag the placeholder so that the upper left corner is at the **1 inch** mark above zero on the vertical ruler and the **4 inch** mark to the left of zero on the horizontal ruler, as shown in **Figure 2**.

■ **Continue to the next page to complete the skill** ➤

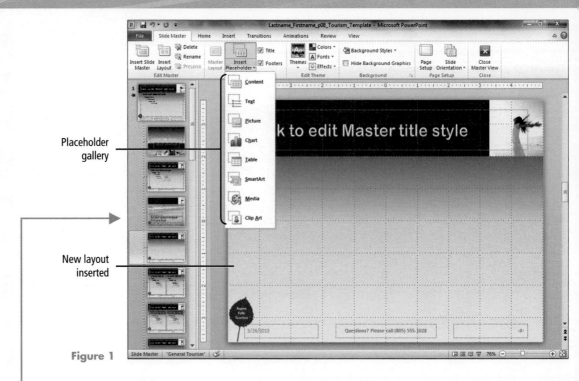

Placeholder gallery

New layout inserted

Figure 1

Table placeholder

Figure 2

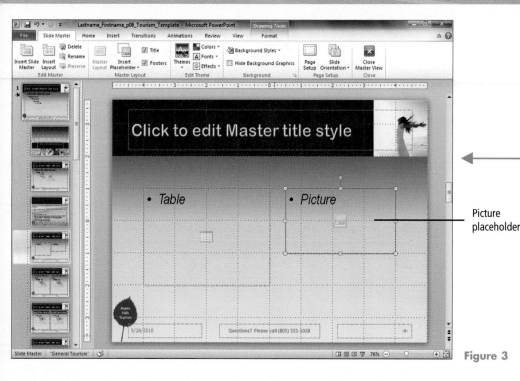

Picture placeholder

Figure 3

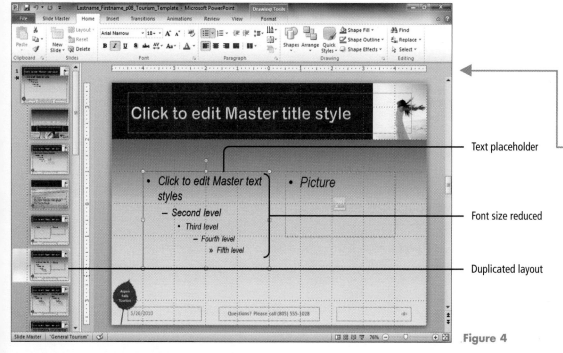

Text placeholder

Font size reduced

Duplicated layout

Figure 4

7. On the **Slide Master tab**, in the **Master Layout group**, click the **Insert Placeholder button arrow**. Click **Picture**, and then draw a picture placeholder **3 inches** in width and **2 inches** in height. Position the upper left corner of the placeholder on the **1 inch** mark on the vertical ruler and the **0.5 inch** mark on the horizontal ruler. Compare with **Figure 3**.

8. With the thumbnail for the new layout still selected, on the **Home tab**, click the lower half of the **New Slide** button, and then click **Duplicate Selected Slides**.

9. Display the **Slide Master tab**, and then repeat the technique used earlier to **Rename** the new custom layout Tourism List

10. Click the table placeholder border, and then press Delete to remove it from the slide.

11. Insert a **Text** placeholder that is **4 inches** in width and **3 inches** in height. Position the text placeholder so that the upper left corner is at the **1 inch** mark on the vertical ruler and the **4 inch** mark to the left of zero on the horizontal ruler. With the placeholder still selected, on the **Home tab**, in the **Font group**, click the **Decrease Font Size** button one time. Compare your screen with **Figure 4**.

12. On the **View tab**, in the **Show group**, clear the **Gridlines** check box.

13. On the **Insert tab**, in the **Text group**, click the **Header & Footer** button. On the **Notes and Handouts tab**, click **Footer** and type the file name and then click **Apply to All**. **Save** 💾 the template.

■ **You have completed Skill 5 of 10**

▶ Placeholders that are used to insert SmartArt can be added to any layout.

▶ Placeholder text and formats can be edited—for example, you can add your own instructions in the placeholder.

1. Scroll to the bottom of the slide thumbnail pane, and then click the fourth-to-last thumbnail—**Title Only** layout.

2. Using the technique practiced previously, rename the layout Tourism SmartArt

3. On the **Slide Master tab**, in the **Background group**, select the **Hide Background Graphics** check box.

    Hiding the background graphics helps the audience focus on the SmartArt.

4. On the **Slide Master tab**, in the **Master Layout group**, click the **Insert Placeholder** arrow, and then click **SmartArt**.

5. With the ⊞ pointer, click anywhere in the slide to insert a **SmartArt** placeholder. On the **Format tab**, in the **Size group**, change the placeholder's **Height** to 4.5" and its **Width** to 9" Position the placeholder approximately as shown in **Figure 1**.

6. In the placeholder, point to the left of the text *SmartArt graphic*. With the Ⅰ pointer, click one time, and then type Click the icon below to insert a SmartArt graphic. Select the SmartArt layout of your choice, and then apply the Cartoon style and Accent 1 colors. Decrease the **Font Size** to **28** points. Compare your screen with **Figure 2**.

    The placeholder text will display when a new slide is created from the Tourism SmartArt layout.

■ **Continue to the next page to complete the skill**

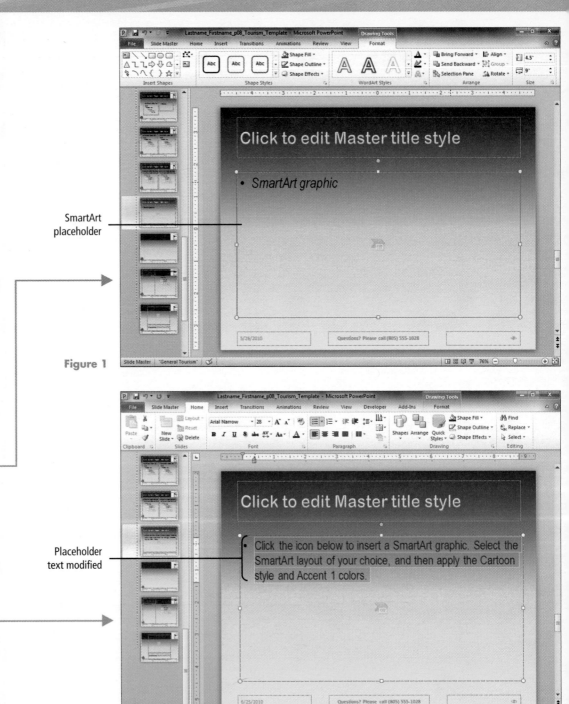

SmartArt placeholder

Figure 1

Placeholder text modified

Figure 2

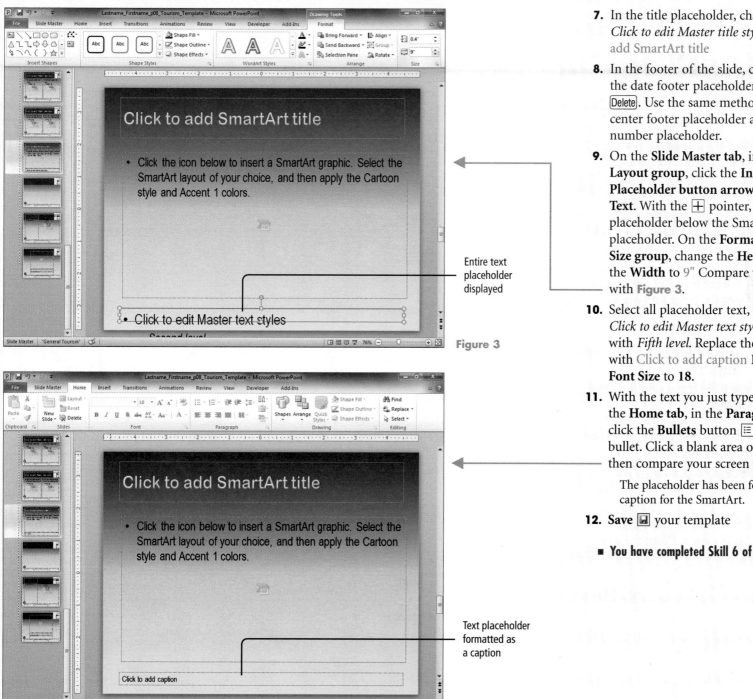

Figure 3

Entire text placeholder displayed

Figure 4

Text placeholder formatted as a caption

7. In the title placeholder, change the text *Click to edit Master title style* to Click to add SmartArt title

8. In the footer of the slide, click a border of the date footer placeholder and press Delete. Use the same method to delete the center footer placeholder and slide number placeholder.

9. On the **Slide Master tab**, in the **Master Layout group**, click the **Insert Placeholder button arrow**, and then click **Text**. With the ⊞ pointer, draw a text placeholder below the SmartArt placeholder. On the **Format tab**, in the **Size group**, change the **Height** to 0.4" and the **Width** to 9" Compare your screen with **Figure 3**.

10. Select all placeholder text, starting with *Click to edit Master text styles* and ending with *Fifth level*. Replace the selected text with Click to add caption Decrease the **Font Size** to 18.

11. With the text you just typed selected, on the **Home tab**, in the **Paragraph group**, click the **Bullets** button ⊞ ▾ to remove the bullet. Click a blank area of the slide, and then compare your screen with **Figure 4**.

    The placeholder has been formatted as a caption for the SmartArt.

12. Save 🔲 your template

    ■ **You have completed Skill 6 of 10**

▶ When presentations contain two or more styles or themes, a slide master is needed for each theme.

▶ Multiple slide masters each have their own set of associated layouts, and each slide master can be customized without affecting the other slide master.

1. Still in Slide Master view, right-click the **General Tourism Slide Master** thumbnail, and then from the shortcut menu, click **Duplicate Slide Master**. Compare your screen with **Figure 1**.

    A second slide master is inserted that inherits the formatting and objects of the first slide master.

2. With the new slide master still selected, on the **Slide Master tab**, in the **Edit Master group**, click **Rename**. Type Sustainable Tourism and then press Enter.

3. In the upper right corner of the Sustainable Tourism master, select the image, and then press Delete. On the **Insert tab**, in the **Images group**, click **Picture**, and then from your student files, insert **p08_Tourism7**. Position the picture in the upper right corner of the slide.

4. Select the text *Click to edit Master title style*. On the **Format tab**, in the **WordArt Styles group**, click the **Text Fill** button ▲, and then under **Standard Colors**, click the fifth color—**Light Green**. Compare your screen with **Figure 2**.

■ **Continue to the next page to complete the skill**

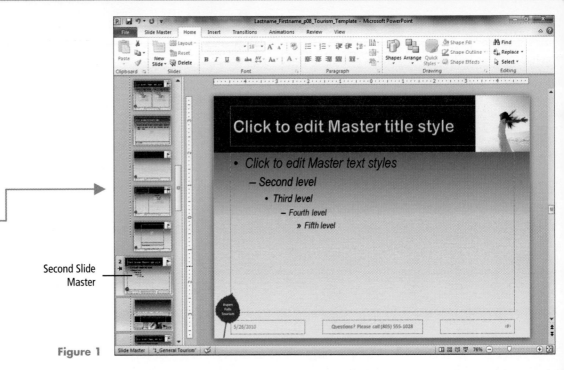

Second Slide Master

Figure 1

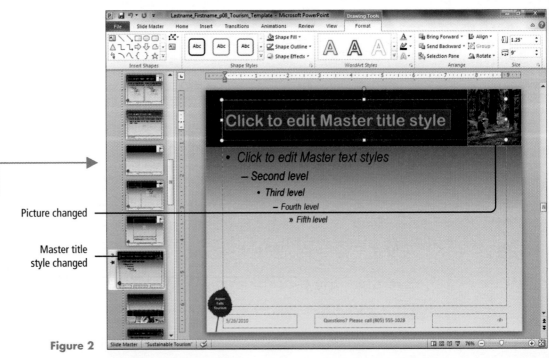

Picture changed

Master title style changed

Figure 2

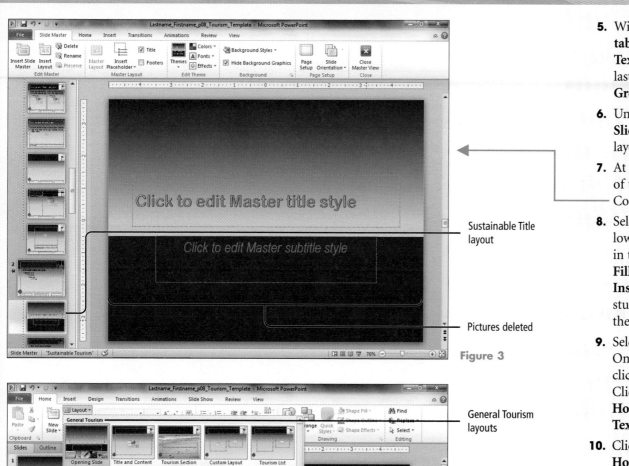

Sustainable Title layout

Pictures deleted

Figure 3

General Tourism layouts

Sustainable Tourism layouts

Figure 4

5. With the text still selected, on the **Format tab**, in the **WordArt Styles group**, click the **Text Outline** button, and then click the last color in the seventh column—**Olive Green, Accent 3, Darker 50%**.

6. Under **Slide Master 2**, click the **Opening Slide** layout thumbnail and rename the layout Sustainable Opening Slide

7. At the lower edge of the slide, select each of the pictures, and then press Delete. Compare your screen with **Figure 3**.

8. Select the blue rectangle shape on the lower half of the slide. On the **Format tab**, in the **Shape Styles group**, click the **Shape Fill** button, and then click **Picture**. In the **Insert Picture** dialog box, navigate to your student files, click **p08_Tourism8**, and then click **Insert**.

9. Select the text in the subtitle placeholder. On the **Home tab**, in the **Font group**, click the **Font Color button arrow**. Click **White, Background 1**. On the **Home tab**, in the **Font group**, click the **Text Shadow** button.

10. Click the **Normal View** button. On the **Home tab**, in the **Slides group**, click the **Layout** button, and then view the available layouts as shown in **Figure 4**.

    Layouts from two slide masters display in the layout gallery—the layouts of the General Tourism slide master and the layouts of the Sustainable Tourism slide master.

11. **Save** the template. Submit the template as directed by your instructor. **Close** the presentation template.

■ **You have completed Skill 7 of 10**

▶ When you double-click a template file in a folder window, a new untitled presentation opens that contains every slide master in the template.

▶ Changes made to the new, untitled presentation will not change the original template.

1. Click **Start** ⊕, and then in the displayed list, click **Computer**. In the folder window, navigate to **Lastname_Firstname_p08_Tourism_Template**. Double-click the file to open a new, untitled presentation as shown in **Figure 1**. ──────────

2. Save the presentation in your **PowerPoint Chapter 8** folder with the name Lastname_Firstname_p08_Tourism_Getaways and verify that the **File Type** is **PowerPoint Presentation**.

   Templates can be used to create new presentations. The new presentations are saved in the .pptx presentation format, and the original .potx template file is not changed.

3. In the title placeholder, type Aspen Falls Press Enter, and then type Oceanside Getaways

4. In the subtitle placeholder, type Presented by Press Enter, and then type Your Name

5. Display **Slide 2**. In the title placeholder, type Accommodations

6. In the content placeholder, add the following bullets, and then compare your screen with **Figure 2**. ──────────
   Seaside Hotels
   Seaside Condos
   Seaside Vacation Homes
   Rental Apartments
   Rental Cottages

■ **Continue to the next page to complete the skill**

New, untitled presentation

Opening Slide layout

Figure 1

Title and content added to Slide 2

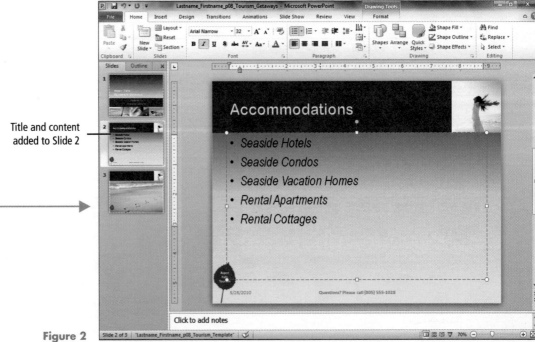

Figure 2

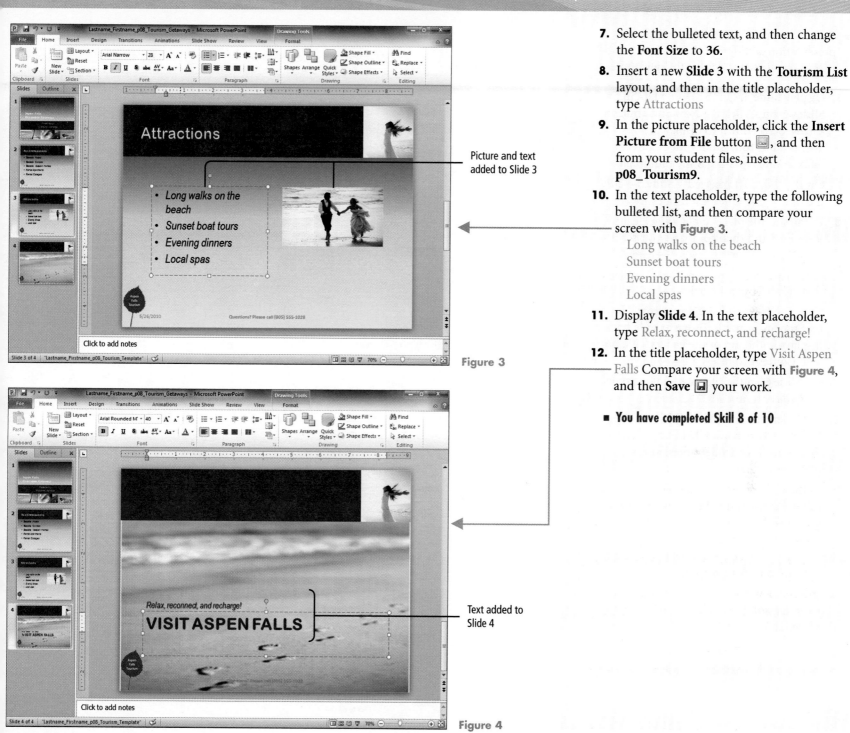

Figure 3

Picture and text added to Slide 3

Text added to Slide 4

Figure 4

7. Select the bulleted text, and then change the **Font Size** to **36**.

8. Insert a new **Slide 3** with the **Tourism List** layout, and then in the title placeholder, type Attractions

9. In the picture placeholder, click the **Insert Picture from File** button, and then from your student files, insert **p08_Tourism9**.

10. In the text placeholder, type the following bulleted list, and then compare your screen with **Figure 3**.

    Long walks on the beach
    Sunset boat tours
    Evening dinners
    Local spas

11. Display **Slide 4**. In the text placeholder, type Relax, reconnect, and recharge!

12. In the title placeholder, type Visit Aspen Falls Compare your screen with **Figure 4**, and then **Save** your work.

■ **You have completed Skill 8 of 10**

► To indicate a change in topic during a presentation, a different slide master can be used to create the slides for the new topic.

1. Display **Slide 4**. On the **Home tab**, in the **Slides group**, click the **New Slide button arrow**. Scroll down to display the **Sustainable Tourism** layouts. Click the **Sustainable Opening Slide** thumbnail.

2. On the slide just inserted—**Slide 5**—add the title Active Outdoor Vacations

3. In the subtitle placeholder, type Healthy Vacations and then compare your screen with **Figure 1**.

   The layouts from the second slide master indicate a change in topic.

4. Click the **New Slide button arrow**. Notice that the **Sustainable Tourism** slide master displays at the top of the gallery. Click **Two Content** to insert a new Slide 6.

5. On **Slide 6**, in the title placeholder, type Activities Abound

6. In the left content placeholder, click the **Insert Picture from File** button, and then from your student files, insert **p08_Tourism10**.

7. In the right content placeholder type the following list and then compare your screen with **Figure 2**.

   Over 100 miles of bicycle trails
   Level of challenge and trail terrain vary
   Something for everyone

8. Insert a new **Slide 7** with the **Tourism Comparison** layout. In the title placeholder, type Area Trails

■ **Continue to the next page to complete the skill**

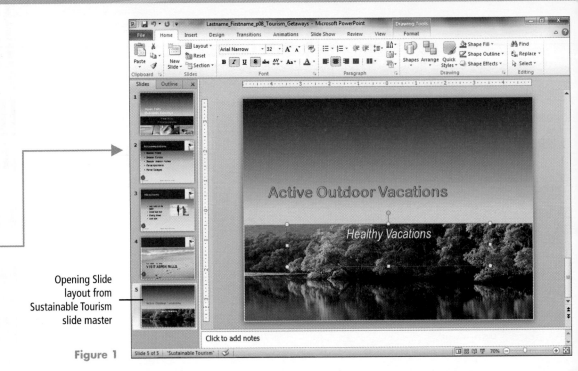

Opening Slide layout from Sustainable Tourism slide master

Figure 1

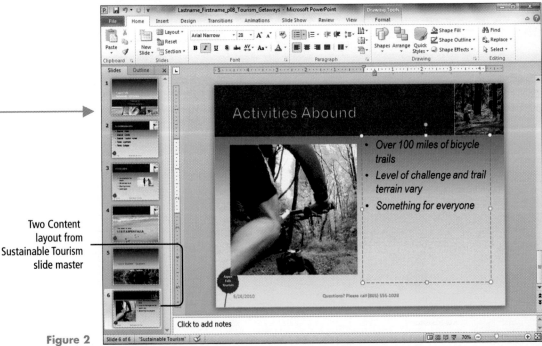

Two Content layout from Sustainable Tourism slide master

Figure 2

	Aspen Lake Trail	**Ocean View Trail**
Family Friendly	Yes	Yes
Pets Allowed	No	No
Rest Facilities	No	Yes
Bicycles Allowed	Yes	Yes

Figure 3

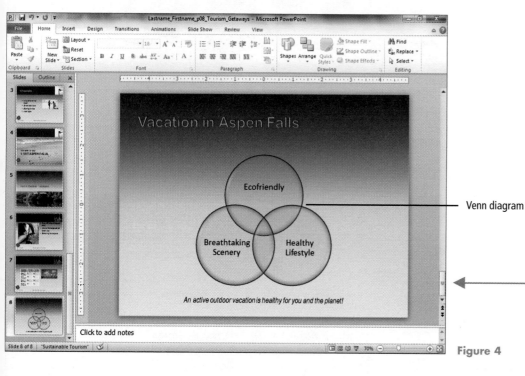

Venn diagram

Figure 4

9. Using the technique practiced previously, in the picture placeholder on the right, insert **p08_Tourism11**.

10. In the table placeholder, click the **Insert Table** button. In the **Insert Table** dialog box, change the number of columns to **3** and in the number of rows to **5**, and then click **OK**. In the table, type the text shown in **Figure 3**.

11. Insert a new **Slide 8** with the **Tourism SmartArt** layout. In the title placeholder, type Vacation in Aspen Falls

12. In the text placeholder below the SmartArt placeholder, click the text *Click to add caption* and type An active outdoor vacation is healthy for you and the planet! **Center** the placeholder text.

13. In the SmartArt placeholder, click the **Insert SmartArt Graphic** button 🖼. In the **Choose a SmartArt Graphic** dialog box, display the **Relationship** layouts, and then click the last layout in the ninth row—**Basic Venn**. Click **OK**.

14. In the upper circle, add the text Ecofriendly In the lower left circle, add Breathtaking Scenery and in the lower right circle, add Healthy Lifestyle

15. Under **SmartArt Tools**, on the **Design tab**, in the **SmartArt Styles group**, click the third choice under 3-D—**Cartoon**.

16. In the **SmartArt Styles group**, click the **Change Colors** button, and then under **Accent 1**, click the last thumbnail— **Transparent Gradient Range - Accent 1**. Deselect the SmartArt, and compare your screen with **Figure 4**.

17. **Save** 🖫 the presentation.

■ **You have completed Skill 9 of 10**

► The *Selection and Visibility task pane* tracks all objects—shapes, pictures, and placeholders—that display on a slide.

► The Selection and Visibility task pane can be used to hide individual components that you do not want to delete.

1. Display **Slide 7**. On the **Home tab**, in the **Editing group**, click the **Select** button, and then click **Selection Pane**.

    The Selection and Visibility task pane lists the shapes on the slide. Next to each item, the eye symbol indicates if the item will be displayed on the slide.

2. In the **Selection and Visibility** task pane, under **Shapes on this Slide**, click **Table Placeholder 7**, and then on the slide, notice the table placeholder is selected.

3. In the **Selection and Visibility** task pane, single click to select, and then double-click **Picture Placeholder 6**. Select the text, and then type Tourism Photo Placeholder Press [Enter] to change the name of the placeholder. Compare your screen with **Figure 1**.

4. In the **Selection and Visibility** task pane, to the right of **Footer Placeholder 3**, click the eye symbol 👁 to hide the footer.

    The appearance of the button changes when an object is hidden. This button can be clicked again to display a hidden object.

5. Switch to Slide Master view. At the top of the slide thumbnail pane, click the **Slide Master**, and then compare your screen with **Figure 2**.

■ **Continue to the next page to complete the skill**

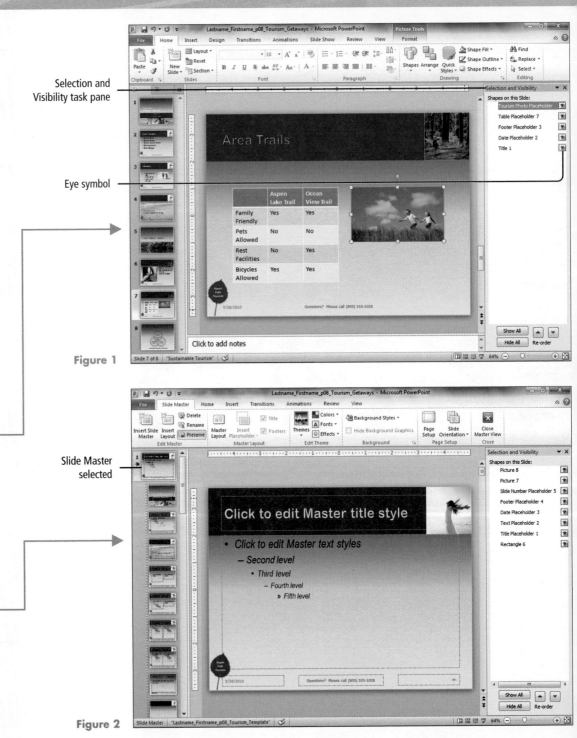

Selection and Visibility task pane

Eye symbol

Figure 1

Slide Master selected

Figure 2

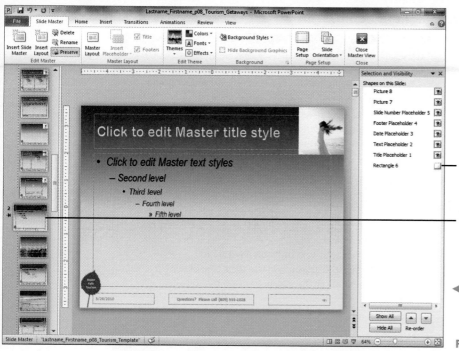

Eye symbol
not visible

Rectangle visible
only in Sustainable
Tourism Slide Master

Figure 3

6. Along the lower edge of the **Selection and Visibility** task pane, click the **Hide All** button to hide all of the objects on the slide master and its associated layouts. Click the **Show All** button to display all slide master objects.

7. In the **Selection and Visibility** task pane, click the **Rectangle 6** eye symbol to hide the shape.

8. In the slide thumbnail pane, scroll down to display the last layouts of the **General Tourism Slide Master** and the first layouts of **Sustainable Tourism Slide Master**. Notice the rectangle is hidden from the first slide master layout and is visible only in Slide Master 2 layout as shown in Figure 3.

9. Return to Normal view, and then **Close** the **Selection and Visibility** task pane. Display **Slide 1**, and then compare your screen with **Figure 4**.

10. Save 🖫 your presentation, and then submit the presentation and template files as directed by your instructor.

Done! You have completed Skill 10 of 10 and
your presentation is complete!

Figure 4

The following More Skills are located at **www.pearsonhighered.com/skills**

More Skills **Create Photo Albums from Templates**

Microsoft PowerPoint 2010 includes templates for creating electronic photo albums. Each template includes a variety of custom slide layouts with which you can create slides that display your own pictures.

In this More Skills activity, you will create a photo album using the Contemporary Photo Album template.

To begin, open your web browser, navigate to www.pearsonhighered.com/skills, locate the name of your textbook, and then follow the instructions on the website.

More Skills **Create Quiz Shows from Templates**

Microsoft PowerPoint 2010 includes a template for creating interactive presentations. The Quiz Show template includes a variety of slide layouts in which you can insert several different types of questions and their answers.

In this More Skills activity, you will create a quiz show using the Quiz Show template.

To begin, open your web browser, navigate to www.pearsonhighered.com/skills, locate the name of your textbook, and then follow the instructions on the website.

More Skills **Add Online Templates to Existing Presentations**

Additional templates can be obtained from the Office.com website.

In this More Skills activity, you will download a template that provides rolling credits and then use the template to add rolling credits to an existing presentation.

To begin, open your web browser, navigate to www.pearsonhighered.com/skills, locate the name of your textbook, and then follow the instructions on the website.

More Skills **Customize the Quick Access Toolbar**

Many commands found on the Ribbon or in dialog boxes have buttons that can be added to the Quick Access Toolbar. Displaying the buttons of frequently used commands speeds access to the tasks you perform most often.

In this More Skills activity, you will add buttons to the Quick Access Toolbar and then use these buttons to perform common tasks such as creating a new slide. You will then reset the Quick Access Toolbar to its original settings. To begin, open your web browser, navigate to www.pearsonhighered.com/skills, locate the name of your textbook, and then follow the instructions on the website.

Key Terms

Custom template 272

Custom slide layout 280

Preserved 277

Slide master 274

Slide layout 273

Selection and Visibility
    task pane 290

Template 272

Online Help Skills

1. Start PowerPoint. In the upper right corner of the **PowerPoint** window, click the **Help** ⊙ button. In the **Help** window, click the **Maximize** button.

2. Click in the search box, type Difference between Templates and Themes and then click the **Search** 🔎 button. In the search results, click **Understand the difference between PowerPoint Templates and Themes**. Compare your screen with **Figure 1**.

Figure 1

3. Read the section, and then see if you can answer the following question: What are two differences between templates and themes?

Matching

Match each term in the second column with its correct definition in the first column by writing the letter of the term on the blank line in front of the correct definition.

_____ **1.** A prebuilt slide or group of slides used to create new presentations.

_____ **2.** Used when a presentation needs two or more different styles or themes.

_____ **3.** Stores the master layout and theme for the slides contained in a presentation.

_____ **4.** The arrangement of objects—like titles and placeholders—on a slide.

_____ **5.** An extension of a vertical or horizontal ruler that spans the slide to help you position objects.

_____ **6.** An object you can use to add information such as text, SmartArt, and pictures to a slide when you create a presentation.

_____ **7.** The top thumbnail displayed when you switch to Slide Master View.

_____ **8.** A task pane used to organize and hide slide elements.

_____ **9.** A button that hides or displays individual slide elements.

_____ **10.** The process of adding a second slide master by copying an existing slide master.

A Duplicate

B Gridline

C Eye symbol

D Layout

E Multiple slide masters

F Office Theme Slide Master

G Placeholder

H Selection and Visibility

I Slide master

J Template

Multiple Choice

Select the correct answer.

1. Templates that have been modified to meet the specific needs of an organization are called this type of templates.
   A. Custom
   B. Downloadable
   C. Master

2. To edit the design or appearance of all slides in a presentation, you must be in this view.
   A. Notes Page
   B. Custom Slide
   C. Slide Master

3. An object inserted on the slide master will display on all of its associated what:
   A. Layouts
   B. Sections
   C. Themes

4. To change the background for all layouts, you should change it in this
   A. Slide master
   B. Themes gallery
   C. Page setup

5. A reusable layout in which you insert your own placeholder, background, and theme sets is called
   A. Slide layout template
   B. Custom slide layout
   C. Content with caption

6. In the slide thumbnail pane, the pushpin indicates that the slide master has been what:
   A. Preserved
   B. Locked
   C. Saved

7. So that more than one design theme can be used in a presentation, you can create multiple slide what:
   A. Masters
   B. Designs
   C. Sections

8. To edit an existing template file, start PowerPoint, and then use this command.
   A. Open
   B. Save & Send
   C. Share

9. A PowerPoint template has this file extension.
   A. .pptx
   B. .potx
   C. .ppsx

10. The command to open the Selection and Visibility task pane is on the Home tab in this group.
    A. Editing
    B. Slides
    C. Drawing

Topics for Discussion

1. How can using templates save an organization time?

2. What are some things you should consider when creating a template?

Skill Check

To complete this project, you will need the following files:

- New, blank PowerPoint presentation
- p08_ContEd1
- p08_ContEd2
- p08_ContEd3
- p08_ContEd4

You will save your files as:

- Lastname_Firstname_p08_ContEd_Template
- Lastname_Firstname_p08_ContEd

1. **Start** PowerPoint 2010 to open a new, blank presentation. On the **View tab**, in the **Master Views group**, click **Slide Master**.

2. On the **Slide Master tab**, in the **Background group**, click **Background Styles**, and then click **Format Background**. Select **Gradient fill**, click the **Color** button, and then under **Standard Colors**, click **Dark Blue**. Click **Apply to All**, and then click **Close**.

3. On the **Office Theme Slide Master**, insert a **Rectangle** shape **7.5** inches in height and **1.3** inches in width. Align the rectangle with right edge of the slide.

4. On the **Office Theme Slide Master**, insert the picture **p08_ContEd1**, located in your student files. Align the upper and right edge of the picture with the upper and right edge of the slide.

5. On the **Slide Master tab**, in the **Edit Master group**, click **Rename**. Type Continuing Ed Theme and then click **Rename**.

6. Select the title placeholder. Drag the middle right sizing handle to align the right edge of the placeholder with the left edge of the rectangle. Repeat this technique to resize the content placeholder.

7. Select the text *Click to edit Master title style*, and then change the **Font** to **Estrangelo Edessa**. Compare your screen with **Figure 1**. —————

8. Click **Save**, and then in the **File name** box, type Lastname_Firstname_p08_ContEd_Template Click the **Save as type box arrow**, and then click **PowerPoint Template**. Navigate to your **PowerPoint Chapter 8** folder. Click **Save**.

9. Display the **Title Slide** layout—the second thumbnail. On the **Slide Master tab**, in the **Background group**, select **Hide Background Graphics**. Insert the picture **p08_ContEd2**. Align the right edge of the picture on the right edge of the slide. Compare your screen with **Figure 2**. —————

- Continue to the next page to complete this Skill Check ▶

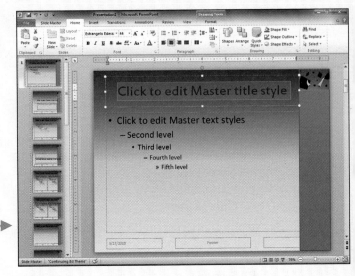

Figure 1

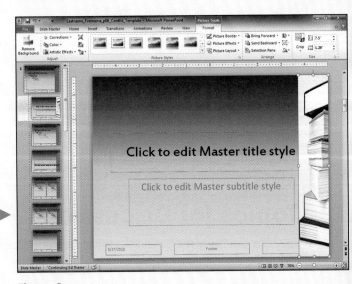

Figure 2

10. On the **Slide Master tab**, in the **Edit Master group**, click **Insert Layout**. Repeat the technique practiced previously to rename the layout Custom Picture

11. In the **Master Layout group**, click the **Insert Placeholder button arrow**, and then click **Picture**. Insert a placeholder that is **5** inches in height and **8.2** inches in width, and then position the placeholder below the title placeholder as shown in Figure 3.

12. Repeat the technique just practiced to insert another layout. Rename the layout Custom SmartArt

13. In the **Custom SmartArt** layout, delete the title placeholder. In the **Master Layout group**, click the **Insert Placeholder button arrow**, and then click **SmartArt**. Draw a placeholder that is **6.6** inches in height and **8** inches in width. Position the placeholder approximately **0.25** inches from the top and left edges of the slide.

14. On the **Slide Master tab**, in the **Edit Master group**, click **Insert Slide Master**.

15. With the newly inserted slide master displayed, in the **Background group**, click **Background Styles**, and then click **Format Background**. With **Solid Fill** selected, click the **Color** button, and then click the third color in the third row—**Tan Background 2, Darker 25%**. Click **Close**.

16. On the second Slide Master, insert **p08_ContEd3**, and then align the picture with the right edge of the slide.

17. Rename the second Slide Master Fall Classes Insert Lastname_Firstname_p08_ContEd into the footer on the Notes and Handouts pages. Switch to Normal view. **Save** your work, and then **Exit** PowerPoint.

18. From your PowerPoint Chapter 8 folder, double-click **Lastname_Firstname_p08_ContEd_Template** to create a new presentation from the template. **Save** the file in your **PowerPoint Chapter 8** folder as Lastname_Firstname_p08_ContEd and verify the **File Type** is PowerPoint Presentation.

19. In Normal view, on **Slide 1**, in the title placeholder, type Continuing Education In the subtitle placeholder, type Your Name

20. On the **Home tab**, in the **Slides group**, click the **New Slide button arrow**, and insert a new slide with the **Custom Picture** layout created previously.

21. In the title placeholder, type Online Learning In the picture placeholder, insert **p08_ContEd4**, and then compare your screen with Figure 4.

22. Display **Slide 1**. On the **Home tab**, in the **Editing group**, click **Select**, and then click **Selection Pane**. In the **Selection and Visibility** task pane, click the eye symbol to the right of **Subtitle 2** to hide the subtitle placeholder, and then **Close** the **Selection and Visibility** task pane.

23. **Save**, and then submit as directed by your instructor.

Done! You have completed the Skill Check

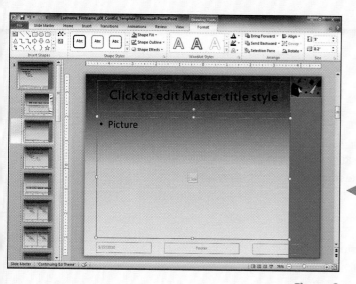

Figure 3

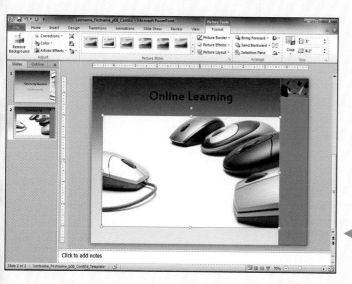

Figure 4

Assess Your Skills 1

To complete this project, you will need the following files:

- New, blank presentation
- p08_Forum1

You will save your files as:

- Lastname_Firstname_p08_Forum_Template
- Lastname_Firstname_p08_Forum

1. **Start** a new, blank presentation, and switch to Slide Master view.

2. For the **Office Theme Slide Master**, change the slide background to a **Solid Fill** of **Blue, Accent 1, Lighter 60%**—the fifth color in the third row of Theme Colors.

3. **Save** the file as a template in your **PowerPoint Chapter 8** folder with the name Lastname_Firstname_p08_Forum_Template

4. **Rename** the Slide Master as Public Forum

5. Select the footer containing the slide number and align the text left.

6. On the slide master, insert the picture **p08_Forum1**. Position the picture's right edge with the bottom right edge of the slide.

7. On the **Title Slide** layout, use Slide Master tab to Hide the Background Graphics. Insert a Clip Art photograph of a lake. Adjust the height and width to match the slide. Adjust the Color to Washout. Then Send to Back.

8. Below the **Title Slide** layout, insert a new slide layout, and then change its name to Custom Text

9. On the **Custom Text** layout, insert a **Text** placeholder that is **2.8** inches in height and **9** inches in width. Position the placeholder between the title and the picture.

10. Display and then **Duplicate** the Public Forum slide master, and then name **Slide Master 2** as Winter Public Forum

11. On **Slide Master 2**, change the background color to **Dark Blue, Text 2, Lighter 80%, Accent 2**—the seventh option in the first row under Theme Colors.

12. **Save**, and then **Close** the template.

13. Create a new, untitled presentation from the file **Lastname_Firstname_p08_Forum_Template**. **Save** the new presentation in your **PowerPoint Chapter 8** folder as Lastname_Firstname_p08_Forum

14. On **Slide 1**, in the title placeholder, type Aspen Falls City Hall Meeting In the subtitle placeholder, type Public Forum

15. Insert a new slide using the **Custom Text** layout from the first slide master. In the title placeholder, type Welcome to City Hall In the text placeholder, type Meetings are open to all citizens Press Enter, and then type Citizen input is welcome Press Enter, and then type Please respect other's opinions

16. Insert a new slide using the **Custom Text** layout from the **Winter Public Forum** slide master. In the title placeholder, type Citizen Concerns

17. Add the file name to the footer on the Notes and Handouts pages.

18. **Save**, and then submit as directed by your instructor.

Done! You have completed Assess Your Skills 1

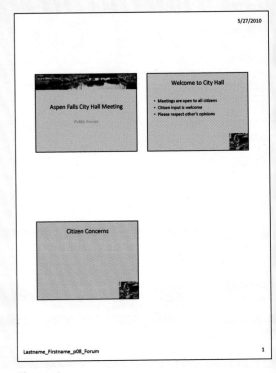

Figure 1

Assess Your Skills 2

To complete this project, you will need the following files:

- p08_Business_Template
- p08_Business_Plan1

You will save your files as:

- Lastname_Firstname_p08_Business_Template
- Lastname_Firstname_p08_Business_Plan

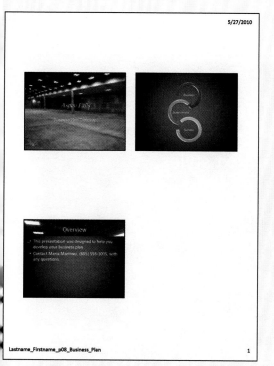

5/27/2010

Lastname_Firstname_p08_Business_Plan   1

Figure 1

1. **Start** PowerPoint, and then open **p08_Business_Template. Save** the template in your **PowerPoint Chapter 8** folder as a template named Lastname_Firstname_p08_Business_Template

2. In Slide Master view, on the **Office Theme Slide Master**, change the master title style font to **Mongolian Baiti**, and then apply **Italic**. Rename **Slide Master 1** Business Plan

3. Display the **Title Slide** layout. Use the **Selection and Visibility** task pane to hide **Striped Right Arrow 7**.

4. Add a custom layout, and then name it Custom SmartArt

5. On the **Custom SmartArt** layout, delete the title placeholder, and insert a **SmartArt** placeholder that is **6** inches in height and **7.5** inches in width. Center the placeholder on the slide.

6. **Duplicate** the **Business Plan Slide Master**. On the duplicate slide master, insert the picture **p08_Business_Plan1**. Align the top edge of the picture with the top edge of the slide, and then click **Send to Back**.

7. **Save**, and then **Close** the template.

8. Create a new presentation from **Lastname_Firstname_p08_Business_Template. Save** the new presentation in your **PowerPoint Chapter 8** folder as Lastname_Firstname_p08_Business_Plan

9. Switch to Normal view. On **Slide 1**, add the title Aspen Falls Add the subtitle Business Plan Template

10. From the Business Plan Slide Master, **Insert** a new **Slide 2** with the **Custom SmartArt** layout.

11. In the SmartArt placeholder, from the SmartArt Cycle gallery, under **Process**, insert a **Circle Arrow Process**. In the first shape, type Business In the remaining shapes, type Government and then Success

12. Change the SmartArt Style to **Polished**— the first option under **3-D**. Use the **Change Colors** button to change the color to **Colorful Range - Accent Colors 2 to 3**— the second option under **Colorful**.

13. Insert a new **Slide 3** with the **Title and Content** layout from the second slide master. In the title placeholder, type Overview

14. In the content placeholder, type This presentation was designed to help you develop your business plan Press Enter, and then type Contact Maria Martinez, (805) 555-1005, with any questions

15. Add the file name to the footer for the Notes and Handouts pages. **Save** the presentation, and then submit as directed.

Done! You have completed Assess Your Skills 2

Assess Your Skills Visually

To complete this project, you will need the following files:

- New, blank PowerPoint presentation
- p08_Community_Share1

You will save your file as:

- Lastname_Firstname_p08_Community_Template

Open a new, blank presentation, and save it in your **PowerPoint Chapter 8** folder as a template named Lastname_Firstname_p08_Community_Template In Slide Master view, create the template shown in **Figure 1**. For the picture along the left edge, insert **p08_Community_Share1** as a shape fill. Edit the Master title style to change the **Font Color** to **Orange**—the third option under **Standard Colors**. Make the title font **Bold**, and add a **Text Shadow**. Resize the title and content placeholders so they do not overlap the picture. Change the background color to **Dark Blue, Text 2, Darker 25%**. Add the text Community Share Program to the center footer, and make the footer font **Italic**. Delete the left and right footer placeholders—the ones containing the date and slide number.

Add the file name to the footer of the Notes and Handouts pages, and then submit the template as directed by your instructor.

Done! You have completed Assess Your Skills Visually

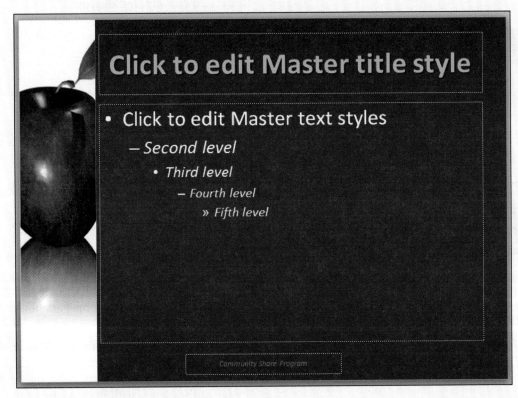

Figure 1

Skills in Context

To complete this project, you will need the following file:

- New, blank PowerPoint presentation

You will save your files as:

- Lastname_Firstname_p08_Aquatics_Template
- Lastname_Firstname_p08_Aquatics_Presentation

The Aspen Falls city government focuses heavily on promoting a healthy lifestyle for all citizens. A series of City Hall meetings have been scheduled to help promote nonprofit fitness programs. Using the skills that you have practiced in this chapter, make a new template that can be used for creating presentations for the series. The template will be used by diverse presenters and should provide a unifying theme of promoting a healthy lifestyle.

Within the template, create a custom layout that can be used to promote the aquatics program. Create a second master in the same template that can be used to promote outdoor excursions.

Use the template to create a new presentation that promotes the city aquatics program. This program includes swimming lessons for children and adults, open swim dates for all citizens, and lifeguard training. Use the second master for at least one slide in the presentation. Name the template Lastname_Firstname_p08_Aquatics_Template and name the presentation Lastname_Firstname_p08_Aquatics_Presentation Submit as directed.

Done! You have completed Skills in Context

Skills and You

To complete this project, you will need the following file:

- New, blank PowerPoint presentation

You will save your files as:

- Lastname_Firstname_p08_College_Template
- Lastname_Firstname_p08_College_Clubs

Using the skills you have learned in this chapter, create a template that can be used by various college campus clubs to promote their events. Rename the slide master using your college's name, and then apply a design using your college colors, logo, and photos if available. Create at least two custom slide layouts, and rename each as appropriate. In the first custom layout, add a table placeholder. In the second custom layout, add several picture placeholders that clubs can use to present pictures of their events. Add the file name to the Notes and Handouts footer. Save the template as Lastname_Firstname_p08_College_Template.

Use the template to create a presentation featuring the club of your choice. Include at least five slides in this presentation: the title slide, two custom layouts that you created, and two other layouts of your choice. Save the presentation as Lastname_Firstname_p08_College_Clubs Add the file name to the Notes and Handouts footer. Submit as directed by your instructor.

Done! You have completed Skills and You

CHAPTER 9

Create Accessible Presentations and Write Macros

▶ To make your presentations more accessible, you can improve the language and design of the presentation and save the presentation in file formats that are designed for sharing.

▶ Inserting ActiveX controls and writing macros adds interactivity and extra functions to your slide shows.

Your starting screen will look like this:

SKILLS

Skills 1-10 Training

At the end of this chapter, you will be able to:

Skill 1 Work with Translation and Language Tools

Skill 2 Make Presentations More Accessible

Skill 3 Prepare Presentations for Kiosks and Save as Slide Shows

Skill 4 Remove Personal Information and Prepare Presentations for Sharing on the Internet

Skill 5 Display the Developer Tab and Add ActiveX Controls

Skill 6 Create and Debug Macros

Skill 7 Write and Test VBA Statements

Skill 8 Add and Edit Comments

Skill 9 Import Slides from Other File Formats and Check Compatibility

Skill 10 Set Passwords and Add Digital Signatures

MORE SKILLS

More Skills 11 Save Presentations as PDF Files

More Skills 12 Create Videos from Presentations

More Skills 13 Send Presentations Using Outlook

More Skills 14 Save Files to SkyDrive

Outcome

Using the skills listed to the left will enable you
to create presentations like these:

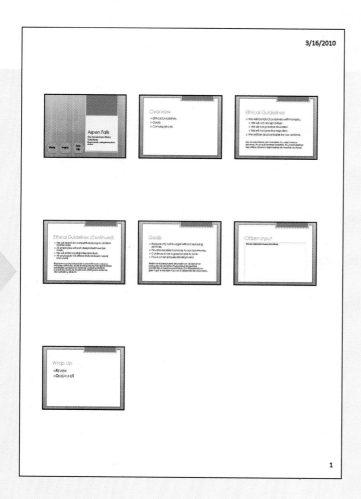

You will save your files as:

Lastname_Firstname_p09_Ethics
Lastname_Firstname_p09_Ethics_Show
Lastname_Firstname_p09_Ethics_Web
Lastname_Firstname_p09_Ethics_Macro

In this chapter, you will create documents for the Aspen Falls City Hall, which provides essential services for the citizens and visitors of Aspen Falls, California.

Introduction

- ▶ When you present to a diverse audience, you can use the Translate tool to provide text in other languages.

- ▶ Presentations can be designed to better meet the needs of those with visual impairments or seizure disorders.

- ▶ Presentations can be saved in formats optimized for sharing, such as the Slide Show and Web page file formats.

- ▶ ActiveX controls and macros can enhance a presentation by enabling audience interaction and automating tasks.

- ▶ You can secure your presentation files by adding passwords or digital signatures.

Time to complete all
10 skills – 50 to 90 minutes

Find your student data files here:

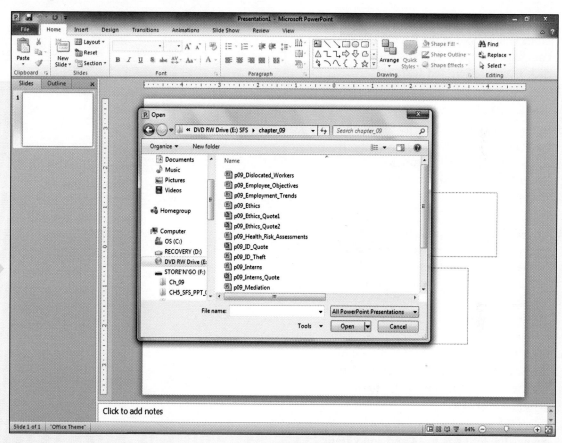

**Student data files needed
for this chapter:**

- p09_Ethics
- p09_Ethics_Notes
- p09_Ethics_Quote1
- p09_Ethics_Quote2

► The *Translate tool* translates text from one language to another.

1. **Start** PowerPoint. From your student files, open **p09_Ethics**. Use the **Save As** dialog box to create a folder named PowerPoint Chapter 9 and then in the folder, **Save** the presentation as Lastname_Firstname_ p09_Ethics

2. On **Slide 1**, select the text *City Government Ethics Guidelines*. On the **Review tab**, in the **Language group**, click **Translate**, and then click **Translate Selected Text**.

   The Research pane can be used to translate 17 different languages.

3. In the **Research** pane, verify that the **From** box value is **English (U.S.)**. Click the **To** arrow, and then click **Spanish (International Sort)**. Under **Microsoft Translator**, view the translation as shown in **Figure 1**.

4. Under **Microsoft Translator**, select and then right-click **Directrices de ética de Gobierno de ciudad**, and then from the displayed shortcut menu, click **Copy**.

   It is a good idea to check the accuracy of translated phrases with an experienced translator.

5. Place the insertion point to the right of the word *Guidelines*, and then press Enter. On the **Home tab**, in the **Clipboard group**, click **Paste**.

6. Select the phrase just pasted, and then change the font size to **14** and apply **Italic**. Compare your screen with **Figure 2**.

7. Display **Slide 3**. Select all of the text in the content placeholder. On the **Review tab**, in the **Language group**, click **Translate**, and then click **Translate Selected Text**.

■ **Continue to the next page to complete the skill**

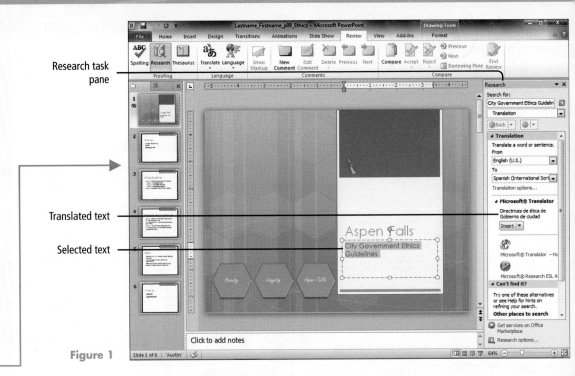

Research task pane

Translated text

Selected text

Figure 1

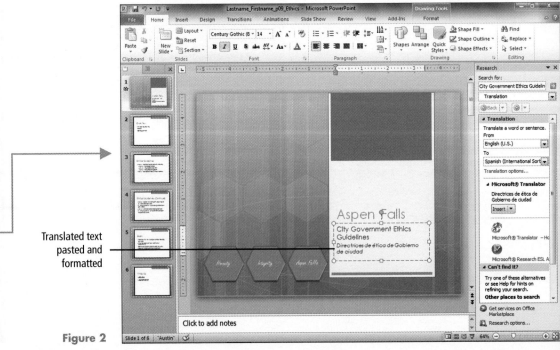

Translated text pasted and formatted

Figure 2

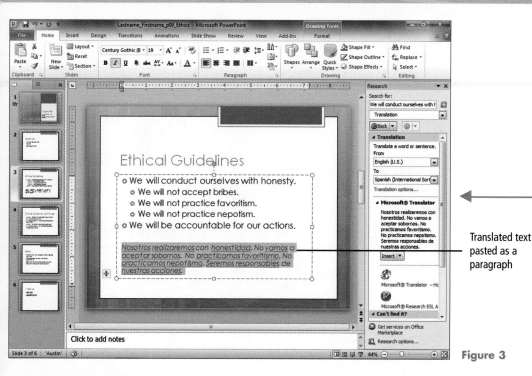

Translated text pasted as a paragraph

Figure 3

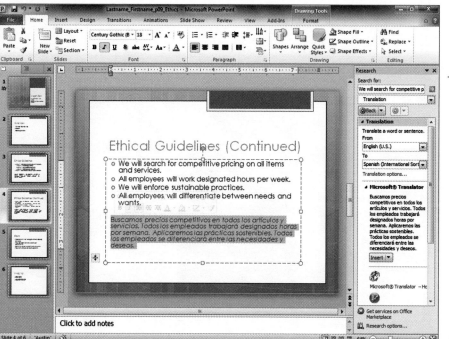

Figure 4

8. In the **Research** pane, repeat the techniques just practiced to copy the suggested translation.

9. Click to the right of the last bulleted point, and then press Enter two times. **Paste** the translated text. For the text just pasted, decrease the font size to **18**, and then apply **Italic**. On the **Home tab**, in the **Paragraph group**, click the **Bullets** button to remove the bullet. Compare your screen with **Figure 3**.

   When you copy translated text from the Research pane, the formatting of the original text is not copied.

10. Display **Slide 4**, and then select all of the text in the content placeholder. On the **Review tab**, in the **Language group**, click **Translate**, and then click **Translate Selected Text**. In the **Research** pane, copy the translated text.

11. Place the insertion point to right of the last bulleted point, and press Enter two times. **Paste** the copied translated text, decrease its font size to **18**, and then apply **Italic** and remove the bullet. Compare your screen with **Figure 4**.

12. Display **Slide 5**, and select all of the text in the content placeholder. Translate the selected text, and then copy the translation.

13. Place the insertion point to the right of the last bulleted point, and then press Enter two times. **Paste** the translated text, and then decrease its font size to **18**. Remove the bullet and then apply **Italic**.

14. **Close** ☒ the **Research** pane, and then **Save** 🖫 the presentation.

   ■ **You have completed Skill 1 of 10**

► When preparing a presentation, consider the needs of your audience. An accessible presentation is one that is effective for all users, regardless of barriers or disabilities.

1. On **Slide 1**, select all of the text in the subtitle placeholder, including the translated phrase.

2. On the **Home tab**, in the **Font group**, click the **Font Color button arrow**. Under **Theme Colors**, select the first color in the second column—**Black, Text 1**.

3. Select the title text, and then under **Theme Colors**, apply the last color in the eighth column—**Blue-Gray, Accent 4, Darker 50%**. Compare your screen with **Figure 1**. ————————————

   To ensure that people with visual impairments are able to view your presentation, choose a font color that contrasts with the background color.

4. With **Slide 1** displayed, and then in the pane that contains the Slide and Outline tabs, click the **Play Animation** star to view the animations added to the slide. Compare your screen with **Figure 2**. ————

5. Press F5 and observe the flashing animation on the title slide.

   Flashing animations that display at a frequency of 15 to 20 times per second can induce seizures for some viewers and should always be avoided. Some research shows that even two flashes per second can induce a seizure in sensitive viewers. For the purpose of demonstration, the shapes on this slide were animated to blink at a rate that would not induce a seizure in such viewers.

■ **Continue to the next page to complete the skill**

Contrast between text and background colors increased

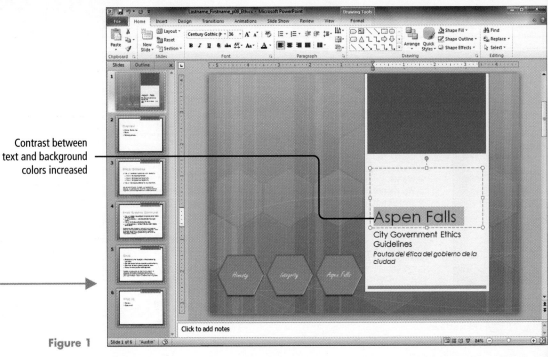

Figure 1

Play Animation star

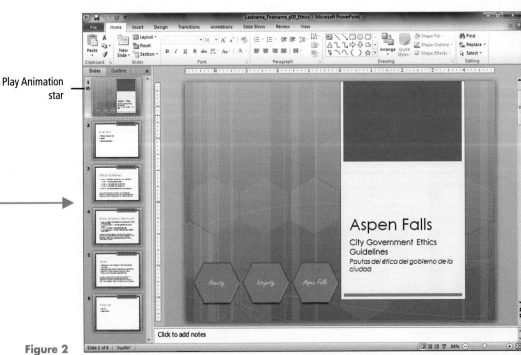

Figure 2

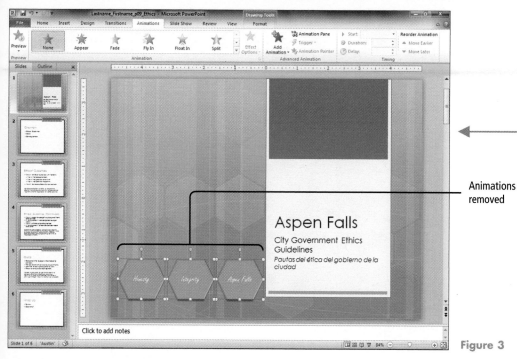

Animations removed

Figure 3

Wrap Up
○REVIEW
○QUESTIONS?

Formatting adjusted to increase readability

Figure 4

6. Right-click the slide, and then click **End Show**. On **Slide 1**, select the first shape, *Honesty*. Press and hold Shift, and then click the *Integrity* and *Aspen Falls* shapes. With all three shapes selected, on the **Animations tab**, in the **Animation group**, click the **More** button, click **None**, and compare your screen with **Figure 3**.

7. With all three shapes still selected, observe the font style and size.

   The fonts used in these shapes are too small, and the script font will be difficult for many viewers to read. The font color needs more contrast with the background color.

8. On the **Home tab**, in the **Font group**, click the **Increase Font Size** A̅ button two times to increase the font size to **24**. Change the font color to **Black, Text 1**, and then change the font to **Gill Sans MT Condensed**.

9. Display **Slide 6**. Select all of the text in the content placeholder, and then click the **Font Dialog Box Launcher** 🗔. Change the **Font style** to **Regular**, and then, under **Effects**, select the **Small Caps** check box. Click **OK**, click a blank area of the slide, and then compare your screen with **Figure 4**.

   Small caps are often easier to read than all caps because the first letter of each word is larger. Removing bold makes the text easier to read because the letters are less crowded.

10. Add the file name to the Notes and Handouts footer for all slides, and then **Save** 🖫 the presentation.

   ■ **You have completed Skill 2 of 10**

▶ Recall that **kiosk presentations** run automatically on public monitors. You can set up a presentation to be viewed at a kiosk, rather than presented by a speaker.

▶ You can save presentations in the Slide Show file format so that the presentation always opens in Slide Show view.

1. In the pane that contains the Slides and Outline tabs, click the **Slide 1** thumbnail.

2. On the **Transitions tab**, in the **Timing group**, under **Advance Slide**, deselect the **On Mouse Click** box, and then select the **After** box. Click the **Up** spin arrow to change the value to **00:07.00**. Click **Apply to All**. Compare your screen with **Figure 1**.

   When creating presentations for viewing at kiosks, consider how long it will take the reader to read all information on each slide and whether all information included on the slides is applicable for viewers who will not interact with a presenter.

3. In the pane that contains the Slides and Outline tabs, select the **Slide 6** thumbnail. Right-click the **Slide 6** thumbnail. Click **Delete Slide**, and then compare your screen with **Figure 2**.

   Because this presentation will be viewed at a kiosk, there is no need for a slide asking for questions or comments.

■ **Continue to the next page to complete the skill**

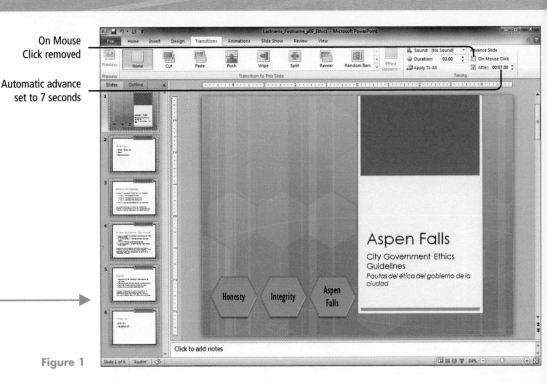

On Mouse Click removed

Automatic advance set to 7 seconds

Figure 1

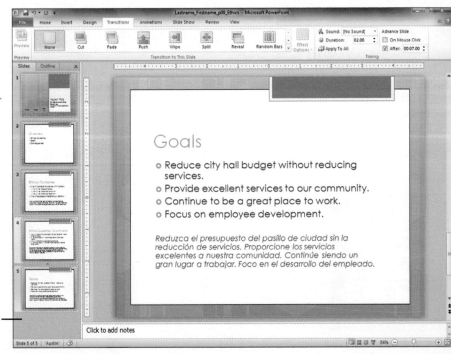

Slide 6 deleted

Figure 2

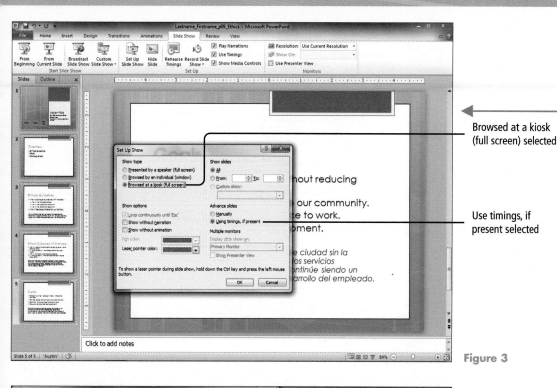

Browsed at a kiosk
(full screen) selected

Use timings, if
present selected

Figure 3

4. On the **Slide Show tab**, in the **Set Up group**, click **Set Up Slide Show**. Under **Show type**, select **Browsed at a kiosk (full screen)**. Be sure that **Using timings, if present** is selected. Compare your screen with **Figure 3**, and then click **OK**.

5. Press [F5] to view the show from the beginning. Note that the slides automatically advance after 7 seconds.

> When the Show type is set to kiosk, the show continually loops through the presentation without the need for a presenter. Clicking the mouse will not advance the slides.

6. After viewing the entire show, press [Esc] to exit the slide show and return to Normal view.

7. Click the **File tab**, and then click **Save As**. In the **Save As** dialog box, click the **Save as type** arrow, and then click **PowerPoint Show**.

8. In the **File name** box, type Lastname_ Firstname_p09_Ethics_Show Compare your screen with **Figure 4**, and then click **Save**.

> The presentation is now saved in the Slide Show format—a file with the .ppsx file extension.

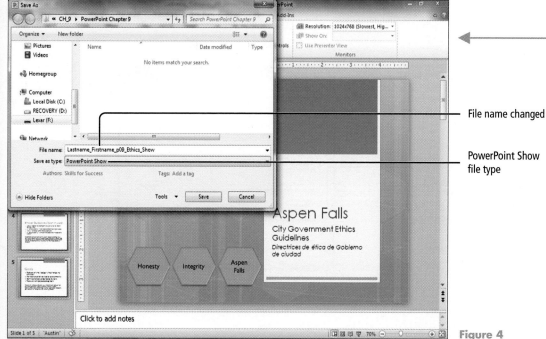

File name changed

PowerPoint Show
file type

9. **Exit** PowerPoint. Click **Start**, and then click **Computer**. In the displayed folder window, navigate to your **PowerPoint Chapter 9** folder. Double-click **Lastname_Firstname_p09_Ethics_Show**.

> Files saved in the Slide Show file format automatically open in Slide Show view.

10. Press [Esc] to end the show and close the displayed folder window.

■ **You have completed Skill 3 of 10**

Figure 4

► Presentations can be inspected to remove certain information before the files are shared over the Internet.

► The *Document Inspector* lists information in presentation files that you may want to remove before making them available on the Internet.

1. **Start** PowerPoint, and then open **Lastname_Firstname_p09_Ethics**. Display **Slide 2**. In the upper left corner of the slide pane, note the Off-Slide Content—a shape containing the words *cell phones*.

2. On the **File tab**, in **Backstage view**, click **Info**, and note the **Properties** listed for the presentation in the right pane.

3. Click **Check for Issues**, and then click **Inspect Document**.

4. In the **Document Inspector** dialog box, select all of the check boxes, including **Off-Slide Content**. Compare your screen with **Figure 1**.

The Document Inspector can be used to check for information in the file that might not display in Slide Show view. This could be personal information, comments that you do not want to make public, or items that are saved in the presentation but not on the slides.

5. Click **Inspect**, and then compare your screen with **Figure 2**.

6. Click **Remove All** to remove the **Document Properties and Personal Information**. Click **Remove All** to remove the **Off-Slide Content**. Click **Reinspect**, click the displayed **Inspect** button, and then click **Close**.

■ **Continue to the next page to complete the skill**

All options selected

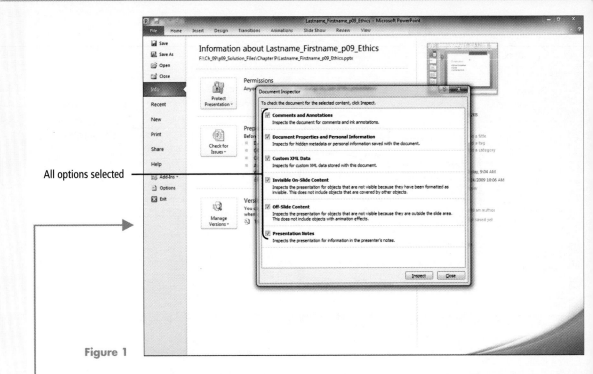

Figure 1

Personal information and Off-Slide Content found in document properties

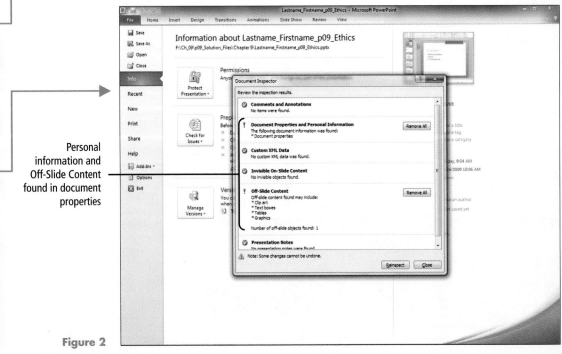

Figure 2

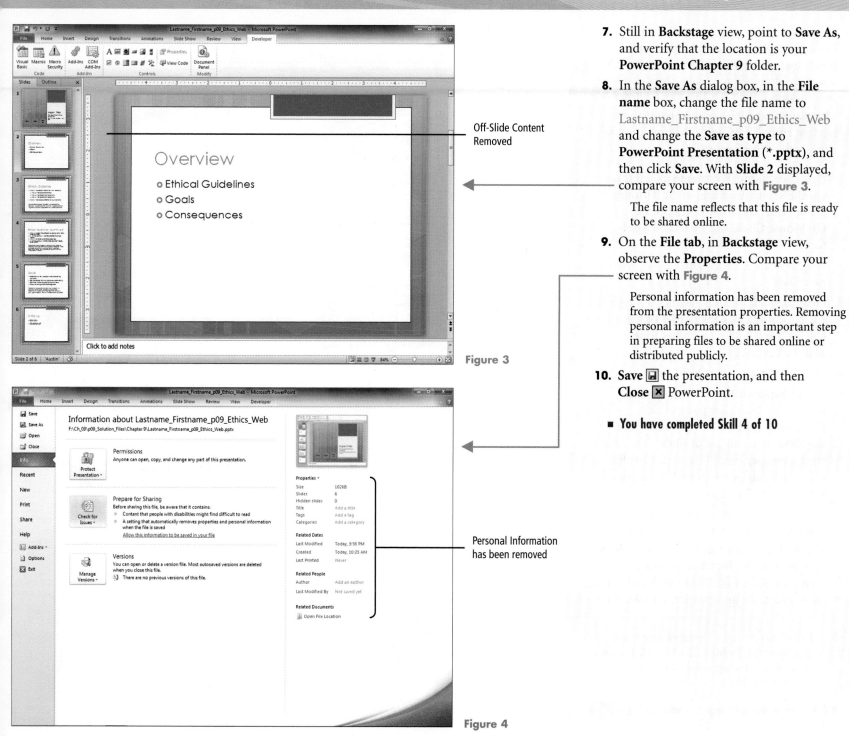

Off-Slide Content Removed

Figure 3

Information about Lastname_Firstname_p09_Ethics_Web

Personal Information has been removed

Figure 4

7. Still in **Backstage** view, point to **Save As**, and verify that the location is your **PowerPoint Chapter 9** folder.

8. In the **Save As** dialog box, in the **File name** box, change the file name to Lastname_Firstname_p09_Ethics_Web and change the **Save as type** to **PowerPoint Presentation (*.pptx)**, and then click **Save**. With **Slide 2** displayed, compare your screen with **Figure 3**.

> The file name reflects that this file is ready to be shared online.

9. On the **File tab**, in **Backstage** view, observe the **Properties**. Compare your screen with **Figure 4**.

> Personal information has been removed from the presentation properties. Removing personal information is an important step in preparing files to be shared online or distributed publicly.

10. **Save** 🔲 the presentation, and then **Close** ☒ PowerPoint.

■ **You have completed Skill 4 of 10**

▶ You can insert ActiveX controls into PowerPoint presentations to gain extra functionality. *ActiveX controls* are prebuilt programs designed to run inside of multiple programs in Office and Internet Explorer.

▶ The *Developer tab* is an optional Ribbon tab that contains the tools that you need to work with ActiveX controls.

1. Open **Lastname_Firstname_p09_Ethics**. On the **Transitions tab**, in the **Timings group**, clear the **After** check box, select **On Mouse Click**, and then click **Apply to All**.

2. Display **Slide 5**. Press ⌨Ctrl + ⌨M to insert a new **Slide 6**.

3. On **Slide 6**, in the title placeholder, type Citizen Input Click the border of the content placeholder two times to select it, and then press ⌨Del.

4. On the **File tab**, click **Options**.

5. In the displayed **PowerPoint Options** dialog box, in the left pane, click **Customize Ribbon**. Under **Customize the Ribbon**, in the list of **Main Tabs**, select the **Developer** check box, and then click **OK**. Click the **Developer tab**. Compare your screen with **Figure 1**.

   The Developer tab displays four groups— Code, Add-Ins, Controls, and Modify.

6. On the **Developer tab**, in the **Controls group**, click the **Text Box (ActiveX Control)** button 🔲. With the ➕ pointer, draw a text box approximately as shown in **Figure 2**.

   Recall that during a typical presentation, typing text is disabled. The ActiveX Text Box control runs during a slide show so that you can type text in its text box.

■ **Continue to the next page to complete the skill**

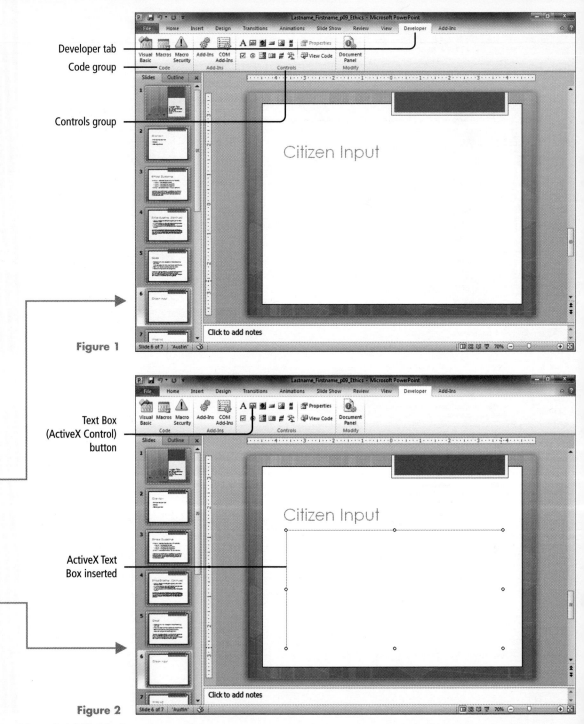

Developer tab
Code group
Controls group

Figure 1

Text Box
(ActiveX Control)
button

ActiveX Text
Box inserted

Figure 2

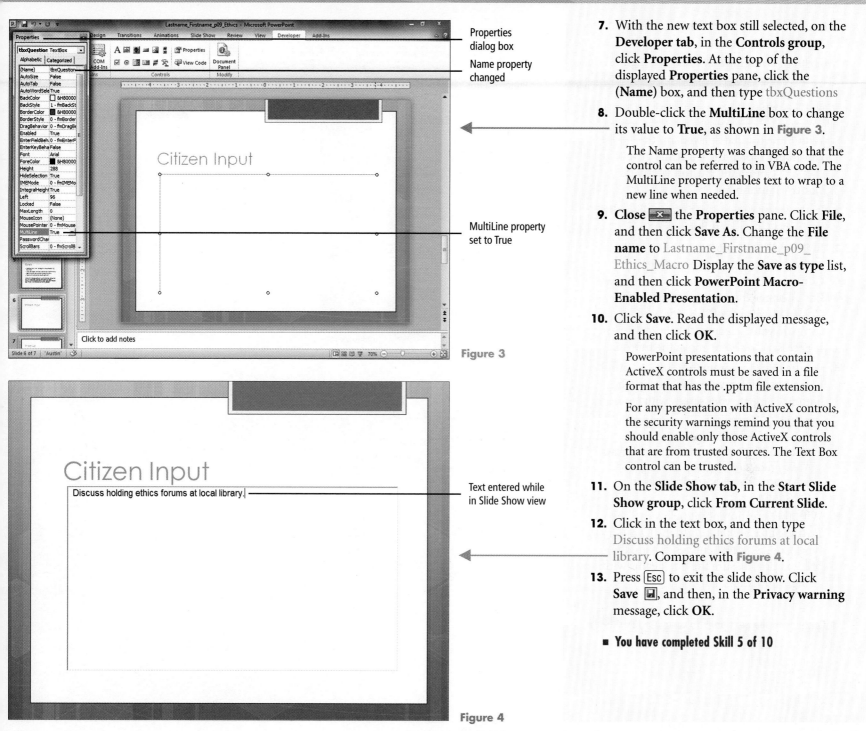

Properties dialog box

Name property changed

MultiLine property set to True

Figure 3

Text entered while in Slide Show view

Figure 4

7. With the new text box still selected, on the **Developer tab**, in the **Controls group**, click **Properties**. At the top of the displayed **Properties** pane, click the **(Name)** box, and then type tbxQuestions

8. Double-click the **MultiLine** box to change its value to **True**, as shown in **Figure 3**.

   The Name property was changed so that the control can be referred to in VBA code. The MultiLine property enables text to wrap to a new line when needed.

9. **Close** [×] the **Properties** pane. Click **File**, and then click **Save As**. Change the **File name** to Lastname_Firstname_p09_ Ethics_Macro Display the **Save as type** list, and then click **PowerPoint Macro-Enabled Presentation**.

10. Click **Save**. Read the displayed message, and then click **OK**.

    PowerPoint presentations that contain ActiveX controls must be saved in a file format that has the .pptm file extension.

    For any presentation with ActiveX controls, the security warnings remind you that you should enable only those ActiveX controls that are from trusted sources. The Text Box control can be trusted.

11. On the **Slide Show tab**, in the **Start Slide Show group**, click **From Current Slide**.

12. Click in the text box, and then type Discuss holding ethics forums at local library. Compare with **Figure 4**.

13. Press [Esc] to exit the slide show. Click **Save** [💾], and then, in the **Privacy warning** message, click **OK**.

   ▪ **You have completed Skill 5 of 10**

► *Macros* are stored sets of instructions that automate common tasks.

► *Microsoft Visual Basic (VBA)* is a high-level programming language that stores sets of instructions. In PowerPoint, macros are written in VBA code.

1. With **Slide 6** still displayed, on the **Developer tab**, in the **Controls group**, click the **Command Button (ActiveX Control)** button 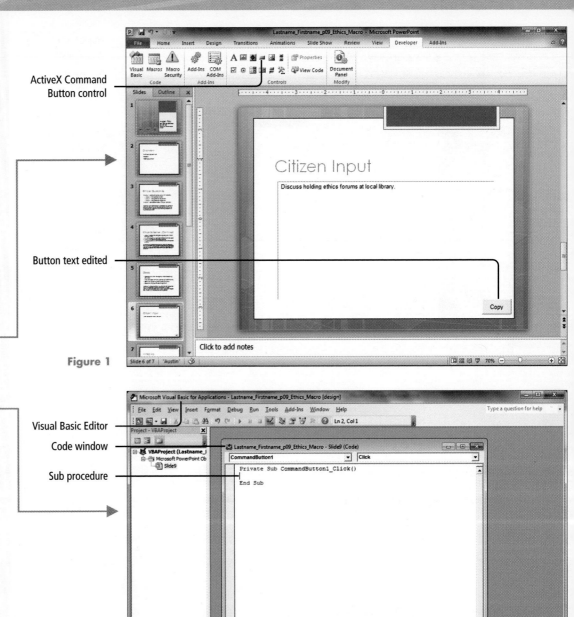.

2. In the lower right corner of the slide, drag to draw a Command Button control.

3. Right-click the button, and then in the displayed shortcut menu, point to **CommandButton Object**, and then click **Edit**. Change the button's text to Copy Click a blank area of the slide, and compare your screen with **Figure 1**. If necessary, resize or move the button.

4. Be sure that the **Command Button** control is not selected, and then double-click the button. Compare your screen with **Figure 2**.

   The Microsoft Visual Basic Editor (VBE) displays. In the Code window, a sub procedure for the command button displays. A *sub procedure* is a group of instructions. Sub procedures are also called *subs* or *procedures*.

5. With the insertion point below the line *Private Sub CommandButton1_Click()*, type 'Copies all text entered during the presentation Be sure the line begins with a single quotation mark.

■ **Continue to the next page to complete the skill**

ActiveX Command Button control

Button text edited

Figure 1

Visual Basic Editor

Code window

Sub procedure

Figure 2

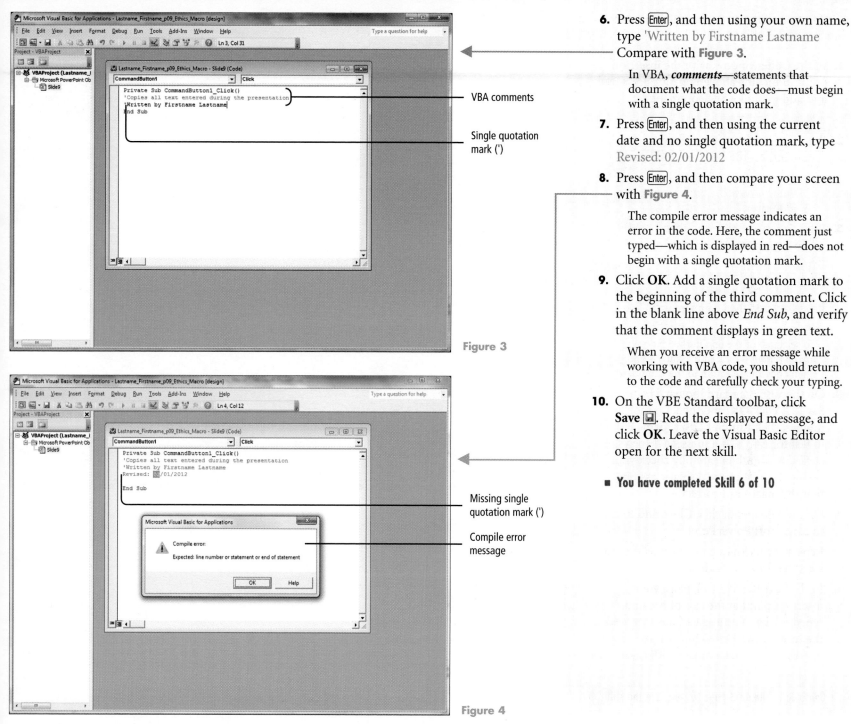

VBA comments

Single quotation mark (')

Figure 3

Missing single quotation mark (')

Compile error message

Figure 4

6. Press [Enter], and then using your own name, type 'Written by Firstname Lastname Compare with **Figure 3**.

   In VBA, *comments*—statements that document what the code does—must begin with a single quotation mark.

7. Press [Enter], and then using the current date and no single quotation mark, type Revised: 02/01/2012

8. Press [Enter], and then compare your screen with **Figure 4**.

   The compile error message indicates an error in the code. Here, the comment just typed—which is displayed in red—does not begin with a single quotation mark.

9. Click **OK**. Add a single quotation mark to the beginning of the third comment. Click in the blank line above *End Sub*, and verify that the comment displays in green text.

   When you receive an error message while working with VBA code, you should return to the code and carefully check your typing.

10. On the VBE Standard toolbar, click **Save** 🖫. Read the displayed message, and click **OK**. Leave the Visual Basic Editor open for the next skill.

▪ **You have completed Skill 6 of 10**

▶ *VBA statements* are the instructions stored in a sub procedure.

――――――――――――

1. In the **Code** window, with the insertion point in the line above *End Sub*, press Enter, and add the following comment:

   'Selects all the text in the text box

2. Press Enter, and type the following statements on the two lines indicated:

   tbxQuestions.SelStart = 0
   tbxQuestions.SelLength = tbxQuestions.TextLength

3. Press Enter two times, and then type the following comment and statement:

   'Copies the text to the system clipboard

   tbxQuestions.Copy

4. Press Enter, and then compare with **Figure 1**. ――――――――▶

   These statements instruct PowerPoint to select all of the text in the text box *tbxQuestions*—created in Skill 5—and then copy the selection to the Clipboard.

5. On the VBE Standard toolbar, click **Save** 🔲, click **OK**, and then, on the toolbar, click **Run Sub/UserForm (F5)** ▶ to test for errors. If a message displays, click **OK**, and then carefully check your typing. If no message displays, assume that the macro ran correctly.

6. On the **File** menu, click **Close and Return to Microsoft PowerPoint**.

7. Repeat the technique practiced earlier to start the show on **Slide 6**.

8. In the **Text Box** control, place your insertion point at the end of the line typed earlier, type a space, and then add the text Involve high schools and colleges in ethics forums. Compare with **Figure 2**. ――――▶

■ **Continue to the next page to complete the skill** ▶

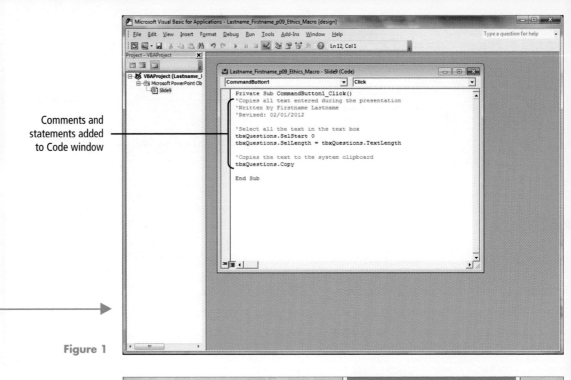

Comments and statements added to Code window

Figure 1

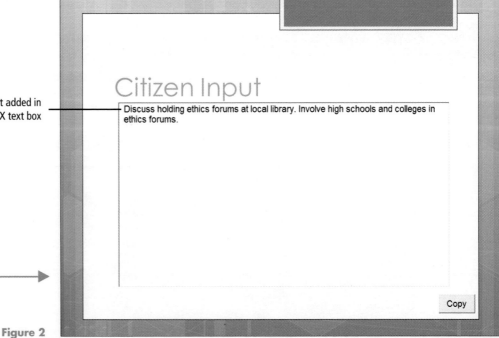

Text added in ActiveX text box

Figure 2

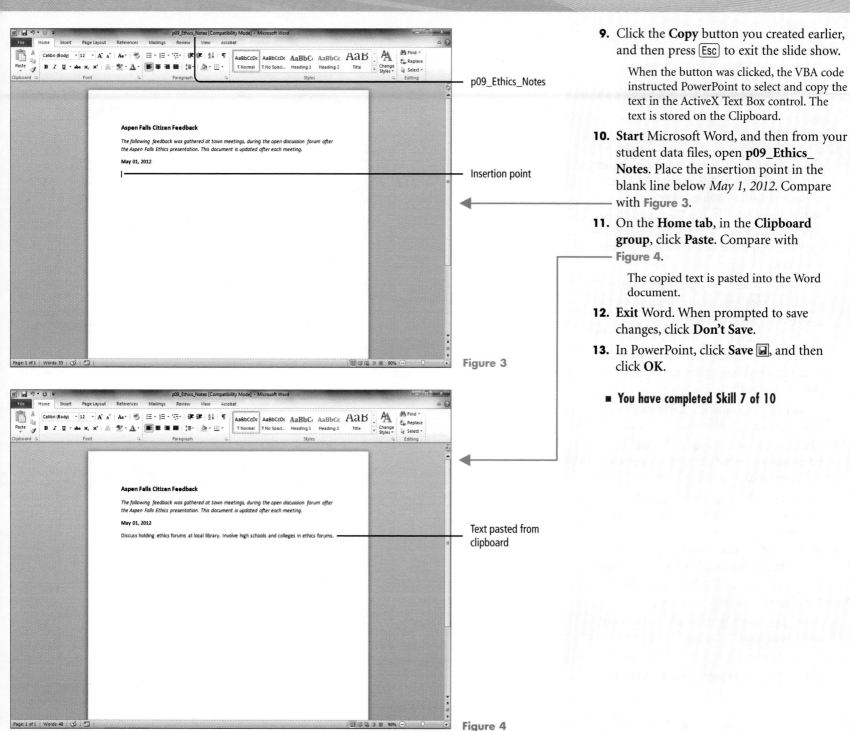

p09_Ethics_Notes

Insertion point

Figure 3

Text pasted from clipboard

Figure 4

9. Click the **Copy** button you created earlier, and then press Esc to exit the slide show.

 When the button was clicked, the VBA code instructed PowerPoint to select and copy the text in the ActiveX Text Box control. The text is stored on the Clipboard.

10. **Start** Microsoft Word, and then from your student data files, open **p09_Ethics_ Notes**. Place the insertion point in the blank line below *May 1, 2012*. Compare with **Figure 3**.

11. On the **Home tab**, in the **Clipboard group**, click **Paste**. Compare with **Figure 4**.

 The copied text is pasted into the Word document.

12. **Exit** Word. When prompted to save changes, click **Don't Save**.

13. In PowerPoint, click **Save** 🖫, and then click **OK**.

■ **You have completed Skill 7 of 10**

▶ In PowerPoint, *comments* are remarks added to a presentation by individuals collaborating to create the presentation.

▶ Comments assist those working on a presentation and do not display in Slide Show view.

1. On the **File tab**, click **Options**. In the **General** options, under **Personalize your copy of Microsoft Office**, note the **User name** and **Initials** values so you can restore them later. In the **User name** box, type your own first and last names, and then in the **Initials** box, type your initials. Click **OK**.

2. On **Slide 6**, select the title, *Citizen Input*. On the **Review tab**, in the **Comments group**, click **New Comment**.

3. In the displayed **Comment**, type Presenters will need to be trained on how to use this text box and macro. Compare your screen with **Figure 1**.

The User name value displays in the comment to identify who makes each comment.

4. Click a blank area on the slide, and then point to, but do not click, the comment indicator as shown in **Figure 2**.

The comment indicator displays your initials and comment number, and when pointed to, it displays the comment.

5. In the lower right corner of the PowerPoint window, click the **Slide Show** button ⬛, and notice the comment does not display.

6. Press [Esc] to exit the slide show and return to Normal view.

■ **Continue to the next page to complete the skill**

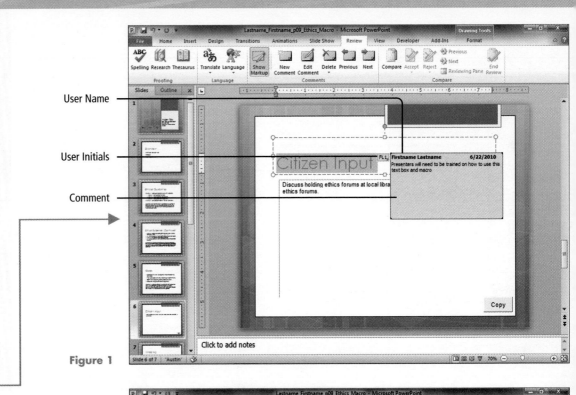

User Name
User Initials
Comment

Figure 1

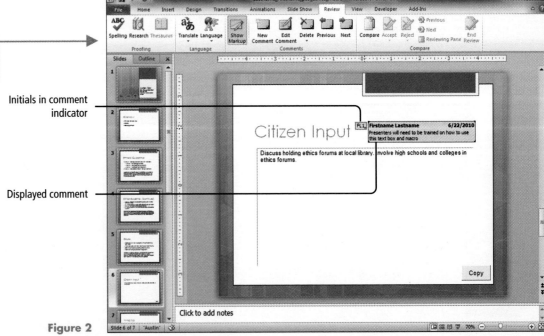

Initials in comment indicator
Displayed comment

Figure 2

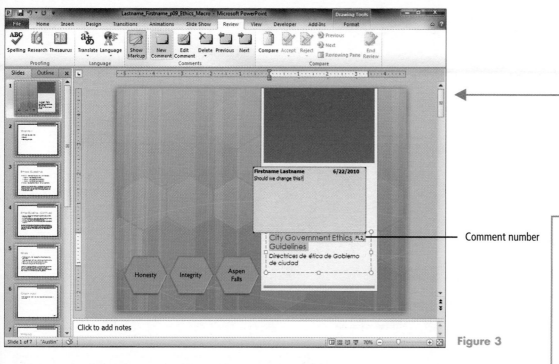

Figure 3

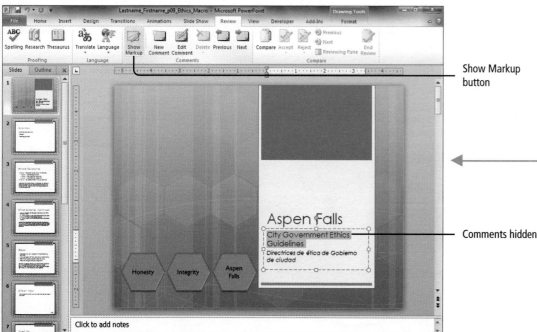

Figure 4

Comment number

Show Markup button

Comments hidden

7. Display **Slide 1**. Select the subtitle *City Government Ethics Guidelines*. On the **Review tab**, in the **Comments group**, click **New Comment**. In the comment box, type Should we change this? Compare your screen with **Figure 3**.

   The comment indicator is numbered, to show that this is the second comment added to this presentation by the current reviewer.

8. On the **Review tab**, in the **Comments group**, click **Show Markup** so that it is not selected, and then compare your screen with **Figure 4**.

   The Show Markup button is used to hide elements such as comments that do not display in Slide Show view.

9. On the **Review tab**, in the **Comments group**, click **Show Markup** to display the comment indicator.

10. On the **Review tab**, in the **Comments group**, click **Edit Comment**. Edit the comment to Should we change this to City Government Ethical Guidelines?

11. Click a blank area of the slide, and then **Save** 🖫 the presentation and click **OK**.

   ▪ **You have completed Skill 8 of 10**

- Slides created in other software or older versions of PowerPoint can be imported into PowerPoint 2010.

- The **Compatibility Checker** verifies that individuals using earlier versions of PowerPoint are able to view your PowerPoint 2010 presentations as you intended.

1. Display **Slide 1**. On the **Home tab**, in the **Slides group**, click the **New Slide button arrow**, and then click **Reuse Slides**.

2. In the **Reuse Slides** task pane, click the **Browse** button, and then click **Browse File**. In the **Browse** dialog box, navigate to your student files, and then double-click **p09_Ethics_Quote1**.

3. At the bottom of the **Reuse Slides** task pane, select the **Keep source formatting** check box, and then compare your screen with **Figure 1**.

   This slide was created in PowerPoint 2002 and saved in the PowerPoint 97–2003 file format, which has the *.ppt* file extension.

4. In the **Reuse Slides** task pane, click the **Slide 1** thumbnail to insert the slide into the existing presentation, and then compare with **Figure 2**.

   The inserted slide uses a design template from PowerPoint 2002.

5. Display **Slide 7**. In the **Reuse Slides** task pane, click the **Browse** button, and then click **Browse File**. In the **Browse** dialog box, navigate to your student files, and then double-click **p09_Ethics_Quote2**.

   This slide was created in a different presentation program and saved in a format that is compatible with Microsoft PowerPoint 2010.

■ **Continue to the next page to complete the skill** ➤

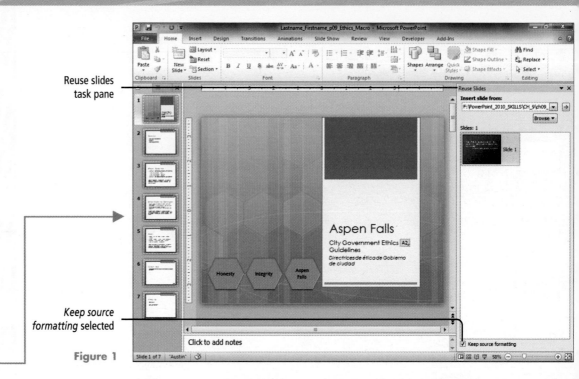

Reuse slides task pane

Keep source formatting selected

Figure 1

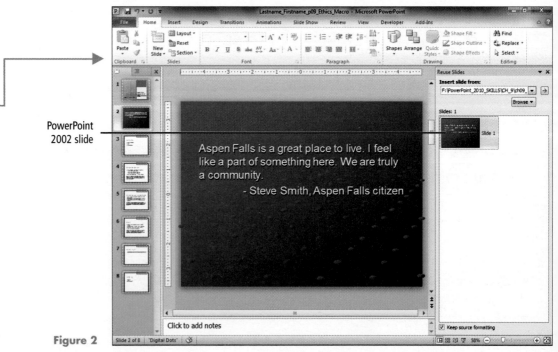

PowerPoint 2002 slide

Figure 2

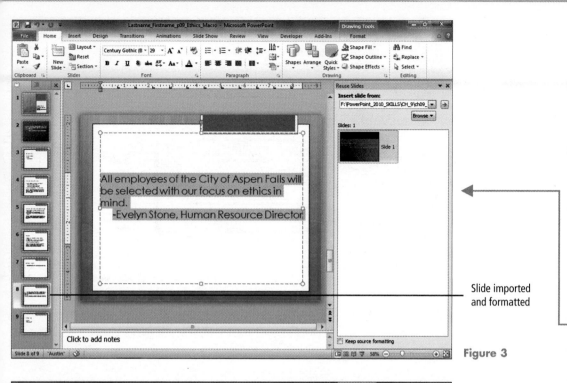

Figure 3

Slide imported and formatted

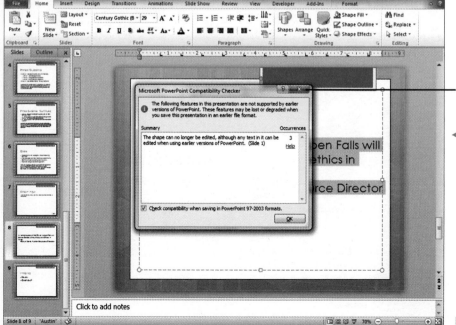

Compatibility Checker

Figure 4

6. At the bottom of the **Reuse Slides** task pane, be sure that the **Keep source formatting** check box is cleared. In the **Reuse Slides** task pane, click the **Slide 1** thumbnail to insert the slide into your presentation.

   When you plan to use slides created by other presentation programs, be sure to save them in a file format that is compatible with PowerPoint 2010.

7. On the slide, select the content placeholder. On the **Format tab**, in the **Size group**, reduce the **Width** of the text box to 8.5" Use the pointer to move the text box and center it over the white area of the slide. Select all of the text on the slide. On the **Home tab**, in the **Font group**, click the **Font Color button arrow**, and then click **Black, Text 1**. Compare with **Figure 3**.

8. **Close** the **Reuse Slides** task pane. Click **File**, and then on the **Info tab**, click **Check for Issues**. Click **Check Compatibility**. Compare with **Figure 4**.

   The Compatibility Checker looks for objects that are not supported in earlier versions of PowerPoint. In this instance, shapes cannot be edited if the presentation is opened in earlier versions.

9. Click **OK** to close the **Compatibility Checker**. Click **Save**, and then click **OK**.

   ■ **You have completed Skill 9 of 10**

► Passwords can be added to files to prevent unauthorized people from viewing or editing your presentations.

► *Digital signatures* are used to identify the author of a file and can be used to verify that any macros in the file are from a trusted source.

1. Display **Slide 1**. Click the **File tab**, and then **Info**. Click the **Protect Presentations** button, and then click **Encrypt with Password**. Compare your screen with **Figure 1**.

   The Encrypt Document dialog box asks for a password and cautions that you need to remember the password.

2. Under **Password**, type 2010Success! Click **OK**, enter the password again, and then click **OK**.

   When encrypting files, use a *strong password*—a password that contains a combination of uppercase and lowercase letters, numbers, and symbols.

3. Click **Save** 🔲, and then click **OK**. Click **Close** to close the presentation and exit PowerPoint.

4. **Start** PowerPoint, navigate to and open **Lastname_Firstname_p09_Ethics_Macro**, and then compare your screen with **Figure 2**.

5. In the **Password** box, type 2010Success! and then press (Enter).

6. Click the **File tab**. On the **Info tab**, click the **Enable Content** button, and then click **Enable All Content**.

7. Click the **File tab**, and then on the **Info tab**, click **Protect Presentation**. Click **Add**

■ **Continue to the next page to complete the skill**

Encrypt Document dialog box

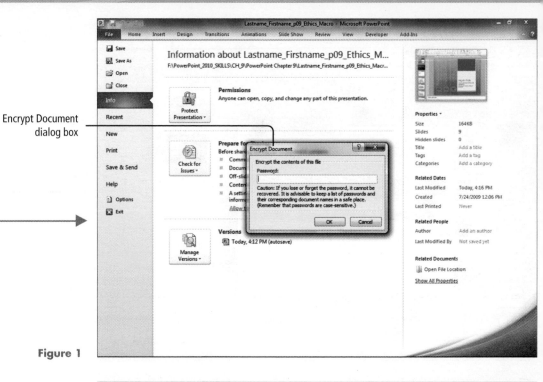

Figure 1

Password box

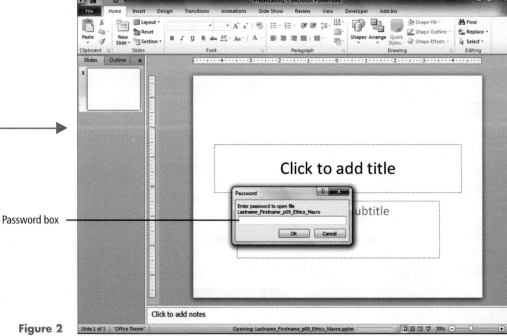

Figure 2

Figure 3

Figure 4

a **Digital Signature**. Read the displayed message, and then click **OK**.

8. In the Get a Digital ID dialog box, click **Create your own digital ID**. Click **OK**. Compare your screen with **Figure 3**.

   In the Create a Digital ID dialog box, verify that your name is displayed. Then add your E-mail address. In the Organization, type your school. In the Location, type your Course name and Section number. Click **Create**.

   A digital signature is created from a unique certificate stored on your computer. This certificate is issued by a certificate agency that verifies your identity before providing you the certificate—typically for a fee.

9. In the Sign dialog box, type the Purpose for signing the document. Click **Sign**. Read the Signature Confirmation message and click **OK**. Compare

   When a digital signature is described as *valid*, the presentation has not been changed since the signature was created. When the digital signature is described as invalid, one or more of the signatures have not been verified.

10. Click the **Home tab**. Compare your screen with **Figure 4**. At the top of your screen, below the tabs, notice that the presentation is **Marked as Final**.

    When a presentation is digitally signed, it is marked as final to discourage editing.

11. Click the **File tab**, and then click **Options**. Restore the **User name** and **Initials** to their original values, and then click **OK**. Close ⊠ PowerPoint.

Done! You have completed Skill 10 of 10 and your document is complete!

The following More Skills are located at **www.pearsonhighered.com/skills**

More Skills Save Presentations as PDF Files

PowerPoint presentations can be saved as Portable Document Format (PDF) files so that they can be viewed without using the PowerPoint program. Presentations saved as PDF files can be viewed with any PDF viewer software. PDF viewer software is available for a variety of operating systems and is typically free.

In More Skills 11, you will save a presentation as a PDF file and then view the file in Adobe Reader—a free PDF viewer program. To begin, open your web browser, navigate to www.pearsonhighered.com/skills, locate the name of your textbook, and follow the instructions on the website.

More Skills Create Videos from Presentations

Videos can be created from a presentation. These videos can contain narration, or other audio, and timings. Videos can be saved in a high-quality format, to be shared on DVD, or saved in a lower quality format, to be shared over the Internet.

In More Skills 12, you will save a presentation as a video, and then you will view the video. To begin, open your web browser, navigate to www.pearsonhighered.com/skills, locate the name of your textbook, and follow the instructions on the website.

More Skills Send Presentations Using Outlook

You can create a new e-mail message from within PowerPoint, and the open file will automatically be attached to the new message. To complete this project, you need to work at a computer where Outlook is installed and configured to send e-mail using your e-mail address.

In More Skills 13, you will send a presentation to your instructor by using Outlook. To begin, open your web browser, navigate to www.pearsonhighered.com/skills, locate the name of your textbook, and follow the instructions on the website.

More Skills Save Files to SkyDrive

Presentations can be saved to SkyDrive so that they can be shared by employees.

In More Skills 14, you will save a file online to SkyDrive. To begin, open your web browser, navigate to www.pearsonhighered.com/skills, locate the name of your textbook, and follow the instructions on the website.

Key Terms

ActiveX control 314

Comments (PowerPoint) 320

Comments (VBA) 317

Compatibility Checker 322

Developer tab 314

Digital signatures 324

Document Inspector 312

Kiosk presentations 310

Macros 316

Microsoft Visual Basic (VBA) . . 316

Procedures 316

Strong password 324

Sub procedure 316

Subs 316

Translate tool 306

VBA statements 318

Online Help Skills

1. **Start** PowerPoint. In upper right corner of the PowerPoint window, click the **Help** ❔ button. In the Help window, click the **Maximize** button.

2. Click in the search box, type Accessibility Checker, and then click the 🔎 button. In the search results, click *Accessibility Checker*. Compare your screen with **Figure 1**.

Figure 1

3. After reading the article, see if you can answer the following question: There are three ways that the Accessibility Checker notifies you of issues that people with disabilities might have with your presentation. Please name these three ways and provide a brief explanation of each.

Matching

Match each term in the second column with its correct definition in the first column by writing the letter of the term on the blank line in front of the correct definition.

____ **1.** A slide show that runs automatically on public monitors.

____ **2.** Checks presentations for comments and annotations, personal information, XML data, Off-Slide Content, and information in the presenter's notes.

____ **3.** Comments, shapes, and text boxes that are saved outside of the slide but within a presentation.

____ **4.** An optional Ribbon tab used to work with macros and controls.

____ **5.** A prebuilt program designed to run inside multiple programs.

____ **6.** A stored set of instructions used to automate a task.

____ **7.** In PowerPoint, macros are created using this type of code.

____ **8.** A remark added to a presentation so individuals can collaborate to create the presentation.

____ **9.** Used to verify that people with earlier versions of PowerPoint can open and use the presentation as intended.

____ **10.** Used to identify the author of a presentation and to check that the file has not been altered.

A ActiveX control

B Comment

C Compatibility Checker

D Developer

E Digital signature

F Document Inspector

G Kiosk presentation

H Macro

I Off-Slide Content

J VBA

Multiple Choice

Choose the correct answer.

1. To ensure that people with visual impairments are able to view your presentation, choose a font that does this with the background color.
   - A. Blends
   - B. Matches
   - C. Contrasts

2. In the Visual Basic Editor, a group of instructions.
   - A. Sub procedure
   - B. Set of code
   - C. Comment

3. Buttons needed to access the tools used for writing code are found on this tab.
   - A. Insert
   - B. Review
   - C. Developer

4. Used to remove personal information before sharing.
   - A. Document Inspector
   - B. User Options
   - C. Developer tab

5. The file extension .pptm indicates that the presentation contains a.
   - A. Macro
   - B. Digital signature
   - C. Metafile

6. Instructions stored in a sub procedure are called VBA what?
   - A. Comments
   - B. Statements
   - C. Code

7. Statements that document what the code does, in VBA.
   - A. Subs
   - B. Comments
   - C. Code

8. A password containing a combination of uppercase and lowercase letters and numbers.
   - A. Strong password
   - B. Impenetrable password
   - C. Complicated password

9. Slides created in other presentation software can be imported into PowerPoint by using this button.
   - A. Reuse Slides
   - B. Insert Picture
   - C. Paste Special

10. To view information about a certificate issuer, point to Info, and then click this button.
    - A. Encrypt Document
    - B. Protect Presentation
    - C. View Signatures

Topics for Discussion

1. What are some of the things you should consider when creating an accessible presentation?

2. What are some advantages of adding digital signatures to a presentation? What are disadvantages?

Skill Check

To complete this project, you will need the following file:

- p09_ID_Theft

You will save your presentations as:

- Lastname_Firstname_p09_ID_Theft_Kiosk
- Lastname_Firstname_p09_ID_Theft_Macro

1. **Start** PowerPoint, and then open **p09_ID_Theft**.

2. On **Slide 1**, select the subheading *Helping citizens protect themselves*. On the **Review tab**, in the **Language group**, click the **Translate** button, and then click **Translate Selected Text**.

3. In the **Research** task pane, verify that the **From** box displays **English (U.S.)**, and then change the **To** box to **French (France)**. Click the **Start searching** button.

4. Select and right-click the translated text, and then click **Copy**. Click to the right of the subheading text, and then press [Enter] two times. On the **Home tab**, in the **Clipboard group**, click **Paste**. For the text just pasted, change the font size to **18**.

5. On **Slide 1**, select the title, and then change the font color to **White, Background 1**. Deselect the text, close the **Research** task pane, and then compare your screen with **Figure 1**.

6. In the pane that contains the Slides and Outline tabs, click the **Slide 1** thumbnail. Press [Ctrl] + [A] to select all the slide thumbnails, and then on the **Transitions tab**, in the **Timing group**, clear the **On Mouse Click** check box. Select the **After** check box, and then change its value to **00:05.00**.

7. On the **Slide Show tab**, in the **Set Up group**, click **Set Up Slide Show**. Under **Show type**, select the **Browsed at a kiosk** option button, and then click **OK**.

8. On the **File** tab, click **Save As**. Navigate to your **PowerPoint Chapter 9** folder, and then change the **File name** to Lastname_Firstname_p09_ID_Theft_Kiosk Click **Save**, and then compare with **Figure 2**.

9. Click **File**, and then on the **Info tab**, click **Check for Issues**. Then click **Inspect Document**. In the **Document Inspector**, click **Inspect**, and then click **Remove All** to remove all personal information. **Close** the dialog box.

10. Click the **Home tab**, and then display **Slide 6**. In the **Slides group**, click the **New Slide button arrow**, and then click **Title Only**.

11. On **Slide 7**, in the title placeholder, type Citizen Concerns

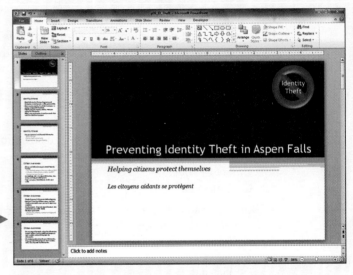

Figure 1

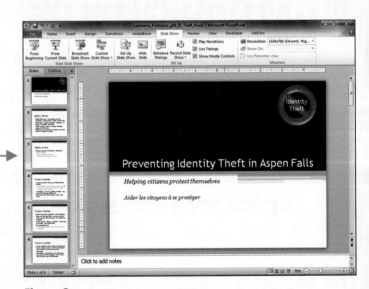

Figure 2

- Continue to the next page to complete this Skill Check

12. On the **Developer tab**, in the **Controls group**, click the Text Box (**ActiveX Control**) button. In the space below the title, draw a text box as shown in **Figure 3**.

13. Right-click the text box, and then click **Properties**. In the **Properties** pane, change the name to tbxInput and change the **Multiline** value to **True**, and then **Close** the **Properties** pane.

14. On the **Developer tab**, in the **Controls group**, click **Command Button (ActiveX Control)**. In the lower right corner of the slide, draw a button.

15. Right-click the button, point to **CommandButton Object**, and then click **Edit**. Change the button text to Copy Input and then click a blank area on the slide. Adjust the size of the button if needed. Compare your screen with **Figure 4**.

16. Double-click the **Command** button you just inserted to open the Visual Basic Editor. In the blank line below *Private Sub CommandButton1_Click()*, type the following VBA comments and statements:

```
'Copies the text
'Written by Firstname Lastname
tbxInput.SelStart = 0
tbxInput.SelLength = tbxInput.TextLength
tbxInput.Copy
```

17. Click **Run** to check for errors, and then correct any errors. From the **File** menu, click **Close and Return to Microsoft PowerPoint**.

18. On **Slide 7**, select the title, *Citizen Concerns*. On the **Review tab**, in the **Comments group**, click **New Comment**. Type For help with this slide, contact Human Resources.

19. In the pane that contains the Slides and Outline tabs, click the **Slide 1** thumbnail. Press [Ctrl] + [A]. On the **Transitions tab**, select **On Mouse Click**.

20. On the **Slide Show tab**, in the **Set Up group**, click **Set Up Slide Show**, and then select **Presented by a speaker (Full Screen)** and then click **OK**.

21. On the **File tab**, click **Save As**. Change the **File name** to Lastname_Firstname_p09_ID_Theft_Macro Change the **Save as type** to **PowerPoint Macro-Enabled Presentation**, and click **Save** and **OK**.

22. Click **File**, and then on the **Info tab**, click **Protect Presentation**. Then click **Encrypt with Password**. In the **Password** box, type 2010Success! Press [Enter], type the password again, and then press [Enter].

23. Add the file name to the Notes and Handouts footer, **Save** the presentation, and then read and click OK on the security message. **Exit** PowerPoint, and then submit your presentation as directed by your instructor.

Done! You have completed the Skill Check

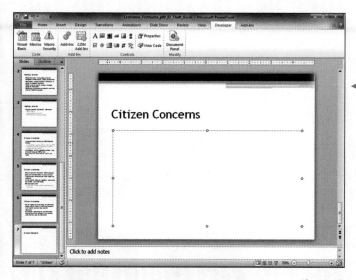

Figure 3

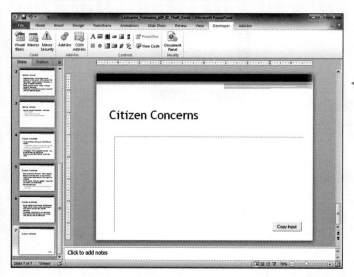

Figure 4

Assess Your Skills 1

To complete this project, you will need the following files:

- p09_Standards
- p09_Standards_Input

You will save your files as:

- Lastname_Firstname_p09_Standards_Show
- Lastname_Firstname_p09_Standards_Macro

1. **Start** PowerPoint, and then from your student files, open **p09_Standards**.

2. On **Slide 1**, change the title and subtitle font to **Perpetua Titling MT**, and then remove the animation from the **Circle Arrow Process** SmartArt shape.

3. Add timings so that the slides advance automatically after 10 seconds. Save the presentation as a **PowerPoint Show** in your **PowerPoint Chapter 9** folder as Lastname_Firstname_p09_Standards_Show

4. Use the **Document Inspector** to remove all personal information from the presentation.

5. Insert a new **Slide 5** with a blank layout.

6. On **Slide 5**, insert a **Text Box (ActiveX Control)** approximately 7 inches wide and 5 inches high and centered.

7. Use the **Properties** pane to change the name of the text box to tbxDiscussion Change the **MultiLine** property to **True**, and then **Close** the pane.

8. Add a **Command Button** to the bottom right corner of the slide. Change the command button text to Copy Input

9. Double-click the button to create a macro sub procedure that copies all of the text in the ActiveX Text Box to the clipboard. Use the same comments and statements used in Skills 6 and 7, but use tbxDiscussion for the control name.

10. Remove the timing from **Slide 5**, and set it to advance **On Mouse Click**.

11. **Save** on the VBA Standard toolbar and click **OK**. **Close** and Return to Microsoft PowerPoint. **Save** the presentation in your **PowerPoint Chapter 9** folder as a **Macro-Enabled Presentation** with the name Lastname_Firstname_p09_Standards_Macro

12. Display the presentation in Slide Show view. On **Slide 5**, in the ActiveX control, type Aspen Falls Community College offers a reasonably priced one-day seminar on business writing.

13. Click the **Copy Input** command button, and then **Exit** the slide show. **Start** Word, and then open **p09_Standards_Input**. Paste the copied text to verify the macro worked. **Exit** Word without saving the file.

14. Substitute your **User name** and **Initials**.

15. Select the title on **Slide 2**. Add this **Comment**: Update to Town Hall Meeting Minutes?

16. Check for compatibility with earlier versions of PowerPoint. Delete any items that cannot be edited in earlier versions of PowerPoint.

17. **Encrypt** the document by using the password 2010Success!

18. Add the file name to the Notes and Handouts footer for all pages.

19. Change the **User name** and **Initials** back to the original setting. **Save** the presentation, and then **Exit** PowerPoint. Submit your presentation as directed by your instructor.

Done! You have completed Assess Your Skills 1

Figure 1

Assess Your Skills 2

To complete this project, you will need the following files:

- p09_Interns
- p09_Interns_Quote

You will save your files as:

- Lastname_Firstname_p09_Interns_Show
- Lastname_Firstname_p09_Interns_Macro

Figure 1

1. **Start** PowerPoint, and then from your student files, open **p09_Interns**.

2. **Save** the presentation in the **PowerPoint Show** file format with the name Lastname_Firstname_p09_Interns_Show in your **PowerPoint Chapter 9** folder.

3. Add timings so that all slides advance every **9 seconds**.

4. On **Slide 2**, translate all of the bulleted text to **Spanish**, and then copy and paste the translation below the bulleted points. Use **Decrease List Level** to make the translation appear at the same bullet level. Apply **Italic** to the translated text. On **Slide 3**, repeat this process.

5. For all slides, except the title slide, change the font color of the text in the content placeholders to **Black, Text 1**.

6. On **Slide 3**, for the four indented bullets, change the font size to **24**, and then **Save** the presentation.

7. Set the **Show type** to **Browsed at a kiosk**. Save your presentation.

8. Use **Save As** to save the presentation in preparation for adding a macro. Name the file Lastname_Firstname_p09_Interns_Macro and change the file type to **PowerPoint Macro-Enabled Presentation**.

9. On **Slide 4**, a **Text Box (ActiveX Control)** in the empty content area of the slide.

10. Use the **Properties** pane to change the name of the text box to tbxSuggestions Change the **MultiLine** property to **True**, and then **Close** the pane.

11. Add a **Command Button** in the lower right corner of the slide, and then change the command button text to Copy

12. Double-click the button to create a macro sub procedure that uses the same comments and statements used in Skills 6 and 7, but use tbxSuggestions for the control name.

13. In Slide Show view, navigate to the fourth slide, and then in the text box, type Marketing Click the **Copy** command button, and then click ⌷Esc⌷ to exit the slide show.

14. **Start** Word, and then in the blank document, paste the copied text to verify that the macro worked correctly. **Exit** Word without saving the file.

15. After **Slide 4**, insert the slide from the file **p09_Interns_Quote** while keeping the source formatting.

16. **Encrypt** the document by using the password 2010Success!

17. Add the file name to the Notes and Handouts footer for all pages.

18. **Save**, and then **Exit** PowerPoint. Submit as directed.

Done! You have completed Assess Your Skills 2

Assess Your Skills Visually

To complete this project, you will need the following file:

- p09_Trends

You will save your presentation as:

- Lastname_Firstname_p09_Trends

Open **p09_Trends**. View the presentation in Slide Show view. Note the readability of the fonts and the animation on the slide. Return to Normal view. Change the font color for all of the text on the slide to **White, Text 1** so that it contrasts with the background, making it easier to read. Increase the size of the title so that it fills the placeholder without dropping onto two lines. Remove the **Bold** effect from the title to make it easier to read. Change the font for all of the bulleted text in the content placeholder to an easy-to-read font, and increase the font size of the same text so that it appears similar to the figure. Remove the **Blink Animation** from the cell phone picture. **Save as** a **PowerPoint Presentation** named Lastname_Firstname_p09_Trends Add the file name to the Notes and Handouts footer. Remove all personal information and **Off-Slide Content**.

Save and submit the presentation as directed.

Done! You have completed Assess Your Skills Visually

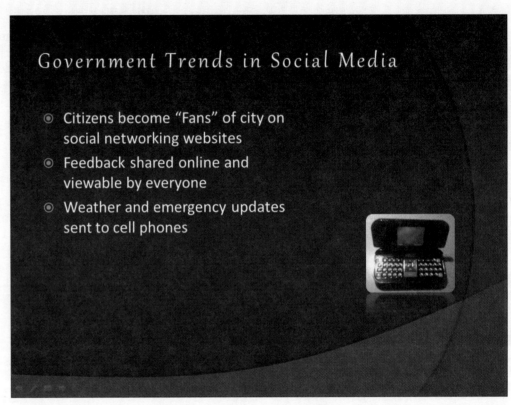

Figure 1

Skills in Context

To complete this project, you will need the following file:

- p09_Concert

You will save your presentation as:

- Lastname_Firstname_p09_Concert

Open **p09_Concert**, and **Save** it in your **PowerPoint Chapter 9** folder as a Macro-Enabled Presentation named Lastname_ Firstname_p09_Concert View the **ActiveX Text Box**. The text box currently allows users to enter text only on one line. Adjust the properties of the text box so that text can be entered on multiple lines.

Use the **Copy Input** command button to open the macro and view the code in Visual Basic for Applications. Run the macro, and locate the errors in the code written for this control. Change the **Revised on** date to today's date. There are three errors—a typographical error, an error involving the name of the textbox, and an error that causes the macro to paste instead of copy. Correct the errors. Return to PowerPoint, switch to Slide Show view, and in the text box, type Explore the possibility of installing a sound barrier between band shell and neighboring condominiums. Use the **Copy Input** button to copy the text on the slide, and then use Word to check that the macro works properly. Add the file name to the footer for the Notes and Handouts page. **Save** and submit your presentation as directed.

Done! You have completed Skills in Context

Skills and You

To complete this project, you will need the following file:

- p09_Featured_Speaker

You will save your presentation as:

- Lastname_Firstname_p09_Featured_Speaker

Open **p09_Featured_Speaker**. **Save** the file in your **PowerPoint Chapter 9** folder as a **Macro-Enabled Presentation** with the file name Lastname_Firstname_p09_ Featured_Speaker This presentation could be used to take notes on a speech that is being delivered remotely. You will add ActiveX Text Boxes to display notes to the audience.

On **Slide 1**, modify the subtitle to reflect a topic that will be presented on your campus within the next 90 days. You could add the subtitle Preparing for a Career Search in Tough Times

On **Slide 2**, use the **Review tab** to add the following comment to the title *Featured Speaker*: Please contact Firstname Lastname for information on using the text boxes below. Add two **ActiveX Text Boxes**, one beneath each title, and size them to fit well in the space provided. Set the **Multiline** property to **True**.

On **Slide 3**, add an **ActiveX Text Box** to the area of the slide below the title, and size it to fit. Set the **Multiline** property to **True**. None of the text boxes need a Copy Command button. In Slide Show view, start the presentation. Add information to each ActiveX Text Box. End the presentation. Add the file name to the footer in the Notes and Handouts pages. **Save** the file, and submit as directed.

Done! You have completed Skills and You

Finalize Presentations

▶ When you prepare for an actual presentation, it is a good idea to obtain feedback from a colleague. You should also consider the computer and projector that will be used during the presentation.

▶ You can collect information from webpages, paste the information into slides, and then credit the sources of the information. When doing so, take care to always observe the intellectual property rights of the original authors.

Your starting screen will look like this:

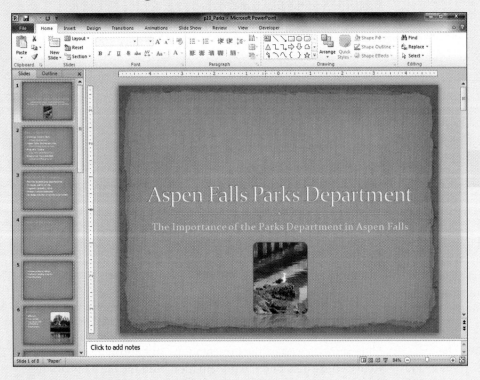

SKILLS

Skills 1-10 Training

At the end of this chapter, you will be able to:

Skill 1 Use Reviewer Feedback to Improve Presentations

Skill 2 Reorder and Hide Slides

Skill 3 Collect Information Using the Clipboard Pane

Skill 4 Paste from Webpages

Skill 5 Create Citations in Word

Skill 6 Cite Sources on a Bibliography Slide

Skill 7 Animate Chart Elements

Skill 8 Mark Up Slides During Presentations and Use the Laser Pointer

Skill 9 Change Presentation Resolution

Skill 10 Package Presentations for CD

MORE SKILLS

More Skills 11 Download and Run PowerPoint Viewer

More Skills 12 Add an Agenda and Change the Orientation of Slides

More Skills 13 Use Presenter View

More Skills 14 Prepare Equipment and Software for Presentations

Outcome

Using the skills listed to the left will enable you
to create a presentation like this:

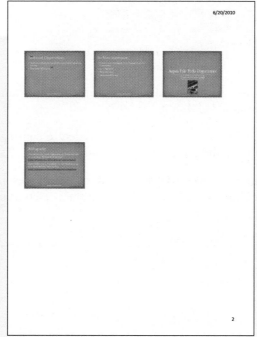

You will save your files as:

Lastname_Firstname_p10_Parks
Lastname_Firstname_p10_Parks_Bibliography
Lastname_Firstname_p10_Parks_CD (a folder)

In this chapter, you will create presentations for the Aspen Falls City Hall, which provides essential services for the citizens and visitors of Aspen Falls, California.

Introduction

- ▶ Preparing to deliver your presentation is nearly as important as the design and information contained within it.

- ▶ Slides can be reordered, animations can be added to charts, and annotations can be added during the presentation to hold the audience's interest.

- ▶ Information can be copied and pasted from other sources. Bibliographies can be created as documents and as slides within the presentation to properly cite the works of other authors.

Time to complete all
10 skills – 50 to 90 minutes

**Student data files needed
for this chapter:**

- p10_Parks

Find your student data file here:

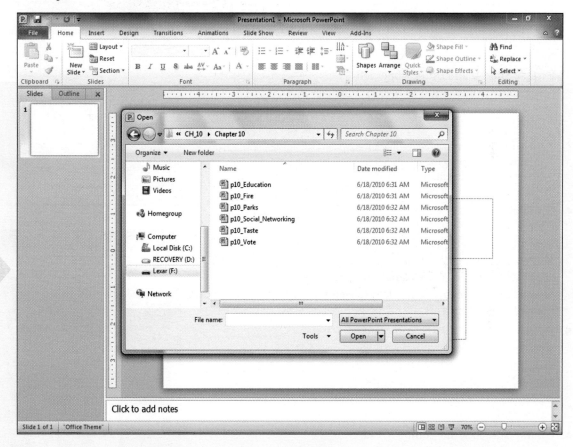

▶ You can improve your presentations by seeking input from people you work with.

1. **Start** 🅟 PowerPoint. From your student files, open **p10_Parks**. On the **File tab**, click **Save As**. Navigate to the location where you are saving your files, create a folder named PowerPoint Chapter 10 and then **Save** the presentation as Lastname_Firstname_p10_Parks

2. Switch to Normal View. Scroll to view all slides in the presentation.

3. Display **Slide 1**, and in the upper left corner of the slide, point to the Comment indicator. Compare your screen with **Figure 1**.

    Evelyn Stone has provided feedback for improving your presentation by adding Comments. Comments are displayed when you point to, or click, the Comment indicator.

4. On **Slide 1**, click the Comment in the upper left corner of the slide to view it. Read the Comment, and then on the **Review tab**, in the **Comments group**, click the top half of the **Delete** button to remove the comment. Click each slide and note Evelyn's comments.

5. Display **Slide 2**. Click the comment to view the feedback, and then with your insertion point in the speaker's notes, type Ask audience members to share their experiences at these parks. Compare your screen with **Figure 2**.

6. On the slide, click the Comment one time to select it, and then on the **Review tab**, in the **Comments group**, click the upper half of the **Delete** button to remove the comment.

■ **Continue to the next page to complete the skill**

Comment containing feedback on presentation

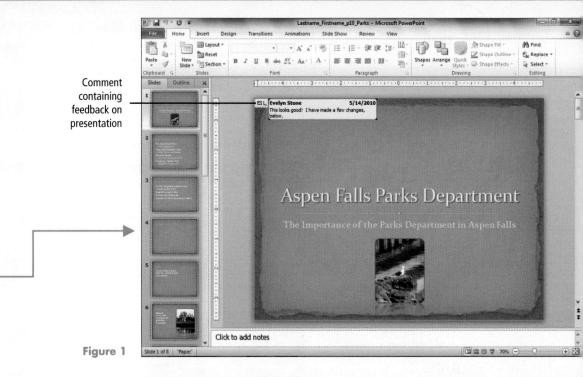

Figure 1

Feedback typed into speaker's notes

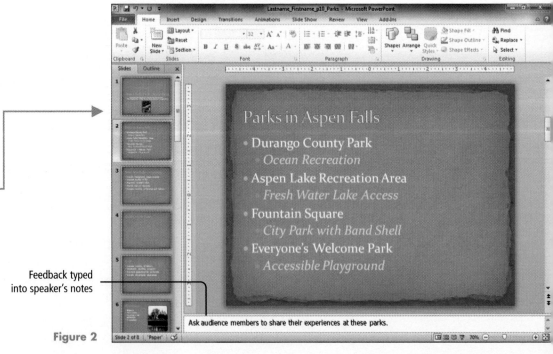

Figure 2

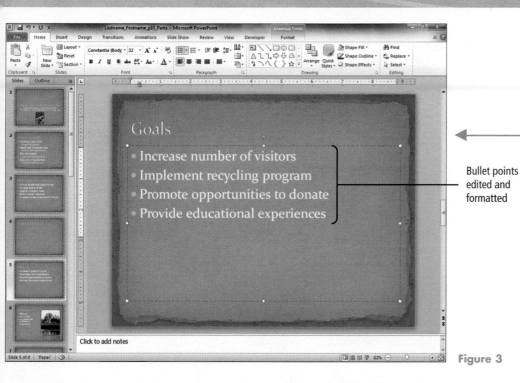

Bullet points edited and formatted

Figure 3

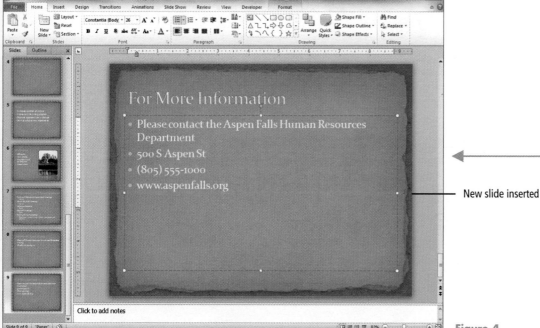

New slide inserted

Figure 4

7. Scroll down to view the feedback for **Slide 5**. Read the Comment, select the text **Raise donations**, and type Promote opportunities to donate

8. With your insertion point at the end of the third bullet point, press Enter, and then type Provide educational experiences

9. Delete the comment on Slide 5. Select all of the bulleted text, and then increase the font size to **32**. Click a blank area of the slide to deselect the text, and then compare your screen with **Figure 3**.

10. Display **Slide 7**. Read the Comment.

    The type of information that Evelyn is asking for is typically found on the last slide of a presentation.

11. Display Slide 8. On the **Home tab**, in the **Slides group**, click the **New Slide** button. In the title placeholder, type For More Information Click the content place-holder, and type all of the contact information listed in Evelyn's Comment. Compare your screen with **Figure 4**.

12. Delete the Comment on **Slide 7**, and then **Save** 🖫 the presentation.

    ■ **You have completed Skill 1 of 10**

▶ Slides can be moved or rearranged to show information in a logical order.

▶ Slides that do not apply to a particular audience can be hidden. In this manner, the hidden slides do not display during the presentation, but they remain a part of the original file.

1. Display **Slide 1**. Scroll to display the feedback for **Slide 6**, and then read the feedback from Evelyn Stone. Return to **Slide 1**. On the bar on the lower right corner of the screen, click the **Slide Sorter** ⊞ button. Alternately, on the View tab, in the Presentation Views group, click Slide Sorter.

2. On the bar on the lower right corner of the screen, click the **Slide Sorter** button. Alternately, on the View tab, in the Presentation Views group, click Slide Sorter.

3. On the **View tab**, in the **Zoom group**, click **Fit to Window**. Compare your screen with **Figure 1**.

   Recall that Slide Sorter view is used to organize presentations and work with transitions between slides. Text and individual slide objects cannot be selected in this view.

4. Drag **Slide 6** to the left so that the insertion indicator displays to the left of **Slide 5**. Compare your screen with **Figure 2**.

   The *Promotion* slide, formerly Slide 6, is now Slide 5.

5. On the **View tab**, in the **Zoom group**, click the **Zoom** button. In the displayed **Zoom** dialog box, select the **66%** option button to return to the original zoom level, and click **OK**.

■ **Continue to the next page to complete the skill** ➤

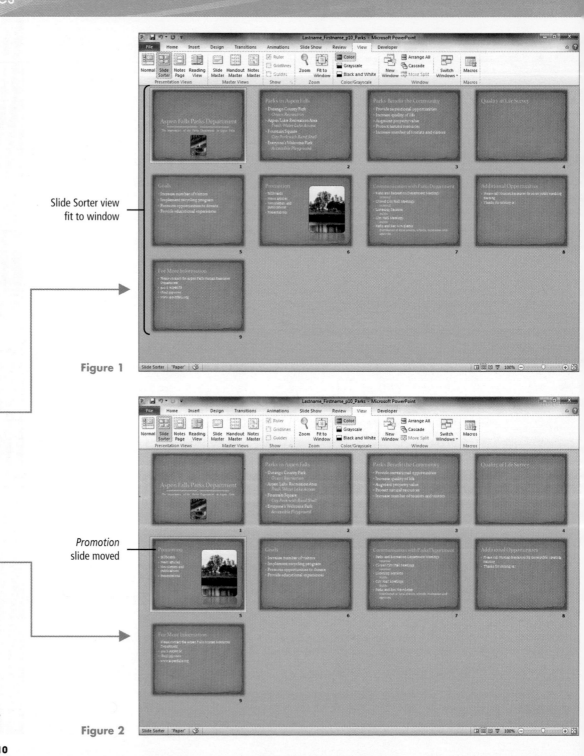

Slide Sorter view fit to window

Figure 1

Promotion slide moved

Figure 2

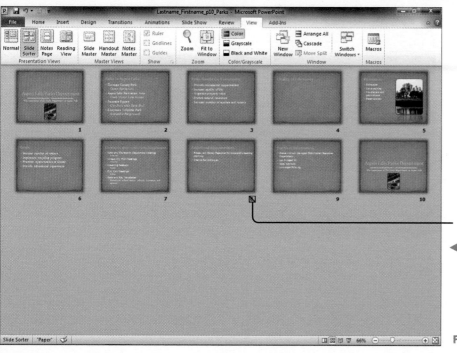

Hidden slide icon

Figure 3

Subtitle changed

Figure 4

6. Point to the **Slide 1** thumbnail. Press and hold [Ctrl] while dragging the thumbnail to the end of the presentation.

   When you hold [Ctrl] and drag an object, the object is copied, and the copy is placed in the location you drag to. Here, Slide 1 has been copied, and the copy has been inserted as Slide 10.

7. Switch to Normal view, and then scroll down to display the feedback for **Slide 8**. Read the feedback.

8. In Slide Sort view, right-click the **Slide 8** thumbnail. From the displayed shortcut menu, click **Hide Slide**, and then compare your screen with **Figure 3**.

   When a slide is hidden, the hidden slide icon displays over the slide number.

9. Click the **Slide 7** thumbnail. On the bar in the lower right corner, click the **Slide Show** button. Click to advance to the next slide, and verify that **Slide 8**, the *Additional Opportunities* slide, does not display.

10. End the show, and display Slide 10 in Normal view. Replace the subtitle text with Thank you for your support! Compare your screen with **Figure 4**.

11. **Save** the presentation.

■ **You have completed Skill 2 of 10**

► You can collect information from the Internet and store it in the Clipboard pane.

1. Display **Slide 3**. On the **Home tab**, in the **Slides group**, click the **New Slide button arrow**, and then click **Two Content**. Repeat this technique to insert another slide with the **Two Content** layout.

2. On the **Home tab**, in the **Clipboard** group, click the **Clipboard Pane Launcher** 🖾 to display the **Clipboard** pane. Click the **Clear All** button to remove any previously copied text.

   Recall that the *Office Clipboard* stores up to 24 items copied from Office programs and other sources. To copy and paste items into the Office Clipboard, you must have the Clipboard open.

3. **Open** your web browser. In the address bar, type www.nps.gov and press Enter. On the displayed page, locate the **Find a Park** textbox. Click the down arrow and select **California**. If this page has changed or moved, click a similar link. Compare your screen with **Figure 1**. Note that webpages change frequently, so your screen might differ from the figure.

4. In the displayed list of parks, click **Channel Islands**. If the webpage has changed or moved, find a page similar to the one shown in **Figure 2**.

5. In the address bar, right-click anywhere on the URL, *http://www.nps.gov/chis/planyourvisit/index.htm*, and then from the displayed shortcut menu, click **Copy**.

   A *URL*, or *Uniform Resource Locator*, is the address used to locate a specific webpage.

■ **Continue to the next page to complete the skill** ➤

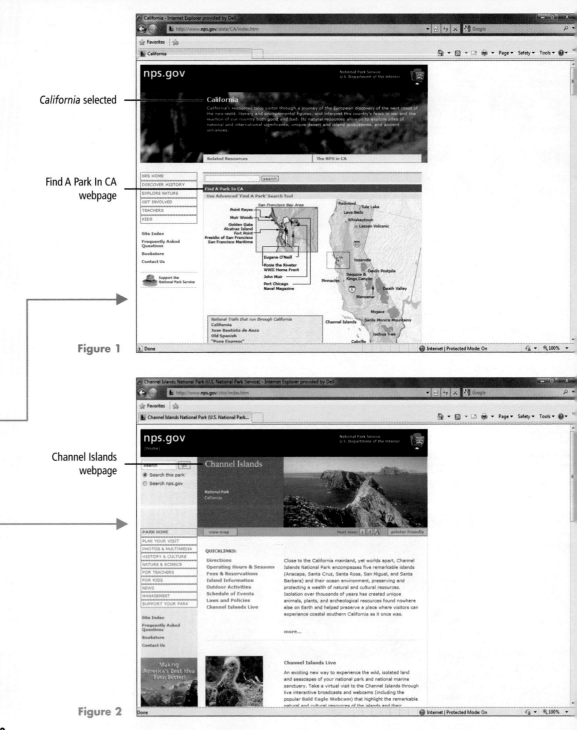

California selected

Find A Park In CA webpage

Figure 1

Channel Islands webpage

Figure 2

Death Valley
webpage

Figure 3

Six items stored
in the Office
Clipboard

Figure 4

6. Select the second sentence of text about the Channel Islands, beginning with *Close to the California Mainland* and ending with *cultural resources*, and then **Copy** the selected text. Click a blank area to deselect the text.

7. Scroll down to locate the photo to the right beneath *Hiking the Channel Islands*. Right-click the picture, and then from the displayed shortcut menu, click **Copy**.

8. In the address bar, type http://www. nps.gov/deva/planyourvisit/index.htm and press Enter. If the webpage has changed or moved, find a page similar to the one shown in **Figure 3**.

9. In the address bar, right-click the URL, and then click **Copy**.

10. Select the sentence beginning with *The salt pan* and ending with *5 miles wide,* and then **Copy** the selected text. Click a blank area to deselect the text.

11. Scroll up to the top of the page and right-click the picture, and then from the displayed shortcut menu, click **Copy**.

12. Switch to PowerPoint. In the **Clipboard** pane, verify that six items display similarly to **Figure 4**.

  In the Clipboard pane, the items are listed in the order they were copied, with the most recent item at the top.

13. On **Slide 4**, in the title placeholder, type Ocean

14. Display **Slide 5**. In the title placeholder, type Inland

15. **Save** 🖫 the presentation.

■ **You have completed Skill 3 of 10**

▶ Information—text, pictures, hyperlinks and URLs—stored on the Office Clipboard can be pasted into your presentation.

▶ Information and photos copied from other sources should include a *citation*—a note crediting the original source or author.

1. On **Slide 4**, click in the left content place-holder. At the bottom of the **Clipboard** pane, click the sentence that you copied about the Channel Islands park to paste it into the placeholder. Press [Enter], and then in the **Clipboard** pane, click the Channel Islands—*www.nps.gov/chis*—URL.

2. Click the border of the right content placeholder to select the placeholder, and then in the **Clipboard** pane, click the image of Channel Islands to paste it. Right-click picture and click **Size and Position**. Increase the Height to 1.5" if necessary. Deselect the picture. Compare your screen with **Figure 1**.

3. In the **Clipboard** pane, point to the thumbnail of the sentence about the Channel Islands, and then click the displayed **arrow**. Compare your screen with **Figure 2**, and then click **Delete**.

   Items can be removed from the Office Clipboard.

4. Repeat the technique just practiced to remove the Channel Islands URL and the Channel Islands image from the Office Clipboard.

■ **Continue to the next page to complete the skill**

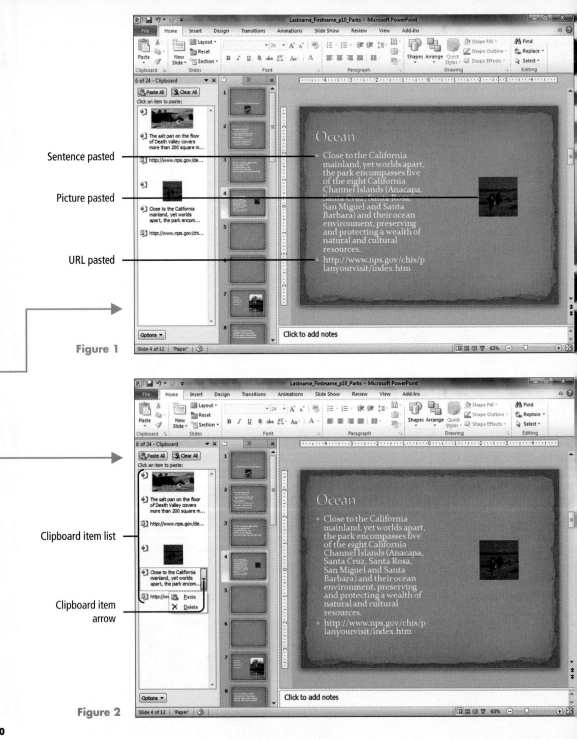

Sentence pasted

Picture pasted

URL pasted

Figure 1

Clipboard item list

Clipboard item arrow

Figure 2

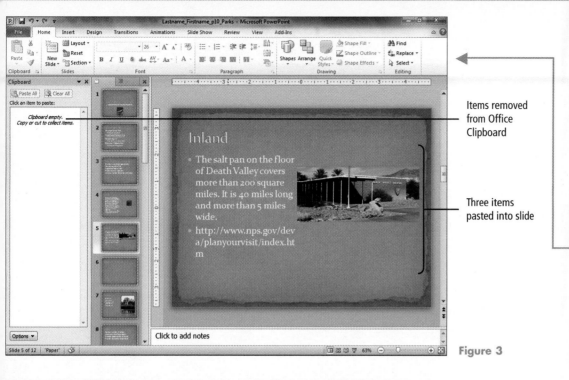

Items removed from Office Clipboard

Three items pasted into slide

Figure 3

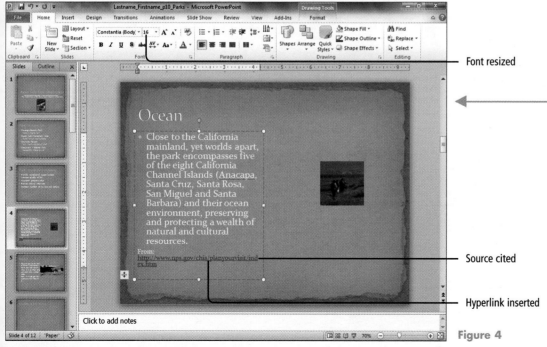

Font resized

Source cited

Hyperlink inserted

Figure 4

5. Display **Slide 5**, and then click in the left content placeholder. In the **Clipboard** pane, click the sentence that you copied about Death Valley. Press Enter, and then in the **Clipboard** pane, click the Death Valley URL.

6. Click the border of the right content placeholder, and then in the **Clipboard** pane, click the image of Death Valley to paste it. Change the picture width to 4". Deselect the picture.

7. In the **Clipboard** pane, click the **Clear All** button. Compare your screen with **Figure 3**. **Close** ☒ the Clipboard pane.

8. Display **Slide 4**, and then place the insertion point between the bullet and the URL. On the **Home tab**, in the **Paragraph group**, click the **Bullets** ☷ button to remove the bullet.

9. Type From: and then press Space. Move the insertion point to the end of the URL, and then press Space. Select *From:* and the entire URL, and change the **Font Size** to 16. Compare your screen with **Figure 4**.

   When you add a space after text that begins with *http://* PowerPoint automatically inserts a hyperlink using the URL.

10. On **Slide 5**, place your insertion before the URL. On the **Home tab**, in the **Paragraph group**, click the **Bullets** ☷ button.

11. Type From: and then press Space. After the URL, add a space to insert the hyperlink. Select *From:* and the entire URL, and change the **Font Size** to 16.

12. **Save** 🖫 the presentation.

- **You have completed Skill 4 of 10**

▶ The Source Manager in Word can be used to create a ***bibliography***—a list of sources referenced in a presentation.

1. **Start** Word. On the **Home tab**, in the **Clipboard group**, click the **Clipboard Pane Launcher** 🔲 to display the **Clipboard** pane.

2. On the **References tab**, in the **Citations & Bibliography group**, click the **Style arrow**, and then select **APA Fifth Edition**. Compare your screen with **Figure 1.**

   APA is a widely used citation style created by the American Psychological Association.

3. In the **Citations & Bibliography group**, click the **Manage Sources** button. In the **Source Manager** dialog box, click **New.**

4. In the **Create Source** dialog box, click the **Type of Source arrow**, and then click **Web site.**

5. In the **Name of Web Page** box, type Channel Islands In the **Name of Web Site** box, type National Park Service

6. Switch to your web browser, and navigate back to the Channel Islands page. Scroll to the bottom of the page, note the date listed, and then in the address bar, **Copy** the URL.

7. Switch to Word, and then in the **Year** box, type the year of the webpage. In the **Month** box, type the month, and then in the **Day** box, type the date that you noted.

8. In the **Year Accessed**, **Month Accessed**, and **Day Accessed** boxes, type values for the current date.

9. In the **URL** box, right-click and then **Paste** the URL you copied. Compare your screen with **Figure 2**, and then click **OK.**

■ **Continue to the next page to complete the skill**

APA style selected

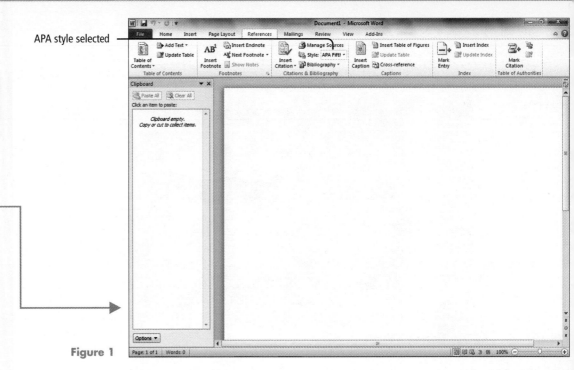

Figure 1

Webpage source information entered into Create Source dialog box

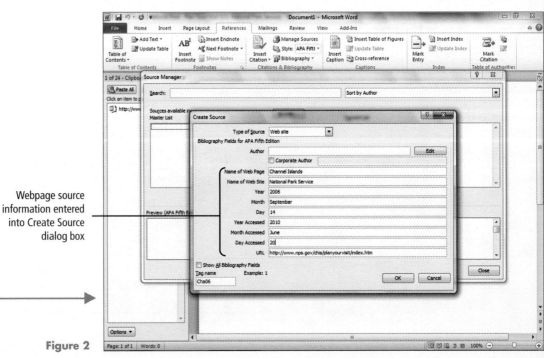

Figure 2

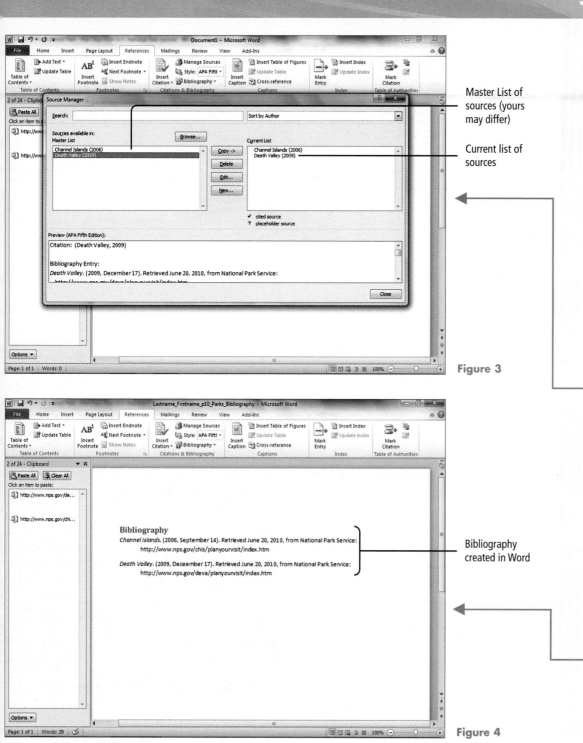

Master List of sources (yours may differ)

Current list of sources

Figure 3

Bibliography created in Word

Figure 4

10. In the **Source Manager** dialog box, click **New**, and then verify that the **Type of Source** is *Web site*.

11. In the **Name of Web Page** box, type Death Valley and then in the **Name of Web Site** box, type National Park Service

12. In your web browser, navigate to the Death Valley page, and then note the date listed at the bottom of the webpage. **Close** the web browser.

13. In the displayed **Create Source** dialog box, in the **Year**, **Month**, and **Day** boxes, type the date values you noted in the previous step. In the **Year Accessed**, **Month Accessed**, and **Day Accessed** boxes, type values for the current date. Please note that your dates will vary from those shown in the screen shots because of website updates.

14. In the **URL** box, right-click and then **Paste** the URL you copied and then click **OK**. Compare your screen with **Figure 3**.

15. **Close** the **Source Manager** dialog box, and then on the **References tab**, in the **Citations & Bibliography group**, click the **Bibliography** button. In the displayed list, click **Bibliography**.

    Using the information stored in the Source Manager, a bibliography is created in APA style. This document can be used as a handout, or information can be copied from it and pasted onto slides.

16. Click the **File tab**, and then click **Save As**. Navigate to your **PowerPoint Chapter 10** folder. In the **File name** box, type Lastname_Firstname_p10_Parks_ Bibliography and then click **Save**. Compare your screen with **Figure 4**.

- **You have completed Skill 5 of 10**

▶ You can copy a bibliography made in Word to a PowerPoint slide. In this manner, you can show your sources during the presentation.

1. Display PowerPoint, and then in Lastname_Firstname_p10_Parks, select the last slide. On the **Home tab**, in the **Slides group**, click the upper half of the **New Slide** button to insert a new **Slide 13** with the **Title and Content** layout.

2. Switch to Word. Click anywhere in the bibliography to select the field. Below the *Bibliography* title, select the two entries beginning with *Channel Islands* and ending with *deva/index.htm*. On the **Home tab**, in the **Clipboard group**, click **Copy**, and then compare your screen with **Figure 1**.

3. **Close** [x] Word.

4. On **Slide 13**, click in the title placeholder, and type Bibliography

5. Place your insertion point in the content placeholder. Display the **Clipboard** pane, and then click the bibliography thumbnail. On the slide, click the **Paste Options** [📋] button, and then click the third option—**Keep Text Only (T)**. Select all text and bullets. On the **Home tab**, in the **Paragraph group**, click the **Bullets** [≡ ▾] button to remove the bullet. Compare your screen with **Figure 2**.

   The bibliography created in Word is pasted into the PowerPoint presentation.

6. **Close** [x] the **Clipboard** pane.

■ **Continue to the next page to complete the skill** ➤

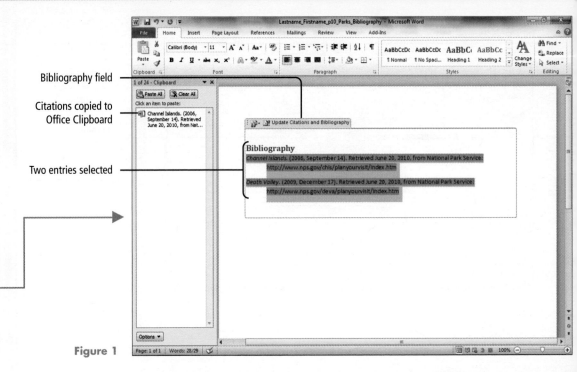

Bibliography field

Citations copied to Office Clipboard

Two entries selected

Figure 1

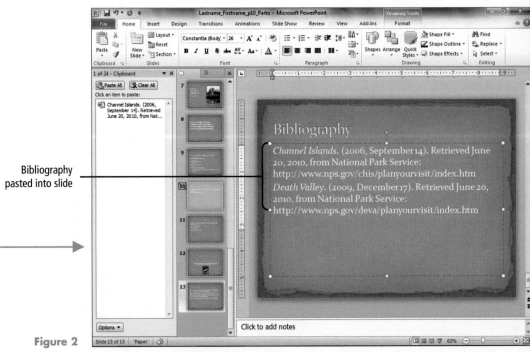

Bibliography pasted into slide

Figure 2

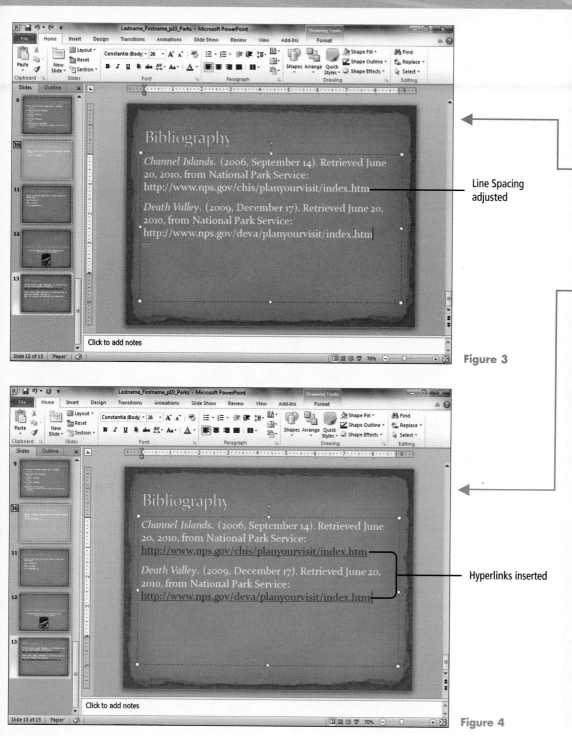

Line Spacing adjusted

Figure 3

Hyperlinks inserted

Figure 4

7. Select all of the text in the content placeholder, and then on the **Home tab**, in the **Paragraph group**, click the **Line Spacing** button. Click **Line Spacing Options**.

8. In the **Paragraph** dialog box, under **Spacing**, change the **After** value to **12 pt**. Click **OK**. Compare your screen with **Figure 3**.

    Twelve points of space has been added between the citations.

9. Place your insertion point at the end of the first citation, and then press Space to insert the hyperlink. Repeat this technique to insert a hyperlink for the second URL, and then compare your screen with **Figure 4**.

10. **Save** the presentation. Click the **Slide Show** button. On the displayed bibliography slide, click the first hyperlink to test the link.

11. On the taskbar, click to display PowerPoint, and then test the second link.

    It is a good idea to check each hyperlink before presenting.

12. **Close** your web browser. If prompted, click **Close all tabs**. **End** the PowerPoint show.

- **You have completed Skill 6 of 10**

▶ You can animate charts to emphasize individual chart elements during a presentation.

1. Display **Slide 6**. In the content placeholder, click the **Insert Chart** 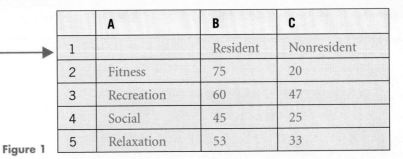 button. In the displayed **Insert Chart** dialog box, under **Column**, click the second choice in the second row—**Stacked Cylinder**—and then click **OK**.

2. In the Excel worksheet, type the data shown in **Figure 1** in columns A, B, and C.

3. In the Excel worksheet, point to the lower right corner of the data range, and then drag so that the range **A1:C5** is selected.

4. **Close** 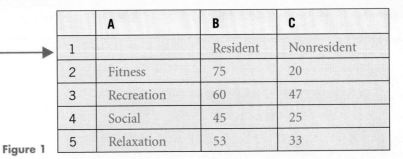 the Excel window. With the chart selected, on the **Chart Tools Design tab**, in the **Chart Layouts group**, click the third thumbnail—**Layout 3**.

5. Click the chart title, and then change the text to Primary Reason for Visiting Park

6. On the **Chart Tools Design contextual tab**, in the **Chart Styles group**, display the **Chart Styles** gallery, and then click the second thumbnail in the fourth row—**Style 26**. Compare your screen with **Figure 2**.

7. Click the chart's border to select the chart without selecting any individual chart element. On the **Animations tab**, in the **Animation group**, click the **Animate arrow**, and then under **Entrance**, click **Random Bars**.

Animation is applied to the entire chart, not the individual elements of the chart.

■ **Continue to the next page to complete the skill**

	A	B	C
1		Resident	Nonresident
2	Fitness	75	20
3	Recreation	60	47
4	Social	45	25
5	Relaxation	53	33

Figure 1

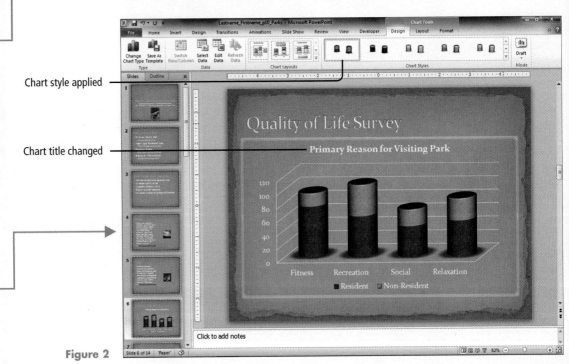

Figure 2

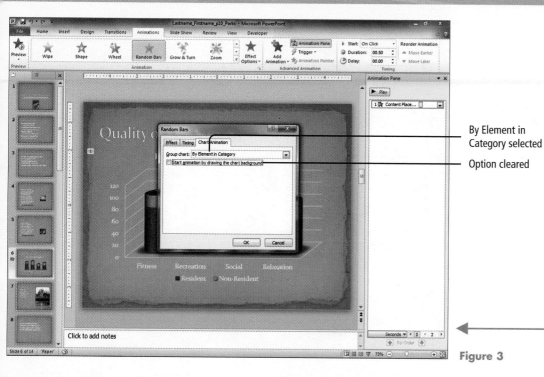

By Element in Category selected

Option cleared

Figure 3

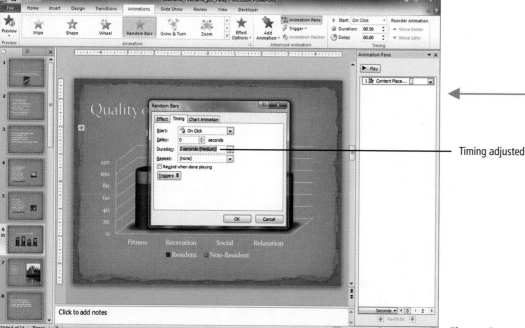

Timing adjusted

Figure 4

8. On the **Animations tab**, in the **Advanced Animation group**, click **Animation Pane**.

The Animation pane is displayed and can be used to enhance the animation effects just added. Animations are listed in this pane. Right-clicking any of these animations, or clicking the arrow, displays a list of available options.

9. In the **Animation Pane**, right-click the animation you just applied—indicated by an animation star and the words *Content Place*—and then click **Effect Options**.

10. In the **Random Bars** dialog box, click the **Chart Animation tab**, click the **Group chart list arrow**, and then select **By Element in Category**. Clear the option **Start animation by drawing the chart background**. Compare your screen with **Figure 3**.

Alternatively, with the chart selected, on the Animations tab, in the Animation group, you can click the Effect Options button to apply an effect.

11. In the **Random Bars** dialog box, click the **Timing tab**. Click the **Duration list arrow**, and then select **2 seconds (Medium)**. Compare your screen with **Figure 4**, and then click **OK**.

12. Close ☒ the **Animation Pane**. Click the **Slide Show** ☑ button, and click to show each chart category. End the show, and then **Save** ⬚ the presentation.

■ **You have completed Skill 7 of 10**

▶ During a presentation, you can make *ink annotations*—highlights, circles, arrows, and other marks that emphasize information during a presentation.

▶ Annotations made during a presentation can be saved or discarded when you end the show.

1. On the **Insert tab**, in the **Text group**, click **Header & Footer**. In the **Header and Footer** dialog box, select the **Slide number** and **Footer** check boxes. In the **Footer** box, type the file name. Select the **Don't show on title slide** check box, and then click **Apply to All**.

2. Display **Slide 1**, and then click the **Slide Show** 🖵 button.

3. In the slide show, advance to **Slide 3**, *Parks Benefit the Community*. Right-click the slide. From the displayed shortcut menu, point to **Pointer Options**, and then click **Pen**.

4. Right-click the slide. From the shortcut menu, point to **Pointer Options**, point to **Ink Color**, and then under **Standard Colors**, click the third color—**Orange**.

5. With the Pen, drag to draw two lines below *recreational*, as shown in **Figure 1**. If you make a mistake, right-click the slide, point to Pointer Options, and then click Erase All Ink on Slide.

6. In the fourth bulleted point, draw a circle around the word *Protect*, as shown in **Figure 2**.

7. Press ⎵Space⎵ to advance to the next slide.

   When the pen is active, clicking the mouse will annotate the slide instead of advancing the slide.

■ **Continue to the next page to complete the skill** ▶

Two lines drawn with Pen

Parks Benefit the Community

- Provide recreational opportunities
- Increase quality of life
- Augment property value
- Protect natural resources
- Increase number of tourists and visitors

Lastname_Firstname_p10_Parks   3

Figure 1

Word circled

Parks Benefit the Community

- Provide recreational opportunities
- Increase quality of life
- Augment property value
- Protect natural resources
- Increase number of tourists and visitors

Lastname_Firstname_p10_Parks   3

Figure 2

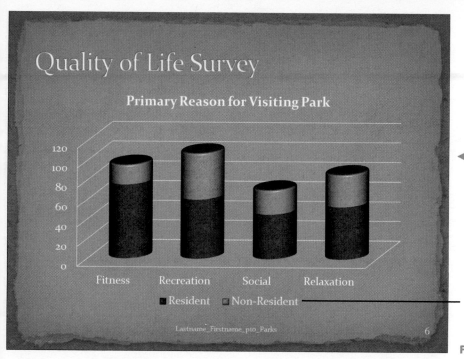

Figure 3

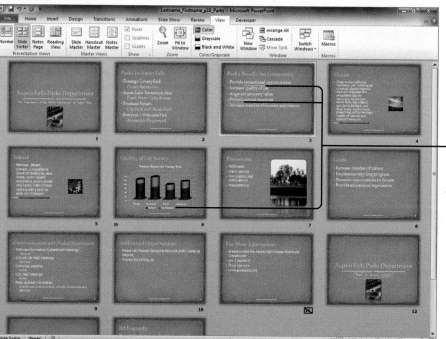

Ink annotations
saved

Figure 4

8. Advance to **Slide 6**, *Quality of Life Survey*. Press Space eight times to display the four categories in the animated chart. Right-click the slide, point to **Pointer Options**, and then click **Highlighter**.

9. With the Highlighter pointer, drag through *Resident* and *Nonresident* to highlight the legend labels. Compare your screen with **Figure 3**.

10. Right-click the slide, point to **Go to Slide**, and then click **12 Aspen Falls Parks Department**.

11. Repeat the technique just practiced to change the pointer to a **Pen**. With the Pen pointer, circle the sentence *Thank you for your support!*

12. Change the pointer from **Pen** to **Arrow**. While on Slide 12, in Slide Show view, press and hold Ctrl and then click, hold, and move your mouse over the text you just circled.

> Pressing Ctrl and then dragging while in Slide Show view causes your pointer to appear on screen as a *Laser Pointer*.

13. Using the techniques practiced previously, advance to the end of the presentation and end the show. In the displayed message, click **Keep** to save your ink annotations.

14. Click the **Slide Sorter** 🔳 button, and then on the **View tab**, in the **Zoom group**, click the **Fit to Window** button, and then compare your screen with **Figure 4**.

> When you keep ink annotations, they remain on the slides after the show is ended.

15. Click the **Normal** view 🔳 button. **Save** 🔲 the presentation.

■ **You have completed Skill 8 of 10**

▶ Before presenting, you might need to adjust your screen's resolution and refresh rate.

▶ **Resolution** affects the way pictures, text, and background images display either on screen or when projected.

▶ The **refresh rate** is the number of times per second that the screen redisplays the screen image.

1. On the **Slide Show tab**, in the **Monitors group**, click the **Resolution arrow**, and then click **640x480 (Fastest, Lowest Fidelity)**. This number can vary.

2. Press F5 to start the show from the beginning, and then compare your screen with **Figure 1**.

   Low Fidelity, or low resolution, results in less clarity—for example, in the text shadow effect and the picture of the seagull.

3. Continue to click through the slide show, noting the difference in resolution. End the show.

4. On the **Slide Show tab**, in the **Monitors group**, click the **Resolution arrow**, and then click **1152x864 (Slowest, Highest Fidelity)**. This number can vary.

5. Press F5 to start the show from **Slide 1**, and then compare your screen with **Figure 2**.

   High Fidelity, or high resolution, causes the slides to display with more clarity. Here, the text shadow effects are crisper, and the image is clearer.

   Before a presentation, try to view the show at different resolutions, using the projector that will be used during the presentation. In this manner, you can pick a resolution that works well with the projector.

■ **Continue to the next page to complete the skill** ▶

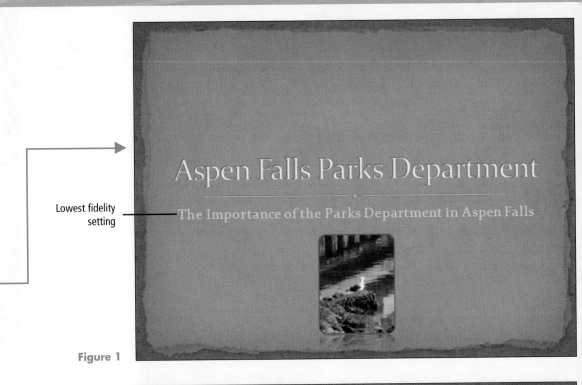

Lowest fidelity setting

Figure 1

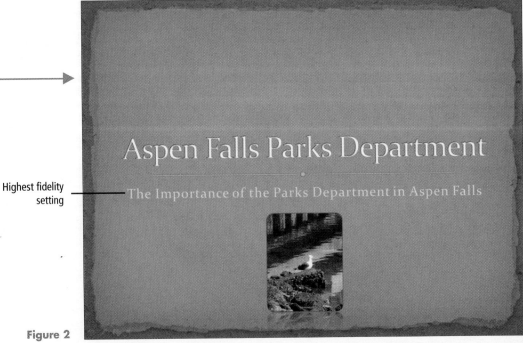

Highest fidelity setting

Figure 2

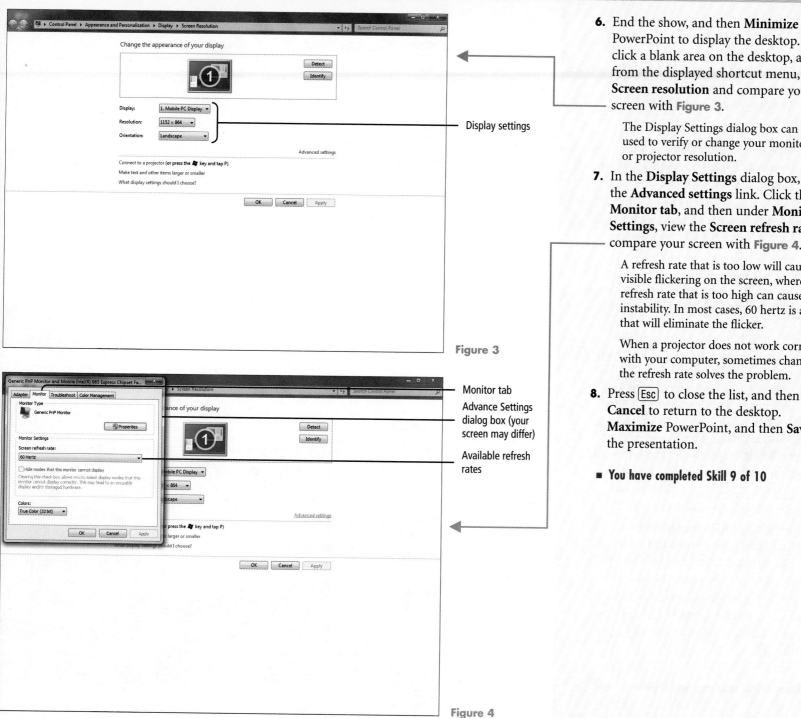

Display settings

Figure 3

Monitor tab

Advance Settings
dialog box (your
screen may differ)

Available refresh
rates

Figure 4

6. End the show, and then **Minimize** PowerPoint to display the desktop. Right-click a blank area on the desktop, and then from the displayed shortcut menu, click **Screen resolution** and compare your screen with **Figure 3**.

   The Display Settings dialog box can be used to verify or change your monitor or projector resolution.

7. In the **Display Settings** dialog box, click the **Advanced settings** link. Click the **Monitor tab**, and then under **Monitor Settings**, view the **Screen refresh rate**, and compare your screen with **Figure 4**.

   A refresh rate that is too low will cause visible flickering on the screen, whereas a refresh rate that is too high can cause system instability. In most cases, 60 hertz is a rate that will eliminate the flicker.

   When a projector does not work correctly with your computer, sometimes changing the refresh rate solves the problem.

8. Press [Esc] to close the list, and then click **Cancel** to return to the desktop. **Maximize** PowerPoint, and then **Save** 🖫 the presentation.

- **You have completed Skill 9 of 10**

► If you are unsure if PowerPoint software will be installed on the computer running your presentation, you can package your presentation for a CD. A presentation packaged for a CD can run the show without having PowerPoint installed on the computer.

1. Click the **File tab**. Click **Save & Send**, and then click **Package Presentation for CD**. Compare your screen with **Figure 1**.

2. Click the **Package for CD** button. In the displayed **Package for CD** dialog box, replace the **Name the CD** value with p10_CD

   CD names are limited to 16 or fewer characters. The Package for CD dialog box has two options for saving these files—to a folder or to a CD.

3. Click the **Add** button. In the **Add Files** dialog box, navigate to your **PowerPoint Chapter 10** folder. At the bottom of the dialog box, click the **Presentations and Shows** button, and then select **All Files**. Click the Word document you created in Skill 5—**Lastname_Firstname_p10_Parks_Bibliography**—and then click **Add**. Compare your screen with **Figure 2**.

   The Bibliography document will be packaged with the presentation.

4. Click the **Copy to Folder** button. Alternatively, if you have a CD available, you might want to insert it now and then adapt these steps to create a CD.

5. In the displayed **Copy to Folder** dialog box, in the **Folder name** box, change the value to Lastname_Firstname_p10_Parks_CD

■ **Continue to the next page to complete the skill** ➤

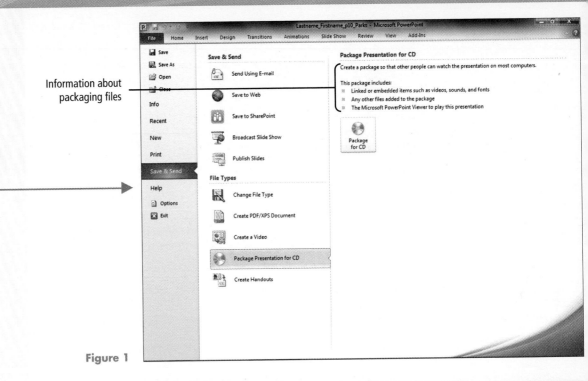

Information about packaging files

Figure 1

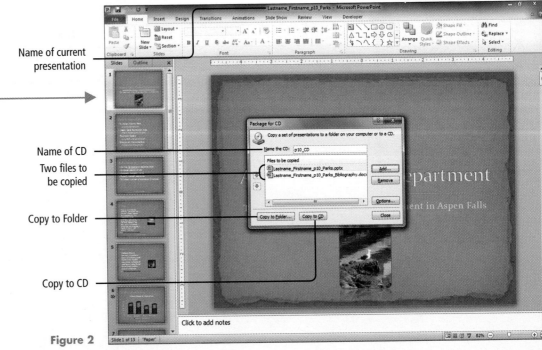

Name of current presentation

Name of CD

Two files to be copied

Copy to Folder

Copy to CD

Figure 2

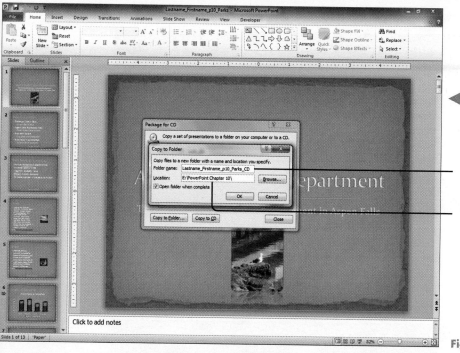

Folder name changed

Path to *PowerPoint Chapter 10* folder

Figure 3

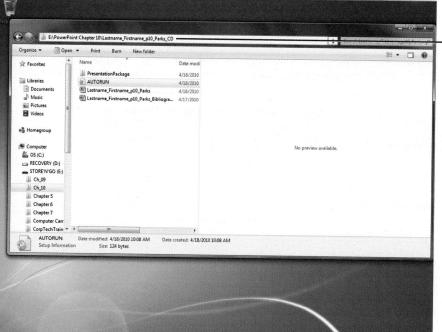

CD folder inside of PowerPoint Chapter 10 folder

Figure 4

6. Still in the **Copy to Folder** dialog box, next to the **Location** box, click the **Browse** button. In the displayed **Choose Location** dialog box, navigate to your **PowerPoint Chapter 10** folder, and then click **Select**, and then compare your screen with **Figure 3**.

   All of the files needed for the presentation are placed in a separate folder within your PowerPoint Chapter 10 folder.

7. In the **Copy to Folder** dialog box, click **OK**. Read the displayed message, and then click **Yes**.

8. Read the next message. Note that when the presentation is packaged, your ink annotations are not included. Click **Continue**. Wait a few moments for the files to be copied, and then view the folder and files created. **Close** the window showing the folder and files.

9. **Close** the **Package for CD** dialog box, and then **Close** ❌ PowerPoint. On the desktop, click **Start** 🔵, and then click **Computer**. In the displayed window, navigate to your **PowerPoint Chapter 10** folder. Open the **Lastname_Firstname_ p10_Parks_CD** folder, and then compare your screen with **Figure 4**.

   All of the files needed to run the presentation without PowerPoint are included in the folder. If you have access to a machine without PowerPoint installed, try opening the presentation on it. If your machine does have PowerPoint installed, the file will open in PowerPoint.

10. **Close** ❌ your folder window. Print or submit your files electronically as directed by your instructor.

Done! You have completed Skill 10 of 10 and your presentation is complete!

The following More Skills are located at **www.pearsonhighered.com/skills**

More Skills Download and Run PowerPoint Viewer

PowerPoint Viewer allows you to view a presentation regardless of whether PowerPoint is installed on the computer. If you are presenting on a computer that does not have PowerPoint installed, you can download and install PowerPoint Viewer so that you can run your show.

In More Skills 11, you will download and install PowerPoint Viewer and then use the program to view a presentation. To begin, open your web browser, navigate to www.pearsonhighered.com/skills, locate the name of your book, and follow the instructions on the website.

More Skills Add an Agenda and Change the Orientation of Slides

Precreated agendas can be converted into SmartArt. By default, slides use the Landscape orientation. When your slides have content that is taller than it is wide, you can change the slide orientation to Portrait.

In More Skills 12, you will open an existing presentation, change the orientation of the slide, and then either print or preview the slides. To begin, open your web browser, navigate to www.pearsonhighered.com/skills, locate the name of your book, and follow the instructions on the website

More Skills Use Presenter View

When you have two monitors connected to the same computer—perhaps one connected to a projector and one connected to a computer monitor—you can use Presenter view to display the show on one monitor, and view notes or other support materials on the other monitor.

In More Skills 13, you will display the show on one monitor and your speaker notes on a second monitor. To complete the skill, you will need access to a computer with two monitors. To begin, open your web browser, navigate to www.pearsonhighered.com/skills, locate the name of your book, and follow the instructions on the website.

More Skills Prepare Equipment and Software for Presentations

Preparation for a presentation is critical to the success of the presenter. To avoid problems or issues with technology, presenters must be prepared to use all of the equipment needed during the presentation. It is a good idea to become familiar with the equipment that you will be using for your presentation.

In More Skills 14, you will check the computer equipment—monitor, speakers, and microphone, for example—needed for a successful presentation. To begin, open your web browser, navigate to www.pearsonhighered.com/skills, locate the name of your book, and follow the instructions on the website.

Key Terms

APA 348

Bibliography 348

Citation 346

High Fidelity 356

Ink annotation 354

Laser Pointer 355

Low Fidelity 356

Office Clipboard 344

Refresh rate 356

Resolution 356

URL 344

Online Help Skills

1. **Start** PowerPoint. In upper right corner of the PowerPoint window, click the **Help** 🔘 button. In the Help window, click the **Maximize** button.

2. Click in the search box, type Broadcast presentation and then click the **Search** button 🔍. In the search results, click *Broadcast your presentation to a remote audience.* Scroll down to view the article, and compare your screen with **Figure 1**.

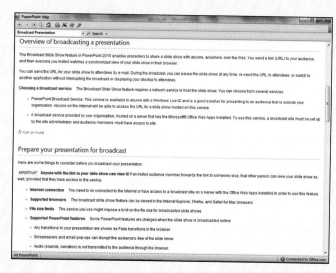

Figure 1

3. Read the article, and then see if you can answer the following questions: What types of information can be included in a presentation that is broadcast through a browser? What types of information might a presentation contain that cannot be broadcast?

Matching

Match each term in the second column with its correct definition in the first column by writing the letter of the term on the blank line in front of the correct definition.

____ **1.** The PowerPoint view that is typically used to reorder slides.

____ **2.** The pane used to copy and paste objects to and from the Office Clipboard.

____ **3.** A note crediting the original source or author.

____ **4.** A list of sources referenced in a presentation.

____ **5.** Elements in a chart can be animated using the Advanced Animations options found in this pane.

____ **6.** Highlights, circles, arrows, and other marks that emphasize information during a presentation.

____ **7.** The term used in the list of available resolutions that refers to the quality of the graphics, text, and pictures.

____ **8.** To change your display options, right-click the desktop, and then click this command.

____ **9.** The number of times per second that the screen redisplays a screen image.

____ **10.** The address of a specific webpage.

A Animation pane

B Bibliography

C Citation

D Clipboard

E Fidelity

F Ink annotations

G Refresh rate

H Screen resolution

I Slide Sorter

J URL

Multiple Choice

Choose the correct answer.

1. Before you give a presentation, it is important to seek this from others.
   A. Input
   B. Backups
   C. Addresses

2. Slides that remain a part of the presentation file but do not display in the slide show.
   A. Hidden
   B. Invisible
   C. Incomplete

3. The acronym URL stands for this.
   A. Universal Resource Locator
   B. Uniform Reform Location
   C. Uniform Resource Locator

4. The Word tool used to create citations in a specific format.
   A. Source Manager
   B. Bibliography Creator
   C. APA Format

5. When annotating a slide show, you can change the marker by right-clicking a slide and then selecting a choice from this list.
   A. Last Viewed
   B. Custom Show
   C. Pointer Options

6. Objects in the Clipboard pane are stored in this Clipboard.
   A. System
   B. 2010
   C. Office

7. When the refresh rate is too low, the screen might do this.
   A. Flicker
   B. Freeze
   C. Lock

8. When you create a chart in PowerPoint, data is entered into this type of worksheet.
   A. PowerPoint
   B. Excel
   C. Database

9. This is the maximum number of characters a CD name can contain.
   A. 16
   B. 32
   C. 8

10. As a part of the process of packaging a presentation on a CD, all related files are placed in this type of container.
    A. Folder
    B. Viewer file
    C. Zipped file

Topics for Discussion

1. By default, all webpages are copyrighted. Under what circumstances can you use images from a webpage in your own presentation?

2. Assume that you will be giving a presentation where you are unsure of what computer and projector will be available. What types of things might cause problems, and what can you do to solve these problems?

Skill Check

To complete this project, you will need the following file:

- p10_Social_Networking

You will save your files as:

- Lastname_Firstname_p10_Social_Networking
- Lastname_Firstname_p10_Social_Networking (a folder)

1. **Start** PowerPoint, and open **p10_Social_Networking**. **Save** the presentation in your **PowerPoint Chapter 10 folder** as Lastname_Firstname_p10_Social_Networking

2. Switch to **Slide Sorter** view. Drag **Slide 10** so that it displays before **Slide 4**.

3. Click the **Normal** view button, and display **Slide 1**. On the **Home tab**, in the **Slides group**, click the **New Slide** button. In the title placeholder, change the **Font Size** to **36**, and then type Growth of Social Networking

4. In the content pane, click the **Insert Chart** button. Under **Column**, click **Clustered Column**, and then click **OK**. Enter the chart data shown in the table in **Figure 1**. Delete the extra data and adjust the data range to **A1:D2**. —

5. **Close** Excel. With the chart selected, on the **Animations tab**, in the **Animation group**, click **Wipe**.

6. In the **Animation group**, click the **Effect Options** button, and then under **Sequence**, click **By Series**.

7. On the **Home tab**, click the **Clipboard Pane Launcher**.

8. **Open** your web browser. In the address bar, type www.usa.gov/webcontent/technology/social_networks.shtml and then press Enter.

9. Select the heading *What are Social Networks?* **Copy** it. Select the entire first paragraph beginning with *Social networking sites are* and then right-click the selected text and **Copy** it. In the address bar, right-click the URL, and **Copy** it. Display PowerPoint, and then compare your screen with **Figure 2**. —

10. Display **Slide 1**. On the **Home tab**, in the **Slides group**, click the **New Slide** button. In the title placeholder, change the **Font Size** to **44**, and then, in the **Clipboard** pane, click **What are Social Networks?**

11. Select the content placeholder, change the **Font Size** to **24**, and then, in the **Clipboard** pane, click the paragraph.

- **Continue to the next page to complete this Skill Check**

	2007	2008	2009
Citizens Using Social Networking	20%	54%	73%

Figure 1

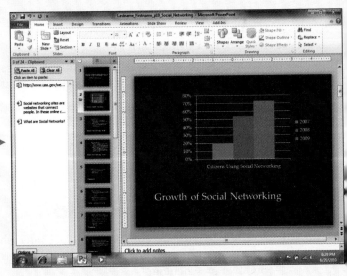

Figure 2

12. Press Enter, change the **Font Size** to **18**, and then, in the **Clipboard** pane, click the URL to **Paste** it onto the slide. Click **Clear All**, and then **Close** the Clipboard.

13. **Start** Word. On the **References tab**, in the **Citations & Bibliography group**, verify that the **Style** value is **APA Fifth Edition**. Click the **Manage Sources** button, and then in the **Source Manager**, click **New**.

14. If necessary, change the **Type of Source** value to **Web site**. In the **Name of Web Page** box, type Social Networks and Government In the **Name of Web Site** box, type WebContent.gov Refer to the webpage, and then enter the year, month, and day the site was last updated in the corresponding boxes. Enter today's date in the **Year**, **Month**, and **Day Accessed** boxes. **Copy** the URL from the website, and paste it into the **URL** box in the **Create Source** dialog box.

15. Click **OK** and then **Close**. On the **References tab**, in the **Citations & Bibliography group**, click the **Bibliography** button, and then click **Bibliography**. Compare your screen with **Figure 3**.

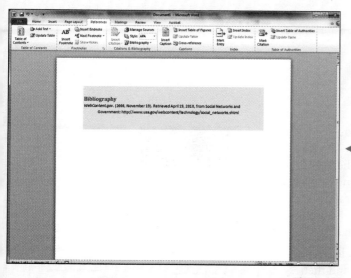

Figure 3

16. **Copy** the all of the text in the Word document, and then in PowerPoint, display the last slide. Place your insertion point in the content pane, and then **Paste** the citation. Select the pasted text, and then on the **Home tab**, in the **Paragraph group**, click **Bullets**.

17. On the **Slide Show tab**, in the **Monitors group**, change the **Resolution** to **800x600**.

18. On the **Insert tab**, in the **Text group**, click **Header & Footer**. Select **Footer**, type the file name, and then click **Apply to All**.

19. Press F5 to start the slide show. Right-click **Slide 1**, point to **Pointer Options**, and then click **Highlighter**. **Highlight** *Expectations and Guidelines for City of Aspen Falls Employees.*

20. Press Space to proceed through the show, and then click to **Keep** the ink annotation.

21. Click the **File tab**, click **Save & Send**, and then click **Package Presentation for CD**. Click the **Package for CD** button.

22. In the **Name the CD** box, type SocialNetworking Click **Copy to Folder**. In the **Folder name** box, type Lastname_Firstname_p10_Social_Networking Click the **Browse** button, navigate to your **PowerPoint Chapter 10** folder, and then click **Select**. In the displayed dialog boxes, click **OK**, click **Yes**, and then click **Continue**. Compare your screen with **Figure 4**.

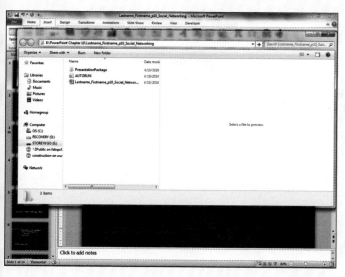

Figure 4

23. **Close** the CD folder window, and then **Close** the **Package for CD** dialog box. **Save** and **Close** your presentation. **Close** all other open windows without saving. Submit as directed by your instructor.

Done! You have completed the Skill Check

Assess Your Skills 1

To complete this project, you will need the following file:

- p10_Education

You will save your file as:

- Lastname_Firstname_p10_Education

1. **Start** PowerPoint, and then open **p10_Education**. **Save** the presentation in your **PowerPoint Chapter 10** folder as Lastname_Firstname_p10_Education

2. Move **Slide 4** so it becomes **Slide 2**.

3. Display the current **Slide 4**. Animate the chart's bars to **Fly In by Series**.

4. Display the **Clipboard** pane, and then **Start** your web browser. Navigate to www.ed.gov. Click the **Funding** link, and then click the **FAFSA** link. Find the **FAFSA Deadlines** information—the deadline date to submit Corrections and Web Applications. **Copy** the title *Federal Student Financial Aid Deadlines* and both paragraphs of information. **Copy** the URL of the page. If necessary, locate and copy similar information. Note the date the page was last updated.

5. On **Slide 5**, in the content placeholder, **Paste** the paragraphs of information you copied, press Enter, and then **Paste** the URL.

6. **Open** Word, and then use the **Source Manager** to create a **Web site** source in the APA style. In the **Name of Web Page** box, type FAFSA - Free Application for Federal Student Aid In the **Name of Web Site** box,

type ED.gov U.S. Department of Education Enter the **Year**, **Month**, and **Day** the site was last updated. Type today's date in the **Year**, **Month**, and **Day Accessed** boxes. In the **URL** box, type the URL. Insert a bibliography, and then **Copy** the entire bibliography, including the title. **Close** Word without saving.

7. On **Slide 6**, in the content placeholder, **Paste** the citation. Select the pasted text, and then remove the bullets. **Clear** the Clipboard and **Close** it.

8. Insert the **Slide Number** on all slides, and add the file name as a footer to all Notes and Handouts pages.

9. Set the **Screen Resolution** to **1152x864** or the setting marked (Slowest, Highest Fidelity).

10. Start the slide show, and then advance to **Slide 2**. Use the **Pen** to circle *PowerPoint 2010*. End the show, and **Keep** your ink annotation.

11. **Save** your presentation and submit your file as directed by your instructor.

Done! You have completed Assess Your Skills 1

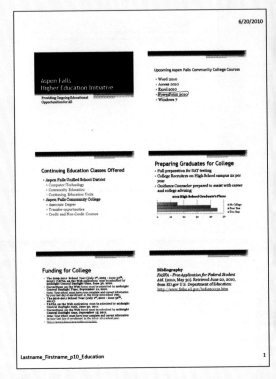

Figure 1

Assess Your Skills 2

To complete this project, you will need the following files:

- p10_Fire
- p10_Fire_Feedback

You will save your files as:

- Lastname_Firstname_p10_Fire
- Lastname_Firstname_p10_Fire_CD (a folder)

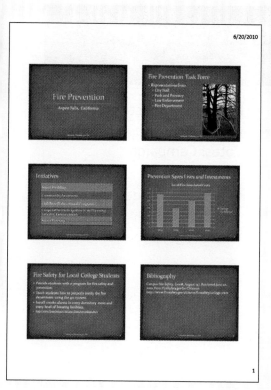

Figure 1

1. **Start** PowerPoint, and then open **p10_Fire**. **Save** the presentation in your **PowerPoint Chapter 10** folder as Lastname_Firstname_p10_Fire

2. Use the **Home tab** and the **Clipboard group** to display the **Office Clipboard**.

3. **Start** your web browser, and then navigate to www.firesafety.gov If this site has moved, find another similar fire-prevention site.

4. Under the **for Citizens** heading, click the **Practice Fire Safety** link, and then click the **Campus Fire Safety** link. Under *Safety Precautions*, **Copy** the first three bullet-pointed paragraphs. **Copy** the URL and note the date the site was last updated.

5. Display PowerPoint **Slide 5**—*Fire Safety for Local College Students*.

6. In the content placeholder, use the Clipboard to **Paste** the copied bullet points.

7. Press Enter, change the **Font Size** to **18**, and then **Paste** the URL.

8. **Start** Word. Use the **Source Manager** in APA format, create a **Bibliography**. In the **Name of Web Page** box, type Campus Fire Safety In the **Name of Web site** box, type FireSafety.gov for Citizens Enter the date the site was last updated. Then enter today's date. In the **URL** box, **Paste** the URL. Insert a bibliography.

9. **Copy** the citation from the bibliography, but not the title, and then **Close** Word without saving.

10. Display PowerPoint **Slide 6**. In the content placeholder, **Paste** the citation. Remove the bullets. Change the **Font Size** to **24**.

11. Hide **Slide 6**, *Bibliography*.

12. On **Slide 4**, animate the chart columns with the **Split** effect applied **By Category**. Use the **Animation** pane to change the **Timing** to **2 seconds (Medium)**. **Close** the Animation pane.

13. Insert a **Footer** with the **Slide Number** and the file name on all slides.

14. Display **Slide 1** and switch to **Slide Show** view. In **Slide 2**, use an orange **Highlighter** to circle around the image of the fire-damaged tree. End the slide show, and **Keep** your ink annotations.

15. Package the presentation for CD. Name the CD FirePrevention. **Copy** the presentation to a folder you create named **Lastname_Firstname_p10_Fire_CD** in your **PowerPoint Chapter 10** folder.

16. **Close** all open dialog boxes, **Save** your presentation, and then submit your files as directed by your instructor.

Done! You have completed Assess Your Skills 2

Assess Your Skills Visually

To complete this project, you will need the following file:

- p10_Vote

You will save your file as:

- Lastname_Firstname_p10_Vote

Animate the chart on the slide to **Fly In By Category**. Set the screen resolution to **1152x864 (Slowest, Highest Fidelity)**. In Slide Show view, use the yellow highlighter and yellow pen to mark up the slide as shown. Keep your ink annotations. **Save** the file as Lastname_Firstname_p10_Vote Add the file name to the **Notes and Handouts** footer, and then **Save** the file. Submit the file as directed by your instructor.

Done! You have completed Assess Your Skills Visually

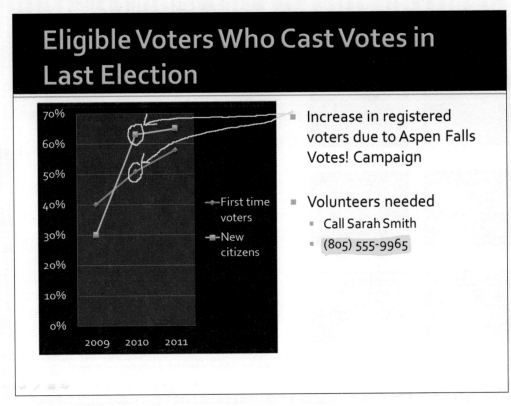

Figure 1

Skills in Context

To complete this project, you will need the following file:

- p10_Taste

You will save your files as:

- Lastname_Firstname_p10_Taste
- Lastname_Firstname_p10_Taste_Bibliography
- Lastname_Firstname_p10_Taste_CD (a folder)

Open **p10_Taste**, and **Save** the presentation in your PowerPoint Chapter 10 folder as Lastname_Firstname_p10_Taste **Animate** the chart on **Slide 2**, using the **Float In By Category** effect. Use the Internet to research a festival in California, and then create a presentation that proposes that the Taste of Aspen Falls festival be cross-promoted with the festival you choose. **Copy** and **Paste** relevant information about the event or festivals in California from *two* different websites to **Slide 3**, inserting an additional slide if needed. Use the copied information to describe the festival that you found or to promote California as a festival location. Use Word to create a

bibliography that cites the sources of your information, and then paste it into the *Bibliography* slide. **Save** the Word document as Lastname_Firstname_p10_Taste_Bibliography. Add the file name to the Notes and Handouts footer. Package the presentation and bibliography document for a CD, naming the CD TastePromo, in a folder named Lastname_Firstname_p10_Taste_CD and then submit the presentation as directed.

Done! You have completed Skills in Context

Skills and You

To complete this project, you will need the following file:

- A new blank PowerPoint presentation

You will save your file as:

- Lastname_Firstname_p10_Speaking

Create a four-slide presentation containing tips about public speaking. Apply a design theme to the presentation. Save the presentation as Lastname_Firstname_p10_Speaking in your PowerPoint Chapter 10 folder. On the title slide, include your name, and in the subtitle, type the class in which you are enrolled. Search the Internet for a quotation about public speaking, and then paste the quotation on Slide 2. Cite the source and leave the webpage open so that you can create a bibliography in Word. Next, search the Internet for ways to overcome common challenges in public speaking. Copy at least three tips, using the Clipboard. On Slide 3, in the title placeholder, type Overcoming Challenges and then in the content placeholder, paste the tips you found and then cite the sources. On Slide 4,

create a bibliography in Word and paste it onto the slide to cite all of the sources you used for the presentation. Hide the *Bibliography* slide. Move the current Slide 2, containing the quote you copied, to the end of the presentation, so that it appears as the last slide. Add the file name to the Notes and Handouts footer, and then save the presentation. If possible, print your presentation in handout format. Ask a peer for feedback on your presentation, make changes as suggested, and save your presentation. Close Word without saving. Close all open browser windows. Submit your presentation as directed by your instructor.

Done! You have completed Skills and You

Glossary

Action setting Settings applied to objects so you can navigate to a specific slide, open a webpage, or play a sound by clicking.

ActiveX control A control, like a text box, radio button, or list that can be placed on a slide for use during a presentation.

After Previous An animation option that begins the animation sequence immediately after the completion of the previous animation.

Alternative text Appears if a graphic does not display correctly.

Animation Visual or sound effects added to an object on a slide.

Animation Painter A feature that copies animation settings from one object to another.

Annotate The action of writing on a slide while the slide show is running.

APA A widely used citation style created by the American Psychological Association.

Background style A slide background fill variation that combines theme colors in different intensities or patterns.

Bibliography A list of sources referenced in a presentation.

Black slide A slide that displays at the end of the slide show to indicate that the presentation is over.

Body font A font applied to all slide text except titles.

Browser Software that is used to view websites and navigate the web.

Bullet point An individual line of bulleted text on a slide.

Caption A text box added to pictures to clarify their purpose or add meaning to the images.

Category label A label that identifies the categories of data in a chart.

Cell The box formed by the intersection of a row and column.

Cell reference A number on the left side and a letter on the top of a spreadsheet that addresses a cell.

Change Picture A Picture tool feature that replaces one image with another.

Character graphic A small graphic character that can be formatted as text.

Character spacing The spaces between letters in titles or bullet points.

Chart A graphic representation of numeric data.

Chart style A prebuilt chart format that applies an overall visual look to a chart by modifying its graphic effects, colors, and backgrounds.

Citation A note in a presentation that refers the viewer to the original source of information.

Clip art A set of images, drawings, photographs, videos, and sound included with Microsoft Office or accessed from Microsoft Office Online.

Clipboard A temporary storage area that holds text or an object that has been cut or copied.

Column chart A chart type useful for illustrating comparisons among related categories.

Comment Remark added to a presentation by individuals collaborating to create a presentation.

Comment (VBA code) Statement that documents what the code does; must begin with a single quotation mark.

Compatibility Checker Verifies individuals using earlier versions of PowerPoint are able to view PowerPoint 2010 presentations.

Compress To change the information stored in a picture file in order to reduce the size of the file.

Containment relationship A relationship that exists within another relationship.

Contextual tool Tools used to perform specific commands related to the selected object.

Contrast The difference in brightness between two elements on a slide, such as the background and the text or the background and a graphic. When a slide background and slide objects or text do not have enough contrast, the message may be lost.

Copy A command that places a copy of the selected text or object in the Clipboard.

Crop To remove unwanted areas along the edges of a graphic or picture.

Custom slide layout A reusable layout in which you insert your own placeholders, backgrounds, and theme sets.

Custom slide show A slide show created within another slide show, containing only selected slides.

Custom template A template designed using custom backgrounds, images, logos, and colors for the specific needs of an organization.

Cut A command that removes the selected text or object and stores it in the Clipboard.

Data label Text that identifies a data marker on a chart.

Data marker A column, bar, area, dot, pie slice, or other symbol that represents a single data point.

Data point A chart value that originates in an Excel worksheet cell, a Word table cell, or an Access field.

Data series In a chart, data points that are related to one another.

Destination file The file to which a source file is linked; when the source file is updated, the destination file is also updated.

Developer tab Contains tools and options used to work with controls and code, including macros.

Dialog box A box where you can select multiple settings.

Digital signature Identifies the author of macros of a file.

Document Inspector Lists information in presentation files that you may want to remove before making them available on the World Wide Web.

Drag To move the mouse while holding down the left mouse button and then to release it at the appropriate time.

Duplicate slide A slide that has been created by making a copy of, or duplicating, an original slide.

Edit To insert text, delete text, or replace text in an Office document, spreadsheet, or presentation.

Emphasis effect Animation that emphasizes an object or text that is already displayed.

Entrance effect Animation that brings an object or text onto the screen.

Equalize Character Height An effect that adjusts all characters so that they are equal in height.

Exit effect Animation that moves an object or text off the screen.

Export To save an object or file in a different file format.

Fill color The inside color of text or an object.

Font A set of characters with the same design and shape.

Footer Text that displays at the bottom of every slide or that prints at the bottom of a sheet of slide handouts.

Format To change the appearance of the text, such as changing the text color to red.

Format Painter A command that copies formatting from one selection of text to another.

Gallery A visual display of choices from which you can choose.

Gradient fill A gradual progression of colors and shades, usually from one color to another or from one shade to another shade of the same color, to add a fill to a shape.

Grayscale A black-and-white effect achieved through a series of shades of gray from white to black.

Grid line A line between the cells in a table or spreadsheet.

Group A collection of multiple objects treated as one unit that can be copied, moved, or formatted.

Grouped object A single object originally made up of several different images and text.

Guides Lines that display in the rulers to give you a visual indication of where the pointer is positioned.

Header Text that prints at the top of each sheet of slide handouts.

Headings font A font applied to slide titles.

High Fidelity A setting in which images appear in high resolution, and colors are accurate; load times may be slow.

Hyperlink Text or other object that displays another document, location, or window when it is clicked.

Indent The amount of space between the placeholder margin and the bulleted text.

Ink Annotation highlights, circles, arrows, and other marks that emphasize information during a presentation.

Insertion point A vertical line that indicates where text will be inserted when you start typing.

Kerning The spacing between characters.

KeyTip An icon that displays in the Ribbon to indicate the key that you can press to access Ribbon commands.

Kiosk presentations Presentations that run automatically on public monitors.

Laser Pointer The mouse pointer displayed in Slide Show view when CRTL is pressed.

Layout The arrangement of the text and graphic elements or placeholders on a slide.

Layout gallery A visual representation of several content layouts that you can apply to a slide.

Legend A box that identifies the patterns or colors that are assigned to the data series or categories in a chart.

List level Levels of text on a slide identified by the indentation, size of text, and bullet assigned to that level.

Live Preview A feature that displays the result of a formatting change if you select it.

Low Fidelity A setting in which images appear in low resolution; load times are fast.

Macro A set of recorded instructions, used to automate a task.

Microsoft Theme File A predesigned, downloadable design template that can be applied to Office files.

Microsoft Visual Basic (VBA) A high-level programming language that stores sets of instructions. In PowerPoint, macros are created with VBA code.

Mini toolbar A toolbar with common formatting buttons that displays after you highlight text.

Motion path An animation effect that moves objects along a line or curve that you draw.

Multimedia object Media objects, including videos, animated clip art, sounds, and action buttons, that are embedded in a presentation to add interest and interactivity.

Multimedia The presentation of information by using a variety of computer-based content such as text, images, sound, and video.

Narration A recorded voice that is applied to slides.

Navigation toolbar A toolbar that is used to navigate to any slide while the slide show is running.

Normal view The PowerPoint view in which the window is divided into three areas—the Slide pane, the pane containing the Slides and Outline tabs, and the Notes pane.

Notes Page A printout that contains the slide image in the top half of the page and speaker notes typed in the Notes pane in the lower half of the page.

Notes pane An area of the Normal View window used to type notes that can be printed below a picture of each slide.

Nudge The action of moving an object in small increments by using the directional arrow keys.

Office Clipboard A feature accessed in the Clipboard task pane that stores up to 24 items copied from any type of Office file.

On Click An animation option that begins the animation sequence when the mouse button is clicked or the Spacebar is pressed.

Organization chart A chart used to show the hierarchy within an organization or process.

Page Layout view A view where you prepare your document or spreadsheet for printing.

Paste Special A command used to create an updateable link between a source file and a destination file; when the source file is updated, so is the destination file.

Paste To insert a copy of the text or an object stored in the Clipboard.

PDF file Portable Document Format file. Can be opened and viewed by users regardless of their operating system and software; PDF files cannot be edited in PowerPoint.

Photo album A presentation composed of pictures.

Picture An image created with a scanner, digital camera, or graphics software that has been saved with a graphic file extension such as .jpg, .tif, or .bmp.

Picture effects Picture styles that include shadows, reflections, glows, soft edges, bevels, and 3-D rotations.

Picture Style A prebuilt set of formatting borders, effects, and layouts applied to a picture.

Pie chart A chart type that illustrates the relationship of parts to a whole.

Pixel The smallest element from which a picture is constructed.

Pixels per inch A measurement for target output of compressed pictures in PowerPoint.

Placeholder A box with dotted borders that is part of most slide layouts and that holds text or objects such as charts, tables, and pictures.

Point Measurement of the size of a font; each point is 1/72 of an inch.

Poster Frame Introductory frame that displays before the video begins playing.

PowerPoint Viewer A stand-alone application that allows you to view presentations without having PowerPoint installed on your computer.

PPI An acronym for pixels per inch.

Preserve A slide master setting that prevents the slide master from accidentally being deleted.

Procedure Abbreviated, or shortened, term for sub procedure.

Protected View A view applied to documents downloaded from the Internet that allows you to decide if the content is safe before working with the document.

RAM The computer's temporary memory.

Read-only mode A mode where you cannot save your changes.

Recolor To apply a stylized color or hue such as black and white or sepia.

Refresh rate The number of times per second that the screen redisplays the original data.

Replace Fonts command A command that finds all occurrences of a font throughout a file and replaces the font with another.

Research task pane A task pane that provides online dictionaries, online encyclopedias, and related websites.

Reset Picture button A Picture tool feature that restores an altered image to its original settings.

Resolution Display setting that affects the way pictures, text, and background images display either on screen or when projected on a screen.

Reuse Slides task pane A task pane that displays slide thumbnails from other presentations; slides from these presentations can be inserted into the current presentation.

Right-click Click the paragraph with the right mouse button.

Screen shot A picture of your computer screen, a window, or a selected region saved as a file that can be printed or shared electronically.

ScreenTip Informational text that displays when you point to commands or thumbnails in the Ribbon.

Selection and Visibility task pane Keeps track of all components—shapes, objects, and placeholders—that display on a slide.

Shortcut menu A list of commands related to the type of object that you right-click.

Sizing handle A small square or circle at the corner or side of a selected object that is dragged to increase or decrease the size of the object.

Slide An individual page in a presentation that can contain text, pictures, tables, charts, and other multimedia or graphic objects.

Slide handout Printed images of a single slide or multiple slides on a sheet of paper.

Slide layout The arrangement of objects—like titles and placeholders—on a slide.

Slide master The top slide in a hierarchy of slides that stores information about the theme and slide layouts of a presentation, including the background, colors, fonts, effects, placeholder sizes, and positioning.

Slide Sorter view The PowerPoint view in which all of the slides in the presentation display as thumbnails.

Slide timings Applied timings, after which a slide advances.

Slide transition A motion effect that occurs in Slide Show view when you move from one slide to the next during a presentation.

SmartArt graphic A designer-quality visual representation of information that you can use to communicate your message or ideas effectively by choosing from among many different layouts.

Snip A screen capture created with the Snipping Tool.

Sound effect Prebuilt sounds that play for specific events such as a slide transition or clicking an object with action settings applied.

Source file The original file, linked to a destination file.

Strong password A password that contains a combination of uppercase and lowercase letters, numbers, and symbols.

Sub Abbreviated, or shortened, term for sub procedure.

Sub procedure A group of instructions; also called subs or procedures.

Synonym A word with the same meaning.

Table Text or numbers displayed in a row and column format to make the information easier to read and understand.

Table style A prebuilt combination of borders and fill colors applied to the entire table in a manner consistent with the presentation theme.

Template A file upon which a presentation can be based.

Text alignment The horizontal placement of text within a placeholder.

Text box An object used to position text anywhere on a slide.

Theme A set of unified design elements that provides a unique look for your presentation, using colors, fonts, and graphics.

Theme color A set of coordinated colors that are applied to the backgrounds, objects, and text in a presentation.

Theme font A theme that determines the font applied to two types of slide text—headings and body.

Thesaurus A research tool that lists words that have the same or similar meaning to the word you are looking up.

Thumbnail A miniature image of a presentation slide.

Timed break slide A break during a presentation in which a timer delays the transition to the next slide.

Toggle button A button used to turn a feature both on and off.

Translate tool Translates words, phrases, or paragraphs by using bilingual dictionaries.

Trimming The process of shortening a video to remove unwanted footage and reduce the file size.

Triple-click Click three times fairly quickly without moving the mouse.

URL An acronym that stands for Uniform Resource Locator and that identifies a web address.

VBA statement Instructions stored in a sub procedure.

Video styles Frames, effects, and other enhancements to a video within the presentation.

Washout effect An effect that lightens color and decreases the contrast of a picture, often used in watermarks.

Watermark A picture that can be added to your entire slide as background or to just part of your slide.

Windows Live A free online storage that can be used to save and open your files from any computer connected to the Internet.

Windows Live ID A unique name and password— a Hotmail or Windows Live e-mail user name and password, for example.

Windows Live network A group of people whom you have invited to share files or to chat using Instant Messenger.

With Previous An animation option that begins the animation sequence at the same time as the animation preceding it or, if it is the first animation, with the slide transition.

WordArt A text style used to create decorative effects in a presentation.

Index

Numbers and Symbols

© **copyright symbol, 255**

A

accessibility of presentations
ActiveX controls, 314–315
comments, 320–321
compatibility of imported slides, 322–323
Developer tab, 314–315
digital signatures, 324–325
increasing, 308–309
on Internet, 312–313
introduction, 304
kiosk presentations, 310–311
macros, debugging, 316–317
outcome, 303
Outlook to send, 326, PowerPoint ch 9,
    More Skills 13
password setting, 324–325
PDF files for, 326, PowerPoint ch 9, More Skills 11
personal information removal, 312–313
skill set, 302
slide shows, 310–311
Translate tool, 306–307
VBA statements, 318–319
videos, 326, PowerPoint ch 9, More Skills 12
Windows Live Skydrive, saving to, 326, PowerPoint
    ch 9, More Skills 14
action settings, 202, 214–215
ActiveX controls, 314–315, PowerPoint ch 6,
    More Skills 14
Advanced tab, on Font dialog box, 24
After Previous animation timing, 150, 153
agendas, 360, PowerPoint ch 10, More Skills 12
alignment
of graphics, 112–113
grid lines for, 243
guides for, 108
of objects, 242–243
All Programs command, 6
alternative text, 251

animations
Animation Painter for, 150–151
appropriate, 156, PowerPoint ch 4, More Skills 14
assessment, 157–165
audiences and, 134
of chart elements, 338, 352–353
duration of, 152–153
effects for, 148–149
introduction, 134
motion paths for, 236, 244–245
outcomes, 133
removal of, 152–153
skill set, 132
slide show navigation, 154–155
timed breaks in, 216
timing for, 150–151
annotations, 154, 338, 354
APA (American Psychological Association) citation
    style, 348
Arrange group, PowerPoint ch 3, More Skills 13
assessment
Office functions, Common Features, 27–29
presentations
    accessibility of, 327–335
    creating, 55–63
    enhancing, 191–199
    finalizing, 361–369
    formatting, 89–97
    graphics, 123–131, 259–267
    multimedia objects for, 225–233
    tables, charts, and animation, 157–165
    templates, 293–301
audiences
animations and, 134
designing for, 54, PowerPoint ch 1, More Skills 14
multimedia for presentations to, 202
for presentations, PowerPoint ch 3,
    More Skills 14
audio, inserting in presentations, 218–219
Autocorrect, 255
automatic playing, of videos, 202

B

backgrounds
formatting, 190, PowerPoint ch 5, More Skills 14
presentation, 74–77
backing up files, PowerPoint ch 10, More Skills 14
Before up spin arrow, 25
bibliographies, 338, 348–351
bitmap (.bmp) images, 212, 240
black slides, 49, 249
body fonts, 73
borders, for pictures, 106–107
Browse Folders button, 10
bulleted lists, 82–83, PowerPoint ch 1,
    More Skills 13
bulleted text, 341
bullet points, 36, 100
By box up spin arrow, 172

C

callouts, 247
captions, 250–251
capturing screens, 26, Common Features,
    More Skills 11
case, of text, 180–181
category labels, of charts, 142
CDs
packaging presentations for, 358–359
songs from, 224, PowerPoint ch 6, More Skills 13
cell references, 12
cells
active, 8–9
Cell Size group for, 139
in tables, 140
Change Case tool, 180
character graphics, 254
character height equalizing, 190, PowerPoint ch 5,
    More Skills 13
character spacing, 80–81, 168, 174–175
charts
animating, 338, 352–353
Excel, 202, 210–211

charts *continued*
  on slides
    assessment, 157–159
    column, 142–143
    formatting, 144–145
    introduction, 134
    outcomes, 133
    skill set, 132
  styles for, 145
Choose A SmartArt Graphic dialog box, 222
citations, 346, 348–349
clip art, 44, 104–105, 220, 240
Clipboard
  to collect information, 344–345
  copying from other presentations by, 172–173
  Excel charts saved to, 210
  Format Painter in, 86–87, 178
  information stored on, 346–347
  overview, 18–19
clustered column charts, 142
colors
  fill, 79
  font, 80–81
  SmartArt, 116–117
  theme, 72–73, 79
  transparency of, 276–277
  video, 120
column charts, 142–143, 352
columns, in presentations, 168, 182–183
comments, 320–321, 340
compatibility, of imported slides, 322–323
compressing graphics, 122, 240, 252–253, ⓒⓦ PowerPoint
    ch 3, More Skills 11
containment relationships, ⓒⓦ PowerPoint ch 7,
    More Skills 13
contextual tools, 44
contrast, in presentation slides, 88, 122, ⓒⓦ PowerPoint
    ch 1, More Skills 14, ⓒⓦ PowerPoint ch 3,
    More Skills 14
controls, ActiveX, 314–315, ⓒⓦ PowerPoint ch 6,
    More Skills 14
copying
  objects, 84–85
  from other programs, 168, 172–173
  text, 18–19, 84–85
copyright symbol (©), 255
Create Source dialog box, 349
Crop button arrow, 106
cropping graphics, 252
Cut command, 84
cutting text, 18–19

Cycle layout, 114

D

data labels, of charts, 147
data markers, of charts, 144
data points, of charts, 144
data series, of charts, 144
debugging macros, 316–317
Define Customer Show dialog box, ⓒⓦ PowerPoint ch 5,
    More Skills 11
deleting
  folders, 26
  PowerPoint slides, 54, ⓒⓦ PowerPoint ch 1,
    More Skills 13
  text, 16
demonstrations, 27
destination files, 212
Developer tab, 314–315
dialog boxes
  Action Settings, 214–215
  Choose A SmartArt Graphic, 222
  Create Source, 34
  Define Customer Show, ⓒⓦ PowerPoint ch 5,
    More Skills 11
  Display Settings, 357
  Font, 24, 254
  Format Picture, ⓒⓦ PowerPoint ch 7, More Skills 12
  Format Shape, 183
  Header and Footer, 239, 354
  Insert Audio, 218, ⓒⓦ PowerPoint ch 6, More Skills 13
  Insert Chart, 352
  Insert Hyperlink, 249
  Insert Picture, 239
  Insert Video, 204
  Open, 14
  overview, 24–25
  Package for CD, 358
  Paragraph, 178
  Print Setting, 12
  Publish as PDF or XPS, ⓒⓦ PowerPoint ch 9,
    More Skills 11
  Random Bars, 353
  Record Slide Show, ⓒⓦ PowerPoint ch 6, More Skills 11
  Replace, 173
  Save as, 15
  Spin, 217
  Symbols, 254
  Trim Video, 204
  Zoom, 342
digital signatures, 324–325
direction, of text, 180–181

Display Settings dialog box, 357
documents (Word)
  bibliographies created in, 338, 348
  citations from, 348–349
  copying from, 170
  presentation slides from outlines of, 88, ⓒⓦ PowerPoint
    ch 1, More Skills 13
Drop Shadow Rectangle style, 22
duplicate slides, 186
duration
  of animations, 152–153
  fade, 206
  of sound effects, 219
  of timed breaks, 216
Duration up spin arrow, 49, 152
DVDs, videos on, ⓒⓦ PowerPoint ch 9, More Skills 12

E

editing
  Editing Group for, 18
  Enable Editing button for, 15
  presentations, 36–37
  text entering and, 16–17
effects
  for animations, 148–149
  for pictures, 106–107
  in presentations, 38, 48–49
e-mail, presentations sent by, ⓒⓦ PowerPoint ch 9,
    More Skills 13
enhancing presentations
  assessment, 191–199
  character height equalizing, 190, ⓒⓦ PowerPoint ch 5,
    More Skills 13
  character spacing, 174–175
  clearing formatting, 176–177
  columns, 182–183
  copying from other programs, 172–173
  font replacement, 188–189
  introduction, 168
  line spacing, 178–179
  online help skills, 191
  outcome, 167
  picture resetting, 190, ⓒⓦ PowerPoint ch 5,
    More Skills 12
  Research Task pane, 170–171
  section addition to slide shows, 190, ⓒⓦ PowerPoint
    ch 5, More Skills 11
  skill set, 166
  slide duplicating, 186–187
  slide title background formatting, 190, ⓒⓦ PowerPoint
    ch 5, More Skills 14

text and shape aligning, 184–185
text direction and case, 180–181
visual skills assessment, 191
Entrance effect, in animations, 148
equipment, for presentations, 360, ⓒⓦ PowerPoint ch 10,
More Skills 14
Exit effect, in animations, 148
exporting grouped objects, 240–241

F

Fade Duration, 206
feedback, from reviewers, 340–341
filenames, 4, 15
files
destination, 212
organizing, 26, ⓒⓦ Common Features, More Skills 13
Paste Special to link, 212–213
sharing, 100
source, 212
Windows Live for, 26, ⓒⓦ Common Features,
More Skills 14
File tab, 13, 25
fill color, 79
fills, gradient, 112–113
finalizing presentations
agenda, 360, ⓒⓦ PowerPoint ch 10, More Skills 12
animating chart elements, 352–353
assessment, 361–369
bibliography slide, 350–351
citations from Word, 348–349
Clipboard to collect information, 344–345
equipment and software, 360, ⓒⓦ PowerPoint ch 10,
More Skills 14
introduction, 338
laser pointer to mark slides, 354–355
online help skills, 361
outcome, 337
package for CD, 358–359
PowerPoint Viewer, 360, ⓒⓦ PowerPoint ch 10,
More Skills 11
Presenter view, 360, ⓒⓦ PowerPoint ch 10,
More Skills 13
resolution, 356–357
reviewer feedback, 340–341
skill set, 336
slide orientation, 360, ⓒⓦ PowerPoint ch 10,
More Skills 12
slide reordering and hiding, 342–343
visual skills assessment, 368
Web pages, pasting from, 346–347
first line indent marker, 242

folders, overview of, 26
Font dialog box, 24, 254
Font Dialog Box Launcher, 24
Font group, 24
fonts. *See also* **symbols**
color of, 80–81
PowerPoint, 38
replacing, 168, 188–189
themes for, 72–73
footers, 50–51, 87
Format Painter, 86–87, 178
Format Picture dialog box, ⓒⓦ PowerPoint ch 7,
More Skills 12
Format Shape dialog box, 183
Format tab, on Ribbon, 22
formatting
clearing, 168, 176–177
slides
charts, 144–145
pictures, 44–45
text, 38–39
title backgrounds, 190, ⓒⓦ *PowerPoint ch 5,*
More Skills 14
text boxes, 250
Free-form Snip, ⓒⓦ Common Features, More Skills 11
Full-screen Snip, ⓒⓦ Common Features,
More Skills 11

G

galleries
Layout, 42
Picture Styles, 22, 221, 247
Transitions, 248
.gif (Graphics Interchange Format) files, 240
gradient fills, 112–113
graphics, 98–131, 234–267
captions, 250–251
indentation, 242–243
introduction, 236
motion paths to animate, 244–245
Notes and Handouts Masters, 256–257
objects
aligning, 242–243
grouping, 240–241
outcome, 235
photo albums, 248–249
picture recoloring, 246–247
presentation size reduction and, 252–253
shapes
custom, 238–239
exporting, 240–241

skill set, 234
slides
alignment of, 112–113
assessment, 123–125
clip art, 104–105
gradient fills, 112–113
introduction, 100
outcome, 99
picture borders and effects, 106–107
for presentations, 102–103
saved as image files, 258, ⓒⓦ *PowerPoint ch 7,*
More Skills 11
shapes, 106–111, 114–115
skill set, 98
SmartArt, 114–117
video files, 118–121
SmartArt
exported as pictures, 258, ⓒⓦ *PowerPoint ch 7,*
More Skills 12
from Nested Target Layout, 258, ⓒⓦ *PowerPoint ch 7,*
More Skills 13
from text, 250–251
symbols, 254–255
WordArt and shapes for text effects, 258, ⓒⓦ PowerPoint
ch 7, More Skills 14
Graphics Interchange Format (.gif) files, 240
grayscale, 76, 120
grid lines, 12, 243, 257
grouping
graphics, 112–113
objects, 236, 240–241
saved as picture files, 122, ⓒⓦ PowerPoint ch 3,
More Skills 12
guides, alignment, 108

H

handouts, presentation, 50–51
Handouts Masters, 236, 256–257
hanging indent marker, 242
hard drive, 10
headers and footers, 27
Header and Footer dialog box, 239, 354
in presentation notes, 87
in presentations, 50–51
headings, 7, 13, 20, 73
help. *See* **online help skills**
hiding slides, 342–343
Hierarchy layout, 114
High Fidelity resolution, 356
highlighting, 24
high resolution images, 240

Home tab, on Ribbon
Editing group, 18
Font group, 24
Styles group, 7, 13, 20
HTML, Paste Special command and, 212
hyperlinks
in Microsoft Office Help, (CW) Common Features, ch 1,
More Skills 12
to photo albums, 249
in presentations, 156, 202, 208–209, (CW) PowerPoint
ch 4, More Skills 12
Research Task pane and, 170

I

Illustrations group, 22
images
altering, 236
bitmap, 212
file formats for, 240
slides as, 258, (CW) PowerPoint ch 7, More Skills 11
indentation, 21, 242–243
ink annotations, 354
Insert Audio dialog box, 218, (CW) **PowerPoint ch 6,**
More Skills 13
Insert Chart dialog box, 352
Insert Hyperlink dialog box, 249
inserting
shapes into slides, 108–109
slides into presentations, 42–43
tables into slides, 136–137
insertion point, 7, 9
Insert Picture dialog box, 239
Insert tab, on Ribbon, 22
Insert Video dialog box, 204
Internet
presentations on, 312–313
videos on, (CW) PowerPoint ch 9, More Skills 12

J

.jpg (Joint Photographic Experts Group) files, 240
Jump List, 10

K

kerning, 172
keyboard shortcuts, 54, (CW) **PowerPoint ch 1,**
More Skills 12
Key Tips, 23
kiosk presentations, 310–311, (CW) **PowerPoint ch 6,**
More Skills 12

L

labels, 142, 147

landscape orientation, 256, (CW) **PowerPoint ch 10,**
More Skills 12
laser pointer, to mark slides, 354–355
layouts
Layout gallery, 42
of presentations, 42-43
of SmartArt types of, 114, 116–117
of tables, 138–139
left indent marker, 242
line spacing, 178–179
linking
Paste Special for, 212–213
updateable, 212
video to presentations, 202
lists
columns for, 182
layout of, 114
levels of, 36, (CW) PowerPoint ch 1, More Skills 11
in presentations, 82–83
Live Preview, 7, 66
locations, presentations designed for, 54, (CW) **PowerPoint**
ch 1, More Skills 14
logos, 238, 256
Low Fidelity resolution, 356

M

macros, 316–317
margins, 12
master slides. *See* slide masters
Matrix layout, 114
Maximize button, 6, 12
menus, shortcut, 24–25
Microsoft Office Help, 26, (CW) **Common Features, ch 1,**
More Skills 12
Microsoft Office Online, (CW) **PowerPoint ch 8,**
More Skills 13
Microsoft Office PowerPoint Security Notice, 213
Microsoft Office theme files, 224, (CW) **PowerPoint ch 6,**
More Skills 14
Microsoft Windows Metafile Format (.wmf) files, 240
Minimize button, 9
Mini toolbar, 17, 21
motion paths, to animate graphics, 236, 244–245
multimedia objects for presentations
action settings for shapes, 214–215
Excel charts, 210–211
hyperlinks, 208–209
introduction, 202
linking files with Paste Special, 212–213
Microsoft Office theme files, 224, (CW) PowerPoint ch 6,
More Skills 14

narration recording, 224, (CW) PowerPoint ch 6,
More Skills 11
outcome, 201
overview, 204
rehearsal timing, 224, (CW) PowerPoint ch 6,
More Skills 12
skill set, 200
SmartArt organization charts, 222–223
songs from CDs, 224, (CW) PowerPoint ch 6,
More Skills 13
sound effects, 218–219
timed breaks for slides, 216–217
video editing, 204–205
video options, 206–207
watermarks, 220–221
multiple windows, opening, 8–9

N

names, file, 4, 15
narration recording, 224, (CW) **PowerPoint ch 6,**
More Skills 11
navigating
Navigation pane, 10, 14–15
Office functions, 6–7
slide shows, 154–155
toolbar for, 154
Nested Target Layout, 258, (CW) **PowerPoint ch 7,**
More Skills 13
New folder button, 10
Normal view, 32, 36, 52, 54, (CW) **PowerPoint ch 1,**
More Skills 13
notes, presentation, 52–53, 176
Notes Masters, 236, 256–257
Notes Pane, 34
nudging objects, 111
numbered lists, 82–83

O

objects
aligning, 242–243
grouping, 236, 240–241
order of, 122, (CW) PowerPoint ch 3, More Skills 13
in presentations, 84–85
Office Clipboard. *See* Clipboard
Office functions, Common Features, 2–28
assessment, 28–29
capturing screens, 26, (CW) Common Features,
More Skills 11
dialog boxes, 24–25
Microsoft Office Help, 26, (CW) Common Features,
More Skills 12

multiple windows open, 8–9

navigating, 6–7

online help skills, 27

opening files, 14–15

organizing files, 26, (CW) Common Features,
More Skills 13

outcome, 3

printing files, 12–13

Ribbon tabs, 22–23

saving files, 10–13

shortcut menus, 24–25

skill set, 2

starting, 6–9

text entering

cutting, copying, and pasting, 18–19

editing and, 16–17

formatting, 20–21

Windows Live, 26, (CW) Common Features, More Skills 14

On Click animation timing, 150

online help skills

Office functions, Common Features, 27

presentations

accessibility of, 327

creating, 55

enhancing, 191

finalizing, 361

formatting, 89

graphics, 123, 259

multimedia objects for, 225

tables, charts, and animations, 157

templates, 293

online templates, 292, (CW) PowerPoint ch 8, More Skills 13

Open dialog box, 14

opening files, 8–9, 14–15

organization charts, SmartArt, 222–223

organizing files, 26, (CW) Common Features, More Skills 13

orientation, landscape, 256

**orientation of slides, 360, (CW) PowerPoint ch 10,
More Skills 12**

**outlines, presentation slides from, 88, (CW) PowerPoint
ch 1, More Skills 13**

**Outline tab, 34, 36, 54, (CW) PowerPoint ch 1,
More Skills 11**

**Outlook to send presentations, 326, (CW) PowerPoint ch 9,
More Skills 13**

P

packaging presentations for CDs, 358–359

Page Layout tab, on Ribbon, 23

Page Layout view, 12

Page Setup group, 12

paperless office, 29

Paragraph dialog box, 178

Parental Controls, 170

passwords, 324–325

paste options, 18–19

Paste Special, linking files with, 212–213

**PDF (Portable Document Format) files, 326,
(CW) PowerPoint ch 9, More Skills 11**

personal information, removal of, 312–313

**photo albums, 156, 248–249, 292, (CW) PowerPoint ch 4,
More Skills 13, (CW) PowerPoint ch 8,
More Skills 11**

pictures

borders of, 106–107

compressing, 122, (CW) PowerPoint ch 3, More Skills 11

effects for, 106–107

file formats for, 240

fill options for, 183

group saved as, 122, (CW) PowerPoint ch 3, More Skills 12

layout of, 114

Picture Styles gallery, 221, 247

positioning order of, (CW) PowerPoint ch 3,
More Skills 13

in presentations, 44–45, 76–77

recoloring, 246–247

resetting, 190, (CW) PowerPoint ch 5, More Skills 12

shapes of, 106–107

as SmartArt graphics, 258, (CW) PowerPoint ch 7,
More Skills 12

styles for, 22, 45

transparent, 202

washout effect for, 220

pie charts, 146–147

pixels per inch (ppi), 253

placeholders

in presentations, 36, 42, 44, 68

for SmartArt graphics, 282–283

.png (Portable Network Graphics) files, 240

points, fonts sized in, 38

Point Size arrow, 21

portrait orientation, (CW) PowerPoint ch 10, More Skills 12

Poster Frame, 205

**PowerPoint Viewer, 156, 360, (CW) PowerPoint ch 4,
More Skills 11, (CW) PowerPoint ch 10,
More Skills 11**

presentations

accessibility of, 302–335

ActiveX controls, 314–315

assessment, 327–335

comments, 320–321

compatibility of imported slides, 322–323

Developer tab, 314–315

digital signatures, 324–325

increasing, 308–309

on Internet, 312–313

introduction, 304

kiosk presentations, 310–311

macros, debugging, 316–317

online help skills, 327

outcome, 303

*Outlook to send, 326, (CW) PowerPoint ch 9,
More Skills 13*

password setting, 324–325

PDF files for, 326, (CW) PowerPoint ch 9, More Skills 11

personal information removal, 312–313

skill set, 302

slide shows, 310–311

Translate tool, 306–307

VBA statements, 318–319

videos, 326, (CW) PowerPoint ch 9, More Skills 12

visual skills assessment, 334

*Windows Live Skydrive, saving to, 326, (CW) PowerPoint
ch 9, More Skills 14*

creating, 30–63

assessment, 55–57

handouts for, 50–51

headers and footers in, 50–51

introduction, 32

notes for, 52–53

opening, viewing, and saving in, 34–35

outcomes, 31

picture inserting and formatting in, 44–45

skill set, 30

spell checking in, 40–41

enhancing, 166–199

assessment, 191–199

*character height equalizing, 190, (CW) PowerPoint ch 5,
More Skills 13*

character spacing, 174–175

clearing formatting, 176–177

columns, 182–183

copying from other programs, 172–173

font replacement, 188–189

introduction, 168

line spacing, 178–179

online help skills, 191

outcome, 167

*picture resetting, 190, (CW) PowerPoint ch 5,
More Skills 12*

Research Task pane, 170–171

*section addition to slide shows, 190, (CW) PowerPoint
ch 5, More Skills 11*

presentations, enhancing *continued*

   skill set, 166

   slide duplicating, 186–187

   slide title background formatting, 190, ⓒⓦ PowerPoint ch 5, More Skills 14

   text and shape aligning, 184–185

   text direction and case, 180–181

   visual skills assessment, 191

  finalizing, 336–369

   agenda, 360, ⓒⓦ PowerPoint ch 10, More Skills 12

   animating chart elements, 352–353

   assessment, 361–369

   bibliography slide, 350–351

   citations from Word, 348–349

   Clipboard to collect information, 344–345

   equipment and software, 360, ⓒⓦ PowerPoint ch 10, More Skills 14

   introduction, 338

   laser pointer to mark slides, 354–355

   online help skills, 361

   outcome, 337

   package for CD, 358–359

   PowerPoint Viewer, 360, ⓒⓦ PowerPoint ch 10, More Skills 11

   Presenter view, 360, ⓒⓦ PowerPoint ch 10, More Skills 13

   resolution, 356–357

   reviewer feedback, 340–341

   skill set, 336

   slide orientation, 360, ⓒⓦ PowerPoint ch 10, More Skills 12

   slide reordering and hiding, 342–343

   visual skills assessment, 368

   Web pages, pasting from, 346–347

  formatting, 64–97

   assessment, 89–91

   introduction, 66

   new, 68–69

   outcomes, 65

   pictures and textures for, 76–77

   skill set, 64

   styles for, 74–75

   text, 84–85

   themes for, 70–71

   WordArt for, 78–79

  graphics, 98–131, 234–267

   alignment of, 112–113

   assessment, 123–131, 259–267

   captions, 250–251

   clip art, 104–105

   gradient fills, 112–113

   indentation, 242–243

   introduction, 100, 236

   motion paths to animate, 244–245

   Notes and Handouts Masters, 256–257

   objects, aligning, 242–243

   objects, grouping, 240–241

   online help skills, 259

   outcome, 99, 235

   photo albums, 248–249

   picture recoloring, 246–247

   picture shapes, borders, and effects, 106–107

   presentation size reduction and, 252–253

   shapes, 108–109, 114–115, 238–241

   skill set, 98, 234

   slides from other presentations, 102–103

   slides saved as image files, 258, ⓒⓦ PowerPoint ch 7, More Skills 11

   SmartArt exported as pictures, 258, ⓒⓦ PowerPoint ch 7, More Skills 12

   SmartArt from Nested Target Layout, 258, ⓒⓦ PowerPoint ch 7, More Skills 13

   SmartArt from text, 250–251

   SmartArt graphics overview, 114–117

   symbols, 254–255

   text in shapes, 110–111

   video files, 118–121

   visual skills assessment, 266

   WordArt and shapes for text effects, 258, ⓒⓦ PowerPoint ch 7, More Skills 14

  headers and footers, 27

   Header and Footer dialog box, 239, 354

   in presentation notes, 87

   in presentations, 50–51

  multimedia objects for, 200–233

   action settings for shapes, 214–215

   assessment, 225–233

   Excel charts, 210–211

   hyperlinks, 208–209

   introduction, 202

   linking files with Paste Special, 212–213

   Microsoft Office theme files, 224, ⓒⓦ PowerPoint ch 6, More Skills 14

   narration recording, 224, ⓒⓦ PowerPoint ch 6, More Skills 11

   online help skills, 225

   outcome, 201

   rehearsal timing, 224, ⓒⓦ PowerPoint ch 6, More Skills 12

   skill set, 200

   SmartArt organization charts, 222–223

   songs from CDs, 224, ⓒⓦ PowerPoint ch 6, More Skills 13

   sound effects, 218–219

   timed breaks for slides, 216–217

   video editing, 204–205

   video options, 206–207

   visual skills assessment, 225

   watermarks, 220–221

slides

  backgrounds, 74–77

  bulleted lists, 82–83

  character spacing, 80–81

  color themes for, 72–73

  font color, 80–81

  font themes for, 72–73

  Format Painter for, 86–87

  inserting and layouts of, 42–43

  numbered lists, 82–83

  objects, 84–85

  slide sorter view for, 46–47

  text editing and replacing in, 36–37

  text formatting in, 38–39

  transitions for, 48–49

tables, charts, and animation, 132–165

  animation effects, 148–149

  animation removal, 152–153

  animation timing, 150–151

  assessment, 157–159

  chart formatting, 144–145

  column charts, 142–143

  introduction, 134

  outcomes, 133

  pie charts, 146–147

  skill set, 132

  slide show navigation, 154–155

  table insertion, 136–137

  table layouts, 138–139

  table styles, 140–141

templates, 268–301

  assessment, 293–301

  custom, 272–273

  introduction, 270

  for new presentations, 286–287

  online, 292, ⓒⓦ PowerPoint ch 8, More Skills 13

  online help skills, 293

  outcome, 269

  photo albums from, 292, ⓒⓦ PowerPoint ch 8, More Skills 11

  Quick Access Toolbar, 292, ⓒⓦ PowerPoint ch 8, More Skills 14

  quiz shows from, 292, ⓒⓦ PowerPoint ch 8, More Skills 12

Selection and Visibility pane, 290–291
skill set, 268
slide layouts, 274–277, 280–281
slide masters, 276–277, 284–285
slides from multiple slide masters, 288–289
SmartArt placeholders, 282–283
transparent colors for, 276–277
visual skills assessment, 300
Presenter view, 360, CW PowerPoint ch 10, More Skills 13
printing
notes for presentations, 52–53
overview, 12–13
Print Setting dialog box for, 12
Process layout, 114
proofreading, 170
Protected view, 15
Publish as PDF or XPS dialog box, CW PowerPoint ch 9, More Skills 11
Pyramid layout, 114

Q

Quick Access Toolbar
customizing, 292, CW PowerPoint ch 8, More Skills 14
overview, 8
saving files on, 11, 17, 21
Undo button on, 17
quiz shows, 292, CW PowerPoint ch 8, More Skills 12

R

RAM (random access memory), 10
Random Bars dialog boxes, 353
Reading view, in PowerPoint, 32, 155
read-only mode, 14
recoloring pictures, 246–247
recording narrations, 224, CW PowerPoint ch 6, More Skills 11
Record Slide Show dialog box, CW PowerPoint ch 6, More Skills 11
Rectangular Snip, CW Common Features, More Skills 11
reducing presentation size, 236, 252–253
refresh rate, 356–357
rehearsal timing, 224, CW PowerPoint ch 6, More Skills 12
reinforcing messages, in presentations, CW PowerPoint ch 3, More Skills 14
Relationship layout, 114
relationships, containment, CW PowerPoint ch 7, More Skills 13
renaming folders, 26
reordering slides, 338, 342–343
Replace dialog box, 173
Replace Fonts command, 188
replacing text, 16

Research Task pane, 168, 170–171
resolution, 356–357
Restore Down button, 9
Reuse Slides task pane, 103, 109, 186–187
reviewer feedback, 340–341
Ribbon tabs
File, 13, 25
Format, 22
Home, 7, 18, 24
Insert, 22
overview, 22–23
Page Layout, 23
Paragraph group, 21
View, 12, 23
right-clicking, 25
rotation, 241

S

saving files
File tab for, 25
as images, 258, CW PowerPoint ch 7, More Skills 11
naming files and, 4
in new folders, 10–11
as PDF (Portable Document Format), 326, CW PowerPoint ch 9, More Skills 11
presentations, 34–35
presentation templates, CW PowerPoint ch 1, More Skills 12
printing and, 12–13
Quick Access Toolbar for, 19, 21
Save as for, 10–11, 14–15
to Windows Live Skydrive, 26, 326, CW Common Features, More Skills 14, CW PowerPoint ch 9, More Skills 14
as XPS, CW PowerPoint ch 9, More Skills 11
screen captures, CW Common Features, More Skills 11
screen elements, 34
ScreenTips, 22, 208
sections, adding to slide shows, 190, CW PowerPoint ch 5, More Skills 11
security, 213
Select button, 18
Selection and Visibility pane, 290–291
selection border, 240
sentences, 168
shapes
action settings for, 214–215
aligning, 184–185
custom, 238–239
exporting, 240–241

on slides
inserting, sizing, and moving, 108–109
of pictures, 106–107
positioning order of, CW PowerPoint ch 3, More Skills 13
in presentations, 114–115
text in, 110–111
for text effects, 258, CW PowerPoint ch 7, More Skills 14
shortcut menus, 24–25, 181
Show/Hide button, 7
sizing handles, 44, 180
slide layouts
custom, 274–275, 280–281
organizing, 276–277
slide masters
editing, 88, CW PowerPoint ch 2, More Skills 11
multiple, 284–285
organizing, 276–277
slides from multiple, 288–289
Slide Pane, 34
slides. See also presentations
animations, 154–155
annotations, 154
backgrounds, 74–77
bibliographies, 338, 350–351
black, 49, 249
bulleted lists, 82–83
character spacing, 80–81
charts
assessment, 157–159
column, 142–143
formatting, 144–145
introduction, 134
outcomes, 133
pie, 146–147
skill set, 132
color themes for, 72–73
compatibility of imported, 322–323
contrast in, 88, 122, CW PowerPoint ch 1, More Skills 14, CW PowerPoint ch 3, More Skills 14
deleting, 54, CW PowerPoint ch 1, More Skills 13
document outlines for (Word), 88, CW PowerPoint ch 1, More Skills 13
duplicating, 186–187
font color, 80–81
font themes for, 72–73
Format Painter for, 86–87
formatting
pictures in, 44–45
text on, 38–39

slides *continued*

graphics

alignment of, 112–113

assessment, 123–125

clip art, 104–105

gradient fills, 112–113

introduction, 100

outcome, 99

picture borders and effects, 106–107

for presentations, 102–103

shapes, 106–111, 114–115

skill set, 98

SmartArt, 114–117

video files, 118–121

hiding, 342–343

as image files, 258, CW PowerPoint ch 7, More Skills 11

inserting

layouts and, 42–43

overview, 42–43

shapes into, 108–109

tables into, 136–137

laser pointer to mark, 354–355

from multiple slide masters, 288–289. *See also* slide masters

navigating, 154–155

numbered lists, 82–83

objects, 84–85

orientation of, 360, CW PowerPoint ch 10, More Skills 12

from other presentations, 102–103

outlines for, 88, CW PowerPoint ch 1, More Skills 13

reordering, 338, 342–343

Reuse Slides Pane, 103, 109

shapes

inserting, sizing, and moving, 108–109

of pictures, 106–107

positioning order of, CW *PowerPoint ch 3, More Skills 13*

in presentations, 114–115

text in, 110–111

tables

applying styles, 140–141

inserting, 136–137

modifying layouts, 138–139

text

editing and replacing in, 36–37

formatting in, 38–39

in shapes, 110–111

timed breaks for, 216–217

title background formatting, 190, CW PowerPoint ch 5, More Skills 14

transitions for, 48–49

Slide Show view

for kiosk presentations, 310–311

navigating, 154–155

as PowerPoint view, 32

sections added to, 190, CW PowerPoint ch 5, More Skills 11

transitions for, 48–49

video shown in, 206

Slide Sorter view, 32, 46–47, 342

Slides tab, 34

SmartArt graphics

exported as pictures, 258, CW PowerPoint ch 7, More Skills 12

from Nested Target Layout, 258, CW PowerPoint ch 7, More Skills 13

organization charts in, 222–223

placeholders for, 282–283

in presentations, 100, 114–117

from text, 250–251

smart tags, 12, CW **Access, ch 10, More Skills**

Snipping Tool, 26, CW **Common Features, More Skills 11**

software, for presentations, 360, CW **PowerPoint ch 10, More Skills 14**

songs from CDs, 224, CW **PowerPoint ch 6, More Skills 13**

sorting, in slide sorter view, 32, 46–47, 342

sound effects, 218–219, CW **PowerPoint ch 4, More Skills 14**

source files, 212

Source Manager (Word), 348–349

spacing

character, 80–81, 168, 174–175

line, 178–179

overview, 24–25

spell checking, 40–41

spin arrows, 25, 49, 152, 172

Spin dialog box, 217

spreadsheets, 8–9. *See also* **workbooks (Excel)**

stacked cylinder column charts, 352

starting Office functions, 6–9

Status bar, 34

storing images, 240

styles

chart, 145

overview, 7, 13, 20

Picture Styles gallery, 221, 247

presentation background, 74–75

SmartArt, 116–117

table, 134, 140–141

video, 120–121, 205

symbols, 254–255

synonyms, 41

T

tables

assessment, 157–165

introduction, 134

layouts for, 138–139

outcomes, 133

skill set, 132

styles for, 140–141

Tagged Image File Format (.tiff) files, 240

templates

custom, 272–273

introduction, 270

for new presentations, 286–287

online, 292, CW PowerPoint ch 8, More Skills 13

outcome, 269

photo albums from, 292, CW PowerPoint ch 8, More Skills 11

presentation, 68, 88, CW PowerPoint ch 1, More Skills 12

Quick Access Toolbar, 292, CW PowerPoint ch 8, More Skills 14

quiz shows from, 292, CW PowerPoint ch 8, More Skills 12

Selection and Visibility pane, 290–291

skill set, 268

slide layout

custom, 274–275, 280–281

organizing, 276–277

slide masters

multiple, 284–285, 288–289

organizing, 276–277

SmartArt placeholders, 282–283

theme, CW PowerPoint ch 6, More Skills 14

transparent colors for, 276–277

temporary memory (RAM), 10

text

aligning, 184–185

alternative, 251

bulleted, 341

case of, 180–181

character height equalizing, 190, CW PowerPoint ch 5, More Skills 13

direction of, 180–181

overview, 8

in slides

aligning, 38

in Outline tab, 54, CW *PowerPoint ch 1, More Skills 11*

in presentations, 36–39, 84–85

in shapes, 110–111

in *SmartArt graphics*, 114–117
WordArt for, 78–79
text boxes, 110, 180, 250
text effects, 258, ⓒⓦ PowerPoint ch 7, More Skills 14
texture (special effects), 76–77, 183
themes, 23, 70–73, 224, ⓒⓦ PowerPoint ch 6, More Skills 14
thesaurus, 40–41
thumbnails, 7, 13, 20, 35, 46, 187
.tiff (Tagged Image File Format) files, 240
Tight setting, for character spacing, 172
timed breaks, for slides, 216–217
timing, rehearsal, 224, ⓒⓦ PowerPoint ch 6, More Skills 12
titles of slides, 190, ⓒⓦ PowerPoint ch 5, More Skills 14
toggle buttons, 7
transitions
   applying, 48–49
   gallery of, 248
   sound effects for, 219
   timed breaks as, 217
   video styles for, 121
   Wipe, 87
Translate tool, 306–307
transparency
   color, 276–277
   image, 240
   of pictures, 202
Trim Video dialog box, 204
triple-clicking, 24

U

Undo button, 17

updateable links, 212
URLs (Uniform Resource Locators), 344, 346–347, ⓒⓦ PowerPoint ch 4, More Skills 12
USB flash drives, 10

V

VBA (Visual Basic for Applications) statements, 318–319
vertical stacking, of text, 180
videos
   editing, 204–205
   inserting, 118–119
   linked to presentations, 202
   options for, 206–207
   from presentations, 326, ⓒⓦ PowerPoint ch 9, More Skills 12
   styles for, 120–121, 205
View buttons, 34
View tab, on Ribbon, 12, 23
visual skills assessment, for presentations
   accessibility of, 334
   creating, 62
   enhancing, 191
   finalizing, 368
   formatting, 96
   graphics, 130, 266
   multimedia objects for, 225
   tables, charts, and animations, 164
   templates, 300

W

washout effect, 220
watermarks, 202, 220–221

Web addresses (URLs), 344, 346–347, ⓒⓦ PowerPoint ch 4, More Skills 12
Web pages, 240, 346–347
Windows Explorer, 10–11, 15
Windows Live Skydrive, 26, 326, ⓒⓦ Common Features, More Skills 14, ⓒⓦ PowerPoint ch 9, More Skills 14
Windows Metafile Format (.wmf) files, 240
Window Snip, ⓒⓦ Common Features, More Skills 11
Wingdings font, 254
With Previous animation timing, 150
WordArt
   in presentations, 78–79
   shapes combined with, 258, ⓒⓦ PowerPoint ch 7, More Skills 14
   styles group for, 110
workbooks (Excel)
   charts from, 202, 210–211
   overview, 8
   slide orientation and, ⓒⓦ PowerPoint ch 10, More Skills 12
   Workbook Views group for, 12
worksheets (Excel)
   overview, 8–9
   PowerPoint charts from, 144–147
Wrap Text button, 23

X

XPS, files saved as, ⓒⓦ PowerPoint ch 9, More Skills 11

Z

Zoom dialog box, 342
Zoom group, 23